THE CAMBRIDGE COMP
THE BEATS

The Cambridge Companion to the Beats offers
the most innovative and popular literary perioc.
Beats were a literary and cultural phenomenon originating in New York City in
the 1940s that reached worldwide significance. Although its most well-known
figures remain Jack Kerouac, Allen Ginsberg, and William S. Burroughs, the
Beat Movement radiates out to encompass a rich diversity of figures and texts
that merit further study. Consummate innovators, the Beats had a profound
effect not only on the direction of American literature but also on models of
sociopolitical critique that would become more widespread in the 1960s and
beyond. Bringing together the most influential Beat scholars writing today,
this *Companion* provides a comprehensive exploration of the Beat Movement,
asking critical questions about its associated figures and arguing for their
importance to postwar American letters.

Steven Belletto is Associate Professor of English at Lafayette College. He is the
author of *No Accident, Comrade: Chance and Design in Cold War American
Narratives* (2012) and a co-editor of *American Literature and Culture in an Age
of Cold War: A Critical Reassessment* (2012). The author of numerous articles
on post-1945 American literature and culture that have appeared in journals
such as *American Literature*, *American Quarterly*, *ELH*, and *Twentieth-
Century Literature*, from 2011 to 2016 he was associate editor of the journal
Contemporary Literature, and is currently an editor there. He is also editor
of the volume *American Literature in Transition, 1950–1960* (2017) and is
currently writing a literary history of the Beats to be published by Cambridge
University Press.

THE CAMBRIDGE
COMPANION TO
THE BEATS

EDITED BY
STEVEN BELLETTO
Lafayette College

CAMBRIDGE
UNIVERSITY PRESS

University Printing House, Cambridge CB2 8BS, United Kingdom

One Liberty Plaza, 20th Floor, New York, NY 10006, USA

477 Williamstown Road, Port Melbourne, VIC 3207, Australia

4843/24, 2nd Floor, Ansari Road, Daryaganj, Delhi – 110002, India

79 Anson Road, #06-04/06, Singapore 079906

Cambridge University Press is part of the University of Cambridge.

It furthers the University's mission by disseminating knowledge in the pursuit of education, learning, and research at the highest international levels of excellence.

www.cambridge.org
Information on this title: www.cambridge.org/9781107184459

10.1017/9781316877067

First published 2017

Printed in the United States of America by Sheridan Books, Inc.

A catalogue record for this publication is available from the British Library.

ISBN 978-1-107-18445-9 Hardback
ISBN 978-1-316-63571-1 Paperback

CONTENTS

CONTENTS

NOTES ON CONTRIBUTORS

STEVEN BELLETTO is Associate Professor of English at Lafayette College. He is the author of *No Accident, Comrade: Chance and Design in Cold War American Narratives* (2012) and a co-editor of *American Literature and Culture in an Age of Cold War: A Critical Reassessment* (2012). The author of numerous articles on post-1945 American literature and culture that have appeared in journals such as *American Literature, American Quarterly, ELH,* and *Twentieth-Century Literature,* from 2011 to 2016 he was associate editor of the journal *Contemporary Literature,* and is currently an editor there. He is also editor of the volume *American Literature in Transition, 1950–1960* (2017) and is currently writing a literary history of the Beats to be published by Cambridge University Press.

NANCY M. GRACE is Virginia Myers Professor of English at the College of Wooster. Her many publications on writers of the Beat Generation include *Girls Who Wore Black: Women Writing the Beat Generation,* co-edited with Ronna C. Johnson (2002); *Breaking the Rule of Cool: Interviewing and Reading Beat Women Writers,* co-edited and written with Ronna C. Johnson (2004); *Jack Kerouac and the Literary Imagination* (2007); and *The Transnational Beat Generation,* co-edited with Jennie Skerl (2012). She was editor of *The Beat Review* from 2007 to 2011, is co-editor of *The Journal of Beat Studies,* and is a founding member of the Beat Studies Association.

OLIVER HARRIS is the world's foremost scholar on the work of William S. Burroughs and is the founding President of the European Beat Studies Network. His ten books include new editions of two trilogies of novels by Burroughs: *Junky: The Definitive Text of "Junk"* (2003), *The Yage Letters Redux* (2006), and *Queer: Twenty-Fifth Anniversary Edition* (2010); and "restored" editions of the Cut-Up Trilogy: *The Soft Machine, Nova Express,* and *The Ticket That Exploded* (2014). He is also the editor of *The Letters of William S. Burroughs, 1945–1959* (1993) and *Everything Lost: The Latin American Notebook of William S. Burroughs* (2008); the author of the critical study *William Burroughs and the Secret of Fascination* (2003); and a co-editor of *Naked Lunch@50: Anniversary Essays* (2009). He has published widely in Beat studies, including essays on Kerouac's mythmaking and Ginsberg's photography, as well as on other subjects, from Hemingway's short stories to the fascination of film noir. He is Professor of American Literature at Keele University.

KURT HEMMER is the editor of the *Encyclopedia of Beat Literature* (2007) and a Professor of English at Harper College. With filmmaker Tom Knoff, he has produced several award-winning films: *Janine Pommy Vega: As We Cover the Streets* (2003), *Rebel Roar: The Sound of Michael McClure* (2008),*Wow! Ted Joans Lives!* (2010), *Keenan* (2011), and *Love Janine Pommy Vega* (2013). His essay on the Beats appeared in *A History of California Literature* (2015).

HILARY HOLLADAY founded both the Kerouac Conference on Beat Literature at the University of Massachusetts-Lowell, which ran from 1995 to 2007, and UMass Lowell's Jack and Stella Kerouac Center for American Studies. Her books include *Wild Blessings: The Poetry of Lucille Clifton* (2004) and *Herbert Huncke: The Times Square Hustler Who Inspired Jack Kerouac and the Beat Generation* (2015). She is currently writing a biography of Adrienne Rich.

MICHAEL HREBENIAK is Director of Studies in English at Wolfson College and Lecturer in English at Magdalene College, Cambridge. He previously taught humanities at the Royal Academy of Music and served as an arts documentary producer. His monograph, *Action Writing: Jack Kerouac's Wild Form*, was published in 2006 and he is currently finishing a book and film on the medieval Stourbridge Fair in relation to cultural memory, habitat, and performance.

RONNA C. JOHNSON is Lecturer in English and American Studies at Tufts University, where she has been Interim Director of Women's Studies. She has written about Jack Kerouac, Joyce Johnson, Lenore Kandel, and Gregory Corso, among others, and has presented papers on Diane di Prima emphasizing gender and ethnicity in Beat movement discourses. She is writing *Inventing Jack Kerouac: Reception and Reputation 1957–2007* and has published *Breaking the Rule of Cool: Interviewing and Reading Women Beat Writers* with Nancy M. Grace (2004), a sequel to their co-edited book *Girls Who Wore Black: Women Writing the Beat Generation* (2002). Johnson is a co-founder of the Beat Studies Association and co-editor of the *Journal of Beat Studies*. Her latest essay, "Gregory Corso's Dada-Surrealist-Absurd Beat Plays," was published in *Beat Drama: Playwrights and Performances of the "Howl" Generation* (2016).

BRENDA KNIGHT began her career at HarperCollins, where she worked with Huston Smith, Paulo Coelho, and His Holiness the Dalai Lama. She served as publisher of Cleis Press, founded Viva Editions, and was named 2015 IndieFab's Publisher of the Year. A prolific writer, Knight is the author of *Women of the Beat Generation* (1996), which won an American Book Award; *Wild Women and Books* (2006), and *The Poetry Oracle* (2008). She leads writing workshops and is an officer of the Woman's National Book Association and is a student of medieval literature and modern poetry.

WILLIAM LAWLOR is the editor of *Beat Culture: Lifestyles, Icons, and Impact* (2005) and the author of *The Beat Generation: A Bibliographical Teaching Guide* (1998). He has received a Summer Study Grant to work on Beat writers from the National Endowment for the Humanities. He has twice been System Fellow at the Institute for Research in the Humanities at the University of Wisconsin-Madison, each time focusing on Beat topics. He is Emeritus Professor of English at the University of Wisconsin-Stevens Point.

A. ROBERT LEE, previously of the University of Kent at Canterbury until 2011 was Professor of American Literature at Nihon University. He edited *The Beat Generation Writers* (1996) and is the author of *Designs of Blackness: Mappings in the Literature and Culture of Afro-America* (1998); *Multicultural American Literature: Comparative Black, Native, Latino/a and Asian American Fictions* (2003), which won an American Book Award; and *Modern American Counter Writing: Beats, Outriders, Ethnics* (2010).

POLINA MACKAY is Assistant Professor of English Literature at the University of Nicosia and Vice President of the European Beat Studies Network. She is the co-editor of several books on modern American literature, including *Authorship in Context: From the Theoretical to the Material* (2007), *Kathy Acker and Transnationalism* (2009), and *The Cambridge Companion to H.D.* (2011). She has also co-edited "The Beat Generation and Europe" (2013), a special issue of *Comparative American Studies*, and will co-edit *Global Beat Studies* (forthcoming in 2017), a special issue of *Comparative Literature and Culture*. Her book on women of the Beat Generation entitled *Aesthetics, Feminism and Gender in Beat Women* is forthcoming with Routledge in 2017. Her articles have also appeared in *Naked Lunch@50* (2009), in *Postcolonial Women's Writing* (2010), and in *Out of the Shadows: Women of the Beat Generation* (2015).

ERIK MORTENSON is a Senior Lecturer at Wayne State University's Honors College. He is the author of *Capturing the Beat Moment: Cultural Politics and the Poetics of Presence* (a Choice Outstanding Academic Title in 2011) and *Ambiguous Borderlands: Shadow Imagery in Cold War American Culture* (2016). He has also published essays on the Beats in a number of journals and in several books.

KIRBY OLSON is Professor at the State University of New York at Delhi. He has written several critical books, including *Gregory Corso: Doubting Thomist* (2002), as well as a book of poems, *Christmas at Rockefeller Center* (2015).

JONAH RASKIN is Professor Emeritus at Sonoma State University, where he taught literature and communications. He is the author of fourteen books, including *American Scream: Allen Ginsberg's "Howl" and the Making of the Beat Generation* (2004). A poet with seven chapbooks to his name, including *Rock 'n' Roll Women* (2012), he performs his work before live audiences and with jazz accompaniment.

DAVID STERRITT is editor-in-chief of *Quarterly Review of Film and Video* and Professor in art history and humanistic studies at the Maryland Institute College of Art. His writing on the Beats has appeared in *The New York Times*, *Cineaste*, and elsewhere, and he is on the editorial board of the *Journal of Beat Studies*. His books include *Mad to Be Saved: The Beats, the '50s, and Film* (1998), *Screening the Beats: Media Culture and the Beat Sensibility* (2004), and *The Beats: A Very Short Introduction* (2013).

TODD F. TIETCHEN is an Associate Professor of American Literature and Culture at University of Massachusetts-Lowell. He is the author of *The Cubalogues: Beat Writers in Revolutionary Havana* (2010). He has also edited three volumes of Jack Kerouac's writings, including *The Unknown Kerouac: Rare, Unpublished and Newly Translated Writings* (2016). Tietchen's *Information Society and the New American Poetry* is forthcoming in the University of Iowa Press's New American Canon series.

REGINA WEINREICH is a co-producer and director of the award-winning documentary *Paul Bowles: The Complete Outsider* (1994) and a writer for *The Beat Generation: An American Dream* (1986). Author of the critical study *Kerouac's Spontaneous Poetics* (1987; 2003), she has also edited and compiled Kerouac's *Book of Haikus* (2003) and wrote the introduction for Kerouac's *You're a Genius All the Time* (2009). A leading scholar of the Beat Generation, she has contributed to numerous essay collections and literary journals including *The Paris Review*, *Five Points*, and *The Review of Contemporary Fiction*. As a journalist, her work has appeared in *The New York Times*, *The Washington Post*, *The Village Voice*, *The Boston Globe*, *The San Francisco Chronicle*, *Talk Magazine*, *Entertainment Weekly*, *American Book Review*, *Hamptons Magazine*, *The Forward*, *The East Hampton Star*, and *The Huffington Post*, among others. In 2009, she co-organized a three-day celebration of the fiftieth anniversary of the publication of *Naked Lunch* in New York. She has taught "The Beat Generation" at Columbia University and at the School of Visual Arts, where she is a professor in the Department of Humanities and Sciences.

JOHN WHALEN-BRIDGE is Associate Professor of English at the National University of Singapore. The author of *Political Fiction and the American Self* (1998), he has co-edited (with Gary Storhoff) the SUNY series "Buddhism and American Culture." This series includes *The Emergence of Buddhist American Literature* (2009), *American Buddhism as a Way of Life* (2010), *Writing as Enlightenment* (2010), and *Buddhism and American Cinema* (2015). Recent essays in *Contemporary Buddhism* and *South Asian Diaspora* explore Tibetan expression and representation, and *Tibet on Fire: Buddhism, Rhetoric, and Self-Immolation* (2015) approaches Tibetan responses to censorship through the lens of Kenneth Burke's notion of dramatism. Whalen-Bridge is currently writing a book about engaged Buddhism and American Beat and post-Beat writers.

Year	Primary Texts	Anthologies, Journals, and Criticism
1948		Jay Landesman, ed., *Neurotica* (1948–1951)
1950	Jack Kerouac, *The Town and the City*	
1952	Chandler Brossard, *Who Walk in Darkness* John Clellon Holmes, *Go* Holmes, "This is the Beat Generation" George Mandel, *Flee the Angry Strangers*	
1953	William S. Burroughs, *Junky*	
1954	Gregory Corso, *This Hung-Up Age*	Robert Creeley, ed., *Black Mountain Review* (1954–1957)
1955	Gregory Corso, *Vestal Lady on Brattle and Other Poems* Lawrence Ferlinghetti, *Pictures of a Gone World* Jack Kerouac, "Jazz of the Beat Generation"	
1956	Allen Ginsberg, *Howl and Other Poems* Michael McClure, *Passage* Kenneth Rexroth, *In Defense of the Earth*	James Harmon and Michael McClure, eds., *Ark II Moby I*
1957	Lawrence Ferlinghetti and Kenneth Rexroth, *Poetry Readings in the Cellar*	"San Francisco Scene" issue of *Evergreen Review*

Year	Primary Texts	Anthologies, Journals, and Criticism
	Jack Kerouac, *On the Road* Norman Mailer, "The White Negro" Marie Ponsot, *True Minds* Kenneth Rexroth, "Disengagement: The Art of the Beat Generation"	
1958	Gregory Corso, "Bomb" Corso, *Gasoline* Lawrence Ferlinghetti, *A Coney Island of the Mind* John Clellon Holmes, *The Horn* Holmes, "The Philosophy of the Beat Generation" Diane di Prima, *This Kind of Bird Flies Backward* Jack Kerouac, *The Subterraneans* Kerouac, *The Dharma Bums* Jack Micheline, *River of Red Wine* Dan Propper, *The Fable of the Final Hour* ruth weiss, *Steps* John Wieners, *The Hotel Wentley Poems*	Gene Feldman and Max Gartenberg, eds., *The Beat Generation and the Angry Young Men* LeRoi and Hettie Jones, eds., *Yugen* (1958–1962)
1959	Alan Ansen, *The Old Religion* William S. Burroughs, *Naked Lunch* William Everson (as Brother Antoninus), *The Crooked Lines of God* Ted Joans, *Jazz Poems* Lenore Kandel, *An Exquisite Navel* Kandel, *A Passing Dragon* Bob Kaufman, "Abomunist Manifesto" Kaufman, "Second April" Jack Kerouac, *Doctor Sax* Kerouac, *Maggie Cassidy* Kerouac, *Mexico City Blues* Tuli Kupferberg, *Beating* Kupferberg, *Snow Job*	Paul Carroll, ed., *Big Table* (1959–1960) Bob Kaufman et al., *Beatitude* (1959–1960; intermittently to 1996)

Year	Primary Texts	Anthologies, Journals, and Criticism
	Philip Lamantia, *Ekstasis* Jay Landesman, Fran Landesman, and Theodore J. Flicker, *The Nervous Set* Ron Loewinsohn, *Watermelons* Christopher Maclaine, *The Time Capsule* Michael McClure, *Hymns to St. Geryon and Other Poems* Kenneth Rexroth, *Bird in the Bush: Obvious Essays* Gary Snyder, *Riprap* Alan Watts, *Beat Zen, Square Zen and Zen* ruth weiss, *GALLERY OF WOMEN* Philip Whalen, *Self-Portrait From Another Direction*	
1960	William S. Burroughs, *Minutes to Go* (with Sinclair Beiles, Gregory Corso, and Brion Gysin) Gregory Corso, *The Happy Birthday of Death* Lawrence Ferlinghetti, *Her* Bob Kaufman, "Does the Secret Mind Whisper?" Jack Kerouac, *Lonesome Traveler* Kerouac, *Visions of Cody* (excerpts) Edward Marshall, *Hellan, Hellan* David Meltzer, *The Clown* Gilbert Sorrentino, *The Darkness Surrounds Us* Gary Snyder, *Myths & Texts* Alexander Trocchi, *Cain's Book* ruth weiss, "The Brink" Lew Welch, *Wobbly Rock* Philip Whalen, *Like I Say* Whalen, *Memoirs of an Interglacial Age*	Donald Allen, ed., *The New American Poetry* Stanley Fisher, ed., *Beat Coast East: An Anthology of Rebellion* Seymour Krim, ed., *The Beats* Shig Murao, ed., *Shig's Magazine* (1960–69) Elias Wilentz, ed., *The Beat Scene*
1961	Alan Ansen, *Disorderly Houses: A Book of Poems* William S. Burroughs, *The Soft Machine*	Gene Baro, ed., *"Beat" Poets* Gregory Corso and Walter Höllerer, eds., *Junge Amerikanische Lyrik*

Year	Primary Texts	Anthologies, Journals, and Criticism
	Gregory Corso, *The American Express*	J.W. Ehrlich, ed., *Howl of the Censor*
	Diane di Prima, *Dinners and Nightmares*	Lawrence Ferlinghetti, Michael McClure, David Meltzer, and Gary Snyder, eds., *Journal for the Protection of All Beings* (1961–1978)
	Lawrence Ferlinghetti, *Starting from San Francisco*	
	Allen Ginsberg, *Kaddish and Other Poems: 1958–1960*	
	LeRoi Jones, *Preface to a Twenty Volume Suicide Note*	LeRoi Jones and Diane di Prima, eds., *The Floating Bear* (1961–1971)
	Seymour Krim, *Views of a Nearsighted Cannoneer*	Thomas Parkinson, ed., *A Casebook on the Beat*
	Tuli Kupferberg, *Beatniks, or The War Against the Beats*	Francis Rigney and L. Douglas Smith, *The Real Bohemia*
	Michael McClure, *Dark Brown*	
	McClure, *The New Book/A Book of Torture*	
1962	William S. Burroughs, *The Ticket That Exploded*	Howard Schulman, ed., *Pa'Lante: Poetry Polity Prose of a New World*
	Gregory Corso, *Long Live Man*	
	William Everson (as Brother Antoninus), *The Hazards of Holiness*	
	Joyce Glassman, *Come and Join the Dance*	
	LeRoi Jones, ed., *Four Young Lady Poets* (Carol Bergé, Barbara Moraff, Rochelle Owens, Diane Wakoski)	
	Jack Kerouac, *Big Sur*	
	Philip Lamantia, *Destroyed Works*	
1963	Williams S. Burroughs and Allen Ginsberg, *The Yage Letters*	LeRoi Jones, ed., *The Moderns: An Anthology of New Writing in America*
	Diane di Prima, *The New Handbook of Heaven*	
	Allen Ginsberg, *Reality Sandwiches: 1953–1960*	
	LeRoi Jones, *Blues People*	
	Jack Kerouac, *Visions of Gerard*	
	Ed Sanders, *Poem from Jail*	

Year	Primary Texts	Anthologies, Journals, and Criticism
1964	William S. Burroughs, *Nova Express* John Clellon Holmes, *Get Home Free* Kay Johnson, *Human Songs* LeRoi Jones, *Dutchman* Michael McClure, *Ghost Tantras* Gilbert Sorrentino, *Black and White* John Wieners, *Ace of Pentacles*	Jack Micheline, ed., *Six American Poets* Fernanda Pivano, ed., *Poesia Degli Ultimi Americani*
1965	Ray Bremser, *Poems of Madness* Herbet Huncke, *Huncke's Journal* LeRoi Jones, *The System of Dante's Hell* Bob Kaufman, *Solitudes Crowded With Loneliness* Jack Kerouac, *Desolation Angels* Joanne Kyger, *The Tapestry and The Web* Michael McClure, *The Beard* McClure, *Poisoned Wheat* David Meltzer, *The Process* Jack Micheline, *In the Bronx and Other Stories* Ed Sanders, *Peace Eye*	
1966	William Everson, *The Blowing of the Seed* Alan Harrington, *The Secret Swinger* LeRoi Jones, *Black Art* Jones, *Home: Social Essays* Lenore Kandel, *The Love Book* Joanne Kyger, *The Fool in April* Philip Lamantia, *Touch of the Marvelous* Michael McClure, *Meat Science Essays* Charles Plymell, *Apocalypse Rose* Kenneth Rexroth, *An Autobiographical Novel* Carl Solomon, *Mishaps, Perhaps* Gilbert Sorrentino, *The Sky Changes*	Hettie Jones, ed., *Poems Now* Gregor Roy, *Beat Literature* (Monarch Notes and Study Guide)
1967	Richard Brautigan, *Trout Fishing in America*	Ann Charters, *Jack Kerouac: A Bibliography*

Year	Primary Texts	Anthologies, Journals, and Criticism
	Ray Bremser, *Angel*	
	John Clellon Holmes, *Nothing More to Declare*	
	Lenore Kandel, *Word Alchemy*	
	Bob Kaufman, *Golden Sardine*	
	Philip Lamantia, *Selected Poems, 1943–1966*	
	Irving Rosenthal, *Sheeper*	
	Philip Whalen, *You Didn't Even Try*	
1968	Kirby Doyle, *Happiness Bastard*	Diane di Prima, ed., *War Poems*
	Allen Ginsberg, *Angkor Wat*	
	Ginsberg, *Planet News: 1961–67*	
	Jack Kerouac, *Vanity of Duluoz*	
	Carl Solomon, *More Mishaps*	
	Gilbert Sorrentino, *The Perfect Fiction*	
	Charles Upton, *Panic Grass*	
	Janine Pommy Vega, *Poems to Fernando*	
	Anne Waldman, *On the Wing*	
1969	Amiri Baraka, *Black Magic*	Paul Carroll, ed., *The Young American Poets*
	Bonnie Bremser, *Troia: Mexican Memoirs*	Anne Waldman, ed., *The World Anthology: Poems From the St. Mark's Poetry Project*
	Charles Bukowski, *Notes of a Dirty Old Man*	
	Diane di Prima, *Memoirs of a Beatnik*	
	Lawrence Ferlinghetti, *The Secret Meaning of Things*	
	Ferlinghetti, *Tyrannus Nix?*	
	Ted Joans, *Black Pow-Wow Jazz Poems*	
	Gary Snyder, *Earth House Hold*	
	Anne Waldman, *O My Life*	
	Lew Welch, *The Song Mt. Tamalpais Sings*	
	Philip Whalen, *On Bear's Head: Selected Poems*	
	John Wieners, *Asylum Poems*	
1970	William S. Burroughs, *The Last Words of Dutch Schultz*	Juliet Mofford, ed., *The Beat Generation*

Year	Primary Texts	Anthologies, Journals, and Criticism
	William S. Burroughs Jr., *Speed*	
	Gregory Corso, *Elegiac Feelings American*	
	Allen Ginsberg, *Indian Journals*	
	Ted Joans, *Afrodisia*	
	Seymour Krim, *Shake It for the World, Smartass*	
	Joanne Kyger, *Joanne*	
	Kyger, *Places to Go*	
	Michael McClure, *The Mad Cub*	
	John Montgomery, *Jack Kerouac: A Memoir ...*	
	Philip Whalen, *Severance Pay: Poems 1967–1969*	
1971	Ray Bremser, *Black Is Black Blues*	Samuel Charters, ed., *Some Poems/Poets*
	William S. Burroughs, *Wild Boys*	Bruce Cook, *The Beat Generation*
	Neal Cassady, *The First Third*	Eric Mottram, *William Burroughs: The Algebra of Need*
	Diane di Prima, *Revolutionary Letters*	
	Edward Dorn, *By the Sound*	
	Ted Joans, *A Black Manifesto in Jazz Poetry and Prose*	
	Michael McClure, *The Adept*	
	Charles Plymell, *The Last of the Moccasins*	
	Leo Skir, *Boychick*	
	Gilbert Sorrentino, *Imaginative Qualities of Actual Things*	
1972	Allen Ginsberg, *The Fall of America: Poems of These States, 1965–1971*	
	Ginsberg, *Gates of Wrath: Rhymed Poems, 1948–1952*	
	Ginsberg, *Iron Horse*	
	Albert Saijo, *The Backpacker*	
1973	William S. Burroughs Jr., *Kentucky Ham*	Donald Allen and Warren Tallman, eds., *The Poetics of the New American Poetry*
	Jack Kerouac, *Visions of Cody*	Ann Charters, *Kerouac*
	Kerouac (with Albert Saijo and Lew Welch), *Trip Trap*	
	Lew Welch, *Ring of Bone*	

Year	Primary Texts	Anthologies, Journals, and Criticism
1974	Allen Ginsberg, *Allen Verbatim* Ginsberg, *Visions of the Great Rememberer* Joanna McClure, *Wolf Eyes* Gary Snyder, *Turtle Island* Janine Pommy Vega, *Journal of a Hermit*	Lawrence Ferlinghetti, ed., *City Lights Anthology* Arthur Knight and Kit Knight, eds., *The Beat Book*
1975	Amiri Baraka, *Hard Facts* Andy Clausen, *Shoe Be Do Be Ee-Op* Diane di Prima, *Selected Poems, 1956–1975* Ed Sanders, *Tales of Beatnik Glory*, Vol. I Anne Waldman, *Fast Speaking Woman and Other Chants*	
1976	Carolyn Cassady, *Heart Beat* Jack Micheline, *North of Manhattan: Collected Poems, Ballads and Songs* John Montgomery, *Kerouac West Coast* Ed Sanders, *Investigative Poetry*	Robert Hipkiss, *Jack Kerouac: Prophet of the New Romanticism*
1977	Neal Cassady and Allen Ginsberg, *As Ever: The Collected Correspondence of Allen Ginsberg and Neal Cassady* William Everson, *Dionysus and the Beat* Dan Propper, *The Tale of the Amazing Tramp* Gary Snyder, *The Old Ways: Six Essays* ruth weiss, *DESERT JOURNAL*	Arthur Knight and Kit Knight, eds., *The Beat Diary* Joseph Masheck, *Beat Art*
1978	Ray Bremser, *Blowing Mouth: The Jazz Poems, 1958–1970* Diane di Prima, *Loba: Parts I–VIII* William Everson, *The Veritable Years, 1949–1966* Allen Ginsberg, *Mind Breaths: Poems 1972–1977* Joyce Johnson, *Bad Connections*	Barry Gifford and Lawrence Lee, *Jack's Book* Arthur Knight and Kit Knight, eds., *The Beat Journey* Anne Waldman and Marilyn Webb, eds., *Talking Poetics: Annals of the Jack Kerouac School of Disembodied Poetics*

Year	Primary Texts	Anthologies, Journals, and Criticism
	Peter Orlovsky, *Clean Asshole Poems & Smiling Vegetable Songs: Poems 1957–1977*	
1979	Ken Kesey, "The Day After Superman Died"	Scott Donaldson, ed., *On the Road: Text and Criticism*
	Janine Pommy Vega, *Journal of a Hermit*	Aram Saroyan, *Genesis Angels: The Saga of Lew Welch and the Beat Generation*
1980	Herbert Huncke, *The Evening Sun Turned Crimson*	
	Dan Propper, *For Kerouac in Heaven*	
	Gary Snyder, *The Real Work: Interviews & Talks 1964–1979*	
1981	Gregory Corso, *Herald of the Autochthonic Spirit*	Lee Bartlett, ed., *The Beats: Essays in Criticism*
	Allen Ginsberg, *Plutonian Ode*	Victor Bockris, *With William Burroughs: A Report from the Bunker*
	John Clellon Holmes, *Visitor: Jack Kerouac in Old Saybrook*	
	Bob Kaufman, *The Ancient Rain: Poem 1956–1978*	Tim Hunt, *Kerouac's Crooked Road*
	Jan Kerouac, *Baby Driver*	Ken Kesey, ed., *Spit in the Ocean #6: The Cassady Issue*
	Joanne Kyger, *Strange Big Moon: The Japan and India Journals, 1960–1964*	Robert Milewski, *Jack Kerouac: An Annotated Bibliography of Secondary Sources, 1944–1979*
	Jay Landesman, *Neurotica: The Authentic Voice of the Beat Generation, 1948–1951*	
1982	Charles Bukowski, *Ham on Rye*	
	Michael McClure, *Scratching the Beat Surface*	
1983	Kirby Doyle, *The Collected Poems of Kirby Doyle*	Glen Burns, *Great Poets Howl: A Study of Allen Ginsberg's Poetry, 1943–1955*
	Joyce Johnson, *Minor Characters*	
	Gary Snyder, *Axe Handles*	Ann Charters, ed., *The Beats: Literary Bohemians in Postwar America, Parts I and II*
	Snyder, *A Passage Through India*	
		Gerald Nicosia, *Memory Babe: A Critical Biography of Jack Kerouac*

Year	Primary Texts	Anthologies, Journals, and Criticism
1984		Arthur Knight and Kit Knight, eds., *The Beat Road*
1985	William S. Burroughs, *The Adding Machine: Selected Essays* Burroughs, *Queer* John Clellon Holmes, *Gone in October: Last Reflections on Jack Kerouac*	Rudi Horemans, ed., *Beat Indeed!* Lewis Hyde, ed., *On the Poetry of Allen Ginsberg* Fred McDarrah, *Kerouac and Friends* Jennie Skerl, *William S. Burroughs*
1986	Alan Ansen, *William Burroughs: An Essay* Joanne Kyger, *Going On: Selected Poems, 1958–1980* Sarah Schulman, *Girls, Visions and Everything*	Ann Charters, *Beats and Company* Warren French, *Jack Kerouac*
1987	Herbet Huncke, *Guilty of Everything*	Roy Carr, Brian Case and Fred Deller, *The Hip: Hipsters, Jazz and the Beat Generation* Park Honan, ed., *The Beats: An Anthology of "Beat" Writing* Arthur Knight and Kit Knight, eds., *The Beat Vision* Regina Weinreich, *Kerouac's Spontaneous Poetics*
1988		Kevin Ring, ed., *The Beat Scene* (1988–)
1989	Gregory Corso, *Mindfield: New and Selected Poems* Maxine Hong Kingston, *Tripmaster Monkey: His Fake Book* Jack Micheline, *Imaginary Conversation with Jack Kerouac* Harold Norse, *Memoirs of a Bastard Angel*	Michael Davidson, *The San Francisco Renaissance*

Year	Primary Texts	Anthologies, Journals, and Criticism
1990	Carolyn Cassady, *Off the Road* Hettie Jones, *How I Became Hettie Jones*	Gregory Stephenson, *Daybreak Boys: Essays on the Literature of the Beat Generation*
1991	Amiri Baraka, *The LeRoi Jones/Amiri Baraka Reader* Seymour Krim, *What's This Cat's Story? The Best of Seymour Krim*	Tim Dean, *Gary Snyder and the American Unconscious: Inhabiting the Ground* John Maynard, *Venice West: The Beat Generation in Southern California* Jennie Skerl and Robin Lydenberg, eds., *William S. Burroughs at the Front: Critical Reception, 1959–1989*
1992		Ann Charters, ed., *Portable Beat Reader* Edward Foster, *Understanding the Beats* James T. Jones, *A Map of Mexico City Blues* Michael Schumacher, *Dharma Lion: A Biography of Allen Ginsberg*
1993		Anne Waldman, ed., *Disembodied Poetics: Annals of the Jack Kerouac School*
1995		David Kherdian, ed., *Beat Voices* Carole Tonkinson, ed., *Big Sky Mind: Buddhism and the Beat Generation* Steven Watson, *Birth of the Beat Generation*
1996	Gary Snyder, *Mountains and Rivers Without End*	Brenda Knight, *Women of the Beat Generation: The Writers, Artists and Muses at the Heart of a Revolution* A. Robert Lee, ed., *The Beat Generation Writers* Anne Waldman, ed., *The Beat Book*

Year	Primary Texts	Anthologies, Journals, and Criticism
1997	Herbert Huncke, *The Herbert Huncke Reader* Albert Saijo, *Outspeaks: A Rhapsody* Ed Sanders, *1968: A History in Verse* Janine Pommy Vega, *Tracking the Serpent: Journeys Into Four Continents*	Timothy Murphy, *Wising up the Marks: The Amodern William Burroughs* Richard Peabody, ed., *A Different Beat: Writings by Women of the Beat Generation* Jack Sargeant, *The Naked Lens: Beat Cinema*
1998	William S. Burroughs, *Word Virus: the William S. Burroughs Reader* Lawrence Ferlinghetti, *A Far Rockaway of the Heart*	David Sterritt, *Mad to Be Saved: The Beats, the '50s, and Film* "The Silent Beat," special issue of *Discourse*
1999	Ted Joans, *Teducation: Selected Poems, 1949–1999* Gary Snyder, *The Gary Snyder Reader: Prose, Poetry, and Translations*	R. J. Ellis, *Liar! Liar! Jack Kerouac, Novelist* James T. Jones, *Jack Kerouac's Duluoz Legend: The Mythic Form of an Autobiographical Fiction* George Plimpton, ed., *The Beat Writers at Work* Michael Skau, *"A Clown in the Grave": Complexities and Tensions in the Works of Gregory Corso*
2000	Allen Ginsberg, *Deliberate Prose* Jack Kerouac and Joyce Johnson, *Door Wide Open: A Beat Love Affair in Letters, 1957–1958* Joan Haverty Kerouac, *Nobody's Wife: The Smart Aleck and the King of the Beats* Janine Pommy Vega, *Mad Dogs of Trieste: New & Selected Poems*	Ben Giamo, *Kerouac, the Word and the Way* Barry Miles, *The Beat Hotel* Thomas Newhouse, *The Beat Generation and the Popular Novel in the United States, 1945–1970* Rod Phillips, *"Forest Beatniks" and "Urban Thoreaus": Gary Snyder, Jack Kerouac, Lew Welch, and Michael McClure* Jennie Skerl, ed., "Teaching Beat Literature" (special issue of *College Literature*) Matt Theado, *Understanding Jack Kerouac*

Year	Primary Texts	Anthologies, Journals, and Criticism
2001	David Amram, *Vibrations: The Adventures and Musical Times of David Amram* Diane di Prima, *Recollections of My Life as a Woman* Lawrence Ferlinghetti, *Love in the Days of Rage* David Meltzer, *San Francisco Beat: Talking With the Poets* Anne Waldman, *Vow to Poetry*	James Campbell, *This is the Beat Generation: New York-San Francisco-Paris* Ann Charters, ed., *Beat Down Your Soul: What Was the Beat Generation?* John Lardas, *The Bop Apocalypse* Lewis MacAdams, *Birth of Cool* Jamie Russell, *Queer Burroughs* Matt Theado, ed., *The Beats: A Literary Reference*
2002		Carmela Ciuraru, ed., *Beat Poets* Jean-François Duval, *Bukowski and the Beats: A Commentary on the Beat Generation* Ronna C. Johnson and Nancy M. Grace, eds., *Girls Who Wore Black: Women Writing the Beat Generation* Kostas Myrsiades, ed., *The Beat Generation: Critical Essays* Kirby Olson, *Gregory Corso: Doubting Thomist*
2003	David Amram, *Offbeat: Collaborating with Kerouac* Harold Norse, *In the Hub of the Fiery Force: Collected Poems, 1934–2003*	Oliver Harris, *William Burroughs and the Secret of Fascination* Manuel Luis Martinez, *Countering the Counterculture*
2004	Neal Cassady, *Collected Letters, 1944–1967* David Meltzer, *Beat Thing*	Nancy M. Grace and Ronna C. Johnson, *Breaking the Rule of Cool* Paul Maher, *Kerouac: The Definitive Biography* Regina Marler, ed., *Queer Beats: How the Beats Turned America on to Sex*

Year	Primary Texts	Anthologies, Journals, and Criticism
		David Scheiderman and Philip Walsh, eds., *Retaking the Universe: William S. Burroughs in the Age of Globalization* Jennie Skerl, ed., *Reconstructing the Beats* David Sterritt, *Screening the Beats* Preston Whaley, *Blows Like a Horn: Beat Writing, Jazz, Style, and Markets in the Transformation of U.S. Culture*
2005		William Lawlor, ed., *Beat Culture: Icons, Lifestyles, and Impact*
2006	Allen Ginsberg, *Collected Poems, 1947–1997*	Stephen Edington, *The Beat Face of God: The Beat Generation as Spirit Guides* Timothy Gray, *Gary Snyder and the Pacific Rim* Kurt Hemmer, *Encyclopedia of Beat Literature* Michael Hrebeniak, *Action Writing: Jack Kerouac's Wild Form*
2007	Jack Kerouac, *On the Road: The Original Scroll* Edie Kerouac-Parker, *You'll Be Okay: My Life With Jack Kerouac* Philip Whalen, *The Collected Poems of Philip Whalen*	Nancy M. Grace, *Jack Kerouac and the Literary Imagination* John Leland, *Why Kerouac Matters* Tony Trigilio, *Allen Ginsberg's Buddhist Poetics*
2008	William S. Burroughs and Jack Kerouac, *And the Hippos Were Boiled in Their Tanks* John Hoffman, *Journey to the End* Philip Lamantia, *Tau* Elizabeth Von Vogt, *681 Lexington Avenue: A Beat Education in New York City, 1947–1954*	

Year	Primary Texts	Anthologies, Journals, and Criticism
2009	Helen Weaver, *The Awakened: A Memoir of Kerouac and the Fifties*	Paul Buhle, ed., *The Beats: A Graphic History*
		Oliver Harris and Ian MacFadyen, eds., *Naked Lunch@50: Anniversary Essays*
		Hilary Holladay and Robert Holton, eds., *What's Your Road, Man? Critical Essays on Jack Kerouac's On the Road*
		Anne Waldman and Laura Wright, eds., *Beats at Naropa*
2010		A. Robert Lee, *Modern American Counter Writing*
2011	Anne Waldman, *The Iovis Trilogy: Colors in the Mechanism of Concealment*	Levi Asher, ed., *Beats in Time: A Literary Generation's Legacy*
		Laurence Coupe, *Beat Sound, Beat Vision: The Beat Spirit and Popular Song*
		Erik Mortenson, *Capturing the Beat Moment*
2012	Lenore Kandel, *The Collected Poems*	Gordon Ball, *East Hill Farm: Sessions With Allen Ginsberg*
		Larry Beckett, *Beat Poetry*
		Sharin Elkholy ed., *The Philosophy of the Beats*
		Nancy M. Grace and Ronna C. Johnson, eds., *Journal of Beat Studies* (2012–)
		Nancy M. Grace and Jennie Skerl, eds., *The Transnational Beat Generation*
		Joyce Johnson, *The Voice Is All: The Lonely Victory of Jack Kerouac*

Year	Primary Texts	Anthologies, Journals, and Criticism
		Todd F. Tietchen, *The Cubalogues: Beat Writers in Revolutionary Havana*
		Paul Varner, *Historical Dictionary of the Beat Movement*
2013	Philip Lamantia, *The Collected Poems of Philip Lamantia*	David Sterritt, *The Beats: A Very Short Introduction*
		Simon Warner, *Text and Drugs and Rock 'n' Roll: The Beats and Rock Culture*
		"The Beat Generation and Europe," special issue of *Comparative American Studies*
2014	Elise Cowen, *Poems and Fragments* Diane di Prima, *The Poetry Deal*	Juan Garcia-Robles, *At the End of the Road: Jack Kerouac in Mexico*
		Tim Hunt, *The Textuality of Soulwork: Jack Kerouac's Quest for Spontaneous Prose*
		John Tytell, *The Beat Interviews*
		Tytell, *Writing Beat and Other Occasions of Literary Mayhem*
2015	Peter Orlovsky, *Peter Orlovsky: A Life in Words* John Wieners, *Stars Seen in Person: Selected Journals* Wieners, *Supplication*	Lawrence Ferlinghetti, ed., *City Lights Pocket Poets Anthology: 60th Anniversary Edition*
		Frida Forsgren and Michael J. Prince, eds., *Out of the Shadows: Beat Women Are Not Beaten Women*
		Mark Gonnerman, ed., *A Sense of the Whole: Reading Gary Snyder's Mountains and Rivers Without End*

Year	Primary Texts	Anthologies, Journals, and Criticism
		Brian Hassett, *The Hitchhiker's Guide to Jack Kerouac*
		Eliot Katz, *The Poetry and Politics of Allen Ginsberg*
		Rich Weidman, *Beat Generation FAQ*
2016		Jimmy Fazzino, *World Beats: Beat Generation Writing and the Worlding of U.S. Literature*
		Deborah Geis, ed., *Beat Drama: Playwrights and Performances of the "Howl" Generation*
		Hassan Melehy, *Kerouac: Language, Poetics, and Territory*
		Bill Morgan, *The Beats Abroad: A Global Guide to the Beat Generation*

STEVEN BELLETTO

Introduction

The Beat Half-Century

Fans of irony will appreciate that *The Cambridge Companion to the Beats* now exists. Cambridge University Press, the world's oldest, telegraphs a certain seriousness and – to some readers – the imprimatur of the academy. And yet, if you know anything about the Beats, you probably know that they were "antiestablishment," that they wrote against conformity, consumerism, and the values of mainstream culture. From a literary perspective, they often positioned their writing against that of the so-called "academic" or "university" poets: in 1961, poet Tuli Kupferberg went so far as to claim that the Beats "destroyed the importance of the Academy in American poetry."[1] Given this history, it may seem a violation of a Beat ethos for scholars to explore their work in a volume published by a university press.

My first response to such objection is that, however much Beat writers insisted on countercultural critique, if you stop to read their work, whether poetry, novels, memoirs, plays, or letters, you quickly find that the chasms separating the mainstream and bohemian cultures, the hip world and the square, are not so wide as is sometimes believed: when it came to the Beats, a dynamic relationship between the two realms always seemed to be at play. It is certainly true, for example, that a phenomenon called "the Beat Generation" would not have risen to public consciousness without the interest of the establishment's publicity wing, mass media, which became fascinated first by the obscenity trial surrounding Allen Ginsberg's great poem "Howl" (1956) and then with the idea that in *On the Road* (1957) Jack Kerouac was speaking for an entire generation of young people. Even as the 1950s media misunderstood Beat writing by confusing it with what journalist Herb Caen dubbed in 1958 the "Beatnik" – the much-repeated caricature of a grubby, bearded loser who pretended to art as a route to sex – few would now deny that contemporary interest in Beat lives and literatures is at least in part a legacy of such largely dismissive media attention. And just as this attention nearly always conflated the cartoon Beatnik with real-life writers and their works, the mid-century academy was generally loathe to admit the Beats were writers at all, let alone good writers, a view that only really began to change in substantive ways in the 1980s. We are at a moment now when the texts and figures associated with the Beat movement, and indeed the very concept of a "Beat Generation," have been subjects of so many doctoral dissertations, scholarly articles, and academic books that it would probably be impossible for one person to have read it all. This suggests that the Beats and the academy are no longer enemies – even as their relationship remains vexed on many levels – and it is my great pleasure to present this volume as one small token of rapprochement. Although one can feasibly account for post-1945 American literature and culture by giving only a passing glance at the Beats, this volume, while not moving them to the center of such an accounting, nonetheless insists that they are essential to understanding the changes and transformations of the period.[2] Far from being merely the exuberant but sloppy writers interested either in vacuous "kicks" or in shocking the middle class, the Beats were a diverse, surprisingly widespread, loosely affiliated literary movement whose formal and aesthetic innovations were as radical as their revolutions in subject matter, a marriage of form and content that has shaped numerous facets of contemporary American literature and culture in ways we are still working to understand.

As will be clear from this introduction and volume as a whole, the enterprise of labeling a diverse range of writers is just as fraught as defining the term Beat or Beat Generation. Over the years, countless arguments and interpretations have been proposed about who or what "Beat" really means, and a favorite opening move of scholars writing on the Beat Generation is to raise the possibility that there was in fact no such thing. This reluctance to attach a fixed meaning to Beat or extend its descriptive power to a generation of course speaks to a fundamental problem with all labels and categories, that they can confuse as much as they clarify, that they are either so specific as to ignore important texts or figures, or so broad as to be meaningless. The Beat writers themselves knew this, which is why John Clellon Holmes, credited with offering the first sustained explanation of the term Beat Generation in a 1952 New York Times article, insisted on "this generation's reluctance to name itself, its reluctance to discuss itself as a group," even as his article did just that.[3] I may therefore seem to beg the question by referring to "Beat writers" when the label "Beat" is itself unstable, what Ronna C. Johnson and Nancy M. Grace call "a famously contingent signifier, characterized by a diversity that is consistent with its wide range of practitioners."[4] Yet even if we accept this contingent status and acknowledge the diversity of its practitioners, the fact remains that the terms Beat and Beat

Generation have had a remarkable cultural and literary life, partly because people have understood and deployed them in wildly different ways.

Here is a straightforward explanation of the Beats that emphasizes their opposition to mainstream culture:

> The Beats were an avant-garde arts movement and bohemian subculture that led an underground existence in the 1940s and early 1950s, gaining public recognition in the late 1950s ... Although influential in many artistic circles and bohemian enclaves and celebrated in the burgeoning youth culture, these writers ... were condemned and ridiculed by mass media journalists, the then-reigning public intellectuals, and by academic critics.[5]

This description is accurate, and a good starting point for getting a handle on the idea of Beat. But as soon as we try to bring it into sharper focus by looking at what Beat writers themselves said, it is immediately apparent that, if the term "Beat" is contingent, when it is linked to the idea of a "generation," things become doubly problematic. The year before he died, Ginsberg reworked definitions of the Beat Generation he had been tinkering with since the early 1980s, explaining that Beat was originally a hip word meaning "exhausted, at the bottom of the world, looking up or out, sleepless, wide-eyed, perceptive, rejected by society, on your own, streetwise," noting also that Kerouac saw the word as rooted in "beatific." From there Ginsberg explores the term in relation to the "Beat generation literary movement," saying first that this phrase refers to "a group of friends who had worked together on poetry, prose, and cultural conscience from the mid-forties until the term became popular nationally in the late fifties," and names specifically Kerouac, Neal Cassady, William S. Burroughs, Herbert Huncke, Holmes, Carl Solomon, Gregory Corso, Lawrence Ferlinghetti, and Peter Orlovsky, later mentioning a subsequent widening of this group to include Michael McClure, Gary Snyder, Philip Whalen, Bob Kaufman, Jack Micheline, Ray Bremser, and LeRoi Jones (known later as Amiri Baraka).[6]

As this loose affiliation radiated outward, Ginsberg argues, one could locate a more widespread Beat ethos defined by "an inquisitiveness into the nature of consciousness, leading to an acquaintance with Eastern thought, meditation practice, art as extension or manifestation of exploration of the texture of consciousness, spiritual liberation as a result" (xv–xvi). These definitions are at once useful and limiting, for though the people Ginsberg names are certainly major figures, he omits many more people (notably women) who were vital to the Beat phenomenon, and the characteristics he cites encompass some but not all of the work associated with the movement. Hardly surprising, then, that other Beat-associated writers had different ideas about what the term meant: in 1959, William Everson argued that the Beat Generation represents "the reemergence in the twentieth century of the Dionysian spirit," and a year later Gary Snyder thought that "The beat generation can be seen as an aspect of the worldwide trend for intellectuals to reconsider the nature of the human individual, existence, personal motives, the qualities of love and hatred, and the means of achieving wisdom."[7] For others such as Diane di Prima, Beat was a fraught label because it ironically reinforced normative ideas about gender. As she wrote of the Beat scene in the 1950s, "as a woman, I was invisible. I took that as a matter of course."[8] Ed Sanders later recalled that "Beatnik and Beat were two of the great pejoratives of the era, but how magnetic and alluring it was to rebellious youth when the squares tossed the word 'beatnik' around with stupid abandon!"[9] One could go on and on listing various interpretations of or reactions to the terms Beat and Beat Generation (Gregory Corso famously claimed that "The Beat Generation is now about everything"), but here I'm pointing to the persistent issues with naming a collectivity so fundamentally diverse and wide-ranging, especially as a key aspect of the supposed members of this generation was a fierce independence and resistance to collectivity, what Holmes called a "reluctance to discuss itself as a group."[10]

One way to think about the problem of the term Beat Generation ascribing collectivity to a diverse range of figures for whom critique of collectivity was paramount is to look at how Kerouac first conceptualized the generation. As is well known, the genesis of the term Beat Generation was a conversation between Holmes and Kerouac in 1948; as Holmes reports it, Kerouac remarked:

> It's a sort of furtiveness ... Like we were a generation of furtives. You know, with an inner knowledge there's no use flaunting on that level, the level of the "public," a kind of beatness – I mean ... we all *really* know where we are – and a weariness with all the forms, all the conventions of the world ... So I guess you might say we're a *beat* generation.[11]

Aside from the assertion of weariness with "conventions," nowhere in this originary definition are the various keywords that have come to be associated with Beatness, but Kerouac does twice mention furtiveness, and uses it to play on a tension between the individual and the collective. In this view, Beatness means both a private interiority unconcerned with the public and critical of convention *and* an identification with a "generation," the idea that "we all" share the same furtiveness. Of all the ways one may define or describe "Beat," then, from the moment the writers Ginsberg names above began sharing social spaces and trading manuscripts, a sense of "insiderness" versus "outsiderness" crystalized: either you felt an intuitive, insider kinship with others weary of convention or you bought in to that convention without thinking too much about it. If the Beats have been perennially cast as outsiders to mainstream culture and its values, they conversely created their own sense of the "inside" that was furtive, secret, invisible to square America. When Kerouac identifies a "generation of furtives," then, he claims another kind of "inside" sensibility premised in part on a secret, unspoken connection to others.

Thus to be Beat wasn't necessarily to be one of four men in New York City in the early 1940s but rather to have an awareness of and identification with the furtive sense of "insiderness" to which Kerouac points. Chandler Brossard, author of *Who Walk in Darkness* (1952), sometimes paired with Holmes's *Go* (1952) as the first Beat novels, claimed in 1958 that the Beat Generation's "very feeling of insideness, of exclusivity (like a secret sect) made anybody on the outside unthinkable, or if not that severe, at least undesirable."[12] Brossard was picking up on the social aspects of the Beat scene, that distance between the hip and square worlds that might possibly be bridged if one came to appreciate the furtive "inner knowledge" Kerouac described. Brenda Frazer/Bonnie Bremser, writing about the gulf between "painfully normal" visitors to Greenwich Village and its Beat residents, used the word "inside" interchangeably with "hip": "As inside or hip residents of the village scene Ray [Bremser] and I were irritated by the stares of tourists who came there just for that, to stare."[13] (Incidentally, by the time she and husband Ray fled to Mexico, where Bonnie would become a sex worker to support him and their infant daughter, she cast Kerouac's language in far darker terms: "From then on I felt hunted, furtive."[14]) In *Minor Characters* (1983), Joyce Johnson would describe her first forays from the relative shelter of her childhood home in Morningside Heights to the Village scene Bremser sketches as "the outside/inside problem."[15]

This sense of "insideness" is exploited for effect in a range of Beat texts, including Ginsberg's "Howl," where, for instance, the poet refers to "N.C., secret hero of these poems."[16] In the mid-1950s, it would have been difficult indeed "on the outside," as Brossard says, to know that these initials referred to Neal Cassady, also the model for Dean Moriarty in *On the Road*. With this line, Ginsberg teases his readers, inviting them to step partway into some imagined "inside" while withholding revelation of who precisely the secret hero is. To appreciate this line of the poem, in other words, one need already be connected to the inside, the irony of our present moment being that such an inside is rendered nearly meaningless when an establishment anthology as august as the *Norton Anthology of American Literature* lets readers in on the secret, dryly explaining that the line refers to "Neal Cassady, hip companion of Jack Kerouac and the original Dean Moriarty."[17] But, just as

Kerouac's "generation of furtives" is paradoxically both idiosyncratic and collective, Ginsberg's "secret hero" is broadcast as secret, so what becomes paramount is the secret itself, and the knowledge that learning it might allow one to move from the outside in. This quality of furtiveness or secrecy announced as such challenges readers who were not there and is an important feature of an early Beat sensibility (which is why, after Holmes recounts Kerouac's coining of the term Beat Generation, he stresses that Kerouac "laughed a conspiratorial, the Shadow-knows kind of laugh," as though the feeling he names is like a secret you either "get" or you don't ["Name" 107]).

A reliance on the trope of secrecy to play with the relationship between "inside" and "outside," the Beat world and square, runs throughout much Beat writing. In briefly citing a few examples, one might begin with Kerouac's famous list of advice for would-be writers of "modern prose," the first item of which is "Scribbled secret notebooks, and wild typewritten pages, for yr own joy."[18] Here again the furtive scribbles away secretly for his own "joy," and yet Kerouac insists on such secrecy when purporting to give writing advice to those interested in participating in a more widespread phenomenon, something flying under the banner of "modern prose." Such a paradox might at first blush seem problematic, were it not for the "generation of furtives" idea he earlier propounded. In *Naked Lunch* (1959), Burroughs introduces the idea of secrecy in his comic, grotesque routines, as when Dr. Benway confuses distinctions between governmental agents and drug users because both have secrets to protect; subject to interrogation with various kinds of drugs, "an agent might be prepared to reveal his secrets but quite unable to remember them, or cover story and secret life might be inextricably garbled."[19] The joke is that Burroughs seems to be revealing all his secrets with *Naked Lunch*, and so what makes it Beat is its invitation to readers to feel included in a furtive world, to think they are participating in a hip underground subculture. Yet, as with the drug-beclouded agent, with Burroughs one can never be sure what is "cover story" and what is "secret life," so real access to the "inside" is always deferred. Bob Kaufman likewise seems to welcome readers into a "secret life" in his poem "Does the Secret Mind Whisper?" (1960), in which he proves himself another of Kerouac's furtives. The poem is a breathless tour de force turning on the titular question to ask whether one can ever really understand another person's "transient ecstasies pains of too personal existences" of another person.[20] The easy answer to the title question is "yes," and the poem seems at first to invite readers on the "inside" of yet another secret, but, like "Howl" and *Naked Lunch*, it may simply propose getting on an "inside" as a tantalizing possibility never truly realizable. The idea of a secret Beat inside became sowidespreadthatbythemid-1970sitcouldserveasanobjectofgentleparody,as in Dan Propper's poem "One, Two, Many Poetry Readings," in which the various characters "on display" at a Beat reading sit "all / secretly knowing themselves the nation's greatest."[21]

Whatever access *The Cambridge Companion to the Beats* does or does not have to a secret "inside" of Beatdom, it assumes the protean virtues of such a construct, however contested, profuse, and slippery it may be. This is a volume by scholars written for students, other scholars, and those looking for deeper analyses of Beat literature that cut through out-sized, romanticized accounts of particular writers' lives. I want to stress that the work to follow is hardly the only way to engage Beat literature and ought not be taken as any manner of final word. That said, because the ensuing chapters have emerged from the broad theoretical and methodological norms of the academy, however they may be deployed by particular contributors, it might be useful to take a tour of some ways the Beats have been conceptualized or constructed in critical editions and anthologies of the past decades, as they clarify the relationship between the Beats and the mainstream academy at various moments in time.

An Introduction to Introductions

For about the past sixty years, there have been anthologies and critical collections designed to showcase, theorize, promote, or challenge a category called "Beat literature." Such texts have been especially useful when planning the shape of this volume, and I want to range over some of this previous work because it demonstrates quite vividly the problems one encounters when attempting to describe the qualities of a Beat writer or an identifiable Beat aesthetic. The earliest printed groupings of Beat-associated writing were in little magazines and literary reviews in the 1950s, some of the most notable of which are *Ark II Moby I* (1956–57), the "San Francisco Scene" issue of *Evergreen Review* (1957), *Yugen* (1958–1962), *A New Folder* (1959), *Beatitude* (1959–60; and intermittently through 1996), and *Big Table* (1959–1960), just to name a few – in 1983 George Butterick compiled a list of 245 "periodicals inspired by the Beat Generation," so this is indeed a mere sample.[22] While little magazines are essential to understanding the development of Beat literature, for the purposes of this introduction, I am interested in those works, either anthologies or collections of critical essays, that wrestled with the consequences of naming something called the Beat Generation and its literatures, and so will leave it to readers to unearth these little magazines from library stacks on their own (a rewarding afternoon).

Instead, let us turn to the first anthology of Beat writing explicitly framed as such, *The Beat Generation and the Angry Young Men* (1958). The volume is illustrative as it emerged from the cultural moment when most readers had a sense of the Beats from *On the Road* and "Howl," and perhaps knew that Ginsberg had dedicated *Howl and Other Poems* to Kerouac and Burroughs, and the poem itself to Carl Solomon, all writers represented in *The Beat Generation and the Angry Young Men* (as is John Clellon Holmes). So far so good, and yet the editors extend their volume to those who had written more broadly about hipsters but were not directly connected to the Beat scene (Anatole Broyard, Chandler Brossard, R. V. Cassill, and George Mandel), and so side-stepped asking whether there were meaningful distinctions between the Beat Generation and other writers interested in American subcultures.[23] Moreover, little in the anthology claims Beat literature as formally or aesthetically distinct from other kinds of writing. The editors focus instead on the Beats as "social phenomena which have found increasing literary expression … In the long run, they may well be the advance columns of a vast moral revolution, one which will transform man from a creature of history to a creature of experience."[24] It is telling indeed that the Beats are conceived first as "social phenomena" and second as writers. Beat literature is worthwhile, this argument goes, because it illuminates the authors' lives, which in turn illuminate more widespread social phenomena, hence the emphasis on "experience" rather than aesthetic form. The texts chosen are then examples that demonstrate the more lurid or outré aspects of bohemian living (Burroughs on heroin use, Kerouac on Times Square, Solomon on life in a psychiatric asylum, and so on). Such a marriage of Beat lives with Beat literature is of course a strong appeal of both for many readers, but, as the example of *The Beat Generation and the Angry Young Men* attests, it also had a hold on the earliest critical constructions of the Beats, which went relatively unexamined for decades.

Beat writing flowered from 1956 to 1960, but, after the publication of *On the Road* in September 1957, the United States entered the Beatnik era, when the cartoon image of a bongo-playing doper reigned in the public imagination. So, even as some of the most complex and consequential Beat work was being published (see the Chronology), the reception of this work was always entangled with the Beatnik image, a fact that again speaks to the dynamic relationship between the Beats and mainstream culture mentioned earlier. Responding to public hunger for all things Beat, by 1960, more anthologies extended or challenged the presentation in *The Beat Generation and the Angry Young Men*. In 1960, *Beat Coast East: An Anthology of Rebellion* included some twenty-five writers (as opposed the earlier nine), some of whom would go on to be recognized as important figures in late twentieth-century letters (Ray Bremser, Gregory Corso, Diane di Prima, LeRoi Jones), as well as a host of others who are now seldom read. The preface asks "What is beat?" but editor Stanley Fisher resists a definitive answer, offering instead a catalog of absurdist questions: "Is it … hopscotch, vaudeville, lecher, grave, holy, lemonade, rebellion, horseradish," a pugnacious rebuke to the scholar's desire to label and categorize that refuses to do either.[25] In this way, the vibe of Fisher's preface is very much in keeping with a Beat ethos (the year before, Michael McClure declared "THERE ARE NO CATEGORIES!").[26] Elaborating his lampoon of a scholarly introduction, Fisher explains that he conducted some light sociological fieldwork, asking "an assortment of squalid squares and plastered saints what they thought the word beat meant" (7). This allows him to offer a numbered list of twenty responses, ranging from "A formal desperation which became a rebellion against all political and literary forms" to "A high level of mentality and awareness of the IDEA and of poetry and a non-involvement with one's awareness" to "A limpid and exhausted jazz rhythm" to "Criminal without a crime" (7–8). By presenting the definitions in this way, Fisher at once adopts a kind of scholarly apparatus and refuses to confirm its value, so readers are left with the impression that Beat *might* be any or none of these things, again reinforcing the potential revelatory power of the secret, insider knowledge I discussed in the previous section.

Even though *Beat Coast East* was more wide-ranging than *The Beat Generation and the Angry Young Men*, because it appeared when the movement was still coalescing, it neglected writers who have since appeared in nearly every accounting of the Beats as a social and literary phenomenon. By contrast, *The Beat Scene* (1960), an important anthology of writing and photographs of the eponymous scene, gives roughly equal attention to the figures named above, but also people such as Lawrence Ferlinghetti, Ted Joans, Tuli Kupferberg, Philip Lamantia, Michael McClure, Jack Micheline, Lew Welch, and Philip Whalen – all of whom are essential to any discussion of Beat writing. *The Beat Scene* was edited by Elias Wilentz, who, with his brother Ted, co-owned the Eighth Street Bookshop in Greenwich Village, a favored gathering place for bohemian literary types throughout the 1950s and thus a vital part of the scene presented in the book. Thanks to Wilentz's intimacy with New York's broader literary pulse, *The Beat Scene* gives readers glimpses of people who circulated in the scene, including those who would probably not self-identify as "Beat." Such figures include Paul Blackburn, Robert Creeley, Paul Goodman, Kenneth Koch, Frank O'Hara, and others less well known. Thus even as the volume's cover is illustrated with Fred McDarrah's now-famous photograph of Kerouac reading at the Artist's Studio, the book's sense of the "Beat scene" went far beyond the Kerouac–Ginsberg–Burroughs triumvirate – Burroughs does not in fact appear at all. This suggests that cross-pollination in the 1950s complicated categories that associated particular writers with larger schools or movements, so that Blackburn and Creeley were not seen as only of the Black Mountain School or O'Hara as only of the New York School. As Ann Charters has put it, "in the creative tumult of the burgeoning literary underground of the 1950s and 1960s, the writers didn't cohere in any absolute lines of allegiance to 'schools' of influence."[27] Charters's observation does not mean that contemporary students of postwar literature ought not find any utility in thinking about the Beat movement, or Black Mountain and New York "schools" of poetry, but that, when the writers who now comprise what we call those schools were associating and producing their work, few thought of themselves as exclusively identified with particular schools or movements.

It therefore makes sense that, in his introduction to *The Beat Scene*, Wilentz emphasized that it was perhaps not possible or even desirable to define any writer as Beat: "You can't lump all writers together – not even the Bohemians. And if you just mean the 'beats,' do you mean *Life* magazine 'beat,' Ginsberg 'beat,' Kerouac 'beat,' or Norman Mailer 'beat'? Each should have to be examined separately to make conclusions – whether aesthetic, political or moral."[28] For Wilentz, defining who or what counted as Beat was already problematic in 1960, and yet his default position was to fall back on the literary energies of the most visible figures: "To a point, the 'beats' are those who identify themselves with the ideas of Allen Ginsberg, Jack Kerouac, Gregory Corso and Peter Orlovsky. The others are whatever they might call themselves – 'underground,' 'Black Mountain,' 'abomunist,' or simply poets and writers" (8). So, to again borrow the terms of the previous section, even for those supposedly most firmly on the "inside" of the Beat phenomenon, it was distinctly possible there was no inside at all. This paradox ran through all the early anthologies of Beat writing and has continued to the present day, for in various intellectual and theoretical moments, scholars have thought factors such as gender or sexuality or race or transnational circulation to be key markers of the Beat experience – factors that would not have occurred to anthologizers in 1960 as relevant.

Seymour Krim, a Beat-associated writer himself, produced yet another anthology in 1960, simply called *The Beats*, which defined the movement as "protest writing, fresh writing, fantastic crazy nutty grim honest liberating fertilizing writing, words and thoughts that come untouched by Madison Avenue's manicured robot hand ... from the experience we have all shared but been too timid to come out and admit."[29] Here we see what became perhaps the hallmark of how the Beats were constructed as such in the late

1950s and early 1960s: using language evoking "Howl," Krim argues that the Beats are at bottom about "protest" – against what, exactly, remains vague, as "Madison Avenue" is shorthand for advertising and thus a culture of consumerism – and yet it is significant that Krim suggests that such protest is rooted in "experience we have all shared." On the one hand, the Beats are protesting the values associated with mainstream culture, and yet on the other, their protest is merely an articulation of what everyone has felt and noticed but is too timid to say. In terms of contributors, like Wilentz, Krim is wide-ranging, so Gary Snyder makes his first appearance in a Beat anthology, yet such range is still limited primarily to men as only two women are represented, Diane di Prima and Brigid Murnaghan, the latter of whom he describes as a "fine upright beat lady" (214). Although the volume includes photographs of other women on the scene, because their work is omitted, readers are left with the impression that they were merely hangers-on, girlfriends and muses, and so women writers who have now come to be recognized as crucial to the development of the Beats in the 1950s are rendered invisible, a gendered myopia that would not be redressed until the 1990s.

One final anthology from this period worth mentioning is Gene Baro's *"Beat" Poets* (1961). Unlike the tenor of these other books, in his introduction, Baro does not focus primarily on the lives of the poets or the Beats as "social phenomena" but instead tries to put his finger on what is distinctive about the writing itself: "The reaction of these writers has been against academism and formality, stiff prosody, controlled ambiguities, precise cultural references, lyrical suppression, and censored emotions."[30] This statement is notable for placing the Beats within the framework of literary history, so that their importance lies not in their personal antics but in what they do in their writing, a thread of Beat scholarship picked up at some moments during this period (Warren Tallman's essay "Kerouac's Sound" [1959] was pioneering in this regard) but that would not gain traction for another fifteen or twenty years. Baro's emphasis on the formal or aesthetic qualities of Beat writing perhaps explains why, in addition to some of the central male writers appearing in other anthologies, he includes a writer such as Ron Loewinsohn, whose brilliant first book *Watermelons* (1959) was given the full Beat treatment – an introduction by Ginsberg *and* a letter of support from William Carlos Williams – but is absent from practically every other critical study or anthology of the Beats.

While not concerned with the Beats per se, two important critical efforts from the early 1960s bear brief discussion for the ways in which, like *"Beat" Poets*, they marked writing – as opposed to "social phenomena" – as the most consequential dimensions of the Beats: Donald Allen's *The New*

American Poetry (1960) and LeRoi Jones's *The Moderns: An Anthology of New Writing in America* (1963). It is hard to overstate the importance of Allen's anthology as it brought more widespread critical attention to a range of poetic practices that had been marginalized by the aesthetic values of the academy throughout the 1940s and 1950s. To describe this "new American poetry," Allen divides poets into "five large groups, though these divisions are somewhat arbitrary and cannot be taken as rigid categories."[31] Allen's categories are Black Mountain, San Francisco Renaissance, Beat Generation, New York poets, and a fifth unaffiliated group that included Whalen, Gilbert Sorrentino, Snyder, McClure, Bremser, Jones, John Wieners, Loewinsohn, and David Meltzer, all of whom are or should be important to any discussion of who or what the Beats were. I mention this because, in 1960, Allen could argue for the importance of the Beats as a group (defined by him as Kerouac, Ginsberg, Corso, and Orlovsky) as well as a wider range of poets who seemed to him significant but were not yet seen as part of an identifiable Beat movement, again underscoring the fluidity and arbitrariness of the groupings named in his preface. Jones positioned *The Moderns* as a prose counterpart to Allen's anthology, and although he concedes that what he calls the "prose restoration" in US letters was "subtler" than the revolutions in poetry for which Allen argues, he nonetheless identifies a unique commonality in the prose he had chosen: "one characteristic that binds most of the writers in this volume together ... is that for the most part they are interested in those personalities (and people) who exist outside the mainstream of the American social organism."[32] Again, although Jones does not write in terms of Beats or the Beat Generation, his sense of what is special about the work in his volume – which has prominent entries by Kerouac, Burroughs, di Prima, and Jones himself, grouped together – is an identifiable and widespread divergence from the "mainstream" of American life, something that, as we have seen, was thought to be *the* central characteristic of Beat writing.[33]

If the perceived opposition between the Beats and the mainstream animated the drive to anthologize the Beats in the early 1960s, as the decade wore on, the media moved away from dissecting the Beatnik as the most recognizable oppositional figure in American culture, and the energies of the youth movement seemed located more in hippie countercultural critique rooted in vocal disapproval of the Vietnam War. There is actually a complex connection between the elder generation of Beat writers and the younger generation of Vietnam War-era activists and writers, and throughout the 1960s, Beat-associated writers continued to produce important work. In this context, anthologies specifically tackling the Beats or the Beat Generation appeared with less regularity – although some are still worth reviewing and are listed in the Chronology.

While a few significant anthologies appeared in the 1970s, notably Arthur, Glee, and Kit Knight's *unspeakable visions of the individual* – which was a compendium of Beat writings, photographs, and criticism that came to encompass what were essentially stand-alone books such as *The Beat Book* (vol. 4, 1974), *The Beat Diary* (vol. 5, 1977), and *The Beat Road* (vol. 14, 1984), as well as critical books such as John Tytell's path-breaking *Naked Angels: Kerouac, Ginsberg, Burroughs* (1976) – it wasn't until the early 1980s that something close to a groundswell of scholarly interest in Beat writing emerged. This was due in part to those individual writers who had begun to receive establishment recognition – Ginsberg won the 1974 National Book Award for *The Fall of America: Poems of These States, 1965– 1971* and Snyder the 1975 Pulitzer Prize for *Turtle Island* – and to the fact that Beat writers themselves were changing the very notion of "the academy," as in 1974, when Ginsberg and Anne Waldman founded the Jack Kerouac School of Disembodied Poetics at the Naropa Institute (now University). As Gregory Corso wrote about a Beat poetry reading at Columbia University in 1975, "16 years ago we were put down / for being filthy beatnik sex commie dope fiends / Now – 16 years later Allen's the respect of his elders / the love of his peers."[34] Otherwise put: by the early 1980s, the critical moment was primed for a more serious critical assessment of the Beats.

Nobody has been more influential in this regard than Ann Charters, a long-time Beat associate and scholar who wrote the first biography of Kerouac (1973) and who edited the hugely important *The Beats: Literary Bohemians in Postwar America* (1983), a two-part reference work that has probably done the most to map the terrain of Beat writing. In addition to thirteen "master entries" on "authors who are generally regarded as major figures in Beat literature," Charters included more than fifty other entries on writers she considered relevant to understanding the Beats as central to the "so-called experimental side of contemporary American literature."[35] No longer, then, could one consider the Beats equivalent to four or five men who knew one another in New York City. Although *The Beats: Literary Bohemians in Postwar America* did not fix a Beat canon as immutable, it powerfully argued for a constellation of "relationships and influences ... related to the Beats" and thus offered a rich body of work into which subsequent scholars could conduct further investigation (xiv). But given that *The Beats* appeared as part of Gale Research Company's Dictionary of Literary Biography series, it was accessible mainly to scholars and college students. Charters's later editorial work, notably *The Portable Beat Reader* (1992) and its companion volume, *Beat Down Your Soul: What Was the Beat Generation?* (2001), were made widely available through Penguin and have been immensely consequential in impressing the importance of the Beats onto the minds of the late twentieth-century reading public.

In 1983, two other books appeared that – while not anthologies – with
Charters's work did much to stir renewed critical interest in the Beats:
Gerald Nicosia's biography of Kerouac, *Memory Babe,* and Joyce Johnson's
memoir *Minor Characters,* which offered a trenchant critique of the Beat
era from a female perspective (and which won the National Book Critics
Circle Award). Taken together with the work of pioneering scholars such
as Tytell, Eric Mottram (*William Burroughs: The Algebra of Need* [1971]),
Tim Hunt (*Kerouac's Crooked Road* [1981]), Regina Weinreich (*Kerouac's
Spontaneous Poetics* [1987]), and Lee Bartlett's edited collection *The Beats:
Essays in Criticism* (1981), these works show that, by the mid-1980s, critical reflection on the Beats was finding its legs. In that decade still more
anthologies of Beat writing appeared, and, with the benefit of thirty years'
hindsight, editors framed Beat writers in historical and political contexts. In
his introduction to *The Beats: An Anthology of "Beat" Writing* (1987), for
example, Park Honan acknowledged the biographical appeal of Kerouac–
Ginsberg–Burroughs but emphasized not their personal exploits but that
they saw themselves as "devoted to art, to technique."[36] Thanks in part to
the wake of *Minor Characters,* Honan also dedicated a section of his introduction to "the female hipster and women's liberation," but included as primary work a lone poem by Sally Stern that had appeared in Wilentz's *The
Beat Scene* in 1960.

Thus despite Rudi Horemans's claim in *Beat Indeed!* (1985) that "the
academic world hardly has any interest for beat writing," by the time his
collection of criticism and commentary appeared and especially into the
1990s, it could not accurately be said that the Beats were lacking critical
attention (although Horemans was right that they still were not warmly
embraced by the academy).[37] By the mid-1990s, with a slowly growing
body of scholarship on which to stand, some critics began to explore
what A. Robert Lee, in his introduction to *The Beat Generation Writers*
(1996), called "the relationship in the Beat phenomenon between art and
politics, the power of the word and the power of the deed."[38] Inquiring
into this relationship represents a pivotal shift in Beat scholarship, which
throughout the 1990s and 2000s focused on various dimensions of the
relationship between "art and politics" that would challenge or otherwise
rethink what had come to be the standard account(s) of the Beats. In
order to address the question he poses, for example, Lee puts pressure on
the idea that the Beats are most profitably understood as apolitical, white
male Americans by noting that "South of the Border to North Africa,
Tibet to Amsterdam, India to London, may all have supplied staging-
posts for Beat gatherings ... [that] the missing, and still only gradually
emerging signatures, point to a generation of 'Beat women' beyond 'the

chicks' ... [and that] Afro-America, its jazz argots, street savvy, risk, are all enseamed in Beat writing" (3). The point of these observations is not to deny the importance of figures like Kerouac or Ginsberg but to read their work by political lights while also turning attention to the diversity of texts and figures that might have claims on the Beat. Such a turn characterized much Beat scholarship over these two decades.

Perhaps the most significant revision in this regard has been with respect to the role of women writers. In the mid-1990s, two important Beat anthologies appeared: Brenda Knight's *Women of the Beat Generation: The Writers, Artists and Muses at the Heart of a Revolution* (1996)—which recognized writers not found in Charters's *The Beats*, including Joan Vollmer Adams Burroughs, Elise Cowen, Hettie Jones, Mary Norbert Körte, and ruth weiss—and Richard Peabody's *A Different Beat: Writings by Women of the Beat Generation* (1997), which included most of these writers as well as Carol Bergé, Eileen Kaufman, Sheri Martinelli, Barbara Moraff, Brigid Murnaghan, and others. Although some people connected to the scene have regarded such anthologies as diluting the idea of Beat to the point of meaninglessness—in 1999, poet Joanne Kyger remarked that they are "a way to put a bunch of women together that were not necessarily, or didn't personally consider themselves beat writers"—the general critical view has been that opening lines of inquiry can only enrich our understanding of the larger movement.[39] Indeed, the Knight and Peabody anthologies were followed by a collection of critical essays (*Girls Who Wore Black: Women Writing the Beat Generation* [2002]) and a collection of essays and interviews (*Breaking the Rule of Cool: Interviewing and Reading Women Beat Writers* [2004]), both edited by Ronna C. Johnson and Nancy M. Grace. Taken together, these and other works from the mid-1990s to the mid-2000s amounted to a revolution in Beat studies.[40] As Johnson and Grace argue in the introduction to *Girls Who Wore Black*,

> Since its advent in the mid-1950s, Beat generation writing has been only partly seen ... Although recent literary studies and anthologies of Beat have admitted a wider range of writers, most have not exceeded minimal recognition of those outside the well-known group of males. The exclusion of female Beat writers diminishes understanding of the Beat literary and cultural movement, creates insufficient representations of the field of Beat literature, and distorts views of the era.[41]

Although Beat women were always "there" in real ways, as Johnson and Grace point out, for many decades they were rendered invisible, excluded from the true "inside" of Beat literature or the Beat Generation, and whether we view the critical turn toward Beat women as expanding the "inside" or positing the existence of multiple, simultaneously extant insides, in the present moment one cannot responsibly define, theorize, or account for the Beats without paying serious attention to women as writers, editors, interlocutors, and scholars.

This is likewise the case, although perhaps to a lesser extent, with writers of color. In the Kerouac–Ginsberg–Burroughs construct, the Beats seem not only overwhelmingly male but also overwhelmingly white.[42] Such an image of the Beats has persisted despite the fact that some well-known Beat figures of the 1950s, Ted Joans in New York and Bob Kaufman in San Francisco, were African American, as was LeRoi Jones/Amiri Baraka, whose editorial eye was essential in the early dissemination of Beat writing. While these figures have been present in accounts of the Beats since the 1950s, only since the mid-1990s have they been understood as progenitors of Beatness rather than as secondary to white men. In her introduction to *Reconstructing the Beats* (2004), for example, Jennie Skerl notes that "African Americans and their art were … an important part of the Beat subculture, [but most criticism] … tends to obscure the fact of a black presence and artistic interchange between black and white artists" (4). Skerl views attention to African American Beats as part of a larger project of "reconstructing the beats," which her collection aims to do largely by examining the Beats from "contemporary critical perspectives," attending to the fluidity and permeability of the Beats with other arts and literary movements, and expanding the "restricted canon of three to six major figures" by "recovering marginalized figures" (2). Such an interrelated reconstruction and revisioning of the Beats has been central to the ongoing development of Beat scholarship, as evidenced by the variety of interests of recent collections such as *Beats at Naropa* (2009), *The Philosophy of the Beats* (2012), *Beat Drama: Playwrights and Performances of the "Howl" Generation* (2016), and the forthcoming *The Hip Sublime: Beat Writers and the Classical Tradition.*

The latest broad turn in Beat scholarship has been toward transnationalism. Following the work of A. Robert Lee and others, collections such as *The Transnational Beat Generation* (2012) and "The Beat Generation and Europe," a special issue of *Comparative American Studies* (2013), have sought to explore the Beats beyond the geographic and psychic bounds of the United States. In their introduction to *The Transnational Beat Generation*, for example, Nancy M. Grace and Jennie Skerl argue that attention to transnationalism encourages one to ask questions about "the differences between tourism and cosmopolitanism, exile, textual hybridity, the legacy of colonialism, and the shared values of freedom and democracy … [and] introduces gender, race, and class into these discussions … and the impact of Beat literature on cultures in Greece, Vienna, Prague,

Nicaragua, and Quebec, Canada."[43] In a chapter titled "Beat International" in *Modern American Counter Writing*, Lee surveys some international Beat associates who might ask such questions, including Alexander Trocchi (Scotland), Michael Horowitz (UK), Jan Cremer and Simon Vinkenoog (both Netherlands), Michael Dransfield (Australia), Kazuko Shiraishi (Japan), and Andrei Voznesensky (Russia), just to name a few.[44] As is evident from this list alone, a contemporary vision of Beat and the Beat Generation is a far cry from the notion of four white guys trading manuscripts in New York City – and, however much it does not deny their importance, this volume still wants readers to understand a much more capacious sense of Beatdom that takes seriously Burroughs's claim that "once started, the Beat movement had a momentum of its own and a world-wide impact."[45]

A Word on the Plan of This Book

Anne Waldman once wrote that editing an anthology of Beat writing is "rather like trying to wrestle a dragon into a matchbox."[46] Having worked on this volume, I can relate. As I hope is clear from the preceding pages, developing a book like this is a balancing act: one wants to acknowledge the importance and influence of the most recognizable figures and texts while still leaving room enough to discuss others that have not been spotlighted for so long. I was therefore reluctant to commission chapters devoted solely to Kerouac, Ginsberg, or Burroughs, partly because so much excellent criticism already exists on these particular writers and partly because I wanted to avoid a reification of the cults of personality that have haunted Beat studies for decades. Interested readers can pretty quickly find out online or through existing works the most famous or notorious incidents of Beat lore; it is less easy to find good analyses and interpretations of the lives and literatures as connected to the cultural, political, and historical moments in and against which these figures wrote. This *Companion* is not, then, finally a compendium of anecdotes and facts, nor a synthetic narrative history.[47] It is rather concerned with interpretation, with understanding Beat literatures and cultures on various registers, rather than with probing the lives of the authors, however compelling those lives may be. Thus the first chapter, by William Lawlor, maps some basic critical terrain, asking how it could be that the Beats' three most famous names could be said to constitute a "generation." From there, in Chapter 2, Jonah Raskin pushes on the definition of the Beat Generation as located primarily in the Kerouac–Ginsberg–Burroughs "inner circle" by demonstrating the deep ties between the Beats in the 1940s and 1950s and what he calls the "ongoing American counterculture" of the 1960s and after, thereby rebuking the notion that Beat relevance had fizzled by the Vietnam Era. In Chapter 3, Regina Weinreich returns to the "inner circle" to speculate about how one might define a Beat aesthetic by looking at some of the principal aesthetic innovations of Kerouac, Ginsberg, and Burroughs. From there, the chapters radiate out while still acknowledging the importance of the "inner circle": in Chapter 4, Nancy M. Grace tackles some lingering myths or misconceptions about the Beats and literary history, demonstrating not only that they tended to be well educated but also that they saw themselves as inheritors of Modernism, a perspective that invites us to rethink the Beats' place in literary history (an invitation extended in many chapters).

Next, the *Companion* offers a series of chapters focalized through well-known Beat figures with the idea that readers might learn something not only about, say, Ginsberg's poetry or Kerouac's novels, but also about what makes such work "Beat," and what counting it as such might mean in terms of genre, cultural critique, and theoretical or aesthetic orientations. In Chapter 5, Erik Mortenson explores how Ginsberg's aesthetic innovations and thematic preoccupations might be connected to other poetry on the scene, showing how his poetics of presence could be said to be paradigmatically Beat. In Chapter 6, I describe five ways of being Beat circa 1958–59 by looking at work by Tuli Kupferberg, Jack Micheline, Ted Joans, Diane di Prima, and Lenore Kandel, suggesting that this work both responds to and actively constructs ideas of Beatness. In Chapter 7, Kurt Hemmer emphasizes that one thing that makes a novel "Beat" is describing a cultural outsider undergoing spiritual crisis, and he amplifies this idea by looking at a range of novels, including those comprising Kerouac's important Duluoz Legend. Even though Kerouac and Burroughs have been yoked together as the two most well-known Beat novelists, even casual readers know that their work could hardly be more dissimilar. Thus, rather than read Burroughs against Kerouac, in Chapter 8, Oliver Harris views Burroughs as a figure modulating uneasily between the broad literary and aesthetic mandates of Beatness and those of postmodernism so that he seems at times to embody both or neither, an exploration that ultimately affirms Burroughs's singularity and his profound influence on a range of later twentieth-century avant-garde literary and artistic practices. In Chapter 9, Brenda Knight turns our attention to another important Beat genre, memoir, by focusing first on Joyce Johnson but then ranging over a wider landscape of those writers, both women and men, who have helped to shape and reshape what we think we know about the Beat phenomenon. This section is rounded out with Chapter 10, in which Hilary Holladay explores the often charged relationship between Beat writers and criticism, paying special attention to the work of scholar Thomas Parkinson, who edited the seminal critical anthology *A Casebook on the Beat* in 1961.

The final group of chapters is organized around themes, issues, or topics important to Beat writing with the idea that contributors might map new directions for understanding a wider diversity of Beat texts and figures while also taking seriously the various categories that have been important to revisionist impulses in Beat scholarship. We deliberately avoided having chapters organized around particular identities such as "women Beat writers" or "African American Beat writers," not only because so doing would ironically reinscribe a white male center but also because issues of gender or race are of course relevant to white men as well as women or people of color. What would happen if scholars did not limit their chapters to particular identities, we wondered, but instead explored what gender or sexuality or race meant to a Beat sensibility broadly imagined? In keeping with the spirit of this question, in Chapter 11, Ronna C. Johnson traces the dynamics of gender across a range of Beat figures and texts to show both how otherwise radical or progressive male Beat writers tended to reproduce misogynistic views of literary production, and how women Beat writers responded to such misogyny to create the conditions for what Johnson calls "gender transcendence." In Chapter 12, Polina Mackay likewise ranges across texts written by both men and women of varying sexual orientations to show how the fluidity of sexuality across Beat literature might be read in terms of political and social critique. In Chapter 13, A. Robert Lee explores the dizzying number of ways "race" circulated in Beat writing to challenge both the facile charge of white writers unthinkingly appropriating racially marked experiences and the notion that Beat writers of color were not creating their own idiosyncratic, historically and politically informed versions of a Beat aesthetic. Picking up on many issues Lee explores, in Chapter 14, Todd F. Tietchen focuses on transnationalism to ask whether the Beat writers were engaging meaningfully and critically with the rest of the world or were merely "global slumming"; ultimately, he suggests, the Beat reaction to US middle-class culture might have been a rejection of whiteness itself in favor of what he calls "an alternative intercultural imaginary." In Chapter 15, John Whalen-Bridge focuses attention on one of the more well-known aspects of the Beat phenomenon, its interest in Eastern religions, particularly Buddhism, to show how Beat writers relied on humor and a camp aesthetic to transmit their knowledge of Buddhism to readers for whom it was foreign and strange. Likewise in Chapter 16, Kirby Olson begins with Gregory Corso to draw attention to another dimension of Beat religiosity, the influence of Christianity, particularly Catholicism, on a Beat ethos that made some Beats – Corso especially – obstinate Americans while others seemed resolutely cosmopolitan. In Chapter 17, Michael Hrebeniak argues that Beat writers' use of jazz idioms and aesthetics transcends "literary homage" to music and rather allows Beat language to hew to the music's "free play of signs, its multipersonal subjectivity, its flexing to assimilate thematically aberrant materials, and its metrical license." Finally, in Chapter 18, David Sterritt reminds us that, beyond their writing, the Beats were deeply interested in visual culture, and he explains the significance not only of visual art produced by the Beats but also of how they have been represented in a range of visual media, from the "Beatsploitation" films of the late 1950s to the admiring biopics and adaptations of the 2000s.

By framing the chapters in this way, I hope that *The Cambridge Companion to the Beats* will be useful both as an introduction for those who are coming to Beat writing for the first time and as a source of new perspectives for those more familiar with primary texts and the broad contours of Beat studies. The chapters endeavor to make connections across texts and figures that encourage us see to them by various lights, thereby creating new critical energies as we continue to read this literature into the twenty-first century.

NOTES

1 Tuli Kupferberg, *Beatniks, or The War Against the Beats* (New York: Birth Press, 1961), np.

2 To cite one example: the *Cambridge Companion to American Fiction After 1945*, ed. John N. Duvall (New York: Cambridge University Press, 2012), mentions Burroughs and Kerouac, two major Beat novelists writing after 1945, only twice and once, respectively. Burroughs is first mentioned by Duvall in his introduction only to say that Burroughs was included as one of twenty-two important American writers in Tony Tanner's influential study *City of Words* (New York: Harper & Row, 1971) but that, if we "base our sense of the canonical" on the current *Norton Anthology of American Literature*, Burroughs no longer remains "relevant to the conversation today" (2). Burroughs is once more name-checked in a chapter on "Science Fiction" (58), and Kerouac is once mentioned in a discussion of Norman Mailer's *The White Negro* (170).

3 John Clellon Holmes, "This is the Beat Generation," *New York Times* (November 16, 1952), 154–166.

4 Ronna C. Johnson and Nancy M. Grace, "Visions and Revisions of the Beat Generation," *Girls Who Wore Black: Women Writing the Beat Generation*, ed. Johnson and Grace (New Brunswick: Rutgers University Press, 2002), 5.

5 Jennie Skerl, "Introduction," *Reconstructing the Beats*, ed. Skerl (New York: Palgrave, 2004), 1.

6 Allen Ginsberg, "Foreword," *The Beat Book: Writings from the Beat Generation*, ed. Anne Waldman (Boston: Shambala, 1999), xiv–xv.

7 William Everson, "Dionysus and the Beat Generation," *Beat Down Your Soul: What Was the Beat Generation?* ed. Ann Charters (New York: Penguin, 2001), 151; Gary Snyder, "Notes on the Beat Generation," *Beat Down*, 521.

8 Diane di Prima, *Recollections of My Life as a Woman* (New York: Viking, 2001), 238.

9 Ed Sanders, *Tales of Beatnik Glory*, Vols. I and II (New York: Citadel, 1990), v–vi.

10 Gregory Corso, "Variations on a Generation," *Portable Beat Reader*, ed. Ann Charters (New York: Penguin, 1992), 183.

11 John Clellon Holmes, "The Name of the Game," *Nothing More to Declare* (New York: E. P. Dutton, 1967), 107.

12 Chandler Brossard, "The Dead Beat Generation," *The Dude* 6.2 (July 1958), 8.

13 Bonnie Bremser, "The Village Scene," *Beat Down*, 26. Note: Brenda Frazer changed her name to Bonnie Bremser, then changed it back to Brenda Frazer. Because she originally published her most well-known work, *Troia: Mexican Memoirs* (1969), under the name Bonnie Bremser, throughout this book, when *Troia* is being discussed, the name Bonnie Bremser will be used.

14 Bonnie Bremser, *Troia: Mexican Memoirs* (1969; New York: Dalkey Archive, 2007), 33.

15 Joyce Johnson, *Minor Characters* (New York, Penguin, 1983), 41.

16 Allen Ginsberg, *Howl and Other Poems* (San Francisco: City Lights Books, 1956), 14.

17 Nina Baym et al., *The Norton Anthology of American Literature, Shorter Eighth Edition* (New York: Norton, 2013), 2543.

18 Jack Kerouac, "Belief & Technique for Modern Prose," *The Portable Jack Kerouac*, ed. Ann Charters (New York: Viking, 1995), 483.

19 William S. Burroughs, *Naked Lunch: The Restored Text*, ed. James Grauerholz and Barry Miles (New York: Grove Press, 2001), 23.

20 Bob Kaufman, *Does the Secret Mind Whisper?* (San Francisco: City Lights Books, 1960), np.

21 Dan Propper, *The Tale of the Amazing Tramp* (Cherry Valley, NY: Cherry Valley Editions, 1977), 35.

22 George F. Butterick, "Periodicals of the Beat Generation," *The Beats: Literary Bohemians in Postwar America, Part II*, ed. Ann Charters (Detroit: Gale Research Company, 1983), 651–688.

23 The term "Angry Young Men" refers to a group of British writers of the 1950s who were critical of mainstream or traditional British culture. As suggested by the pairing in *The Beat Generation and the Angry Young Men*, the two associations have some broad affinities, but are generally understood as distinct.

24 Gene Feldman and Max Gartenberg, "Introduction," *The Beat Generation and the Angry Young Men*, ed. Feldman and Gartenberg (1958; New York: Dell, 1959), 12.

25 Stanley Fisher, "Preface," *Beat Coast East: An Anthology of Rebellion*, ed. Fisher (New York: Excelsior Press, 1960), 7.

26 Michael McClure, *Hymns to St. Geryon and Other Poems* (San Francisco: Auerhahn Press, 1959), 50.

27 Ann Charters, "Introduction," *Beat Down*, ed. Charters, xxxiv.

28 Elias Wilentz, "Introduction," *The Beat Scene*, ed. Wilentz (New York: Corinth Books, 1960), 11.

29 Seymour Krim, "Introduction," *The Beats*, ed. Krim (Greenwich, CT: Gold Medal Books, 1960), 10.

30 Gene Baro, "Introduction," *"Beat" Poets*, ed. Baro (London: Vista Books, 1961), 6.

31 Donald Allen, "Preface," *The New American Poetry*, ed. Allen (New York: Grove Press, 1960), xii.

32 LeRoi Jones, "Introduction," *The Moderns: An Anthology of New Writing in America*, ed. Jones (New York: Corinth Books, 1963), xi, xiii–xiv.

33 For a detailed discussion of what is perhaps the most influential critical collection on the Beats from this period, Thomas Parkinson's *A Casebook on the Beat* (New York: Crowell, 1961), see Chapter 10.

34 Gregory Corso, "Columbia U Poesy Reading – 1975," *Mindfield: New and Selected Poems* (New York: Thunder's Mouth Press, 1989), 161.

35 Ann Charters, "Foreword," *The Beats: Literary Bohemians in Postwar America, Part I*, ed. Charters (Detroit: Gale Research, 1983), xiv.

36 Park Honan, "Introduction," *The Beats: An Anthology of "Beat" Writing*, ed. Honan (London: Dent & Sons, 1987), xv.

37 Rudi Horemans, "Introduction," *Beat Indeed!* ed. Horemans (Antwerp: Exa, 1985), 11.

38 A. Robert Lee, "Introduction," *The Beat Generation Writers*, ed. Lee (London: Pluto Press, 1996), 7.

39 "Particularizing People's Lives" [Linda Russo interviews Joanne Kyger], *Jacket* (April 11, 2000), http://jacketmagazine.com/11/kyger-iv-by-russo.html (accessed October 17, 2016).

40 See also Frida Forsgren and Michael J. Prince, eds., *Out of the Shadows: Beat Women Are Not Beaten Women* (Norway: Portal Books, 2015).

41 Johnson and Grace, "Visions and Revisions of the Beat Generation," 1–2.

42 Although some scholars have challenged this view, noting, for example, Ginsberg's Jewishness (see Chapter 13) or what Hassan Melehy calls Kerouac's identification with "the colonized but in-between status of the Québécois" ("Jack Kerouac and the Nomadic Cartographies of Exile," *The Transnational Beat Generation*, ed. Nancy M. Grace and Jennie Skerl [New York: Palgrave, 2012], 48). See also Chapter 14.

43 Nancy M. Grace and Jennie Skerl, "Introduction," *The Transnational Beat Generation*, ed. Grace and Skerl (New York: Palgrave, 2012), 7.

44 A. Robert Lee, *Modern American Counter Writing: Beats, Outsiders, Ethnics* (New York: Routledge, 2010), 70–83.

45 Quoted in Ann Charters, ed. "Introduction," *Portable Beat Reader*, ed. Charters, xxxi.

46 Anne Waldman, "Editor's Introduction," *The Beat Book: Writings from the Beat Generation*, ed. Waldman (Boston: Shambala, 1999), xxii.

47 For works that offer reliable accounts of the facts, see Ann Charters, ed., *The Beats: Literary Bohemians in Postwar America* (Detroit: Gale Research, 1983); Matt Theado, ed., *The Beats: A Literary Reference* (New York: Carroll & Graf, 2003); William Lawlor, ed., *Beat Culture: Icons, Lifestyles, and Impact* (Santa Barbara: ABC CLIO, 2005); Kurt Hemmer, *Encyclopedia of Beat Literature* (New York: Facts on File, 2007); and Paul Varner, *Historical Dictionary of the Beat Movement* (Lanham: Scarecrow Press, 2012).

I

WILLIAM LAWLOR

Were Jack Kerouac, Allen Ginsberg, and William S. Burroughs a Generation?

Recognizing Generations: Lost and Beat

Connecting the term "generation" with a cultural movement is alluring, imprecise, and indelible. John Clellon Holmes, whose novels and essays make him a key interpreter of the Beat Generation, declares that such labeling is "unrewarding" and that specifying "a word that crystalizes an entire generation" is "a thankless task."[1] Malcolm Cowley, whose memoirs, poetry, and work as an editor make him an insightful commentator on the Lost Generation, a literary group that was a precursor to the Beats, stands back cautiously when assessing literary generations: "A generation is no more a matter of dates than it is one of ideology. A new generation does not appear every thirty years."[2] Despite these reservations, the fact remains that generational labels – particularly the label Beat Generation – garner attention and stir debate about central figures and the ideas that make a generation cohere.

The Lost Generation, a label made famous by Ernest Hemingway in one of two epigraphs in *The Sun Also Rises* (1926), persists as a descriptive phrase for artists emerging near the end of World War I and between the wars, but the phrase is inexact. In "Une Génération Perdue," Hemingway cites Gertrude Stein, reporting that Stein picked up the phrase in a repair shop.[3] According to Hemingway, a young mechanic was ineffectual in repairing Stein's "old Model T Ford," and the shop's director reprimanded the mechanic: "You are all a *génération perdue*" (29). Stein subsequently turned the phrase on Hemingway: "That's what you are. All of you young people who served in the war. That's what you all are. You are a lost generation" (29). Hemingway rejected this language and later reflected privately that "all generations were lost by something and always had been and always would be"; he appreciated Stein but dismissed "her lost-generation talk and all the dirty, easy labels" (30–31). Despite Hemingway's dismissal, the epigraph attributed to Stein appeared in *The Sun Also Rises* and proved infectious.

Disquieted, Hemingway wrote to his editor and friend Max Perkins that the novel ought to be read as a "damn tragedy with the earth abiding for ever [sic] as the hero."[4] Hemingway thought the second epigraph, the one from Ecclesiastes, was more to the point, but the die was cast and the novel endured as a testament of the Lost Generation.

Like the label Lost Generation, the label Beat Generation became inextricably associated with a particular book: Jack Kerouac's *On the Road* (1957). Coined by Kerouac, the phrase, according to Holmes, was uttered in conversation in November 1948.[5] Kerouac's first written use of the word "beat" as an adjective is found in an entry in his journal dated July 3, 1948.[6] Referring to Times Square hustler Herbert Huncke as "the most miserable of men, jailed & beaten and cheated and starved and sickened and homeless," Kerouac insisted that Huncke was "still alive, and strange, and wise, and beat" (*Windblown* 100). This appreciation of Huncke reveals that what is Beat involves an act of perception: there is Huncke, who exudes the Beat state of being, but there is also Kerouac, whose receptive eye appreciates the Beat figure.

According to Holmes, for Kerouac Beat referred to "furtiveness" and "a weariness with all the forms, all the conventions of the world" ("Name" 54). In "This Is the Beat Generation," Holmes assesses the factors that formed the Beats: "Brought up during the collective bad circumstances of a dreary depression, weaned during the collective uprooting of a global war," the Beats had no faith in "collectivity" (59). Even with the war over, the Beats, according to Holmes, found that the "peace they inherited was only as secure as the next headline" (59). However, writing retrospectively in *The Voice Is All* (2012), Joyce Johnson makes a distinction between Holmes's view and Kerouac's. Johnson says that for Holmes "the Beat Generation signified a revolution in the mores, values, and sexual behavior of the children of the white middle class, who were searching for something to believe in and refusing to conform to a repressive cold war culture"; in contrast, for Kerouac the Beat Generation was "a subterranean revolution quietly going on outside of politics."[7] According to Johnson, in Kerouac's eyes some of the Beats "were anarchists by nature and had already done jail time"; other Beats "were hipsters, coolly impervious to society's demands" (301). Unlike Holmes, Kerouac maintained "a crucial place" in the Beat Generation for blacks, "notably the young beboppers" who told Kerouac "how fed up they were feeling" (301–302). Nevertheless, Johnson reveals that Kerouac apparently lost faith in the ongoing survival of the Beat Generation: "In August 1957, just weeks before the publication of *On the Road*," Kerouac wrote "in his diary ... that the Beat Generation had ceased to exist" by 1949, "when the people who had inspired the idea began disappearing either into jails" or into "domesticity and more settled lives" (302).

Ironically, soon after Kerouac rued the generation's passing, the Beats were launched into American consciousness with the publication of *On the Road* in September 1957. In the *New York Times*, Gilbert Millstein argued that *On the Road* was "a major novel" and insisted on a parallel with the Lost Generation. Millstein wrote that "as, more than any other novel of the Twenties, *The Sun Also Rises* came to be regarded as the testament of the 'Lost Generation,' so it seems certain that *On the Road* will come to be known as that of the Beat Generation."[8] On the surface, Millstein saw "the frenzied pursuit of every possible sensory impression, an extreme exacerbation of the nerves, a constant outraging of the body," while, beneath the surface, the Beats had "a spiritual purpose" that was "still to be defined" and "unsystematic" (27).

Before the public could discover and digest the interpretations of the Beat Generation offered by Holmes, Kerouac, and Millstein, the Beats rode a wave of sensationalism, endured attacks, went through metamorphoses, and grew. Writing in the now-famous "San Francisco Scene" issue of *Evergreen Review* (1957), Kenneth Rexroth remarked, "There has been so much publicity recently about the San Francisco Renaissance and the New Generation of Revolt and Our Underground Literature and Cultural Disaffiliation that I for one am getting a little sick of writing about it."[9] Even as early as 1957, Rexroth could note, "Certainly there is nothing underground about it anymore" (5). In periodicals such as *Nation* and *Partisan Review*, Herbert Gold, John Hollander, Norman Podhoretz, Diana Trilling, and others insisted that the Beats were delinquents or pretenders without any substantive intellect or artistry. In *Life*, Paul O'Neil responded to "Squaresville U.S.A. vs. Beatsville," a photo essay previously published in *Life* that showed young women in Hutchinson, Kansas, hungry for the coolness of the Beats in Venice Beach, California. To cut such coolness down, O'Neil's own photo essay, "The Only Rebellion Around," mocked the apparent trashiness of the Beats.[10] In the *San Francisco Chronicle*, Herb Caen coined the term "beatnik" in his column on April 2, 1958, establishing a caricature of the Beats as lazy, dirty rebels who were also probably communist. Hollywood produced exploitative movies such as *The Beat Generation* (1959), *A Bucket of Blood* (1959), and *The Beatniks* (1960), all focusing on the perceived sordid wildness of the Beatniks, with little to no attention to literary or artistic productions. (For more on such films, see Chapter 18.) Caricatures of the Beats appeared on television in programs such as *Alfred Hitchcock Presents*, *The Twilight Zone*, and *The Many Loves of Dobie Gillis*, the last of which featured Maynard G. Krebs – a likable Beatnik, but a demeaning caricature nonetheless.

In the wake of media misinterpretation and exploitation, in a letter to Allen Ginsberg dated March 24, 1959, Jack Kerouac remarked that the *American College Dictionary* had drafted a definition of Beat Generation and asked him to review and revise it. In the draft, the Beats were "certain members of the generation that came of age after World War II" who displayed "detachment from moral and social forms and responsibilities, supposedly due to disillusionment."[11] In revising, Kerouac added the Korean War as an influence. He said that the Beats united for "a relaxation of social and sexual tensions" and favored "anti-regimentation, mystic disaffiliation and material-simplicity values, supposedly as a result of Cold War disillusionment" (427). Kerouac's revision reveals the enduring contrast between popular views of the Beats and the views the Beats had of themselves.

The "Inner Circle" vs. a Broad Spectrum

If one aims to identify the principal literary figures in the Beat Generation, the group seems either too small (three principal figures, usually Kerouac, Ginsberg, and Burroughs) or too large (dozens and dozens of participants). Bill Morgan quotes Gregory Corso, another central figure, who remarks that "three people do not make a generation."[12] In the introduction to *Beat Down Your Soul* (2001), Ann Charters reports that Gary Snyder told her, "There was no Beat Generation – it consisted of only three or four people, and four people don't make up a generation."[13] Taking a broad view, Ann Charters herself is the editor of *The Beats: Literary Bohemians in Postwar America* (1983), a two-volume work that refers to dozens of writers associated with the Beat Movement. Similarly, Kurt Hemmer's *Encyclopedia of Beat Literature* (2007) provides information on an even wider range of Beat writers. Whether viewed narrowly or broadly, the Beat Generation, now a phenomenon for more than seven decades, lives on, with the label revealing remarkable flexibility and resilience. Can one turn to Jack Kerouac, Allen Ginsberg, and William S. Burroughs and find that they constitute the Beat Generation? Or is the label Beat Generation not established by three central literary figures and instead engendered by other factors?

Jack Kerouac, perhaps more than any other writer, is central to the Beats. *On the Road* is the bible of the Beats, and Kerouac, prolific as a novelist, poet, essayist, and writer of stories, is noteworthy for *The Dharma Bums* (1958), *Mexico City Blues* (1959), *Lonesome Traveler* (1960), *Big Sur* (1962), and *Visions of Cody* (1973). Kerouac's work reaches into memory and the subconscious to bring to the surface what he refers to in the narrative of *Pull My Daisy* (1959) as "secret scatological thought" – a frank and candid expression in a style based on spoken American English and the melodies, rhythms, and syncopations of jazz.[14] Kerouac discovers in the inspiring individuality and resourcefulness of Americans and in the continent's wondrous topographies and climates his basis for being the Suffering Servant who redeems and blesses the world through a personal literature.

Robert Frank, who was the photographer for the film *Pull My Daisy* and who traveled across the nation to shoot his collection of photographs *The Americans*, especially admires Kerouac's "descriptions of the landscape in the morning, the little towns, which he describes with such exquisite beauty – the love for America."[15] In John Antonelli's film *Kerouac* (1985), Allen Ginsberg remarks on Kerouac's tenderness, referring to "a compassionate, open understanding" and an "old-ladies-in-the-park empathy." In "The Origins of the Beat Generation," Kerouac says,

> I want to speak out *for* things, for the crucifix I speak out, for the Star of Israel I speak out, for the divinest man who ever lived who was a German (Bach) I speak out, for sweet Mohammed I speak out, for Buddha I speak out, for Lao-tse and Chuang-tse I speak out, for D. T. Suzuki I speak out.[16]

He concludes, "This is Beat. Live your lives out? Naw, *love* your lives out" (32). As Kerouac told Steve Allen on his show in 1959, to be Beat is to be "sympathetic." For Kerouac, then, to be Beat is to see others and recognize with imaginative insight their history, backgrounds, values, goals, predicaments, joys, satisfaction, and sorrows. To be Beat is not to intrude but to savor compassionately and understand appreciatively a primordial past and a heavenly future.

Standing at the coffin of Kerouac in Lowell, Massachusetts, in October 1969, Ginsberg said to Ann Charters, "I think Jack dreamed us all."[17] In his dedication to *Howl and Other Poems* (1956), Ginsberg credits Kerouac for the title "Howl" and salutes him as the "new Buddha of American prose," the creator of a "spontaneous bop prosody and original classic literature."[18] Burroughs, in *What Happened to Kerouac?*, recognizes Kerouac as the inspiration for the entire Beat Generation – "a worldwide cultural revolution absolutely unprecedented."[19] According to Burroughs, even though social transformation was not Kerouac's intention, Kerouac started the movement that penetrated "even the Arab countries," a group of nations that were "really a hermetic society." Historian David Halberstam in *The Fifties* declares that "if anyone was the center of the group, it was Kerouac. He hungered to be a writer, not so much for fame, but for people to listen to him, to take his words and his ideas seriously."[20] In the film version of *The Fifties*, Halberstam recognizes Kerouac's sweeping influence, pairing him with Elvis Presley, seeing the two as icons of youthful American spirit. For these observers at least, the Beat Generation has one figure – Jack Kerouac – at its core. He embodies the myth, spirit, faith, and social influence that make the Beat Generation an unmistakable force.

With Kerouac appropriately acknowledged, one must also recognize the key role of Allen Ginsberg. *Howl and Other Poems* (1956) preceded *On the Road* (1957), and the subsequent obscenity trial created widespread publicity. Ginsberg channeled his talents in communications, marketing, and oratory through a broad network of personal and public connections. Revering the artistic and spiritual power of Kerouac and carrying it forward, even as Kerouac himself retreated from the public sphere and descended into death, Ginsberg, long after Kerouac's death, was a sustaining force for both Kerouac and the Beats.

Ann Charters argues that Ginsberg "brought the whole Beat Generation into being with the strength of his vision of himself and his friends as a new beginning – a new generation."[21] Like Charters, Bill Morgan asserts that the Beat Generation was "essentially a group of friends" who were in contact with Allen Ginsberg (xix). Instead of searching for thematic or artistic points of common ground, Morgan argues that Ginsberg was a magnet for "interesting and talented people through the power of his inclusive, supportive nature and nurturing personality" (xx). Like Morgan, Halberstam in *The Fifties* sees Ginsberg as the "social glue" of the Beat movement (299).

Ginsberg, sustaining the Beats as he evolved, complemented the anguish of "Howl" (1956) and "Kaddish" (1961) with humorously introspective poems such as "Mugging" (1974), "Personals Ad" (1987), "Homework" (1980), and "C'mon Pigs of Western Civilization Eat More Grease" (1993). Always a dissenter, he incorporated environmental awareness and meditation in a quest for peace and spiritual health.

Like Kerouac or Ginsberg, William S. Burroughs, with works such as *Junky* (1953), *Queer* (written 1951–53; pub. 1985), and *Naked Lunch* (1959), might be deemed the key Beat. Being older, Burroughs introduced his companions to experimental and innovative approaches to history, civilization, art, philosophy, and psychology. Without Burroughs, the Beats might not have been so influenced by Marcel Duchamp, Wilhelm Reich, or Oswald Spengler. Moreover, Burroughs linked the Beats to Times Square and the underworlds of addiction, sexuality, and petty crime. With his conservative dress and understated demeanor, Burroughs was an agent bent on undermining the conventional.

Jennie Skerl writes that Burroughs's "aesthetic – the Beat aesthetic – is one that defines art as consciousness. For Burroughs, the perceptions that become literature are as much an aesthetic experience as the words on the page."[22] She adds, "The hip principles of honesty, clarity, spontaneity, and improvisation dictate that autobiography is the only literature" and "recording one's consciousness as vision or story is to create legend" (18).

Oliver Harris acknowledges that Robin Lydenberg's *Word Cultures* (1987) and Timothy Murphy's *Wising up the Marks* (1997) do not refer to Kerouac at all, and Harris remarks, "It is tempting to free Burroughs from the Beat Generation altogether, to quite simply disregard the context."[23] However, that temptation, according to Harris, leads to misunderstanding because in "the Beat context, Burroughs ... occupies that indeterminate space 'somewhere between' Ginsberg and Kerouac" (4). Ann Douglas appreciates the experimental style of Burroughs, remarking, "Jump cuts replace narrative transitions; straight chronological quasi documentary sequences are spliced with out-of-time-and-space scenes of doom-struck sodomy and drug overdoses."[24] Douglas finds that Burroughs "used the word 'beat' sparingly and literally, to mean 'no fire, no intensity, no life,' while Kerouac and Ginsberg said it meant 'high, ecstatic, saved'" (xxv–xxvi). As Ted Morgan reports, in 1983 Burroughs attended an induction ceremony at the American Academy of Arts and Letters, endured a cold reception, and concluded afterwards that the induction was not significant.[25] Therefore, for Harris, Douglas, and Morgan, Burroughs was a central Beat because of his quiet disassociation and determined experimentation.

The Legend of Neal Cassady

Neal Cassady, yet another central figure, put forth incalculable energy and restless fervor. As Gregory Stephenson writes, "The Cassady figure is an embodiment of transcendental primitivism – the American response to the cultural-spiritual crisis of Western civilization to which such movements as dadaism, surrealism, and existentialism have been the European response."[26] Cassady, though not a prolific writer himself, inspired others to write prolifically about him. In *Go* (1952), a novel by Holmes, Cassady is Hart Kennedy, and Stephenson observes that "there is no attempt in the novel to reconcile or resolve the creative and destructive aspects of Hart Kennedy, but by virtue of his duality and ambiguity he becomes ... something elemental, a force more than a man – ultimately an enigma" (156).

For Kerouac, Cassady had a broad impact, inspiring the characters of Dean Moriarty in *On the Road* and Cody Pomeray in *Visions of Cody* (written 1951–52), *Book of Dreams* (written 1952–60), *The Dharma Bums* (1958), *Desolation Angels* (written 1956–1961), and *Big Sur* (1962). In *On the Road*, Dean flashes with "a kind of holy lightning," and Sal says that in the West, Dean spent "a third of his time in the poolhall, a third in jail, and a third in the public library."[27] In *Visions of Cody*, Cody is "a young guy with a bony face that looks like it's been pressed against iron bars to get that dogged rocky look of suffering."[28] In *Pull My Daisy*, Cassady is Milo, the railroad worker with "tortured socks" (21) whose Beat friends confound his wife and the visiting bishop. Tim Hunt suggests that Kerouac saw that faithfully rendering Cassady was a frustrating challenge that led to "artistic despair."[29] In a letter to Hunt, Holmes states that Kerouac's "fascination with Neal's persona" and the "mystery of Neal's character" led Kerouac to perpetually review his writing about Cassady and to renew efforts to capture Cassady truly (118–119).

In an interview in *Paris Review*, Kerouac refers to Cassady's legendary Joan Anderson letter, which Kerouac says is "forty-thousand words long" and is "a whole short novel."[30] According to Kerouac, the "vast letter" is "all about a Christmas weekend in the pool halls, hotel rooms, and jails of Denver, with hilarious events throughout and tragic, too" (6). The letter is "the greatest piece of writing" Kerouac ever saw, and because of it he created the spontaneous style of *On the Road* (5). However, Charters observes that Kerouac "had been getting [Cassady's] letters for years and already had a sense of Neal's style." Beyond the voice, the letter's "extended narrative" inspired Kerouac to develop an "autobiographical style" with Cassady's letter as a touchstone.[31]

Like the Beats, who began in the 1940s and 1950s and inspired a counterculture in the 1960s and 1970s, the literary Cassady begins his quest in the pages of Holmes, Kerouac, and Ginsberg and becomes part of the subsequent counterculture in Ken Kesey's play "Over the Border," his story "The Day after Superman Died," and his novel *One Flew over the Cuckoo's Nest* (1962). Cassady's exploits with the Merry Pranksters also appear in Tom Wolfe's *The Electric Kool-Aid Acid Test* (1968). Cassady, therefore, is a central Beat because he embodies intensity, pursuit of the intangible, and the mystic sorrow of being beyond comprehension.

Beyond the "Inner Circle": The Reading at the 6 Gallery

The reading at the 6 Gallery in San Francisco on Friday, October 7, 1955, suggests, at least in part, the breadth rather than the narrowness of the Beat movement. Kenneth Rexroth, the master of ceremonies, introduced Ginsberg, Michael McClure, Philip Lamantia, Snyder, and Philip Whalen. The spirited audience included Cassady, Lawrence Ferlinghetti, and Kerouac. This reading underscores the importance of Beat oratory, for it was after Ginsberg's powerful performance of "Howl" that Ferlinghetti prompted him to send the manuscript for publication by City Lights Books. Described in

Kerouac's *The Dharma Bums*, the reading ignited the San Francisco Literary Renaissance.

Important as it was, this reading hardly captures the full scope of Beat literature. Gregory Corso, whose humor and disruptive behavior contrasted with the angst and confession of Ginsberg, won audiences with poems such as "Bomb" (1958) and "Marriage" (1959). Bob Kaufman, who brought theatrics and Surrealism into the streets of San Francisco, engaged audiences with "Bagel Shop Jazz" and "The Ancient Rain." In *This Kind of Bird Flies Backward* (1958), Diane di Prima was defiant and compassionate. With LeRoi Jones (later known as Amiri Baraka), di Prima published *The Floating Bear*, a forum for many Beat writers. On Manhattan's Lower East Side, Anne Waldman and Ed Sanders later fomented a second generation of Beats at St. Mark's Church and the Peace Eye Bookstore.

The Generation Seen Through a Lens

More than any other generation, the Beat Generation was photographed. Images of the Beats, sometimes sharp and clear, sometimes blurred and dim, capture attention and spark speculation. The photos, for the most part black and white, reveal personalities, explore environments, denote coolness, and grant instant and imaginative entrance to the Beat world. The photography in *Life*, *Look*, and *Mademoiselle* gave widespread visual recognition to the Beats. One picked up the generation at the newsstand, carried it anywhere, and spread out the images for friends. Anthologies included photos, as is shown in *The Beat Scene* (1960) and in the "San Francisco Scene" issue of *Evergreen Review* (1957). Individual photographers became Beat specialists, among them Fred McDarrah, Harry Redl, Ann Charters, Chris Felver, Larry Keenan, and Gordon Ball. Hettie Jones observes, "To be Beat, you needed a B-movie graininess, a saintly disaffection, and a wild head of hair like the poet Tuli Kupferberg, or a look of angst like Jack Micheline. Ted Joans was another Beat picture, a black man always dressed in black, from a black beret on down."[32]

The greatest insider photography of the Beats was done by Ginsberg, whose relentless picture taking is revealed in *Snapshot Poetics* (1993), *Allen Ginsberg: Photographs* (1990), and *Beat Memories: The Photographs of Allen Ginsberg* (2013). Stylized with detailed handwritten captions, Ginsberg's photography captures daily life in the spirit of naturalism, yet he writes, "My motive for taking these snapshots was to make celestial snapshots in a sacred world."[33]

The Women of the Beat Generation

For Joyce Johnson, the "whole Beat scene had very little to do with the participation of women as artists themselves. The real communication was going on between the men, and the women were there as onlookers."[34] Nevertheless, Johnson remarks that she and Kerouac "talked a lot about writing," and Kerouac "was very interested" in her novel and "very encouraging" (236). While Johnson's observation about the exclusion of women as artists is true, she unveils the significance of women in her recollection of Kerouac. In Manhattan in the 1940s, the Beats came together at several apartments leased by Joan Vollmer Adams and Edie Parker. Hilary Holladay writes that "Joan's apartment on West 115th Street" became "the incubator for the Beat Movement."[35] Holladay suggests that "Without Joan, the gathering of restless, ever-questing minds might never have achieved the critical mass necessary to spur a real literary movement" (118). Ann Douglas astutely observes that, in his introduction to *Queer*, Burroughs clarifies that Joan's tragic accidental death created a "lifelong struggle" for Burroughs, a struggle he managed through writing ("Punching" xvii).

In addition to Joan Vollmer Adams and Edie Parker, numerous other Beat women were crucial to the Beat literary movement. Hettie and LeRoi Jones produced *Yugen* (1958–62), a little magazine; as Hettie Jones writes, "From a quick first look at *Yugen* 4, you'd say Beat, as the three Beat gurus – Kerouac, Corso, and Ginsberg – were represented" (*How* 74). However, Jones explains that the magazine also featured a broader selection of writers: "Basil King, Joel Oppenheimer, and Fielding Dawson, the poets Robert Creeley, John Wieners, and Charles Olson were out of Black Mountain College … Frank O'Hara … was a poet of the 'New York School.' Gilbert Sorrentino lived in Brooklyn, Gary Snyder in Japan, Ray Bremser in a Trenton, New Jersey, prison" (74).

With the novel *Come and Join the Dance* (1963), Joyce Glassman (later Joyce Johnson) revealed a young woman tormented by the imposing forces of parents, school authorities, and men. About Joyce, Hettie writes, "We shared what was most important to us: common assumptions about our uncommon lives. We lived outside, as if. As if we were men? As if we were newer, freer versions of ourselves? There have always been women like us. Poverty, and self-support, is enough dominion" (*How* 81).

The shaping force in Allen Ginsberg's life was another woman: his mother, Naomi, who introduced him to compassionate communism. In "America," Ginsberg writes, "America when I was seven momma took me to the Communist Cell meetings," where "everybody was angelic" (*Howl* 63). Naomi's loss of mental health and Ginsberg's childhood connection to that loss are profoundly disclosed in "Kaddish." In "White Shroud" Naomi again is the center of Ginsberg's art.

A source of stability, Gabrielle Kerouac provided her son with the orderly environment for a writer's work. At his father's deathbed, Kerouac promised to care for his mother, and, despite alcoholism, he did (Charters, *Kerouac* 61). With the deaths of Kerouac's father, brother, and sister, Kerouac and his mother were sole survivors, so one understands Kerouac's unswerving allegiance. Depicted as Sal's aunt in *On the Road*, Kerouac's mother is exemplary. The aunt's traditional life is a foil to Sal's wandering. At the end of Part One, Sal returns from the road with his book unfinished; in contrast, the aunt, who has stayed home, has completed an artistic rag rug with scraps of clothing from family members (107–108).

But, beyond these maternal influences on male writers, Beat women actually kept the Beats from extinction. Well into the 1980s, with the notable exception of Ann Charters, academics often reinforced previous dismissive attitudes. And yet, affirming the Beat experience, Joyce Johnson wrote *Minor Characters* (1983), a memoir about her coming of age and her love relationship with Jack Kerouac. Accepted for its excellence, this memoir revised interpretations of the Beats. Similarly, Carolyn Cassady's *Off the Road* (1990) and Hettie Jones' *How I Became Hettie Jones* (1990) expanded attention to Beat women and the Beat Generation. When the Beats seemed destined for oblivion, Beat women became prominent, ushering the movement into the more receptive 1990s.

During the 1990s, the serious consideration of the Beats was largely established by women scholars. Brenda Knight's *Women of the Beat Generation* (1996) and Richard Peabody's *A Different Beat* (1997) showcased Beat women. At City Lights Books, Nancy Peters became an influential editor. Ann Charters, Ann Douglas, Nancy M. Grace, Hilary Holladay, Ronna C. Johnson, Robin Lydenberg, and Jennie Skerl contributed substantially to a growing body of scholarship on the Beats. Without the contributions of women, the Beats would not have been taken as seriously as they are today.

Who or What Makes a Generation?

Multiple factors make the Beat Generation cohere. One does not need to accept Kerouac, Ginsberg, and Burroughs as triumvirs because any one of them alone, or even another figure, such as Cassady, might be construed as the single central figure. However, the Beat Generation, to be adequately assessed, must include a broad range of participants. Photography reveals this broad range, capturing not only Kerouac, Ginsberg, Burroughs, and Cassady but also a cultural scene of writers as well as of actors, dancers, musicians, painters, filmmakers, and photographers. The photography, whether plain, stylized, or artistic, invokes the coolness that connects people to the Beat spirit. Even so, the photographic record of the Beats ought not overshadow women, who were prominent in the Beats' incunabular period. If Burroughs, Ginsberg, and Kerouac were instigators, they were so because Joan Vollmer Adams, Naomi Ginsberg, and Gabrielle Kerouac dominated their thinking. If the Beat movement has enduring literary, intellectual, and cultural significance, it has such significance because women writers and scholars sustained the Beat spirit and established inclusivity not only for women but also for members of other inadequately recognized groups. The Beat Generation involves both individualism and community, and, as part of the American tradition, the Beats are nontraditional. They challenge America because they love it, and, in doing so, they are inseparable from it.

NOTES

1 John Clellon Holmes, "This Is the Beat Generation," *Passionate Opinions* (Fayetteville: University of Arkansas Press, 1988), 58; Holmes, "The Philosophy of the Beat Generation," *Passionate*, 66.

2 Quoted in Albin Krebs, "Malcolm Cowley, Writer, Is Dead at Ninety," *New York Times* (March 29, 1989), www.nytimes.com/1989/03/29/obituaries/malcolm-cowley-writer-is-dead-at-90.html?pagewanted=all (accessed October 17, 2016).

3 Ernest Hemingway, "Une Génération Perdue," *A Moveable Feast* (New York: Scribners, 1964), 29.

4 Matthew Bruccoli, ed., *The Only Thing That Counts: The Ernest Hemingway / Maxwell Perkins Correspondence, 1925–1947* (New York: Scribners, 1996), 51.

5 Holmes, "Name of the Game," *Passionate*, 53–55.

6 Jack Kerouac, *Windblown World: The Journals of Jack Kerouac, 1947–1954*, ed. Douglas Brinkley (New York: Penguin, 2004), 100.

7 Joyce Johnson, *The Voice Is All: The Lonely Victory of Jack Kerouac* (New York: Viking, 2012), 301.

8 Gilbert Millstein, "Book of the Times [review of *On the Road*]," *New York Times* (September 5, 1957), 27.

9 Kenneth Rexroth, "San Francisco Letter," *Evergreen Review* 2 (1957), 5.

10 Paul O'Neil, "The Only Rebellion Around," *Life* (November 30, 1959), 114–115.

11 Jack Kerouac, *Jack Kerouac and Allen Ginsberg: The Letters*, ed. Bill Morgan and David Stanford (New York: Viking, 2010), 427.

12 Bill Morgan, *The Typewriter Is Holy: The Complete, Uncensored History of the Beat Generation* (New York: Free Press, 2010), xxi.

13 Ann Charters, "Introduction," *Beat Down Your Soul: What Was the Beat Generation?* ed. Charters (New York: Penguin, 2001), xv.

14 Jack Kerouac, *Pull My Daisy* (New York: Grove Press, 1960), 23.

15 Quoted in Nicholas Dawidoff, "The Man Who Saw America," *New York Times Magazine* (July 5, 2015), www.nytimes.com/2015/07/05/magazine/robert-franks-america.html (accessed October 17, 2016).

16 Jack Kerouac, "The Origins of the Beat Generation," *Playboy* (June 1959), 32.

17 Quoted in Ann Charters, *Beats and Company: A Portrait of a Literary Generation* (Garden City, NY: Doubleday, 1986), 24.

18 Allen Ginsberg, *Howl and Other Poems* (San Francisco: City Lights, 1956), np.

19 Richard Lerner and Lewis MacAdams, dir. *What Happened to Kerouac?* (Sony, 2003).

20 David Halberstam, *The Fifties* (New York: Villard Books, 1993), 299.

21 Ann Charters, *Beats and Company*, 24.

22 Jennie Skerl, *William S. Burroughs* (Boston: Twayne, 1985), 18.

23 Oliver Harris, *William Burroughs and the Secret of Fascination* (Carbondale: Southern Illinois University Press, 2003), 3.

24 Ann Douglas, "Punching a Hole in the Big Lie: The Achievement of Williams S. Burroughs," *Word Virus: The Williams S. Burroughs Reader*, ed. James Grauerholz and Ira Silverberg (New York: Grove, 1998), xiv.

25 Ted Morgan, *Literary Outlaw: The Life and Times of Williams S. Burroughs* (New York: Holt, 1988), 1–13.

26 Gregory Stephenson, *The Daybreak Boys: Essays on the Literature of the Beat Generation* (Carbondale: Southern Illinois University Press, 1990), 170.

27 Jack Kerouac, *On the Road* (1957; New York: Penguin, 1991), 7.

28 Jack Kerouac, *Visions of Cody* (New York: Penguin, 1993), 48.

29 Quoted in Tim Hunt, *Kerouac's Crooked Road* (1981; Berkeley: University of California Press, 1996), 117.

30 Jack Kerouac, "Kerouac: The Art of Fiction No. 41," *Paris Review* (summer 1968), 6.

31 Ann Charters, *Kerouac* (New York: St. Martin's, 1987), 125.

32 Hettie Jones, *How I Became Hettie Jones* (New York: E. P. Dutton, 1990), 45–46.

33 Allen Ginsberg, *Allen Ginsberg: Photographs* (Altadena, CA: Twelvetrees Press, 1990), np.

34 Quoted in Barry Gifford and Lawrence Lee, *Jack's Book: An Oral Biography of Jack Kerouac* (New York: St. Martin's, 1978), 235–36.

35 Hilary Holladay, *Herbert Huncke: The Times Square Hustler Who Inspired Jack Kerouac and the Beat Generation* (Tucson: Schaffner Press, 2015), 117.

2

JONAH RASKIN

Beatniks, Hippies, Yippies, Feminists, and the Ongoing American Counterculture

This chapter addresses the challenges that have faced historians and biographers who have chronicled the permutations and incarnations of the Beat Generations – plural – as they unfolded from the 1950s to the 1990s and beyond. It maps the multilayered Beat narrative thematically as well as chronologically, and textually as well as contextually. It also suggests some cultural influences and lineages, from Ginsberg and Kerouac to Bob Dylan – *the* pivotal countercultural figure of the 1960s – to Abbie Hoffman and the Yippies across racial, gendered, and generational divisions, a move that suggests there is no single, correct way to understand the Beats.

After fifty years of scholarship, a shift away from the four Beat giants has long been needed. Indeed, biographers have chronicled almost ad infinitum and nearly ad nauseam the fledgling adventures of Jack Kerouac, Allen Ginsberg, William S. Burroughs, and Neal Cassady. Steven Watson's *The Birth of the Beat Generation* (1995), James Campbell's *This Is the Beat Generation* (2001), and Bill Morgan's *The Typewriter Is Holy* (2010) – to name three important interpretations – emphasize the period from 1945 to 1959. But, on the whole, these books neglect to say that, while the Beats tipped from 1956 to 1959, they tipped again and again in the ongoing saga of what is probably the longest running, continually evolving literary movement in American history.

If this narrative rings true, then it is vital to understand how the raucous politics of the 1960s severed the Beats from one another in ways that the politics of the 1940s and 1950s never did, and as multiple threads of the Beat narrative blossomed and splintered along various fault lines. What had been originally enacted in private homes was transformed into a public spectacle, and what had germinated in New York's Greenwich Village and San Francisco's North Beach morphed into a global outcry against regimentation and repression that echoed from London to Liverpool (birthplace of the Beatles) and from Prague to Mexico City.

Many Beat Generations

Seventy-plus years after Burroughs, Kerouac, and Ginsberg first met, it's clear that chronology, while useful, might not be the best way to tell their story. Instead, one might begin the Beat narrative in 2013, with the cinematic version of *Big Sur* (1962) – Kerouac's last masterpiece – and work backward to 1943, when he and Ginsberg rendezvoused in Times Square with hipster Herbert Huncke, who introduced them to subterranean New York and its argot. Or else one might begin in 1993 with the publication of *Snapshot Poetics*, a collection of Ginsberg's never-before-seen black-and-white photos of himself and his friends, and then move back to the heady days of World War II when Lucien Carr went to prison for manslaughter and Burroughs and his wife, Joan Vollmer Adams, provided a home of sorts for the wayward boys who left their nuclear families to forge a brotherhood of their own.

For a time, it seemed as though the core group would hold through war and peace, social crisis and personal crack-up, alcoholism and drug addiction. Yet soon after 1951, when Burroughs accidentally shot and killed Adams in Mexico City and then fled to Morocco, the initial Beat bubble burst. Death and tragedy, along with the seismic shifts in American society during the Cold War, divided the core members of the group from one another. No one would come to be more critical of Kerouac and Cassady than Burroughs, and no one was more devoted to the Beat ethos than Ginsberg. Ineluctable threads held them together despite class divisions. Friendships provided long-lasting foundations that defied ideological differences and transcended divergent lifestyles. In popular legend, Burroughs, Kerouac, and Ginsberg were tireless, timeless road warriors and loyal literary musketeers bound to one another, a narrative that never quite held together as the years wore on. Indeed, by the 1960s, even the core group had splintered. After the publication of *On the Road* (1957), Kerouac slowly but steadily severed connections to Ginsberg and Burroughs, though all through the 1960s he continued to chronicle his Beat misadventures in autobiographical novels such as *Desolation Angels* (1965) and *Vanity of Duluoz* (1968), in which Ginsberg and Burroughs appear as fictional characters named Irwin Garden and Bill/Will Hubbard.

Not long after the publication of *Naked Lunch* (1959), Burroughs left Tangiers, ventured out on his own, and forged seminal literary relationships with two Englishmen, Brion Gysin and Ian Sommerville. Using montage, collage, and cut-ups, he pushed his literary experiments into new territories in the trilogy made up by *The Soft Machine* (1961), *The Ticket That Exploded* (1962), and *Nova Express* (1964). In the second half of the twentieth century, rock groups, filmmakers, and science-fiction authors would borrow the Burroughs mystique and enshrine him as the quintessential American hipster, sexual outlaw, and grandfather of punk.

Ginsberg morphed faster than Burroughs and Kerouac to keep pace with the trends and fads of the 1960s, which Kerouac often disdained and ignored. After the publication of *Howl*, Ginsberg came out of the closet, embraced his queer identity, and explored overtly sexual and sadomasochistic themes in poems such as "Please Master," collected in *The Fall of America: Poems of These States, 1965–1971* (1972). Eager for allies in the culture wars, he joined forces with Timothy Leary, an ousted Harvard professor, and insisted that LSD would transform human consciousness and usher in a brave new harmonious world. Then, too, Ginsberg moved in the rarified atmosphere of the Beatles and Bob Dylan, the Minnesota-born folk singer who carried on Kerouac's legacy and echoed Ginsberg in such lines as "He not busy being born is busy dying," in the song "It's Alright, Ma (I'm only Bleeding)" (1965), which spoke to the widening generation gap of the 1960s.

Along with Dylan and the antiwar student radicals, the Beats helped to thaw the icy culture of the Cold War and to defuse the anticommunist crusade that petrified many 1930s lefties, drove writers such as Dalton Trumbo into exile, and led to the imprisonment of Dashiell Hammett, the father of the noir detective story and one of Burroughs's heroes. Unlike Trumbo and Hammett, the Beats went into exile and to jail not because they belonged to so-called subversive organizations (such as the American Civil Liberties Union) but because they were themselves (or rubbed shoulders with) common criminals and defied the rules of bourgeois society. When, for example, Ginsberg first met and befriended Gregory Corso in the early 1950s, Corso had just been released from jail; when poet Ray Bremser sent his work to Corso and LeRoi Jones, he was serving a six-year sentence for armed robbery. Ginsberg himself aided and abetted a gang of thieves who used his apartment to stash stolen goods. Kerouac helped Lucien Carr dispose of the knife he used to murder David Kammerer, an act that almost led to his conviction as an accessory to murder. Burroughs was famous for violating the drug laws that turned him, he argued in books like *Junky* (1953) and *Naked Lunch*, into a victim of what he regarded as the American totalitarian state.

"America when will you be angelic?" Ginsberg asks in "America," a short lyrical poem in *Howl and Other Poems* that moves from anger ("Go fuck yourself with your atom bomb") to humor ("When will you take off your clothes?") to mock enthusiasm ("I'm putting my queer shoulder to the wheel").[1] Dylan escalated Ginsberg's subversive wit. In the aforementioned song "It's all right, Ma (I'm Only Bleeding)," Dylan proclaimed,

"Even the president of the United States / Sometimes must have to stand naked."[2] If Whitman's free verse lurks behind Ginsberg's long, prosy lines, so too does Ginsberg's role as bard lie behind Dylan's 1960s persona as rambling poet and prophet who denounced war makers. In the opening scenes of D. A. Pennebaker's documentary *Dont Look Back* (1967), a bearded Ginsberg stands on a street corner behind Dylan as he exhibits and discards a series of placards with the lyrics to "Subterranean Homesick Blues" (1965), for a time the theme song of the Weather Underground, the 1970s clandestine organization that placed bombs in buildings such as the US Capitol, helped Leary escape from jail, and evaded the FBI for a decade; the scene is emblematic of Beat staying power into the tumultuous 1960s and after.

1960s: Fracturing and Reconnecting a Movement

By the 1960s, Gary Snyder moved away from Kerouac's values in texts such as *Earth House Hold* (1969), in which he called for a utopian society that would be Buddhist, matriarchal, and communist. All through the 1960s, Ginsberg put himself at the center of various countercultural movements, denounced both the White House and the Kremlin, and practically begged to be investigated by the FBI *and* the KGB. In communist Czechoslovakia he was crowned "Kral Majales" or May King, and in Cuba officials deported him because he befriended homosexuals in Havana. At the start of the decade, Ginsberg shared with Dylan a genuine admiration for the Old Left and folk artists, who would soon be replaced both by rock 'n' roll stars such as Mick Jagger who praised street-fighting men and by the flesh-and-blood street-fighting men and women themselves who rioted in Chicago in 1968 during the Democratic National Convention and again in 1969 during the Conspiracy Trial. Given their visible presence at these and other events, Ginsberg, Burroughs, and Snyder deserve some of the credit for the ensuing chaos.

All through the era of the Vietnam War (1962–1975), Ginsberg was perhaps *the* key living link between the radicalism and bohemianism of his parents' generation and the counterculture that reached an apotheosis at the Woodstock Festival of peace and love in August 1969 and again during Dylan's 1975–1976 Rolling Thunder Revue, which included Joan Baez and Joni Mitchell along with Ginsberg, who adroitly marketed the Beat literary movement and later the countercultures of the 1960s and 1970s. As Lawrence Ferlinghetti argued in 1999, "Without him there would be great writers in the landscape, but not a Beat Generation."[3] Perhaps so, but it's best not to underestimate the reach and the influence of the mass media, independent of Ginsberg's strategies.

With ideas borrowed from advertising and public relations, Ginsberg promoted modest poetry readings in the 1950s. By the 1960s, they had blossomed into mega-poetry festivals that brought together Russians such as Andrei Voznesensky; Americans such as Ferlinghetti, a poet and the owner of City Lights Books; and Gregory Corso, a New Yorker and ex-con. Ferlinghetti and Corso published their first books – *Pictures of a Gone World* and *The Vestal Lady and Other Poems*, respectively – in 1955, and both emerged as mainstays of the 1960s counterculture. The International Poetry Incarnation, which took place in London in June 1965 at the Royal Albert Hall, assembled an array of talent from around the world and animated the global poetry scene from Latin America to Eastern Europe.

The mega-readings linked writers from different countries and cultures and helped to widen the generation gap that separated the young (who were busy being born) from the old (who seemed to be busy dying or merely existing). Dylan accelerated the speed of social change with songs such as "Blowin' in the Wind" (1963) and by turning from acoustic to electric guitar at the 1965 Newport Folk Festival. As a visionary artist with ties to pop culture, he understood Beat idioms that academics rarely if ever appreciated. In fact, academics had long denigrated the Beats for mixing the irreverent and the reverential, two cornerstones of the counterculture that found expression on college campuses, in ashrams, and in communes. Seymour Krim, the hipster intellectual and writer for the *Village Voice*, stood out from the crowd of academics who found texts such as *On the Road* unintelligent and unintelligible. His sassy essays, including "What's This Cat's Story?" (1961) and "Norman Mailer, Get Out of My Head" (1969), caught much of Kerouac's energy and invective.

Like Krim, Dylan offered astute insights into the Beats. "Ginsberg is both tragic & dynamic, a lyrical genius, con man extraordinaire and probably the single greatest influence on American poetry since Whitman," he noted in the blurb that appears on the back of Ginsberg's *Collected Poems*.[4] The Ginsbergian sense of tragedy – so antithetical to the underlying optimism and utopianism of the 1960s – is perhaps best expressed in "Kaddish" (1961), a long lament for Naomi Ginsberg, the poet's mother, and an elegy for a generation of immigrant Jews who struggled to survive in the alien world of America. Throughout the 1960s, Ginsberg helped to revive and reshape left-wing Jewish traditions even as he encouraged Jews to become Buddhists or to embrace all the world's religions as one. He wrote elegiac poems and essays in the 1960s about his Beat brothers, including Kerouac and Neal Cassady. He also honored guerrilla warriors such as Che Guevara (in *The Fall of America*) and praised his own literary mentor, William Carlos Williams, the modernist poet who had taken him under his wing in the

1950s and who wrote an effusive preface to *Howl and Other Poems*. Then, too, as New Age movements swept across America, long after the passing of the 1960s, Ginsberg greeted them enthusiastically in works such as "C'mon Pigs of Western Civilization Eat More Grease" (1993) and "Put Down Your Cigarette Rag (Dont Smoke)" (1971; 1992).

Yet, even as Ginsberg and the Beat Generation reinvented themselves, journalists continued to write obituaries about them. In 1997, the *New York Times* declared both that "The last year has been pretty much the end of the road for the Beat Generation" and that "The beats' defiance of authority and their experimentation with drugs and sex helped set a generation on course for the counterculture of the 60's."[5] As this article suggests, even in the 1990s, the mass media continued to emphasize the sex and drugs while minimizing radical political protest and genuine spirituality.

Beat Women in the 1960s and Beyond

The flowering of the Beats in the 1960s and after was perhaps most dramatically evident among at least two generations of women who often wrote about their harrowing experiences long after the fact and who dissected the biases and assumptions of the movement's founding fathers and brothers. Brenda Knight's landmark anthology *Women of the Beat Generation* (1996) touted a dozen or so unsung Beat women writers and helped to pave the way for two long-simmering narratives, Edie Kerouac-Parker's *You'll Be Okay: My Life With Jack Kerouac* (2007) and Helen Weaver's *The Awakened: A Memoir of Kerouac and the Fifties* (2009), both of which take a nostalgic look back at the past. The "boy gang," as Ginsberg called it, was busy being reborn in literature and legend as a circle that featured girls and women. Lenore Kandel's *The Love Book* (1966), Kerouac's daughter Jan Kerouac's *Baby Driver* (1981), and Carolyn Cassady's *Off the Road* (1990) revised Beat narratives and added their own female and feminist voices to the male chorus. Joyce Johnson (*Minor Characters* [1983], Hettie Jones (*How I Became Hettie Jones* [1990]), Anne Waldman (*Fast Speaking Woman* [1974]), and writers such as Joanne Kyger and Janine Pommy Vega plunged into unchartered territories that often eluded Beat men.

Diane di Prima played a leading role in the political and spiritual rebellion of her contemporaries, stripping aside the halos that surrounded her Beat brothers and pointing out that women usually did the cooking, shopping, cleaning, and more. Perhaps the preeminent Beat female writer, di Prima published more than two dozen books and enjoyed a following in feminist, ecological, and anarchist circles. Born in 1934, she came of age just as *On the Road*, *Howl*, and *Naked Lunch* appeared in print. In

Memoirs of a Beatnik (1969), she acknowledges the impact of *Howl* as a poem and Ginsberg as a person on her imagination and on the consciousness of a generation. He had "broken new ground" she insisted, yet she refused to accept the role of Beat playmate that Beat playboys aimed to impose on her.[6]

Not surprisingly, given her intellectual and artistic stance, di Prima promulgated an account of the genesis and evolution of the Beats that diverged from male narratives. From her point of view, the Beat Generation was a state of mind that continued after 1969, the year she landed in San Francisco and the year in which Kerouac died at forty-six. Ken Regan's iconic photos of Dylan and Ginsberg at Kerouac's grave in 1975 bring together the poet and the singer-songwriter and speak volumes about the Beats: the vagabond Kerouac was dead and buried in his hometown, but his spirit went marching on; his cultural heirs paid homage to him and his search for freedom and authenticity.

For di Prima, as for veterans of the Vietnam War, college dropouts, and readers who had come of age on *Howl*, *On The Road*, and *Naked Lunch*, 1969 signaled yet another tipping point in the Beat narrative, as the 1960s cascaded into the 1970s. In *Memoirs of a Beatnik* – which might be called a feminist parody of male pornography – and in *Recollections of My Life as a Woman*, (2001), a genuine memoir that scrambles chronology, di Prima looks back at New York in the 1950s and offers a complex story in which the Beat Generation runs parallel to and mixes with Marxism, feminism, surrealism, African American jazz, and the blues. Her roots in the Italian American community and her awareness of the Mafia's economic role in Greenwich Village kept her from idealizing bohemia. Raised in Brooklyn, she later joined with Peter Coyote and the Diggers and helped to create the counterculture that thrived in San Francisco in the 1970s, an era when hippie and Beat manners and mores drifted into white working-class communities and when men and women with blue-collar jobs smoked marijuana, and wrote and read poetry in coffeehouses. Di Prima's own overtly political poems collected in *Revolutionary Letters* (1971) spoke to members of the counterculture in the polyphonic voices of the counterculture itself.

When read on rural communes and in urban collectives, di Prima's raucous verse sounded more in keeping with the turbulent 1960s than *On the Road* and *The Dharma Bums* (1958), in which Kerouac famously called for a "rucksack revolution," for America's youth to drop out from society by hitting the road fitted only with backpacks. Indeed, *Revolutionary Letters* makes no apologies for violent upheaval. Dedicated to Bob Dylan, the volume urges readers – in capital letters for emphasis – to "SMASH THE

MEDIA" and "BURN THE SCHOOLS."[7] Ginsberg and Kerouac had never been quite as inflammatory. "Revolution" in the Maoist sense of the word echoes across the pages of di Prima's work, and yet she still managed to wear her Buddhism more comfortably than Kerouac ever did.

Di Prima's sexual revolution, unlike Kerouac's, dovetailed with feminism and women's liberation. Like many male Beats, di Prima wrote about her lovers, but unlike them she described pregnancy, childbirth, and the lives of her five children, all while she traced the evolution of her life as an independent woman, a poet, and the author of *Loba* (1978), perhaps her masterpiece, a paean to the feminine, to the sacred, and to goddess worship. Throughout a career that stretched from the 1950s to the 2010s, di Prima resisted the urge to fix labels such as Beat, beatnik, and hippie to movements and individuals, though she defined the 1950s "rule of Cool," as she called it, as effectively as any cultural historian. In "the midst of terrifying indifference," "sentimentality," and "media mush," she argued, the 1950s rule of cool enabled artists to maintain their integrity, survive, and continue to be creative (*Memoirs* 126).

From Beats to Hippies to Everyone Else

By the 1990s, the line from 1950s Beats to 1960s hippies had long been accepted as conventional wisdom. In a 1981 essay titled "A Definition of the Beat Generation," Ginsberg argued that the Beats initiated a half-century of American liberation movements. He noted that he and his friends "refreshed the bohemian culture," disseminated "ecological consciousness," generated "opposition to the military-industrial machine civilization," pushed "rhythm and blues into rock 'n' roll," and sowed the seeds for causes that improved the lives of gays, African Americans, and women.[8] For Ginsberg, there wasn't a niche in the second half of the twentieth century where he didn't discern Beat influences, and, while overstated, his exaggerations encouraged students and teachers to consider the ripples that emanated from the initial Beat disturbances in the placid American landscape.

In *The Portable Beat Reader* (1992), the first comprehensive anthology of Beat writing, Ann Charters, Kerouac's groundbreaking biographer, offers snippets from the writings of John Clellon Holmes, Peter Orlovsky, Lew Welch, and other core Beats. She also extends boundaries to include writers far beyond the original "inner circle." Dylan's "Blowin' in the Wind" and "The Times They Are A-Changin'" (1964) both appear in the *Reader* (though "Masters of War" [1963], a sober indictment of the military–industrial complex, would probably have been a better choice). Charters includes the work of more than two dozen writers, including

African American poet, playwright, and editor Amiri Baraka (LeRoi Jones), Charles Bukowski, and Ken Kesey. These are perhaps odd literary bedfellows, as Baraka and Bukowski wore the Beat label reluctantly, if at all. Ed Sanders and the Fugs – the band that included poet Tuli Kupferberg, who appears anonymously in "Howl" – provided a musical link between 1950s Beats and 1960s hippies and were among the first pop icons of the counterculture. Songs such as "Slum Goddess" (1965) and "Kill for Peace" (1966) helped pave the way for the popularity of troubadour Phil Ochs and poet-songwriter Lou Reed, famous for "Walk on the Wild Side" (1972), a paean to sex, drugs, and defiance.

But just because the writers named above were associated with the Beat movement did not mean that they hewed closely to what Beat meant in the 1950s. Baraka embraced the early literary experimentalism of the Beats, but by the end of the 1960s he adopted the politics and the aesthetics of Black Nationalism, which put him in a world tangential to Ginsberg's, Kerouac's, and Burroughs's. In California, Bukowski steered the subterranean Beat vehicle into the backstreets of noir Los Angeles in nonfiction books such as *Notes of a Dirty Old Man* (1969), novels such as *Ham on Rye* (1982), and in movies such as *Barfly* (1987). Seedier than Ginsberg and Kerouac, he reveled in the unromantic world of un-beatific men and women who seemed permanently lost and lonely. Two still-underappreciated black writers, Bob Kaufman, one of the founders of *Beatitude* magazine, and Ted Joans, a musician and a performance poet, fused Beat lingo with African American jazz idioms and the blues and helped to set the stage for rap.

Again and again the core members of the group reincarnated themselves as though reincarnation was a way of life. After his release from San Quentin in 1960, Neal Cassady, the real-life hero of *Howl* and *On the Road*, dusted himself off and joined Ken Kesey and the Merry Pranksters. With the aid of LSD and a brightly colored bus called "Furthur," the Pranksters turned the Beats into a traveling circus and medicine show. For a time, Ginsberg joined with them and with Kesey and even rubbed shoulders with Sonny Barger and the Hell's Angels, the notorious California motorcycle gang, whom he persuaded not to assault antiwar protesters in Oakland, California, in 1965.

By the end of the twentieth century, there were almost too many poets and performers to add to the extensive list of Beat friends and fellow travelers. One could name figures such as ruth weiss, who performed with jazz musicians and published distinguished books over a half-century, including *Gallery of Women* (1959) and *Can't Stop the Beat* (2011), the title of which suggests the irrepressible force of the movement. Born in Germany in 1928, weiss came to the United States in 1939, settled in San Francisco, befriended Jack Kerouac in the 1950s, and published her work in *Beatitude*. As she approached her ninetieth birthday, she continued to perform the spoken word before appreciative audiences and to entertain listeners with tales of her adventures with Kerouac and Cassady.

Not surprisingly, cultural pundits were hard-pressed to ascertain where, if at all, the Beats stopped and where a host of other groups and movements began, including neo-Beats, post-Beats, hippies, freaks, pranksters, the Ann Arbor (Michigan) White Panthers, and anarchist groups such as the San Francisco Diggers. The Beats created their own mythology, which became a new reality. Burroughs's face appears on the cover of the seminal Beatles album *Sgt. Pepper's Lonely Hearts Club Band* (1967), along with Lenny Bruce, Dylan Thomas, Marlene Dietrich, and others. If the Beats played a role in the genesis of rock, rock shaped them and their art – Kerouac considered renaming *On the Road* to *Rock 'n' Roll Road*. Ginsberg described the Rolling Stones as angels and found inspiration in Mick Jagger's theatrics. He also joined John Lennon and Yoko Ono in Montreal for the 1969 recording of "Give Peace a Chance," which helped to swell the antiwar movement.

Beat influences appear almost everywhere that literary historians look. One movement blurred into another as the 1950s flowed into the 1960s, and later as Beats morphed into punks, a story that Victor Bockris tells in *Beat Punks* (1998).[9] Decades earlier, when Richard Brautigan arrived on the scene with short lyrical books such as *Trout Fishing in America* (written in 1961; published in 1967), he seemed to speak directly to the newborn hippies, though he'd crafted his minimalist art long before hippies arrived in the Haight-Ashbury, the neighborhood that replaced North Beach as the go-to destination for kids from the suburbs and that the media turned into a spectacle for middle-class tourists. No wonder then that the Diggers staged a funeral for "Hippie," complete with a coffin they carried through the streets of San Francisco. Although he appeared in the pages of *Beatitude* in the late 1950s, Brautigan didn't need the Beat label or the mystique of the Haight-Ashbury to find success, nor did his success stop him from committing suicide, an act that reflected badly on the world of bohemians and their descendants.

In the late 1950s, the Beats and the phenomenon of the media-created "Beatniks" were blamed for juvenile delinquency, drug overdoses, and the collapse of middle-class morality. In later decades, the Beats would be credited for their trenchant social criticism and lauded for the success of artists and performers who developed only in part under their aegis.

Singer-songwriter Tom Waits collaborated with William Burroughs on the opera *The Black Rider* (1990), but Waits boasted a unique voice and style that couldn't be subsumed under the Beat umbrella. Jerry Garcia of the Grateful Dead found inspiration in Kerouac's tales of the highway and translated them into songs such as "Truckin'" (1970), but he, too, created his own brand of popular music. Still, it's fair to say that the influence of the Beats extended far beyond literature; one finds their imprint in music (David Amram), painting (Larry Rivers), and film and photography (Dennis Hopper and Robert Frank, whose book *The Americans* [1958] boasts an introduction by Kerouac).

And yet for decades the mass media continued to trivialize the Beats as mindless, antisocial adolescents. Case in point: the June 2015 multimedia event in San Francisco, sponsored by the Beat Museum, was promoted as a "Beatnik Shindig." Many of the Beat faithful were horrified by what seemed to be blatant pandering to a tabloid mentality, but even Beat loyalists rose to the defense of the much-maligned Beatniks and heralded them as a vital link between the 1950s and 1960s. Un-American and "spaced out," at least by middle-class standards, the Beatniks hid in plain view with sunglasses, berets, black leotards, and their iconic beards. At jazz clubs they nodded heads and snapped fingers to the music of Miles Davis and the Modern Jazz Quartet. Madison Avenue borrowed Beatnik cool and turned it into a marketing tool that sold products and lifestyles.

In *Memoirs of a Beatnik*, di Prima suggests that all cultures on the edge inevitably become mainstream and diluted. As though to forestall her own co-optation, she joined the Diggers and aimed to radicalize the hippies of the Haight-Ashbury. Hunter S. Thompson brought the Beat idiom into the field of "Gonzo" journalism with its drugs, guns, and revulsion for the wealthy and the powerful. In *Fear and Loathing in Las Vegas* (1972), Thompson, a.k.a. Raoul Duke, and his buddy go on the road across an alienated, drugged-out, war-weary nation bulging with police officers. Kerouac's odyssey never expressed as much desperation and despair. *Fear and Loathing* offered a critique of the Kerouac road and reinvented it, too.

Looking Back, Looking Forward

If a single member of the Beat Generation led to the commercialization and the popularization of the counterculture it was probably Kerouac, the photogenic all-American male who felt like an alien in his own country and who insisted in *Lonesome Traveler* (1960) and elsewhere that he was more comfortable among the peasants of Asia and Africa than with the citizens in his own country. In that sense he was a harbinger of the 1960s hippies who trekked to Asia and Latin America in search of spiritual revelation ("the primitive") and aimed to live in tribes with their rites and rituals. As Burroughs noted: "Kerouac opened a million coffee bars and sold a million pairs of Levis to both sexes. Woodstock rises from his pages."[10]

What the Beats began in apartments and coffeehouses reached critical mass at rock concerts with the Grateful Dead and the Rolling Stones in the late 1960s and 1970s. Psychedelic drugs took the place of alcohol. Gloomy and depressed, Kerouac agonized about the end of American innocence and the loss of genuine patriotism and yet the hippies cast him as an eternal hero and envisioned a bright future on earth, which they described as a kind of space ship cruising toward paradise. Burroughs provided an antidote to hippie utopianism and offered a dark, menacing world that met the needs of apocalyptic-minded readers.

In the second half of the twentieth century, few major American writers aimed to be more subversive than Burroughs. "All of my work is directed against those who are bent, through stupidity or design, on blowing up the planet or rendering it uninhabitable," Burroughs explained in 1965.[11] In his experimental novels, in his inimitable interviews and irreverent essays, and in his satirical self, Burroughs aimed to subvert the kind of mind control that he saw in both capitalist and communist nations. In place of regimentation, he encouraged critical thinking and aimed to liberate the citizens of the world through a combination of shock, satire, and a sense of the absurd. Like di Prima, he championed the transcendent power of the human imagination.

Although 1960s activists rarely evoked Burroughs, all through the era of protest, *Howl* and *On the Road* propelled white northern students such as Abbie Hoffman and Tom Hayden into the Civil Rights Movement in the South. West Coast Beats lured East Coast kids to the San Francisco Bay Area, where they joined Californians to decry capital punishment and the execution of Caryl Chessman at San Quentin in 1960, and to continue denouncing the hearings of the House Committee on Un-American Activities. In Golden Gate Park in January 1967, Beat veterans and Berkeley radicals joined with rock 'n' rollers at the "Human Be-In," which was dubbed a "Gathering of the Tribes." The event featured the Jefferson Airplane, Janis Joplin, the Grateful Dead, Timothy Leary, and Allen Ginsberg along with Lenore Kandel and Gary Snyder, who had made his first public appearance at the 6 Gallery reading in 1955 before his long sojourn in Japan. African Americans, including Dick Gregory and Dizzy Gillespie, joined the other performers on stage in Golden Gate Park, while members of the audience danced, smoked marijuana, and performed their own rituals. More than any other single event, the Human Be-In dramatized the coming of age of the counterculture and carried with it the imprint of the Beats.

From about 1965, the first year of mass antiwar protests in the streets, to 1975, when the Vietnam War ended, the kinds of young men and women who might have listened to jazz and poetry a decade or two earlier found themselves at marches and demonstrations with rocks, bottles, and rage. It is only a short step from Ginsberg to Abbie Hoffman, the author of *Revolution for the Hell of It* (1968) and perhaps the most boisterous defendant (save for Black Panther Party co-founder Bobby Seale) at the Chicago Eight trial, which brought Beat non-conformity and 1960s defiance to a boil in a federal courtroom. In August 1968 in Lincoln Park, Ginsberg sat, meditated, chanted "Om," and urged protesters to adopt nonviolence – not Hoffman's way or Tom Hayden's, but unpredictably effective, as it really did calm the crowd, albeit briefly. In the winter of 1969–1970, Ginsberg testified for the defendants in Judge Julius Hoffman's federal courtroom and read from *Howl*, his epic poem about a generation "destroyed by madness" that became the anthem for a generation in the 1960s.

Not surprisingly, *Howl* continued to sell well at City Lights and elsewhere all through the decade of defiance, though by 1969 Ferlinghetti would complain that the novels of Richard Brautigan sold more copies than Ginsberg's poetry (quoted in *San Fransisco Beat*, 75). Ferlinghetti agonized about the vast wasteland of the counterculture that didn't read books and preferred recorded music and illustrated novels. Aliterate hippies – those who could read but chose not to – displaced the literary Beats who had been raised on T. S. Eliot, Marcel Proust, and James Joyce. Television took the place of radio, the mass media that had shaped Kerouac, Burroughs, and Ginsberg in the 1940s. Baby boomers nurtured on popular shows such as *Dragnet*, *Gunsmoke*, and *The Many Loves of Dobie Gillis* (in which Bob Denver plays Beatnik Maynard G. Krebs) embraced television, the medium that the Beats saw as an ominous sign of brain washing. (See, for example, Ginsberg's "Television Was a Baby Crawling Toward That Deathchamber" collected in *Planet News: 1961–1967* [1968].)

"During the Korean War ... a sinister new kind of efficiency appeared in America," Kerouac explained in "About the Beat Generation" (1957), perhaps his best essay. The society that mass-produced nearly everything, he argued, "was the result of the universalization of Television and ... the Polite Total Control of Dragnet's 'peace' officers."[12] In 1968, he briefly overcame his revulsion for television and appeared on William Buckley's *Firing Line*, though Burroughs had warned him not to. Drunk, Kerouac offered anti-Semitic remarks and insisted that he ought not to be linked with Ginsberg, who embraced him at the end of the show and whispered a last farewell. Kerouac's heroes had been the hobos of the 1930s and the "crazy, illuminated" hipsters of the 1940s who were, he explained, "characters of a special spirituality who didn't gang up but were solitary Bartlebies staring out the dead wall window of our civilization" (559).

Time and again, the antiwar and anti-bomb sentiments of the Beats were echoed in one generation of Americans after another as the nation sent troops to fight in countries around the world and continually tried to contain and control African Americans and other minorities all through the twentieth and early twenty-first centuries. Moreover, the Beat emphasis on originality encouraged young poets and novelists to write in the first person, to validate and express their own experiences, and to communicate with fearlessness even when outnumbered, their roars often overwhelmed by the big commercial slogans of the corporate world.

The Beats taught the hippies to honor their own hearts. Along with the later punks and rappers, they rediscovered the roots of American bohemianism, which went back to Whitman. Moreover, they offered alternatives to Main Street consumerism and shrill patriotism, valorizing a genuine tradition of dissent and nonconformity that had long flowered in Greenwich Village. The Beats and the beat went marching on and on. Indeed, nearly every counterculture born in the 1950s and 1960 still thrives in the twenty-first century on Main Street, in isolated pockets nearly everywhere, and in far-flung corners of the world. Howling has never gone out of fashion. Going on the road has never lost its appeal, and Burroughs's soft machine and nova express still take intrepid travelers all the way to the end of the line.

NOTES

1 Allen Ginsberg, *Collected Poems, 1947–1997* (New York: Harper Perennial, 2006), 154–56.
2 Bob Dylan, *Bringing It All Back Home* (Columbia Records, 1965).
3 Quoted in David Meltzer, ed., *San Francisco Beat* (San Francisco: City Lights, 2001), 101.
4 Bob Dylan, in Allen Ginsberg, *Collected Poems, 1947–1980* (New York: Harper Perennial, 1988), np.
5 George Judson, "Naked Lunches and Reality Sandwiches: How the Beats Beat the First Amendment," *New York Times* (August 10, 1997), www.nytimes.com/books/oo/02/13/specials/burroughs-first.html (accessed October 17, 2016).
6 Diane di Prima, *Memoirs of a Beatnik* (Paris: Olympia, 1969), 127.
7 Diane di Prima, *Revolutionary Letters* (1971; San Francisco: Last Gasp, 2007), 22.
8 Allen Ginsberg, *Deliberate Prose: Selected Essays, 1952–1995*, ed. Bill Morgan (New York: Perennial, 2001), 238–39.

9 See Victor Bockris, *Beat Punks* (Boston: Da Capo, 1998).

10 William S. Burroughs, "Remembering Jack Kerouac," *The Adding Machine: Selected Essays* (New York: Arcade, 1993), 180.

11 Quoted in Jonah Raskin, *Allen Ginsberg's "Howl" and the Making of the Beat Generation* (Berkeley: University of California Press, 2004), 113.

12 Jack Kerouac, "About the Beat Generation," *The Portable Jack Kerouac*, ed. Ann Charters (New York: Viking, 1995), 280.

3

REGINA WEINREICH

Locating a Beat Aesthetic

"It is impossible to conceive a new philosophy until one creates a new language."
–Norman Mailer, "The White Negro"

This chapter attempts to formalize a definition of Beat with a focus on the aesthetic principles of this controversial mid-century literati. Unlike most literary coteries, the writers known as Beat have endured, and the three most visible Beat authors, Jack Kerouac, William S. Burroughs, and Allen Ginsberg, are read today within and outside academic institutions. Their work still has the aura of subversive cadences, delivering sacred truth, articulating the private and less-often-spoken-about aspects of the human condition. Today readers are familiar with their use of language – certain "unmentionable words," as they were deemed in the trials, that were prohibited in the 1950s, the highpoint of Beat literary production, but that are perfectly acceptable today on cable television. But, as contemporary life becomes less and less communicative, more about sound bites, confined to 140 characters, limited by the technology that enables it, Beat subject matter becomes more rare: Beat as in beatific, for Jack Kerouac; Beat as telepathic, for William S. Burroughs; or Beat as tender, as Allen Ginsberg may have termed it. All favor aspects of instinct over intellect, fresh experience over canned. All worked in that most rarified and poetic place, working to express human experience that may be beyond the radar of most people, whom they viewed as hypnotized by the language of advertising and commodification. Today the strictures of society may be different from what they were in the heyday of the Beat movement, but the most important influence of the Beats was to provide a roadmap for transcendence still very much relevant today. For the purposes of this chapter, I'm going to look at some characteristic aesthetics of the Beat Movement's three most well-known writers in order to suggest why people have thought their work to be so consequential to the changing landscape of twentieth-century letters.

The New Vision: "Everything is Collapsing"

Jack Kerouac's advice to "never afterthink to 'improve' or defray impressions" – that is, his refusal to revise – was at once his most visible aesthetic choice and his most controversial.[1] Many critics found the long, sweeping sentences of *On the Road* (1957) or *The Subterraneans* (1958) ragged and grammatically derelict.[2] Revision being the artist's chief control, this stance was seen as a rebellion against language itself, especially according to the norms of New Criticism and what the critic and Beat associate Seymour Krim termed "the critical straitjacket of post-T. S. Eliot letters."[3] In some ways the most experimental Beat writer of all, Kerouac composed manuscripts on scrolls, one long road-like paragraph coming in at over 200 pages when paginated, eschewing changes and doing away with the encumbrance for readers of turning a single page. When he insisted, however, that *On the Road* be published in scroll form, his former publisher, Robert Giroux, refused. The novel languished until it was picked up for publication by Viking in 1957, edited, paginated, and revised. According to editor Malcolm Cowley, Kerouac revised well.[4] As we now know, Kerouac's unique way of revision was to simply write another version, and each variation became its own singular book.

Kerouac explained his quest for pure, unadulterated language, the truth of the heart unobstructed by the lying of revision in essays published in the *Evergreen Review*: "Essentials of Spontaneous Prose" (summer 1958) and "Belief and Technique for Modern Prose" (spring 1959). On the grammatically irreverent sentences, Kerouac extolled a "method" eschewing conventional punctuation in favor of dashes. In "Essentials of Spontaneous Prose," he recommended the "vigorous space dash separating rhetorical breathing (as jazz musician drawing breath between outblown phrases)"; the dash allowed Kerouac to deal with time differently, making it less prosaic and linear and more poetic. He also described his manner of developing an image beginning with the "jewel center," from which he wrote in a "semitrance," "without consciousness," his language governed by sound, by the poetic affect of alliteration and assonance until he reached a plateau, initiating a new "jewel center," stronger than the first and spiraling out as he riffed (in an analogy with a jazz musician) ("Essentials" 484–485). He saw himself as a horn player blowing one long note, as he told his interviewers for *The Paris Review* in 1968.[5] His technique explains the unusual organization of his writing, not haphazard or sloppy but systematic in the most individualized sense. His "spontaneity" allowed him to develop his distinct voice freed from what he called, pejoratively, "Craft" (485), or literary lying.

Seeking visual possibilities in language, Kerouac combined spontaneous prose with a technique he called sketching, suggested by Ed White, a
friend from his Columbia University days: sketch "like a painter, but with
words."[6] *Visions of Cody*, a variation of *On the Road*, used the sketching
technique. Note, for example, a rather famous passage describing Hector's
Cafeteria. Allen Ginsberg called this sequence a Homeric hymn in his
introduction:

> But ah, the counter! as brilliant as B-way outside! Great rows of it – one vast
> L-shaped counter – great rows of diced mint jellos in glasses; diced straw-
> berry jellos gleaming red, jellos mixed with peaches and cherries, cherry
> jellos top't with whipcream, vanilla custards top't with cream; great straw-
> berry shortcakes already sliced in twelve sections, illuminating the center
> of the L – Huge salads, cottage cheese, pineapple, plums, egg salad, prunes,
> everything.[7]

As I demonstrated in *Kerouac's Spontaneous Poetics* (1987), Kerouac
"sketches" the counter, his eye moving like a camera panning, drawing a
picture that also doubles the neon images of Broadway outside.[8] The sketching is far from random, or stream-of-consciousness, but governed by a
specific sound system of repetition, alliteration, and assonance (note, for
example, the repetition of "jellos" and the return to the L-shaped counter). The sequence is further governed by oscillating emotive tropes, the
exclamation of the glorious food juxtaposed with the novel's hero, Cody, as
drab onlooker: "Poor Cody, in front of this in his scuffled-up beat Denver
shoes, his literary 'imitation' suit he had wanted to wear to be acceptable
in New York cafeterias which he thought would be brown and plain like
Denver cafeterias, with ordinary food" (11).

Another aspect of Kerouac's development of a spontaneous aesthetic is
how it connected to what he perceived as a jazz idiom. Perhaps the best
example of this aesthetic is found in *The Subterraneans* (written 1953; published 1958). For example, in the famous single paragraph in which Kerouac
describes a party at the Red Drum, he sees "up on the stand Bird Parker with
solemn eyes who'd been busted fairly recently and had now returned to a
kind of bop dead Frisco but had just discovered or had been told about the
Red Drum, the great new generation gang wailing and gathering there" to
hear him blow "his now-settled-down-into-regulated-design 'crazy' notes."[9]
The passage underscores the structures of jazz as it mimics the musical constructs in words (for more on Kerouac's and the Beats' relationship to a jazz
aesthetic, see Chapter 17).

After meeting the poet Gary Snyder in 1955, Kerouac and other Beats
were introduced to Japanese haiku, a form mostly unknown to Americans

because the poetry of Basho, Buson, Issa, and Shiki had not been translated into English until the pioneering work of R. H. Blyth in 1949. Kerouac's mastery of the art of haiku is described in *The Dharma Bums* (1958). While Ezra Pound had modeled his two-line poem "In a Station of the Metro" (1913) after the spirit of Japanese haiku, Kerouac redefined the form, setting off an American haiku tradition departing from the seventeen-syllable, three-line strictures. In his essay "The Origins of Joy in Poetry" (1958), he extols the haiku form as "pointing out things directly, purely, concretely, no abstractions or explanations, wham wham the true blue song of man."[10] In the posthumously published collection *Scattered Poems* (1971), he proposes that the "Western haiku" simply say a lot in three short lines. "Above all, a Haiku must be very simple and free of all poetic trickery and make a little picture and yet be as airy and graceful as a Vivaldi Pastorella."[11] In his pocket notebooks, Kerouac wrote and rewrote haiku, revising and perfecting them. He also incorporated his haiku into his prose. He told his *Paris Review* interviewers, "A sentence that's short and sweet with a sudden jump of thought is a kind of haiku" ("Jack Kerouac, The Art of Fiction"). Thus he writes a sequence in *The Dharma Bums*: "The storm went away as swiftly as it came and the late afternoon lake-sparkle blinded me. Late afternoon, my mop drying on the rock. Late afternoon, my bare back cold as I stood above the world digging shovelsful into a pail. Late afternoon, it was I not the void that changed."[12]

Kerouac turned to Buddhist study and practice after his "road" period, from 1953 to 1956, in the lull between composing *On the Road* in 1951 and its publication in 1957. When he finished *The Subterraneans* in the fall of 1953, fed up with the world after the failed love affair upon which the book was based, he read Thoreau and fantasized a life outside civilization. He immersed himself in the study of Zen, beginning his genre-defying book, *Some of the Dharma*, in 1953 as reader's notes on Dwight Goddard's *Buddhist Bible* (1938); the work grew into a massive compilation of spiritual material, meditations, prayers, haiku, and musings on the teaching of Buddha. In an attempt to replicate the experience of the reclusive Chinese poet Han Shan, Kerouac spent sixty-three days atop Desolation Peak in Washington State. Kerouac recounted this experience in *Desolation Angels* (1965) using haiku as bridges, connectives as in jazz, between sections of spontaneous prose. In 1956 he wrote a sutra, *The Scripture of the Golden Eternity*, and, extending that practice to his literary concerns, he thought of his entire oeuvre, Legend of Duluoz, as a "Divine Comedy of the Buddha," thereby combining Eastern and Western traditions.

In 1982 at the Naropa Institute, at the twenty-fifth anniversary of *On the Road*'s publication, Diane di Prima spoke about Kerouac as an immigrant writer, and this footage later appeared in the documentary film *The Beat Generation: An American Dream* (1986). The most recent scholarship on Kerouac's prose sees him in the context of the Franco-American origins of his language. The struggle to find Kerouac's unique American voice is in fact the work of an immigrant outsider, which explains too his identification with his *Visions of Cody* hero, Cody Pomeray.[13] Dealing with Kerouac's "poetics of exile," Hassan Melehy brings a new understanding to Kerouac's "road" adventure, revealing that, after the novel's 1951 composition, "Jean-Louis Lebris de Kerouac wrote several novels set in his native Lowell, MA whose first-person narrator speaks to himself and others in French."[14] What this reminds us is that Kerouac grew up in a bilingual community, and his traditional English studies were augmented by half-day studies in French. This understanding goes far to informing the Lowell novels: *Doctor Sax* (1959), *Maggie Cassidy* (1959), and *Visions of Gerard* (1963). As Kerouac's writing was for him an enterprise in ever-changing process, Kerouac studies are likewise in a continual state of flux.

Burroughs's Redemption from the Ugly Spirit

William S. Burroughs claimed the accidental killing of his wife Joan Vollmer in Mexico City made him a writer: he needed to redeem what he called the "ugly spirit." He avowed his urgency to expiate the ugly spirit, to atone for the killing of Joan by becoming a writer, as he explained in the introduction of *Queer* (1985), published decades after the manuscript was originally penned. The introduction reads like a mea culpa, wherein he further spins his own theories of coincidence, taking the accidental crippling of the writer Denton Welch as an example of how a minute here or there can change a life. His time-and-space experiments emerged from these intellectualizations. We might well ask: was this simply a facile excuse, or perhaps a heartfelt quest for forgiveness for a horrific act? While this question is perhaps impossible to answer, it is clear that, if Kerouac personalized his aesthetic by linking his wild forms to his own subjectivity, at various moments in his long career, Burroughs certainly viewed writing as connected to personal expiation, and his radical experiments with form might be viewed as attempts to make sense of the fundamentally complex yet confounding nature of human experience.

Burroughs's most well-known aesthetic innovation is the "cut-up method," which he developed with the artist Brion Gysin in the late 1950s. As he said in 1980, "The future of writing is in Space, not Time."[15] He and Gysin collaborated on a kind of time–space how-to manual, *The Third*

Mind (1977; 1978), which explains to some degree a procedure for bringing these together. A provocative philosophical document, its tenets had been revered for years in the French *oeuvre croissées*. Regarded as a new Sartre in France and as something of a New Age philosopher in Switzerland, where a German-language publication *RADAR* celebrates the Burroughsean slogan "Time is running out," the Burroughs–Gysin "third mind" entity contributed an idiom of consciousness to existential tradition: the cut-up.

Visual artists are familiar with the techniques of collage and montage. "Writing is fifty years behind painting," Brion Gysin declared.[16] The first cut-up experiments applied painters' techniques to writing:

> Cut right through the pages of any book or newsprint ... lengthwise, for example, and shuffle the columns of text. Put them together at hazard and read the newly constituted message. Do it for yourself. Use any system which suggests itself to you ... Words have a vitality of their own and you or anybody can make them gush into action. (34)

In this illustration, a percussive poem reads something like a mantra:

PROCLAIM	PRESENT	TIME	OVER
PROCLAIM	PRESENT	TIME	
OVER	PROCLAIM	PRESENT	
TIME	OVER	PROCLAIM	
PRESENT	TIME[17]		

The words dart off the page in pulsating word/images. Fixed on the page but not in syntactical position, they can be read in any combination. Meaning is conveyed in camera clicks. Words flash. As Burroughs explains, this typography attempts to bring word and image together, to close the gap between writing and its origins in calligraphy and hieroglyphics – picture language. The grid is therefore useful as words and paintings increasingly become formulas and spells intended to produce specific effects in the reader/viewer. The word is thus invested with new powers: Reichean orgone, Joycean epiphany, orgasm – energy-packed images in spurts. Wrested from the restrictions of the linear sentence, and thus free of cause and effect, the word conjures a variety of image associations, dynamic déjà-vu. A practical example: once I was walking down a Greenwich Village street thinking of a friend named Perry. A man carrying a pizza box nudged me and asked, "Where's Perry?" Jarred, I thought: how could this man be reading my mind? Of course he meant Perry Street, the next one over, where he was probably to deliver the food. A coincidence, or perhaps a telepathic connection? In Burroughs-speak, this coincidence should be taken as an aspect of consciousness, toward a radiant vision of the future.

And this is precisely how the urban mind flows; the cut-up is a manifest-ation of stream-of-consciousness, a literary montage of the mind cut con-stantly by random factors. Cut-ups emphasize the randomness of life. *The Third Mind* suggests that coincidence is not only frequent but also patterned, "if people keep their eyes and ears open" (136). Thus, the cut-up theory not only provides an alternative to linear thinking, to the sentence and the per-vasive blandness of the straitjacket novel, but is also aesthetic rebellion. Yet, just as Kerouac was criticized for his spontaneous method, Burroughs's non-linear prose calls attention to itself and was difficult for the writer to defend. Far from promulgating a cult of unintelligibility, Burroughs endeavored to explain his aesthetic theories in earlier esoterica, such as "White Subway," "Snack," and "The Job."

Brion Gysin was experimenting with montage techniques in 1959 when Burroughs was looking for a new method of writing that would rescue his *Naked Lunch* leftovers. Gysin's own *Minutes to Go* (with Burroughs, Sinclair Beiles, and Gregory Corso [1960]) contains unedited newspaper clippings arranged at random that emerge as meaningful and coherent prose. Although this was a radical aesthetic that seemed to rob the writer of authorial agency, it created new kinds of meaning that would be found in Burroughs's subsequent work, such as *Soft Machine* (1961), *Nova Express* (1964, 1966), and *Ticket That Exploded* (1962, 1967). Seemingly frag-mented narrative requires the reader's participation in completing it. In the best sense, readers can wrest themselves from the program they were born into, thus breaking a fundamental element of control – of language, cultural norms, institutions, authority.

Looking back to Burroughs's earlier work, it might be tempting to think the cut-up explains the fragmentary structures of *Naked Lunch*. If *Junky* was an attempt to explain the street life of heroin in a linear way, *Naked Lunch* expresses the junky's imaginative, interior journey or trip. The title, which means literally the ability to see clearly the food at the end of one's fork, may have been a misreading for "naked lust." Kerouac famously sug-gested this was a good title, after Ginsberg was reading aloud from the man-uscript of *Queer* and misread "naked lust" for "naked lunch."[18] But, despite such surface similarities between the cut-up method and the fragmentary nature of *Naked Lunch*, Burroughs did not develop the cut-up technique until after *Naked Lunch* was composed: although he wrote that "You can cut into *Naked Lunch* at any intersection point," this does not mean that his most famous work was composed with what would become his most dis-tinctive method, the cut-up.[19] However, in his last trilogy – *Cities of the Red Night* (1981), *The Place of Dead Roads* (1983), and *The Western Lands*,

(1987) – Burroughs returns to linearity, his authorial persona a writer living in a boxcar, mired in his own clichés. The wildly executed flourishes of the early literature give way to neat sentences – paranoia, yes, but the sensibility of a man growing old.

Burroughs was always interesting, his discourse perhaps the least mired in clichés. Younger, Kerouac and Ginsberg thought of him as their guru. And he recommended books to them, instructing them in science, and even for a time gave Kerouac some psychoanalysis. In the mid-1940s, after the David Kammerer murder, Kerouac and Burroughs attempted a hard-boiled novel, based on the scandal. In alternating chapters, the two novelists tell a true story in fictional form of their mutual friend Lucien Carr's fatal stabbing of his stalker in Riverside Park. The work, finally published in 2008 as *And the Hippos Were Boiled in Their Tanks*, shows the early talents of each, and a commitment to writing as a shared experience. The history shows mutual respect as writers, a continuous dialogue in person and in letters regarding their texts, even the practical. When Burroughs needed to complete the manuscript for *Naked Lunch*'s publication by Maurice Girodias of Olympia Press, he called upon his friends to help. Kerouac began the typing-up process in Tangier, and was followed by Ginsberg and Peter Orlovsky. The typing of *Naked Lunch* itself didn't necessarily influence Kerouac's fiction writing, only his regard for Burroughs. Being in Tangier, however, gave him nightmares. Burroughs's later literary experiments influenced Kerouac and Ginsberg, especially in their emphasis upon the visual. "When you start thinking in images," Burroughs told one interviewer, "without words, you're well on the way" (*The Third Mind* 2).

Allen Ginsberg's Long Line: From Whitman's "Barbaric Yawp" to "Howl"

Allen Ginsberg's "courage teacher" was not his father, Louis Ginsberg, a poet and educator, but Walt Whitman, stretching back to a century prior. Ginsberg's lyric "A Supermarket in California" (1956) is an overt homage, as his persona follows the predecessor poet up and down the aisles of the image marketplace of democracy, noting each and every item selected and added to his shopping cart. Clearly this impulse is shared by the American consumer culture that would name a shopping mall on Long Island after the bard of American letters. But Ginsberg's appreciation is poet to poet, a Freudian son to surrogate father, and a revelatory key to his own poetry, especially the epic for which he is most known, "Howl" (1956). Is not a howl, like the poem "Howl," a scream of rage, a mad call to arms, a rebellious announcement of revolt?

Reading "Howl," what is perhaps most immediately clear is Ginsberg's aesthetic of the long line, which he inherited from Whitman and made his own. Calling his long lines "strophes," after the Greek, Ginsberg notes his own poetic strategies and innovations in the poem itself, even as he mimics and then breaks from the Whitmanesque long line in the creation of his own voice: "who dreamt and made incarnate gaps in Time & Space through images juxtaposed, and trapped the archangel of the soul between 2 visual images and joined the elemental verbs and set the noun and dash of consciousness together jumping with sensation of Pater Omnipotens Aeterne Deus."[20] Here Ginsberg uses a jazz aesthetic comparable to the use of jazz in Kerouac's "blowing," as Kerouac put it in his long, breathless lines, riffing in the repetition of "who" as the point of departure, a "jewel center," to use Kerouac's term, for the extended imagery and description of his characters, the "mad" ones, including Carl Solomon, and others who might also be defined as "hip" or "psychopaths" in Norman Mailer's era-defining essay "The White Negro" (1957).

Ginsberg articulated "The New Vision" in "Howl," just as Kerouac had in his "true-life" novels. And, just as Burroughs's cut-up was an attempt to re-view time–space relationships, so too does Ginsberg define his process in these "Howl" strophes, moving toward a cut-up, or collaged image, "images juxtaposed ... between 2 visual images and joined the elemental verbs and set the noun and dash of consciousness together jumping with sensation ... to recreate the syntax and measure of pure human prose." (*Howl* 20)

In many ways, this "human prose" represents American cadences, and, in his important poem "Wichita Vortex Sutra" (written 1966; published 1968), Ginsberg sweeps across the Western landscape, almost his own version of *On the Road*, noting the sights and sounds of the road in close detail. But, as Greil Marcus has aptly pointed out, the repetition of the word "Prophesy" speaks to Ginsberg's meaning and purpose, and, if I may enlarge the concept, to the Beat aesthetic as invented and practiced by Kerouac, Burroughs, and Ginsberg[21] For Ginsberg, the idea of prophesy is always connected to the uses (and abuses) of language; as he writes in "Wichita Vortex Sutra":

> Flashing pictures Senate Foreign Relations Committee room
> Generals faces flashing on and off screen
> mouthing language
> State Secretary speaking nothing but language
> McNamara declining to speak public language
> The president talking language,
> Senators reinterpreting language.[22]

Amid all the dangerous language of those politicians in power, which further embroiled the United States in the Vietnam War and which the poem calls "Black Magic Language" (*Howl* 409), Ginsberg counterpoints his own poetic language, which he imbues with a mystical prophetic power. In fact, by the end of the poem, he symbolically declares an end to the Vietnam War through the act of making a "Mantra of American language now" (415). Prophesy, being related to ideas of becoming, of seeing a future as yet unseen, a moving toward transcendence, thus also suggests notions of the spiritual, of beatitude, or Beat in its most blessed form.

In a letter to Ginsberg from Mexico City dated May 18, 1952, when he was visiting Burroughs, Kerouac asserted his "sketching" technique as suggested by Ed White as "the only way to write," and likened it to the "poetry you write" (*Letters* 356). In the same letter, Kerouac writes of Burroughs's "Junk or Queer." Clearly, a kinship had developed among these three, beyond just their fueling one another's work. In this early fomenting of the Beat literary aesthetic, the writers were collaborating on an expression of the present ethos. But the Beat aesthetic is also a road map for others. Burroughs insisted upon the loss of control, literally cutting through the linear sentence and thought. Kerouac's wild form (from the sketching method) and Ginsberg's long line created possibilities for extending the American language, creating more radiant, spontaneous, and free idioms for a contemporary consciousness. They understood that what writers write is always in the becoming, in the shimmering aspiration of creation. The enduring value of the Beat aesthetic is its reach for the eternal in the expression of the next American moment.

NOTES

1 Jack Kerouac, "Essentials of Spontaneous Prose," *The Portable Jack Kerouac*, ed. Ann Charters (New York: Viking, 1995), 485.

2 Although we now know that the version of *On the Road* published in 1957 was not exactly the same as the one typed on a scroll in three weeks in 1951; see, for example, Tim Hunt, *Kerouac's Crooked Road* (1981; Berkeley: University of California Press, 1996).

3 Seymour Krim, "Introduction," Jack Kerouac, *Desolation Angels* (1965; New York: Bantam, 1966), 3.

4 Barry Gifford and Lawrence Lee, *Jack's Book: An Oral Biography of Jack Kerouac* (New York: Penguin, 2012), 206.

5 Ted Berrigan, "Jack Kerouac, The Art of Fiction No. 41 [interview with Kerouac]," *Paris Review* (summer 1968), www.theparisreview.org/interviews/4260/the-art-of-fiction-no-41-jack-kerouac (accessed September 9, 2016).

6 Jack Kerouac, *1940–1956*, Vol. II of *Selected Letters*, ed. Ann Charters (New York: Penguin, 1996), 356.

7 Jack Kerouac, *Visions of Cody* (1972; New York: Penguin, 1993), 10.

8 Regina Weinreich, *Kerouac's Spontaneous Poetics: A Study of the Fiction* (1987; New York: Thunder's Mouth Press, 2001), 62–74.

9 Jack Kerouac, *The Subterraneans* (New York: Grove, 1958), 13.

10 Jack Kerouac, "The Origins of Joy in Poetry," *Good Blonde & Others* (San Francisco: Grey Fox, 1993), 74.

11 Jack Kerouac, *Scattered Poems* (San Francisco: City Lights, 2001), 69.

12 Jack Kerouac, *The Dharma Bums* (1958; New York: Penguin, 1976), 189.

13 See, for example, Joyce Johnson, *The Voice Is All: The Lonely Victory of Jack Kerouac* (New York: Viking, 2012) and Hassan Melehy, *Kerouac: Language, Poetics, and Territory* (London: Bloomsbury, 2016).

14 Hassan Melehy, unpublished abstract for *Kerouac: Language, Poetics, and Territory*.

15 William S. Borroughs, "Dinner with Susan Sontag, Stewart Meyer, and Gerard Malanga: New York 1980," Victor Bockris, *With William Burroughs: A Report from the Bunker* (1981; New York: St. Martin's, 1996), 2.

16 William S. Burroughs and Brion Gysin, *The Third Mind* (New York: Viking, 1978), 34.

17 Burroughs and Gysin, "In Present Time," *The Third Mind*, np.

18 Oliver Harris, "Introduction," William S. Burroughs, *Queer* (New York: Penguin, 2010), xviii.

19 William S. Burroughs, *Naked Lunch: The Restored Text*, ed. James Grauerholz and Barry Miles (New York: Grove Press, 2001), 187.

20 Allen Ginsberg, *Howl and Other Poems* (San Francisco: City Lights, 1956), 20.

21 Greil Marcus, *The Shape of Things to Come: Prophecy and the American Voice* (New York: Farrar, Straus, 2007), 276–77.

22 Allen Ginsberg, *Collected Poems, 1947–1997* (New York: Harper Perennial, 2006), 410.

4

NANCY M. GRACE

The Beats and Literary History
Myths and Realities

Parasitic Narratives and the Beats as Bugs

In the 1950s and 1960s, critical consensus remained steadfast in its condemnation of Beat literature and Beat culture. At that nascent stage in Beat literary reception, no one out-demonized the Beats more than Norman Podhoretz, a cultural critic and former Columbia University classmate of poet Allen Ginsberg. Podhoretz's now infamous essay "The Know-Nothing Bohemians," published in the spring 1958 issue of the *Partisan Review*, leveled punch after punch at the Beats for being indecent, violent, racist, solipsistic, and anti-intellectual. Above all, Podhoretz vitriolically characterized Beat bohemians as full-out anti-civilization. According to Podhoretz, Beats defied belief in "intelligence, cultivation, [and] spiritual refinement" and were instead "young men who can't think straight and so hate anyone who can" (he was ignorant of the fact, or didn't care, that women also belonged to the Beat Generation).[1] For Podhoretz and many other detractors, Beat writing was unrehearsed, willfully anti-intellectual (i.e. opposed to intellect and reason in favor of action and emotion) and anti-academic (i.e. opposed to scholarly activities associated with colleges and universities), as well as shocking for the sake of being shocking, a situation proving that the Beats wallowed in ignorance of preceding literary movements, lineages, and ancestors. That same spring, San Francisco columnist Herb Caen had derogatorily written off the Beats with a reference to the Soviet satellite Sputnik: "*Look* magazine," he wrote, "hosted a party in a No. Beach house for 50 beatniks, and by the time word got around the sour grapevine, over 250 bearded cats and kits were on hand, slopping up ... free booze."[2] Beats refused, as *Life* magazine writer Paul O'Neil remarked little more than a year later, "to sample the seeping juices of American plenty and American social advance [preferring to] scrape their feelers in discordant scorn of any and all who do."[3] Such characterizations ground a historical narrative positioning Beat writers as archetypal villains, as abominations assaulting the defenders of cultural "goodness and light," a modern-day version of the ancient trope of a heroic king, prince, or knight fighting off the worst that vindictive gods or men can throw at him. From a distance of almost sixty years, we can laugh at the unsubstantiated fear expressed in such cultural declarations, possibly admiring the passion with which these texts were written (and, in the case of Podhoretz, acknowledging that despite his many prejudices he nailed Beat racism for exactly what it was) while pitying the fact that Beat critics got so much of it so wrong.

But it would be unjust to solely blame literary critics and journalists for this version of history. Jack Kerouac carries some of this burden, based on treatises such as "Belief & Technique for Modern Prose" (1959), in which he set forth writerly prescriptions calling for "no time for poetry but exactly what is" and "composing wild, undisciplined, pure, coming in from under, crazier the better."[4] Dictates like these built on earlier statements from Beat literature itself, in particular Kerouac's creation of Dean Moriarty as the anti-intellectual, streetwise, street-hardened visionary angel, a crazy, Christ-like figure around whom lesser lights, such as narrator Sal Paradise, circled in search of wisdom. Allen Ginsberg's "Howl" (1956) best epitomizes the Beat Generation, described by the speaker as "a lost battalion of platonic conversationalists," holy victims of Molochian capitalism, who were expelled from the academy, used drugs, partied endlessly, wandered aimlessly across America, and ended up dead or in mental hospitals.[5] Even the earliest pronouncements on "Beatdom" sowed the narrative seed. John Clellon Holmes, author of the first Beat novel, *Go* (1952), said as much in his 1952 essay "This Is the Beat Generation," published in the *New York Times Magazine*. Identifying the average GI, secretary, and hotrod driver as members of the Beat Generation, he heralded their "ever-increasing conviction that the problem of modern life is essentially a spiritual problem; and that capacity for sudden wisdom which people who live hard and go far, possess."[6] Comparing them to the youth of Dostoyevski's 1880s Russia, Holmes suggested that the Beats were a serious threat to the status quo.

These passages are poetic pronouncements and opinions, not scientific evidence or biographical data, but even the latter at times functioned to reify the grotesque image of Beat writers as despicable insects. For instance, the contributor's note for Ginsberg's longtime lover Peter Orlovsky, published in Donald Allen's *The New American Poetry* (1960), reads like a line from "Howl": "Grew up with dirtyfeet and giggles. Cant [sic] stand dust so pick my nose ... Quit high school in middle of last term & and got lost working in Mental hospital old man's bed slopy [sic] ward."[7] In contrast to the Podhoretzian emplotment of Beat elements, these passages narrativize the anti-academic/anti-intellectual Beat as the quintessential American: the poor, everyday, and shat-upon who out of desperation or primitive wisdom sets out to slay the evil oppressor.

This narrative has long driven American cultural history, dating back at least to Ralph Waldo Emerson's call for a truly American poet "with tyrannous eye, which kn[ows] the value of our incomparable materials, and s[ees], in the barbarism and materialism of the times, another carnival of the same gods whose picture he so much admires in Homer."[8] This poet Emerson eventually discovered in Walt Whitman. That call was again answered at the turn of the century by Ezra Pound, credited by many as almost single-handedly revolutionizing twentieth-century poetics.[9] Pound's poetics, the product of an extraordinary intellect, are finely wrought but fundamentally articulated as a belief in common speech and free verse economically expressed, the freedom to choose one's subject matter, and artistic invention as the beacon of civilization. Many young writers of the mid-twentieth century, especially Ginsberg, Diane di Prima, and Anne Waldman among the Beats, inheriting an aesthetic world awash in border crossings and boundary violations, responded to Pound as Whitman did to Emerson, constructing a historical narrative of their own lives to flow with the "tyrannous" one(s) that had come before.

However, it was the "abomination-must-be-destroyed" narrative that dominated American discourse. Literary declarations such as Podhoretz's were coupled with governmental efforts to quash Beat publishers and writers through obscenity laws. Alongside the US Postal Service's failed efforts to ban James Joyce's *Ulysses* (1922) now stand the 1957 "Howl" trial; the 1966 *Naked Lunch* trial; the 1960 censorship of Kerouac's *Old Angel Midnight* and selections from Burroughs's *Naked Lunch* in the literary magazine *Big Table*; New York City police raids in 1964 of di Prima and LeRoi Jones's The Poet's Theatre; the San Francisco police suppression of Michael McClure's play *The Beard* in 1965; and the 1966 seizure of Lenore Kandel's *The Love Book* in San Francisco.[10] Of these, the "Howl" and *Naked Lunch* trials, together with the obscenity-defying publications of D. H. Lawrence's *Lady Chatterley's Lover* and Henry Miller's *Tropic of Cancer* by Barney Rossett's Grove Press, contributed to unshackling imaginative literature from formal restrictions on First Amendment rights.

This same confrontation played out in "anthology wars" involving public and private sectors of the US educational system and business community, especially concerning secondary-school textbooks and literary collections aimed at serious producers and consumers of poetry. In the early post-war decades, most young Americans learned about literature through class lessons drawn from bulky anthologies purchased by local school boards. In the early 1960s, the heyday of Beat notoriety, high school textbooks featured poets such as Browning, Burns, Frost, Shakespeare, Tennyson, Whitman, and Wordsworth; long fiction was frequently represented by excerpts from Charles Dickens's *Great Expectations* and George Eliot's *Silas Marner*. As late as 1989, major anthologies used in US high schools, while featuring more female and African American writers, contained no texts by Beat or Beat-associated writers.[11] Through this lens, one could conclude that public schools had successfully eradicated the Beat "abomination" before the GenXers ever had a chance to hear about it.

A review of major literary anthologies leads to the same conclusion. *New Poets of England and America*, published in 1957 and edited by the poet-critics Donald Hall, Robert Pack, and Louis Simpson, used the cut-off of forty years of age to identify new poetic voices in the Anglo-American tradition.[12] Of the fifty-two poets published in the anthology, none was part of the Beat, San Francisco Renaissance, Black Mountain, or New York schools. The selections represented a university-focused philosophy of poetics expressed in Robert Frost's introduction to the volume: "[a] large part of reading in school always has been and still is poetry" (10), he wrote, wistfully concluding, "many of us like school and want to go there" (12).

Hall and Pack's *New Poets of England and America, Second Selection* (1962) ramped up the attack. The editors included Denise Levertov, Sylvia Plath, Adrienne Rich, and Anne Sexton – significant marginalized female voices – but Pack's introduction to the American section drew a sharp line between academic American and Beat poets, between "good and bad, honest and pretentious writing."[13] Beat writers were, wrote Pack, "conventionally irreverent [and] push[ed] a poor substitute for satirical humor, while their sympathies c[a]me too easily ... as if the goof-off, the slob, the criminal, were more human and more lovable than anyone else" (177). Blaming media interest in the Beats for misdirecting attention from the poem to the poet, Pack denounced Beat coffeehouses and little magazines as venues incapable of nurturing good and honest writing as well as good and honest readers, staking out the university as the only place qualified to nurture poetry, since it stood alone as a "place where past and present live together" (182).

At the same time, the cultural power of the "abomination-as-savior" counternarrative had not been lost upon either the legal community or the publishing industry. The voice of the unwashed American, exemplified by the "Howl," *Naked Lunch*, and *Big Table* rulings, has frequently been protected, no doubt to some degree by the persistent presence of counterculture publications reminding civil authorities of their fundamental responsibility to protect the voices of the powerless. Some of the earliest Beat works were published by mainstream presses – Holmes's essay by the *New York Times* and *Go* by Scribner (1952), Kerouac's first novel *The Town and The City* (1950) by Harcourt Brace, and *On the Road* (1957) by Viking. But, simultaneously, the existence of most Beat writing depended upon small literary presses. Among the best known are Ferlinghetti's City Light Books; *The Evergreen Review* (1957–73; 2016–); *Yugen* (1958–62), produced by LeRoi and Hettie Jones; *Beatitude* (1959–60; sporadically through the 1990s), founded by Bob Kaufman, Ginsberg, John Kelly, and William Margolis; *Big Table* (1959–60), produced by Paul Carroll; *Kulchur Magazine* (1960–65), founded by Marc Schleifer and named for Ezra Pound's *Guide to Kulchur*; *The Floating Bear* (1961–71), produced by LeRoi Jones and Diane di Prima; *Fuck You: A Magazine of the Arts* (1962–65), produced by Ed Sanders; and *Angel Hair Sleeps With a Boy in My Head* (1966–69), produced by Anne Waldman and Lewis Warsh. As Anne Waldman reflected, these countercultural publications gave "a younger generation cognizance that you can take your work, literally, into your own hands … They signify meticulous human attention and intelligence, like the outline of a hand in a Cro-Magnon cave."[14] Many of the magazines were literally constructed on kitchen tables by the writers themselves, defying the mainstream gate-keeping publishing protocols of periodicals such as *Esquire, Kenyon Review, Paris Review, Poetry Magazine*, and *Yale Review*.

At the level of commercial publishing, this charge was led by Donald M. Allen, the editor of *The New American Poetry*, published in 1960 by Grove Press. Allen's anthology bridged the Beat late 1950s and the hippie 1960s with the bold declaration that the young poets included in the volume, those born in and after the 1920s including Kerouac, Ginsberg, Ferlinghetti, Corso, Orlovsky, Whalen, McClure, Ray Bremser, and Jones, shared "one common characteristic: a total rejection of all those qualities typical of academic verse" (xi). Allen did not identify those qualities, but, based on poetic statements that conclude the collection, he probably had these in mind: closed verse, form-driven content, description, and rhetoric. Significantly, as Majorie Perloff points out, "Allen introduce[d] the 'new' American poetry, not as an 'alternative' to anything else but as the *successor* [emphasis mine] of two preceding generations."[15] Here "successor" in the context of Allen's introduction readily connotes a takeover by a new regime rather than a friendly and agreed-upon transition of power.

Almost a decade later, Paul Carroll, also included in Allen's volume, edited *The Young American Poets*, which included Waldman and

Warsh. (Interestingly, Carroll writes in "Note about the Selection" that he would have included works by Beat-associated writers Ed Sanders and Bob Dylan but neither replied to the two invitations he sent them.)[16] In the introduction, the poet James Dickey found in these young voices hope for "a wild, shaggy, all-out, all-involving way of speaking where language and [the poet] engage each other at primitive levels, on ground where the issues are not those of literary fashion but are quite literally those of life and death," a stunning validation of the literary "abomination-as-savior" narrative (7).

Over time, as the United States moved out of Cold War McCarthyism, the Vietnam War, the Civil Rights and women's movements, and Reaganomics and into the world of neoliberal globalism, nationalistic populism, and cyberspace technology, the Beat "abomination-as-savior" narrative has become de rigueur boilerplate language, found in book chapters and essays as well as paratexutal materials. For instance, the dust-jacket text to Viking's 2007 publication of the "scroll" typescript of *On the Road* claims that the publication "represents the first full expression of Kerouac's revolutionary aesthetic."[17] Erik Mortenson opens his study of the Beats by stating that their experimentation went "beyond the desire simply to 'make it new.' Rather it seeks to alter the categories of subject, body, and language in a manner that transcends their modernist predecessors."[18] The introduction to *The Philosophy of the Beats* (2012) contends that "The Beats initiated a radical break with the old formalistic forms of expressions, introducing a new relation to power and language, particularly the poetic voicing of personal experience and the articulation of positions of marginality."[19] The publisher's abstract for *The Beat Generation FAQ* (2015) repeats this trope: "The Beat writers shared a vision for a new type of literature, one that escaped the boundaries of academia and employed an organic use of language."[20]

Truth resides in these statements. Beat writing continues to remake our visions of the world through an intentional blending of so-called high and low cultural practices and artifacts, a de facto defining of the academic and intellectual production of art as desperately in need of resuscitation, if not resurrection. But the apparent ease with which such a characterization now appears – in effect, a noncontested vision of Beat history – is disconcerting, since it implies that the "abomination-as-savior" narrative has been effectively subsumed *and therefore disempowered* by the very academic, legal, and commercial entities that tried to wipe it out. Additionally, an uncritical reliance on the Beat savior story can allude to American culture as dependent neither upon the eradication of the mainstream nor upon the eradication of the counterculture. This is exactly what Christopher Gair in *The American Counterculture* describes as the "slippery and often uneasy relationship between [the] 'mainstream' and [the] 'marginal.' "[21] Paradoxically parasitic, each feeds on the other's oppositional and *undesirable* nature, *ingesting and propagating* the other in order to exist. Ironically, then, Beat writers join the experimental (Emerson's tyrannous eye that appreciates the barbarity of the new; Pound's fixation on the new and the free) with the conventional (Emerson's poet who admires the gods in Homer; Pound's reverence for the mythic and arcane). These ancestral lines emerge from a nexus of literary and cultural planes essentializing Beat avant-garde art as a by-product of, a resource for, and a source of US democracy.

What the Beats Learned From Modernism

Since histories are destined to be written and rewritten, I present in this section alternatives, correctives of sorts, to illustrate what Beat realities might have looked like within the interstices of the abomination narratives. The first is a factual response to Podhoretz's claim that Beat writers were anti-academic. A few – Gregory Corso, Peter Orlovsky, Herbert Huncke, Neal Cassady, and Ray Bremser (none except Corso writers of significant output) – fit the stereotype of the Beat autodidact, having educated themselves through prison library reading or other means. But the majority enjoyed what only about five percent of the American population from the 1930s through 1950 could afford: a college education of at least several terms, if not graduation.[22] For example, Jack Kerouac attended Columbia and the New School for Social Research; Burroughs received a degree in English from Harvard; Ginsberg graduated from Columbia with a degree in English; Edward Dorn attended the University of Illinois and Black Mountain College; Ferlinghetti earned a *doctorat de l'universite* with a *mention tres honorable* from the Sorbonne; LeRoi Jones attended Howard University and Columbia, earning a master's degree in German literature from the New School for Social Research; Gary Snyder graduated from Reed College and studied at Indiana University and the University of California; Philip Whalen attended Reed College; di Prima studied at Swarthmore for several terms; Lew Welch attended College of the Pacific, Reed College, and pursued graduate study at the University of Chicago; Hettie Jones graduated from Mary Washington College; Joyce Johnson was one course shy of graduating from Barnard College; Waldman graduated from Bennington College; Michael McClure earned a bachelor's degree from San Francisco State College; Philip Lamantia studied at Berkeley; Holmes, who did not graduate from high school, attended Columbia and the New School for Social Research; and Ed Sanders graduated from New York University with a degree in Greek.

Beat connections to higher education also include Holmes's tenure at the University of Arkansas, where he taught from 1976 to 1987 and established a creative writing program; Ginsberg and Waldman's 1974 founding of the Jack Kerouac School for Disembodied Poetics at Naropa; and Ginsberg's position at Brooklyn College as Distinguished Professor of English from 1986 until his death in 1997. McClure taught at the California College of Arts and Crafts in Oakland, where he eventually became a full professor. Snyder is a professor emeritus of English at the University of California – Davis. Other Beat writers did not so hate the academy that they refused to occasionally speak there: Kerouac appeared at Harvard, and Burroughs appeared at the University of Kansas and the University of the New World (Switzerland) and taught at the City College of New York (Theado 325).

Beat–academy relationships were fraught with ambivalence on both sides, but the two had to have known that each needed the other. For instance, the Buddhist poet Philip Whalen remarked, "I do not put down the academy but have assumed its function in my own person, and in the strictest sense of the word – *academy:* a walking grove of trees."[23] Snyder, in a 1974 interview with James MacKenzie, described the academy as "one of the most creative and potentially revolutionary structures in this society … They're like giant kivas that people descend into for four years to receive the transmission of the lore."[24] While most Beat writers distanced themselves from the academy, they never fully erased those experiences from their biographies, and, if a number of them downplayed privileged backgrounds that had allowed them into the academy, whatever anti-academic baggage they carried did little to stop them from pursuing lives of rich intellectual rigor – as well as fame.

Many writers can serve as brief case studies, but Kerouac is ideal, since of the three major Beats he is often considered the least academic and intellectual. Even a cursory survey of his juvenilia, however, transforms the image of the working-class "Canuck" into an exceptional mind relentlessly pursuing a vocation as a major American writer. As a teenager and young man, Kerouac read and wrote voraciously, using his voluminous journals to practice his art. At the age of eighteen, he wrote an entry on "A Play I Want to Write," a charming text revealing the caricature of the "great American writer" that he had internalized, including smoking cigarettes (but not inhaling them!) to help him write, and reading over his play "at night by the lamp." Confidently, he concludes that "life as life is" will be his theme and that he will win both the Pulitzer and Nobel literature prizes.[25] In another entry, he becomes the literary critic, taking on Joyce's *Ulysses* in an astute reading of Paddy Dignam, a minor character in the novel (226).

Throughout his life, Kerouac carried with him knowledge of and admiration for Joyce, filtering Joycian interior monologue and wordplay through the conversational style of Neal Cassady's epistolary voice to create the unique world of Jack Duluoz. This voice matured as the multigenre novels *Doctor Sax* (1959) and *Visions of Cody* (1973); the spontaneous prose of *The Subterraneans* (written 1953; published 1958), confessing racial, gender, and sex-based prejudices; the *Finnegans Wake*-like disembodied voice(s) of *Old Angel Midnight* (1960); and the lyrical onamatapoetics of the section "The Sea" in *Big Sur* (1962).

Other early texts demonstrate Kerouac's literary experiments with sports writing, music reviews, lyric poetry, autobiography, socialism, dialogue, and his own Québécois dialect. The convergence of literary planes of influence repeatedly appear in these early texts as both literary experiments and meta-discourse. His journal titled "Book of Symbols 1944" details one of the more specific, a composition regimen based on authors and literary styles, such as "Galloway – Joycean period," "The Haunted Life – Wolfean period," "I Bid You Lose Me – Neitzschean period (Neo-Rimbaudian)," "The Sea is My Brother – American period (Dos Passos)." These he prefaces with the certitude that "[t]he modern artist must discover new forms or he will perish by the hand of action," the entry signifying his place at the head of long lines of new visions.[26]

As Kerouac's indebtedness to Joyce and others illustrates, the Beats' innovation was a product of knowledge of their literary predecessors and their willingness to learn from those predecessors. No single line of influence culminates in Beat poetics. More accurately, Beat figures and aesthetics exist within a complex web or honeycomb of literary traditions. Enumeration of these lineages for even Kerouac, Burroughs, and Ginsberg is beyond the scope of this chapter, but a *mise en abyme* composed of the influences on women Beat writers can illuminate these complex heritages – literary, philosophical, religious, musical, and others.

Joyce Johnson, for instance, claims Henry James as literary mentor; Hettie Jones credits LeRoi Jones; ruth weiss acknowledges Anaïs Nin, Edgar Allen Poe, Rainer Maria Rilke, Gertrude Stein, François Truffaut, and Virginia Woolf; di Prima cites H. D., Robert Duncan, Ginsberg, Keats, Olson, Paracelsus, Pound, Buddhism, and goddess myths; Anne Waldman names Jane Austen, the Brontës, Ginsberg, Bernard Malamud, Howard Nemerov, Pound, Edith Sitwell, Williams, and Woolf; Joanne Kyger credits Descartes, Duncan, Homer, Olson, Jack Spicer, and Buddhism; and Brenda Frazer/Bonnie Bremser turned to Kerouac. This list barely scratches the surface but nonetheless reflects the larger scope of Beat ancestries and intersections conjoining the men and women. This tiny mirror also reveals, not through reflection but rather through the absence of reflection, the significance of a coterie of writers as influences upon each other. Women Beat writers wrote in isolation during their formative years, compared to many of the male writers who were not only friends but also helped to develop and promote one another's work.[27]

This same *mise en abyme* also underscores Modernism as the most prominent of literary heritages out of which Beat writers worked, which makes sense, since many were born at the height of Modernism and inherited the experimental traditions of that American-Anglo-European revisionist period. Pound, as already noted, was particularly important. However, Eliot, twin to Pound as Modernist titan, was a formidable presence, who, as Burroughs recalled, "was very much something that people were into" in the late thirties when he, Burroughs, was an undergraduate at Harvard (Theado 320). For postwar Beats, Eliot loomed large as a master of lyric free verse but even more troubling as a specter of high Modernism in exclusive literary circles. As Terrence Diggory contends, Eliot's "The Waste Land" (1922) signaled through its heavy reliance on multiple cultural and linguistic traditions the return of poetics to academics, to those with "the knowledge to translate Eliot's many foreign phrases and explicate his mythical allusions," which dramatically shifted poetics from the act of writing to the act of reading.[28] The institutionalization of this priority from the 1920s to the 1950s produced the type of "academic verse that Donald Allen oppose[d]" (60). For Beat writers such as Kerouac, finely attuned to Modernist poetics, Eliot prompted a bi-furcated assessment: Kerouac found his poetry "sublime" but dismissed him as an academic quibbler who had betrayed the bardic tradition of Homer with "dreary negative rules like the objective correlative ... which is just a lot of constipation and ultimately emasculation of the pure masculine urge to freely sing."[29] Eliot, for better or worse, was transmogrified into a scapegoat for a Beat rhetoric that championed automatic writing, performativity, Absurdism, and popular forms of American English, that which would save American literature from its own past.

Modernism – hardly a monolith propagandizing a universal narrative via the construction of a stable self that some critics still insist it is – featured these very concepts through the many schools situated under its umbrella, and Beat writing claims this heritage as well. In both, we find creation of multi- and interdisciplinary forms of art (Dadaism, Surrealism); a search for truth by disengaging from cultural norms of time and space in favor of dream and nightmare (Dadaism, Surrealism, Absurdism); reliance upon randomly composed or found constructions (Dadaism); juxtaposition of language to create a barrage of sensory data (Surrealism, Absurdism); a focus on the subjective (Expressionism) and childlike as purer and closer to truth and freedom (Surrealism); the belief in a pre-verbal or alchemical space where everyone is an artist (Dadaism); an emphasis on ideas and objects of the contemporary moment, including film, pulp fiction, jazz, and Vaudeville (Imagism, feminism, Surrealism), coupled with common speech, new rhythms, and distortion of common syntax (Imagism, Surrealism, Absurdism); and the search for human equality and freedom (feminism). This list is not comprehensive but provides evidence of Modernist philosophies that simultaneously threatened the American status quo (this time, an "abomination" from without, the Franco-European) and had become that very status quo that the counterculture "abomination" had to defeat. Hence, as Joanna Pawlick notes, a Beat such as Ginsberg could appropriate a Modernist school such as Surrealism while simultaneously denouncing it, just as did Kerouac with Eliot.[30]

Some of these practices are more evident in Beat literature than others, one of the most obvious being the Dadaist connection between Tristan Tzar's cut-up procedure, detailed in "to make a dadist poem," picked up by Brion Gysin and Burroughs, and later modified as their fold-in method, used extensively in the *Nova Trilogy*.[31] Imagism via Pound and William Carlos Williams grounded the practices of Corso, di Prima, Ginsberg, LeRoi and Hettie Jones, Kyger, Waldman, and others who took seriously the focus on a heteroglossia of language systems used freely in the open space of the page to blend form and content. Beat women writers carried forward the first-wave feminist agenda of modernists such as Djuna Barnes, Mina Loy, Gertrude Stein, and Virginia Woolf, echoing in poetry and fiction the white, middle-to-upper-class feminist rhetoric of the Anglo-American suffragist tradition emphasizing economic and legal equality and the right of a woman to control her own body. A few, such as Hettie Jones, dared to revise that narrative to legitimize and embrace the working class and women of color.

The impact of André Breton's Surrealism, part of the pervasive influence of French intellectual culture on post-World War II aesthetics in the United States, joined Beat poetics in the October 7, 1955, performance at the 6 Gallery, which brought Beat writing to national attention. Ginsberg read along with Lamantia, McClure, Snyder, and Whalen, who drew inspiration from Surrealists Antonin Artaud, Salvador Dalí, and Joan Miró. Lamantia's poetry, now collected in the fifty-ninth volume in City Lights' Pocket Poets series along with John Hoffman's, also reflects a Surrealist/Beat focus on what Garrett Caples, in his introduction to Lamantia's *Tau*, calls "spiritual self-interrogation" and "rapturous faith." Caples notes that the manuscript of *Tau* includes performance notes and musical notations, illustrating the bardic link between certain Modernist and Beat practices.[32] Lamantia chose not to read his own poetry at the 6 but instead works by John Hoffman, who had died in Mexico in 1952. Lamantia placed Hoffman in the tradition of Rimbaud, and Caples introduces Hoffman's poems by describing him as a deeply religious person who believed in mystical experiences as a pathway to truth. Of the other poems read that evening, "Howl" openly celebrates its Surrealist ancestors, but it was Whalen's "Plus Ça Change," the subtly humorous conversation between two birds-as-humans or humans-as-birds, that spoke most directly to the early Beat embrace of Surrealism.

Surrealism's continued influence on Beat opposition to American "militarism, conformity, racism, homophobia and materialism," admittedly a different historical constellation than what European surrealists confronted (Pawlik 4), is found in Burroughs's creations of dystopias; Ginsberg's Buddhist poetics;[33] Kerouac's spontaneous prose, which draws implicitly on Surrealistic psychic automatism; the jazz- and Surrealist-inspired poetry of Ted Joans and Bob Kaufman (known as the Black Rimbaud); the early poetry of di Prima, such as "Brass Furnace Going Out: Song After an Abortion"; ruth weiss's reliance on cut-up composition practices and dreamlike imagery in her long poem *Desert Journal* (1977); and Bonnie Bremser's narrative of her life as a mother, wife, and prostitute: *Troia: A Mexican Memoir* (1969). Other vestiges of Modernist practices include the fusion of Surrealist and Absurdist images and themes, which can be found in di Prima's early plays, including *Rain Fur* (1959) and *Murder Cake* (1960), as well as ruth weiss's film *The Brink* (1961).

The Modernism that the Beats inherited, of course, was a partial return to Anglo-American Romanticism, a heritage crucial to an understanding of the "abomination" narratives guiding this chapter. Much has been written about the Beats' indebtedness to the Romantics, but what has remained virtually unrecognized is an ancestral line extending back from Beat literature to Modernism into Romanticism and culminating in the Greco-Roman tradition. That this particular lineage has been elided in Beat literary histories is not surprising, since it undercuts the now dominant abomination-as-savior narrative, which is aligned with the historical reality that, by the 1950s, the classical tradition in the United States had long been under siege. But, as already noted, Beat writers via Modernism came in contact with the Western classics – Ginsberg claiming, perhaps half jokingly, that he and his "confreres" would never have known about them if it hadn't been for Pound.[34] In the Romantics they again encountered a tradition steeped in Hellenic materials, including Emerson's demand for a new poet for the new world, one who could do for America what Homer did for Ancient Greece: "resemble a mirror carried through the street, ready to render an image of every created thing" ("The Poet"). It was this bardic tradition that many Beats explicitly acknowledged.

But, as with Modernism, Beat recognition of this heritage was conflicted. Ginsberg, for example, ridiculed the Greco-Roman tradition as obsolete and culturally narrow, chastising publishers of translations of classic literature for censoring queer and other sexualized identities. His disdain, however, did not stop him from translating works by Catullus, which he then used, according to Matthew Pfaff, as a "guarantor of valid social identities."[35] Ever tolerant of all forms of literature, by 1964, when he completed a survey for *Arion*, a journal of the classics, he concluded that "square" classicists "made the Classics an oppressive bore. The Classics themselves are fine" (*Arion* 56). Others took it upon themselves to keep the classics alive: Kenneth Rexroth's translations were published as *Poems From the Greek Anthology, Translated* (1962);[36] Ed Sanders translated and set to music verses by Sappho;[37] Whalen encouraged his fellow poets to read deeply in Aeschylus, Aristophanes, Cicero, Homer, Horace, Virgil, and others, and his own poetry relied heavily on classical allusions.[38] Still other Beat writers engaged in imitations and/or adapted subject matter from classical traditions to express post-World War II values: most striking is the way female writers embraced the second-wave feminist project of revising classical narratives, exemplified by Kyger's *The Tapestry and the Web* (1965), di Prima's *Loba* (1978), and Waldman's *Iovis Trilogy* (2011).

Finally, the classics served some as an obligatory curriculum legitimizing their later break from those very traditions. Kerouac's early work *Orpheus Emerged* illustrates the pattern. Published posthumously in 2000, *Orpheus* is the story of a mid-twentieth-century young man who "abandons his human self" to seek God or Eternity, ultimately realizing that "the highest state he can attain is that of the 'Lyre of God,'" – that is, Orpheus, "the artist-man" (157–58). Through this modern revisioning of the Orpheus myth, the young Kerouac generated a seed crystal for his "new vision." While Kerouac quickly abandoned the classical paradigm, elements of that early education appear in the Duluoz Legend, scattered throughout as cultural touchstones.

Thus, through a focus on the Beat–Modernist–Romantic–Hellenic lineage(s), one can see the many ways in which Beat writers found homes both permanent and temporary in the interstices of many cultural practices extending as far back as the days of the ancients. In some cases, these traditions elevated the Beat artist as counterculture savior; others legitimized that same artist as culturally safe and reliable; still others negated or affirmed the existence of both. In all cases, Beat scholarship has now embraced the project of disentangling and complicating the two fundamental "abomination" narratives that have for decades preserved Beat art.

NOTES

1 Norman Podhoretz, "The Know-Nothing Bohemians," *Partisan Review* (spring 1958), reprinted in Matt Theado, ed., *The Beats: A Literary Reference* (New York: Carroll & Graf, 2003), 81.

2 Herb Caen, "Pocketful of Notes," *San Francisco Chronicle* (April 2, 1958), www.sfgate.com/news/article/Pocketful-of-Notes-2855259.php (accessed October 17, 2016).

3 Paul O'Neil, "The Only Rebellion Around," *Life* (November 30, 1959), reprinted in Theado, *The Beats*, 85.

4 Jack Kerouac, *1957–1969*, Vol. II of *Selected Letters*, ed. Ann Charters (New York: Penguin, 2000), 483.

5 Allen Ginsberg, *Howl and Other Poems* (San Francisco: City Lights, 1956), 11.

6 John Clellon Holmes, "This Is the Beat Generation," *Nothing More to Declare* (New York: E. P. Dutton, 1967), 115.

7 Donald M. Allen, ed., *The New American Poetry* (New York: Grove, 1960), 443.

8 Ralph Waldo Emerson, "The Poet," *Ralph Waldo Emerson Texts* (January 26, 2016), www.emersoncentral.com/poet.htm (accessed September 9, 2016).

9 Ezra Pound, *Literary Essays of Ezra Pound*, ed. T. S. Eliot (New York: New Directions, 1954), xi.

10 Ronna C. Johnson, "Lenore Kandel's *The Love Book*: Psychedelic Poetics, Cosmic Erotica, and Sexual Politics in the Mid-sixties Counterculture," *Reconstructing the Beats*, ed. Jennie Skerl (New York: Palgrave, 2004).

11 Arthur N. Applebee, *A Study of High School Literature Anthologies* (Albany, NY: National Research Center on English Learning & Achievement, 1991).

12 Donald Hall, Robert Pack and Louis Simpson, eds., *New Poets of England and America* (New York: Meridian, 1957).

13 Donald Hall and Robert Pack, eds. *The New Poets of England and America, Second Selection* (Cleveland, OH: World Publishing, 1962), 181.

14 Anne Waldman, "Introduction," *Jacket*, 16 (March 2002), www.jacketmagazine.com/16/ah1-wald.html (accessed September 9, 2016).

15 Marjorie Perloff, "Whose New American Poetry: Anthologizing in the Nineties," *Electric Poetry Center* (July 2005), http://epc.buffalo.edu/authors/perloff/anth.html (accessed September 9, 2016).

16 Paul Carroll, ed., *The Young American Poets* (Chicago: Big Table, 1968), 13.

17 Jack Kerouac, *On the Road: The Original Scroll*, ed. Howard Cunnell (New York: Viking, 2007), np.

18 Erik Mortenson, *The Beat Moment, Cultural Politics and the Poetics of Presence* (Carbondale: Southern Illinois University Press, 2011), 6.

19 Sharin Elkholy, "Introduction," *The Philosophy of the Beats*, ed. Elkholy (Lexington: University of Kentucky Press, 2012), 3.

20 See publisher's abstract on Amazon.com for Rich Weidman, *The Beat Generation FAQ: All That's Left to Know About the Angelheaded Hipsters* (St. Andrews: Backbeat, 2015).

21 Christopher Gair, *The American Counterculture* (Edinburgh: Edinburgh University Press, 2007), 2.

22 US Census Bureau, "Education," *US Census Report 2000* (2000), www.census. gov/population/www/cen2000/censusatlas/pdf/10_Education.pdf   (accessed September 9, 2016).

23 Philip Whalen, *The Collected Poems of Philip Whalen*, ed. Michael Rothenberg (Middletown, CT: Wesleyan University Press, 2007), 153.

24 Gary Snyder, "Moving the World a Millionth of an Inch [interview with James MacKenzie]," *The Beat Diary: The Unspeakable Visions of the Individual*, Vol. XIV, ed. Arthur Knight and Kit Knight (California, PA: Knight, 1977), 149.

25 Jack Kerouac, *Atop an Underwood: Early Stories and Other Writings*, ed. Paul Marion (New York: Viking, 1999), 28–29.

26 Jack Kerouac, *Orpheus Emerged* (New York: Simon & Schuster, 2000), 158–59.

27 Ronna C. Johnson and Nancy M. Grace, "Visions and Revisions of the Beat Generation," *Girls Who Wore Black: Women Writing the Beat Generation*, ed. Johnson and Grace (New Brunswick, NJ: Rutgers University Press, 2002), 17.

28 Terence Diggory, "Why the New American Poetry Stays News," *The New American Poetry Fifty Years Later*, ed. John R. Woznicki (Bethlehem, PA: Lehigh University Press, 2015), 60.

29 Jack Kerouac, "The Origins of Joy in Poetry," *Good Blonde & Others*, ed. Donald Allen (San Francisco: Grey Fox, 1993), 74.

30 Joanna Pawlik, "Surrealism, Beat Literature and the San Francisco Renaissance," *Literature Compass* 10.2 (2013), 97–110.

31 Tristan Tzara, *Dada Manifesto on Feeble Love and Bitter Love* (1921), www.391.org/manifestos/1920-dada-manifesto-feeble-love-bitter-love-tristan-tzara.html#.V_akxLXr5ow (accessed October 17, 2016).

32 Garrett Caples, "A Note on *Tau*," *Tau by Philip Lamantia and Journey to the End by John Hoffman* (San Francisco: City Lights, 2008), 12–13.

33 Tony Trigilio, *Allen Ginsberg's Buddhist Poetics* (Carbondale: Southern Illinois University Press, 2007), 40.

34 Allen Ginsberg, in Anonymous, "An Arion Questionnaire: The Classics and the Man of Letters," *Arion*, 3 (winter 1964), 56.

35 Matthew Pfaff, "The Invention of Sincerity: Allen Ginsberg and the Philology of the Margins," *The Hip Sublime: Beat Writers and the Classical Tradition*, ed. Ralph Rosen and Sheila Murnaghan (Columbus: Ohio State University Press, 2017), 118.

36 Kenneth Rexroth, *Poems from the Greek Anthology, Translated* (Ann Arbor: University of Michigan Press, 1962).

37 Jennie Skerl, "Sappho Comes to the Lower East Side: Ed Sanders, the Sixties Avant-Garde, and Fictions of Sappho," *Hip Sublime*, ed. Rosen and Murnaghan, np.

38 Jane Falk, "Philip Whalen and the Classics: 'A Walking Grove of Trees'," *The Hip Sublime*, ed. Rosen and Murnaghan, 345.

5

ERIK MORTENSON

Allen Ginsberg and Beat Poetry

In April of 1971, Allen Ginsberg was discussing his poetic practice with students at Kent State University. Ginsberg was trying to impress on them the idea of writing as an unrepeatable act occurring at the point where mind and body encounter the world. In order to make his point, Ginsberg recalled an anecdote about a visit from Black Mountain poet Robert Duncan. Ginsberg was living in the Beat enclave of North Beach in San Francisco at the time, and had pinned a copy of Jack Kerouac's artistic statement "Essentials of Spontaneous Prose" to the wall of his apartment. Kerouac's piece called for a writing that began "not from preconceived idea of what to say about image but from jewel center of interest in subject of image at *moment* of writing."[1] As Ginsberg explained to the students, he asked Duncan, "'Well, what do you think – how could you possibly just write without revising?'" Despite Ginsberg's skepticism, Duncan agreed with Kerouac's point and asked for a copy of the statement, explaining, "'Well, look, I've taken a step across the room; how can I go back and revise my step? I've already done it. How can I go back in time and revise the step?'"[2] By relating this anecdote, Ginsberg wanted the class to see poetry not as a product crafted to produce certain effects but rather as an ongoing process of revelation. Ginsberg saw the act of writing as a means of exploring consciousness as it reacted to the ever-changing conditions of the present.

Ginsberg was the public face of the Beats. Although the term "Beat Generation" created a heated debate in both cultural and poetic circles in the postwar era, Ginsberg used this media attention as a key into a public arena that he became deft at manipulating. An important lynchpin of the Beat movement, Ginsberg tirelessly edited and promoted his friends' writing and worked to gain attention for the Beat movement and those underneath its banner. In the early 1950s, he helped to generate interest in the manuscript of what would become Kerouac's *On the Road* and was an early supporter of Gregory Corso's work; in the mid-to-late 1950s, he helped to type and edit William S. Burroughs's *Naked Lunch*; and throughout this period he produced numerous prose articles articulating his positions and defining the "Beat Generation" for the public. By the 1960s, he had become one of the most recognizable spokespersons for a variety of countercultural causes. All of this promotion has paid dividends – Ginsberg's work is instantly recognizable and has come to stand at the center of Beat poetry. Bill Morgan has gone so far as to argue that "We should think of the Beat Generation as a social circle created by Allen Ginsberg and his friends instead of as a literary movement."[3] Though this might be overstating the case a bit, Ginsberg's highly visible presence in the countercultural scene and a career writing and performing that lasted into the 1990s has meant that his poetry has come to epitomize what we think of as "Beat." Ginsberg's corpus represents a compendium of the styles, approaches, and thematic interests of Beat poetry, and his continued presence in anthologies and central importance for the myriad films, graphic novels, and other cultural reproductions of the Beats and their legacy means that each new generation is sure to discover this poet as central to our understanding of the movement.

Despite Ginsberg's public championing of the Beats, ultimately it is his insistence on the act of writing as a means of capturing the immediacy of the world around him that lies at the heart of Beat poetry and, indeed, the Beat lifestyle. In his discussion with Kent State students, Ginsberg went on to talk about the connection between both the San Francisco Renaissance writers he met in the city and those of the New York school such as Frank O'Hara and John Ashbery, stating that the common theme is the "first steps of exploration of the contents of present consciousness during the moment of composition" (*Allen Verbatim* 149). This is likewise a good definition of Beat poetry broadly imagined, and indeed of much of the postwar arts scene in general. This chapter explores Ginsberg's presentist concerns in some of his classic work as well as in his obscurer pieces, to show how he was able to use this desire for living and writing the present not only as a means of offering resistance to a repressive Cold War culture but also as a means of developing a rubric for understanding Beat poetry in general. A ceaseless innovator, Ginsberg encapsulates the Beat approach to poetry as a means of self-exploration conducted through the printed page. Ginsberg experimented relentlessly with novel states of consciousness and new means of expressing them, making for a writing practice that was always open to new influences, impulses, and the desire to question one's own beliefs and assumptions. Ginsberg's oeuvre maps his personal development as it follows its own twists and turns. While not everyone will agree on a Beat canon or even the need for the term, Ginsberg's thinking on poetics is crucial for understanding Beat poetry and the question of what makes it distinctive: he epitomizes the spirit of inquiry that is at the heart of Beat Generation writing, and his attempts to remain aware of and record the present moment mark him as perhaps the most "Beat" Beat of all.

Early Influences

As the Kent State anecdote demonstrates, Ginsberg was not always a proponent of such spontaneous aesthetic practices. In fact, in his early work, Ginsberg struggled to find his own voice by writing in traditional rhyme and meter forms. The tightly controlled poems collected in *The Gates of Wrath: Rhymed Poems, 1948–52* (published 1972) offer an interesting counterpoint to a poet generally known for his exuberance and expansiveness. But Ginsberg was an astute student of poetics, and, like many of his fellow Beat poets, drew on the work of his Modernist predecessors for inspiration (on this point, see Chapter 4). The most important of these influences was William Carlos Williams. While Ginsberg claims he was influenced by Ezra Pound's ability to measure his line by speech as it issued from the human body and that he absorbed Gertrude Stein's interest in modalities of consciousness and Marianne Moore's ability to play with line breaks, it was Williams's admonition "No ideas but in things" that helped to propel Ginsberg's early work in exciting new directions.[4] Ginsberg thus reads Williams's poem "The Red Wheelbarrow" as emblematic of this attention to the numinous quality of the world: "his whole mind depends on the image ... just being there completely mindful" (*Composed* 134). Armed with these insights, Ginsberg began crafting shorter lines that attempted to capture his impression of the world around him in a direct, American style of speech. As he advises, "Don't treat the object indirectly or symbolically, but look directly at it and choose spontaneously that aspect of it which is most immediately striking – the striking flash in consciousness or awareness, the most vivid, what sticks out in your mind – and notate that."[5] Many of these early Williams-inspired pieces written between 1946 and 1951 would be published later in *Empty Mirror* (1961), and Ginsberg continued to work in this mode. "The Green Automobile" (1953), Ginsberg's tribute to his lover and Beat icon Neal Cassady, is an important early work that employs this directness of style, and the long poem "Siesta in Xbalba" (1954) finds the poet chronicling his thought processes in a series of short lines as ideas percolate to the surface of consciousness.

Ginsberg's most well-known and widely acclaimed poem, "Howl" (collected in *Howl and Other Poems* [1956]), owes its existence to Williams's mentorship. According to the poet, "Howl" is the result of a fusion between the short, imagistic line inspired by Williams and what Ginsberg called his "Hebraic-Melvillean bardic breath" derived from Ginsberg's other poetic touchstone, Walt Whitman. "Howl" is built through the addition of these smaller units into the poem's characteristic long line. Take, for example, the line that runs

> Peyote solidities of halls, backyard green tree cemetery dawns, wine drunken-ness over the rooftops, storefront boroughs of teahead joyride neon blinking traffic light, sun and moon and tree vibrations in the roaring winter dusks of Brooklyn, ashcan rantings and kind king light of mind.[6]

Ginsberg bombards the reader with a series of images meant to convey the drug-like emotional state of the "best minds of my generation" to his read-ers (134). Although Ginsberg experimented with other forms such as the song lyric and would return to rhymed poetry later in his career, the major-ity of his oeuvre can be divided into shorter, more imagistic work and poems that combine them into the long-line format.

Despite Ginsberg's insistence on spontaneity, he did revise, as a glance at *Howl: Original Draft Facsimile* (2006) amply proves. Much of this revision, however, was geared toward condensing the poem to make it sparser, and led to Ginsberg's characteristic style that omits prepositions, articles, and other less-necessary parts of speech. Ginsberg's revision process does not detract from his belief in the importance of capturing the immediacy of the world in his poetry. As long as these smaller units "register the contents of one consciousness during that time period" they can be tied together "in the sense that hopefully the consciousness has a bottom."[7] Although many questioned whether Ginsberg's work found this "bottom" and others saw it as formless or unfocused, Ginsberg's technique rested on the belief that, when done openly and sincerely, there was always something "there" that the reader would experience, and thus his poetry need not be revised into a coherent whole. Capturing immediacy was at the core of Ginsberg's prac-tice – revision simply meant tidying up.

Ginsberg was nothing if not eclectic in his borrowings. While he cites a litany of American Modernist poets, he was also influenced by a host of other artists working in various media. Ginsberg's interest in presenting the sort of transcendent states he himself experienced in his 1948 visions of William Blake began with his study of Paul Cézanne, whose landscape paintings Ginsberg scrutinized at the New York Museum of Modern Art. Cézanne attempted to represent states of being on the canvas, and Ginsberg strove to capture these "petite sensations" in his own work. Ginsberg was also influenced by Surrealism. In "Howl"'s celebrated phrase "hydrogen jukebox," for instance, Ginsberg is able to create a dense web of allusion

Immediacy + Surrealism.

that reverberates in the reader's own mind. "Hydrogen" recalls the atomic bomb, which was an omnipresent feature of Cold War life, while "jukebox" evokes the ecstatic celebration of jazz, which was a major influence on Beat poetry and an impetus for the term "Beat" itself. Ginsberg credits the discovery of this "surrealist jolt" to a dream he had of Joan Vollmer, Burroughs's deceased wife, and the quick, almost filmic, cut to her gravestone that he captured in the poem "Dream Record: June 8, 1955."

Dreams, visions, and other transcendent states were an important source of inspiration for many Beat poets. In a constraining postwar society that sought to harness the rationality of the expert to placate social fears, the irrational was seen by many Beat poets as a refuge of authentic and spontaneous thought. Surrealism allowed Beat poets to tap into the unconscious mind in order to create juxtapositions meant to challenge and provoke readers into questioning accepted beliefs. In a tribute to Philip Lamantia, Ginsberg writes that "his interest in techniques of surreal composition notoriously antedates mine and surpasses my practice in a quality of untouched-news, nervous scatting, street moment purity" (*Deliberate* 442–43). The surrealist impulse is also present in the work of Ted Joans (who wrote an unfinished autobiography called "I, Black Surrealist") and Bob Kaufman, both African American poets who questioned the racial discourse of the time. Gregory Corso, though less interested in Surrealism per se, drew on the irrational most famously in his poem "Bomb" (1958), which goaded readers into rethinking their approach to this anxiety-producing device.

While Ginsberg pays homage to his predecessors, ultimately his turn toward immediacy as a basis for his poetics owes its existence to his contemporaries. Spontaneity and improvisation were in the air during the 1950s, as artists working in a variety of media experimented with forms meant to challenge the rigid thinking of the times. As Daniel Belgrad notes in his informative study *The Culture of Spontaneity*, this impulse to create work in opposition to both mass and high culture could not be traced to one single event, person, or movement. Jazz, especially in its experimental bebop variety, was perhaps the most important touchstone for Beat poets. Not only did it offer a model for poetic improvisation in the moment of composition but it also influenced Beat ideas of performance, with poets such as LeRoi Jones/Amiri Baraka experimenting with voice as an instrument and Beats such as ruth weiss and Kerouac taking the stage to read to jazz accompaniment. Spontaneous artistic practices were a means to break free from the rigid thinking of the times and tap into a more vibrant form of being. Ginsberg cites Kerouac's work specifically as a direct inspiration, especially his series of jazz-inspired Buddhist poems collected as *Mexico City Blues* (composed 1954–57; published 1959), claiming "He taught me everything I knew about writing. It took a long time, a couple of years I think, for me to appreciate his ability there and even a longer time for me to begin practicing in spontaneous composition." He also saw Kerouac's method as a crucial influence for "Howl" (*Composed* 79–80). But Kerouac was not the only postwar poet to "discover" this style of writing.

Although the mutual influence between Kerouac and Ginsberg is well documented, less remembered is the impact of other schools of poetry.[8] For example, Ginsberg credited poets associated with Black Mountain College in North Carolina, particularly Charles Olson and Robert Creeley, with inspiring this turn toward the immediate. As Ginsberg relates, "I learned mostly from Kerouac, and then put a patina of literary categorization over it later on having dealt with Williams and Creely and Olson" (*Improvised* 27). Ginsberg turns Olson's statement in his highly influential essay "Projective Verse" (1950), "FORM IS NEVER MORE THAN AN EXTENSION OF CONTENT," into "Form is always an extension of content," which Olson himself credits to Creeley and Ginsberg believes illustrates "the interconnectedness of the spontaneous gesture" (*Allen Verbatim* 162). Ginsberg would likewise turn Williams's "No ideas but in things" into the call to pay attention to how the mind reacts to the world in "Notice what you notice" (*Collected Poems* 954). This emphasis on the importance of everyday events, activities, and observations was widespread. For some poets, such as Joanne Kyger, Gary Snyder, and Philip Whalen, the quotidian present became the site for meditational concerns, while for others, such as New York School poets Ted Berigan and O'Hara, this dailiness was more observational and campy. But, in both cases, the importance of the mundane was that it offered an opportunity to rethink one's attitude toward the world.

Reaching Out to Others

But "Howl" was not just a literary breakthrough for Ginsberg. It also catapulted him to fame as a spokesperson for the Beats, their writing, and indeed for the underground lifestyle that the poem chronicles. Ginsberg's notoriety began at the celebrated 6 Gallery, where he debuted the poem in 1955 along with Lamantia, Michael McClure, Kenneth Rexroth, Snyder, and Whalen. Despite the triumphant reception the poem received in the San Francisco poetry community, Ginsberg's national and indeed international fame was the result of the censorship trial that followed the reading and the poem's publication by fellow Beat poet and longtime editor and publisher of Ginsberg's works Lawrence Ferlinghetti. Much of the brunt of media interest in the Beat Generation fell on Ginsberg. With Kerouac growing frustrated with media portrayals and Burroughs living abroad in Tangier, it was Ginsberg who picked up the mantle of Beat Generation spokesperson.

Ginsberg certainly relished his role. This comes as little surprise from a former market researcher who explained the value of "theater" in his essay "How to Make a March / Spectacle" (1965). In keeping with his mantra "Candor ends paranoia," Ginsberg was fond of disrobing at social gatherings as a means to figuratively expose his own self to the world and to challenge others to give up their inhibitions. Ginsberg's public and poetic statements often rang of sensationalism and were sometimes a bit off-putting. Promoting the Beats was also a means of promoting his own work, and many fellow poets felt that Ginsberg was cheapening poetry by advertising it. The rise of the Beat Generation also caused strife within the poetic community among those who felt the Beats were eclipsing others in the scene. Nevertheless, Ginsberg's championing of the Beat Generation label helped many poets to get their work published and gave them access to public forums unavailable in the past.

As poetry that sought to turn intensely personal observation and feeling into public statement, it is unsurprising that Ginsberg's work met with resistance. Confessional writing, a term coined by M. L. Rosenthal to describe the work of the poets John Berryman, Robert Lowell, Sylvia Plath, and Anne Sexton, came under attack in the late 1950s and early 1960s as sensational, self-promoting, and lacking in literary merit. While not directly linked to this group, Ginsberg's work was treated similarly. The extremely personal nature of Ginsberg's works as well as the prophetic voice he often used to turn personal revelation into cultural critique transgressed the lines of social and literary propriety. In "Kaddish" (1961), for example, Ginsberg returns to his Whitmanesque long line to chronicle his feelings toward his mother, Naomi. Like Ginsberg, she too experienced psychological issues, and Ginsberg authorized her institutionalization and lobotomization. Ginsberg used the poem to work through his own traumatic memories, writing the main draft while weeping in a two-day marathon session. Ginsberg spares the reader nothing:

> One time I thought she was trying to make me come lay her – flirting to herself at sink – lay back on huge bed that filled most of the room, dress up around her hips, big slash of hair, scars of operations, pancreas, belly wounds, abortions, appendix, stitching of incisions pulling down in the fat like hideous thick zippers – ragged long lips between her legs – What, even, smell of asshole? I was cold – later revolted a little, not much – seemed perhaps a good idea to try – know the Monster of the Beginning Womb –

(227)

Ginsbe~~~   ~~~f was initially unsure whether this was poetry or self-
~~~   ~~~nd John Wieners, who studied at Black Mountain but
~~~   ~~~Beat circles for his *Hotel Wentley Poems* (1958), ques-
~~~   ~~~..dish." A fellow gay poet who also tried to capture a numinous
~~~   ~~~cy in his writings, Wieners nonetheless found the poem boring.[9]
Spontaneous writing shared much with Sigmund Freud's "talking cure,"
which made the patient responsible for working through psychological
issues by revealing inner, hidden compulsions and desires. But, for Beats
like Ginsberg, Freud was unnecessary – writing itself became the means of
personal revelation. The question became whether others really needed to
read it.

Ginsberg clearly felt that they should. Writing focused on the present not
only helped to reveal writers to themselves; it also made for a poetry that
everyone could understand. Ginsberg reasoned that, since personal and
familial traumas were universal, poems such as "Howl" or "Kaddish" could
be appreciated by a wide audience. As Ginsberg claims, "If it's at all spontaneous, I don't know whether it even makes sense sometimes. Sometimes I do
know it makes complete sense, and I start crying. Because I realize I'm hitting
some area which is absolutely true. And in that sense applicable universally,
or understandable universally."[10] Focusing on the present was instrumental
in Ginsberg's attempts to reach out to others through his poetry, to form a
bridge through the written word. Ginsberg had struggled with feelings of
isolation, and thus his need to connect was palpable. The personal became
the political in the postwar years, as direct action in the political field gave
way to attempts to change attitudes and opinions in the culture at large.
The immediacy of Ginsberg's work and other Beat poetry was an attempt
to engage the reader by speaking directly to universal experience. The hope
was that such writing could become a catalyst for "raising the consciousness" of readers by forcing them to confront their own true fears and desires
and thus rethink their lives.

This two-fold function of poetry as both revelation and inspiration can
been seen in the frank portrayal of homosexuality that runs throughout
Ginsberg's corpus. Chronicling his desires, urges, and homosexual acts
in detail and with candor, Ginsberg explored the often conflicted feelings that accompanied them. Depictions of homosexuality are scattered
throughout Ginsberg's work, with the line "who let themselves be fucked
in the ass by saintly motorcyclists, and screamed with joy" from "Howl"
and the twin phalluses that enclose Robert LaVigne's art work for "Kral
Majales" being the two most famous instances (136).[11] But, in the Beat
spirit of inquiry, Ginsberg explored his feelings toward homosexuality in

a number of poems. His willingness to reveal his sexual desires heralded an openness to a subject many wanted closed. Nor was Ginsberg alone in his desire to explore sexual desire. Lenore Kandel's *The Love Book* (1966) explored female sexuality in language uninhibited by convention, and, like "Howl," Kandel's book was confiscated for obscenity. McClure's first book-length poem, *Dark Brown* (1961), often sold under the counter in a brown wrapper, argued for sexuality based not on mind or soul but on bodies. Even in contemporary US society, where much of the Beats' rebellious attitude has been absorbed into the culture, such graphic depictions remain shocking (see Chapter 12 for an in-depth discussion of Beat sexualities).

In much the same way that Beat poetry used sexuality to explore new modes of being and, with them, new ways to write, Ginsberg championed drug experimentation as a means to experience and represent an altered reality. In a time when the possession of drugs carried stiff penalties and was derided as a threat to national security, Ginsberg openly questioned American drug policy and made public pitches for the mind-expanding qualities of marijuana and LSD. Some of our most iconic images of Ginsberg come from this period, such as the photo of him in a cold New York street with a sandwich board that reads "Pot is a reality kick." Ginsberg pursued drug decriminalization, but ultimately his interest lay elsewhere – in universal mind expansion. As he explains on the last page of *Kaddish and Other Poems* (1961), where many of his drug-inspired works are collected, "The message is: Widen the area of consciousness." Drugs were a useful tool for exploring new states of being and, along with them, new ways to write. Writing in the moment of inebriation in order to capture the effects of drugs on perception, Ginsberg chronicled his drug experiments extensively in his notebooks, in his journals, and in poems such as "Laughing Gas" (1958), "Mescaline" (1959), "Lysergic Acid" (1959), "Aether" (1960), "Magic Psalm" (1960), "The Reply" (1960), and, most importantly, "Wales Visitation" (1967), where Ginsberg best conveys his experience of LSD. Not all drugs were equal. Ginsberg was vehemently opposed to the amphetamine use that had a negative impact on his lover and fellow Beat poet Peter Orlovsky and other Beat poets such as Janine Pommy Vega, and felt that heroin addicts such as Herbert Huncke, the man who introduced the Beats to both the term and the lifestyle, should be treated compassionately. In countercultural circles, drug use was widespread. But Ginsberg was one of the few poets to systematically explore both the social issues surrounding drugs and their effects on consciousness and writing.

Ginsberg and the 1960s

Despite Ginsberg's increasing fame and literary accomplishments, by the early 1960s the poet had hit a wall. Ceaselessly experimenting with altered states of consciousness, Ginsberg was trying to recapture the Blake visions he had experienced in New York in 1948 and that had so far defined his spiritual and poetic path. Unfortunately, all this experimentation had backed him into a corner. This attempt to test the limits of consciousness, along with a constant schedule of public appearances and readings, had left Ginsberg exhausted, and so he turned his sights to the East. His journey to India, while personally engaging and a catalyst for sending a legion of hippies and seekers to the country in search of spiritual enlightenment, was really more of a "dark night of the soul" for the poet. Ginsberg had traveled abroad before and would continue to do so throughout his life, but his roughly two years spent in India were a lacuna, with very little writing and much soul searching. Traveling with Orlovsky and meeting up with Snyder and Kyger (the latter of whom was frustrated with Ginsberg's misogyny), Ginsberg did produce a journal that was published as *Indian Journals* (1970), but it is a work that the poet himself dismisses: "My trip wasn't very spiritual, as anybody can see if they read *Indian Journals*. Most of it was spent horsing around, sightseeing and trying the local drugs. But I did visit all of the holy men I could find and I did encounter some teachers who gave me little teachings then that were useful then and now."[12] Nevertheless, *Indian Journals* deserves closer attention. In it, Ginsberg struggles to find a means of representing the overwhelming experience of India, and the journal is replete with "photo descriptions," snippets of poems, and detailed observations that never quite add up. Ginsberg is searching for both a guru to guide him and a means of representing the unrepresentable, and only finds it when he leaves India for Japan. On a train bound for Tokyo, Ginsberg realizes that he has overlooked the body itself as a means of meaningfully engaging the world. As Ginsberg chronicles in "The Change: *Kyoto-Tokyo Express*" (1963):

> Open the portals to what Is,
> The mattress covered with sheets,
> soft pillows of skin,
> long soft hair and delicate
> palms along the buttocks
> timidly touching. (332)

The return to the body as a site for a poetic practice that focuses on the moment of composition is a leitmotif in Beat poetry. Inspired mainly by the breath rhythms of jazz but also by Charles Olson's idea of poems as energy conduits and Wilhelm Reich's concept of orgasmic release, Beat poets turned to writing done through the body in order to attain a more authentic relationship to both their lines and their lives. Some, like McClure, took this stance to its extreme. In *Ghost Tantras* (1964), McClure wrote in what he called a "beast language" that was located "somewhere between human speech and animal sounds."[13] Kyger, like McClure, linked her line to her body as well, claiming it was "an extension of [her] arm" (188). Of course, in a postwar society where gender difference and racial segregation were rife, the desire to occupy the body as a privileged site for poetry also created difficulties. Diane di Prima, in her collection *Dinners and Nightmares* (1961), details a domestic argument over who will do the dishes. Di Prima grudgingly capitulates to gender expectations and goes to the kitchen to do them, demonstrating that living the body in the present moment is not always an emancipatory act. Nevertheless, the importance of the body for both Beat poetics and politics cannot be overstated.[14]

For Ginsberg, this return to the body as a basis for poetic practice would have a lasting effect not only on his writing but also on his life. The "change" he experienced in Japan heralded an extremely productive period of literary and political activity in the mid-to-late 1960s, providing many of the now-classic conceptions of Ginsberg as hippie guru. Much of his output was part of a series of travel poems he called "A Long Poem on These States" that were published as *The Fall of America: Poems of These States, 1965–1971*, which won the National Book Award in 1974. Returning from his sojourn abroad, Ginsberg participated in two important events: the Vancouver Poetry Conference in 1963, where he read with Creeley, Duncan, Denise Levertov, Olson, and Whalen, and the Berkeley Poetry Conference in 1965, where he read with Baraka, Creeley, Duncan, Kyger, Olson, Jack Spicer, Lew Welch, and Wieners. These conferences were catalysts for the idea that Ginsberg's poetry could have a more direct impact on life in America, and they became precursors to the famous "be-ins" Ginsberg would participate in later in the decade (he opened San Francisco's 1967 Human Be-In with Snyder).

With a renewed focus on the body and its interaction with the world, Ginsberg set off in a series of cross-country trips meant to record the tenor of an America embroiled in the Vietnam War. One of the best-known results was the long poem "Wichita Vortex Sutra" (written 1966; published 1968). Using an Uher tape recorder given to him by Bob Dylan, Ginsberg recorded his immediate impressions of both the American heartland he experienced and the media representations coming over the Volkswagen bus's radio in order to both question and counter the war language of the State Department. The travelogue format was used by other Beat poets as well.

Snyder employs a similar format in his poem "Night Highway 99" (from *Mountains and Rivers Without End*, begun 1956 and finished 1996), and Kerouac's collaboration with Welch and Albert Saijo, *Trip Trap: Haiku on the Road* (1973), records their 1959 trip from San Francisco to New York in a series of Buddhist haikus. Ginsberg's travel poems such as "Wichita Vortex Sutra" were even more successful, due to their extensive circulation in often colorfully illustrated draft versions throughout the underground press before being collected in *Planet News* (1968). Much of Ginsberg's work in this period, such as "Television Was a Baby Crawling Toward That Deathchamber" (1961), "Angkor Wat" (1963), and "Wales Visitation" (1967), experienced similar publication histories, solidifying Ginsberg's status as a premier underground poet with an international reputation.

Buddhist Mindfulness

Ginsberg's return to the body was also a catalyst for a deeper commitment to Buddhism. Although his study of Buddhism began as early as 1953, it wasn't until 1972 that he took formal Buddhist vows with Chögyam Trungpa Rinpoche and deepened his meditative practice. Tony Trigilio, in his excellent study *Ginsberg's Buddhist Poetics* (2007), sees the poems "Angkor Wat" and "The Change" as an important shift in Ginsberg's early Buddhist-inspired writings. Ginsberg's return to the body reinforces his commitment to the practice of mindful attention to the passing moment that is essential in the letting go of attachment to the world and its phenomena. Unsurprisingly, this focus on meditative Buddhist practice finds expression in Ginsberg's poetry. "Mind Breaths" (1973) and "Thoughts Sitting Breathing" (1973) chronicle the images and ideas that flow through Ginsberg as he sits meditating, while "Ego Confession" (1974) and "What would you do if you lost it" (1973) find Ginsberg trying to implement the Buddhist practice of nonattachment.

Two Reed College poets Ginsberg first met in San Francisco were catalysts in this turn toward Buddhist writing: Gary Snyder and Philip Whalen. Snyder, a lifelong Buddhist whose work shared an interest in writing meant to reveal the poet's connection to place, was an important mentor. Whalen, whose definition of poetry as a "graph of a mind moving" fit perfectly into Ginsberg's own ideas, offered another example of Buddhist practice becoming poetry.[15] Borrowing from his mentor Trungpa, Ginsberg coined another mantra, "First thought best thought," to emphasize the importance of letting the mind itself determine the path that poetry would take rather than forcing it into preconceived directions. Buddhism taught a letting go that allowed poetry access to a self that, in its nakedness, could be understood by everyone (for more on the connection between the Beats and Buddhism, see Chapter 15).

Ginsberg's interest in Buddhism was instrumental in his later turn to questions of ecology. While earlier work such as the poems "To Poe: Over the Planet; Air Albany-Baltimore" and "Ecologue," both collected in *The Fall of America*, raised the issue of humankind's destructive exploitation of the world, issues of environmental sustainability become foregrounded when Ginsberg bought his Cherry Valley Farm in upstate New York in 1968. Ginsberg saw Cherry Valley as both a respite from the stresses of the city and its temptations and a foray into self-sustainable organic farming. Gordon Ball, Ginsberg's friend and editor, chronicles this period in his memoir *East Hill Farm: Seasons With Allen Ginsberg* (2012), including the ups and downs of life on a farm as poets, musicians, friends, and fans came to visit, collaborate, and sometimes fight. Eschewing the consumer lifestyle, Ginsberg admonishes those seeking to change the world while overlooking its practicalities: "It's impossible for French Parisian kids or New York kids to conceive of a blueprint for a new society if they don't even know where water comes from, if they've never seen a tomato grow, if they've never milked a cow, if they don't know how to dispose of their shit, how can they possibly program a human future?" (*Composed* 91). This interest in environmental issues resulted in another of Ginsberg's famous protest poems, "Plutonian Ode," published in a volume of the same name in 1982. Completed on the day Ginsberg, Orlovsky, Anne Waldman (who co-founded the Jack Kerouac School of Disembodied Poetics at the Naropa Institute with Ginsberg), and others sat meditating on the railroad tracks in defiance of the Rockwell Corporation's Plutonium bomb trigger factory in 1978, Ginsberg addressed this deadly substance as Corso addressed the nuclear warhead in his famous poem "Bomb" (1958), personifying and addressing it in a cathartic act of exorcism.

Ginsberg used his fame to garner attention to his causes, but what is often overlooked are his more self-reflective works where he questions his role as countercultural guru. Despite Ginsberg's desire to publically confess, condone, and condemn, his work is replete with the humorous, playful, and self-mocking. Ginsberg turned his inquisitive gaze inward in poems such as "Birdbrain!" (1980), where he castigates his own desire for power, and in "Salutations to Fernando Pessoa" (1988), where he takes himself to task for his pretensions: "Every time I read Pessoa I think / I'm better than he is I do the same thing / more extravagantly – he's only from Portugal, / I'm American greatest Country in the world" (976). Yet Ginsberg is also willing to confront the difficult and unpleasant moments of life with an intimate and often painful honesty. Even as he is experiencing a deterioration of his body as he approaches death, Ginsberg remains fixed on his Buddhist practice as a means of staying awake to the present. In "Scatological Observations" (1997), Ginsberg laments, "Shit machine shit machine / I'm an incredible shit machine" (1147). One senses the exasperation but also the humor, as Ginsberg follows his own admonishment to return to the body but finds the body has taken on new meaning as a site for deterioration rather than exaltation. Undaunted, however, Ginsberg continues to explore this breakdown in poems such as "Sphincter" (1986) and "Here We Go 'Round the Mulberry Bush" (1994). Creeley, a poet equally concerned with the here and now of writing, acknowledges this ability to keep "the world both intimate and transcendent" in his foreword to Ginsberg's final collection, *Death & Fame* (1999).[16] Even at the end, Ginsberg stays true to his own advice to students that writing should be seen as a meditative practice, a humble recording of life all the more valuable for its transitory nature.

Ginsberg's desire to write and live the present offers a useful means of understanding what the Beats were trying to accomplish with their writing. Beat poetry is meant as a direct intervention into readers' lives, and, in order to achieve this, Ginsberg and other Beat poets felt that nothing less than the attempt to capture the world as it was experienced and lived would do. In one of the last poems of his life, "Objective Subject" (1997), Ginsberg playfully but seriously declares, "It's true I write about myself / Who else do I know so well?" (1137). But, rather than falling into solipsism, the intensely personal nature of Ginsberg's work is precisely what allows his readers to form a connection with the poet. Such personal writing speaks directly to readers, opening up new ways of living, thinking, and being. Beat poetry was, from its very outset, political, meant to challenge readers to question their own position in the world. Ginsberg chronicles the grand experiment that is life, recording it in minute detail so that others might gain from both his insights and his failures. And, in the end, what is more Beat than that?

NOTES

1 Jack Kerouac, "Essentials of Spontaneous Prose," *The Portable Jack Kerouac*, ed. Ann Charters (New York: Viking, 1995), 485.

2 Quoted in *Allen Verbatim: Lectures on Poetry, Politics, Consciousness*, ed. Gordon Ball (New York: McGraw-Hill, 1974), 146.

3 Bill Morgan, *The Typewriter Is Holy: The Complete, Uncensored History of the Beat Generation* (New York: Free Press, 2010), 155.

4 For Ginsberg's discussion of Pound and Stein, see *Allen Verbatim*, 180 and 157 respectively. For his discussion of Moore, see *Composed on the Tongue*, ed. Donald Allen (Bolinas, CA: Grey Fox Press, 1980), 21. Ginsberg's invocation of Williams's "no ideas but in things" occurs in numerous essays and interviews.

5 Allen Ginsberg, *Deliberate Prose: Selected Essays 1952–1995*, ed. Bill Morgan (New York: Harper, 2000), 266.

6 All references to Ginsberg's poems are from *Collected Poems: 1947–1997* (New York: Harper Perennial, 2007). Readers should be aware that the *Collected Poems* organizes Ginsberg's work by chronological date of composition rather than by date of publication (134).

7 Allen Ginsberg, *Improvised Poetics*, ed. Mark Robison (San Francisco: Anonym Press, 1971), 12.

8 For an extended discussion of the importance of a shared dream of a "shrouded stranger" on Kerouac's and Ginsberg's early poetic development, see Erik Mortenson, *Ambiguous Borderlands: Shadow Imagery in Cold War American Culture* (Carbondale: Southern Illinois University Press, 2016).

9 John Wieners, *Lost & Found: The CUNY Poetics Document Initiative*, 3.3.ii:19 (2012), 24.

10 Interview with Tom Clark in *Spontaneous Mind: Selected Interviews 1958–1996*, ed. David Carter (New York: HarperCollins, 2001), 26.

11 "Kral Majales" appears in *Collected Poems*, 361–63.

12 Interview with Peter Barry Chowka in *Spontaneous Mind*, 386.

13 Michael Davidson, *The San Francisco Renaissance: Poetics and Community at Mid-Century* (Cambridge: Cambridge University Press, 1991), 85.

14 For a more detailed discussion of the importance of the body and its relationship to the trope of orgasm in Beat writing, see the third chapter of Erik Mortenson, *Capturing the Beat Moment: Cultural Politics and the Poetics of Presence* (Carbondale: Southern Illinois University Press, 2011).

15 Philip Whalen, *Memoirs of an Interglacial Age* (San Francisco: Auerhahn Press, 1960), 49.

16 Robert Creeley, "Foreword," in Allen Ginsberg, *Death & Fame: Poems 1993–1997* (New York: HarperFlamingo, 1999), xv.

6

STEVEN BELLETTO

Five Ways of Being Beat, Circa 1958–59

What happens if we decenter the notion of "Beat literature" from the Ginsberg–Kerouac–Burroughs triumvirate? After all, what constitutes Beat literature or the Beat Movement is hardly limited to the most well-known, reproduced, or written-about texts. While still acknowledging those texts' importance, in this chapter I want to take the opportunity to offer five brief sketches of other writers "on the scene" circa 1958 and 1959: Tuli Kupferberg, Jack Micheline, Ted Joans, Diane di Prima, and Lenore Kandel. None are particularly obscure figures, but they tend to be spoken about either as writers emerging in the 1960s (Kupferberg, Kandel) or as secondary lights (Micheline, Joans), or in the case of di Prima as the supposedly lone Beat woman writing in the 1950s. None of these characterizations are exactly correct, as all five writers were active in their own ways throughout the 1950s. While each of these writers invoked their connections to the Beat scene via their knowledge of or intimacy with more visible writers such as Allen Ginsberg or Jack Kerouac, rather than merely mimicking the work of such figures in derivative ways, what characterizes their writing is a self-conscious analysis and critique of the Beats as both literary phenomenon and cultural construct. Moreover, in attuning ourselves to the ways these writers formulated Beatness, we find that their work makes broadly political interventions, an idea that challenges conventional wisdom, which holds that Beat writing, at least circa 1958 and 1959, was resolutely apolitical.

"The War Against the Beats"

Tuli Kupferberg has long been associated with both the broader Greenwich Village literary scene and the Beats in particular, although he has received relatively scant critical attention. When critics do mention Kupferberg, it tends to be in connection to the 1960s incarnation of Beatness, when he and Ed Sanders fronted the Fugs, a satirical band devoted to equal parts poetry and rock 'n' roll that became known for its anti-Vietnam War songs like "Kill for Peace" (1966; written by Kupferberg). In his "complete, uncensored history" of the Beats, for example, Bill Morgan only mentions Kupferberg once, in a passage about the Fugs in a final chapter called "The End of the Road."[1] From such discussions, readers might be left with the impression that Kupferberg was only associated with the Beat movement later, connecting to it via the hippie scene with works such as *1001 Ways to Beat the Draft* (1966), when in fact he had been a visible presence since at least the mid-1950s. Born in 1924, between Kerouac (1922) and Ginsberg (1925), Kupferberg was long recognized by those in the know as the model for the figure in Ginsberg's "Howl" (1956) "who jumped off the Brooklyn Bridge this actually happened and walked away unknown and forgotten."[2] Although Kupferberg wasn't named in *Howl and Other Poems*, in later, annotated editions of "Howl," Ginsberg included glosses quoting Kupferberg, who explained that

> In the spring of 1945 at the age of 21, full of youthful angst, depression over war and other insanities and at the end of a disastrous love affair, I went over the side of the Manhattan Bridge... Thruout the years I have been annoyed many times by "O did you really jump off the Brooklyn Bridge?" as if that was a great accomplishment. (128)

Despite Kupferberg's annoyance at being asked, presumably by Ginsberg aficionados, whether he was indeed the real-life model for that line of "Howl," the reasons he lists for his attempted suicide – "youthful angst," "depression over war," "disastrous love affair," and unspecified "insanities" – can in fact be read as typically Beat, so it's perhaps unsurprising that Kupferberg had a longer and more self-conscious engagement with the scene than is often remembered.

This chapter discusses two of Kupferberg's publications from 1959, *Beating* and *Snow Job*, both of which explicitly theorize the meaning of Beat or "Beat Generation," a preoccupation to which Kupferberg would return in later work such as *Beatniks, or The War Against the Beats* (1961). *Beating* was published in the summer of 1959 by Kupferberg's boutique, essentially one-man Birth Press (also the publisher of *Snow Job*). For those interested in how Beat-associated writers defined the phenomenon circa 1959, *Beating* is a treasure trove of analyses of the burgeoning social and literary movement. *Beating* opens with a list of "THE SUBJECTS OF BEAT poetry":

> 1) sex
> 2) narcotics & alcohol
> 3) jazz
> 4) insanity
> 5) the Negro

6) homosexuality

7) hoboes & bums; travelling (new places)

8) anti-politics

9) anti-institutions (the army & war, the fuzz & prison, the mass media, the school, the job)

10) writing (& creative act) itself.[3]

Read with the caveat that plenty of other writers who had nothing to do with the Beats were interested in these topics, taken together, the list is actually a pretty good representation of a Beat sensibility circa 1959, and is impressively clear-eyed about the stakes and diversity of Beat writing. If sex had been explored by, say, Grace Metalious in *Peyton Place* (1956), or "the Negro," by, say, Ralph Ellison in *Invisible Man* (1952), the Beats were interested in these subjects as they related both to each other and to the whole constellation of concerns on Kupferberg's list. Thus far from the titillating escapades in a middlebrow novel like *Peyton Place*, for Kupferberg, sex was always bound up in political and social questions, so that "sexual 'delinquency' ... is one of the few healthy signs in American life today" (np). If for Ellison blackness renders African Americans invisible to white America, for Kupferberg blackness is connected to social and political revolution, as "The Beats link themselves & are linked to the new rising energies of Africa & Asia, to the primitive current life-loving peoples of Mexico & the Caribbean" (np). Even drug use is not for Kupferberg strictly recreational as it heightens the ways in which the Beats are "outside of society," and those squares who refuse drugs for "Fear of law and of 'society' ... are [actually manifesting] fear of sex, fear of excitement, fear of life" (np). In other words, although Kupferberg claims the Beats were "anti-politic[al]," *Beating* demonstrates that Beat writing was in fact shifting what could count as "political," not merely in its subject matter but also in the specific framing and treatment of its content.

When he moves on to an analysis of "Beat Poietics," Kupferberg takes "Howl" as paradigmatic, confessing that his first reading of the poem mirrored that of "America at large," so he was "repelled" and found it "shocking," "disgusting," "exhibitionist," and "infantile." But, since that first reaction, Kupferberg explains, he reexamined his attitudes and realized "Howl" is necessary to the healthy functioning of contemporary America. He elaborates:

> because ["the Beat poet"] takes himself seriously and openly, he is willing to discuss & to air *him*self & his writings ... Because he is interested in creating a society of friends and believes in poetry as an instrument of joy he wants the living contact of the spoken word and the living audience. (np)

Such interest in "creating a society of friends" is one way to view what constituted the tissue of Beatness in 1959, a willingness to present oneself "seriously and openly" for the mutual benefit of a like-minded community.

This is why, in a poetry collection like *Snow Job*—which includes poems written between 1946 and 1959—Kupferberg focuses so often on constructions and depictions of bohemianism. The collection evinces a wide range of references and poetic styles, from allusions to Jewish mysticism, the Old Testament, Leon Trotsky, and Federico García Lorca to experiments with form, such as plays on haiku and alphabet poems. "Intimations on Pound's *Immorality*" is a double allusion to William Wordworth's "Ode: Intimations of Immortality" and Pound's poem "An Immorality"; given Kupferberg's progressive social views, it's hardly surprising that his ironic rejoinder to Pound's poem struggles, as many have, with reconciling Pound's poetic reputation and his support of the Fascist regime in Italy: "Poetry and politics / Like hate and love / Should never mix" (np).

Interspersed with such responses to broader literary histories are poems in which Kupferberg theorizes the contemporary Beat scene and how it does or does not fit into other literary trajectories. This is the case, for example, in "The Abominable Snow Job," which includes a parody of the famous final line of *The Communist Manifesto* (1848) ("Workers of the World: Unite!"):

> Fuzz of all countries
> You bite!
> I'd like to turn you on!
> Whos gonna protect you guys fun yourselves?
> Certainly not the beat(niks)?
> Someday you all might arrest *each other*
> *Its not beyond the possibility of a doubt*
>
> Never underestimate the power of a poet
>
> ...
>
> Authors note: I would of continued this
>   poem more beatly but just
>   as I'm writing this line
>   the fuzz is entering the doo.[4]

In this passage, Kupferberg plays with the distinctions between the "mainstream" and the Beats by inverting Marx and Engels's rallying cry to the world's exploited working classes. Here it is Kupferberg speaking with authority: it is not legal, political, or economic authority but a kind of countercultural creative authority ("Never underestimate the power of a poet") that can confidently claim that the police or "fuzz" bites. But, however much this authority is asserted in the context of the poem itself, it is nonetheless ironically undercut in the poem's final line, when the "real world" intrudes in the form of a police raid, literally cutting the poet off mid-word. Like-minded play is also found in poems such as "Washington Square," concerning "Tramps of feeling" and "The Bohemians [who] have gone into the sand-pit to drink sand" (np); "For a Poet Scheduled to Die Young," which describes a "Landsman, cocksman, buddy of my balls" (np); "The Ballad of the Rienzi Ladies," which is set at Café Rienzi, a bohemian hot-spot where earnest young men woo ladies with dubious lines like "I have changed you into a poem" (np); and "Square," which reverses the popular notion that the Beats were violent by imputing such violence to the titular "Square":

> Tankstrut down the
> slippering street
> he'll bang you into
> a plateglass hell
> ...
> Fags & beautiful poets
> watshit!he'll rune
> on you. (np)

Just as "Square" bluntly opposes squares to "beautiful poets" to argue for the cultural violence done to Beats by mainstream culture, taken together, *Beating* and *Snow Job* comprise an important articulation of a Beat ethos in 1959. Indeed, these works illustrate Kupferberg's fluency not only with literary, cultural, and political history but also with the particular ways "Beat" was being circulated in contemporary US culture, and the two works deserve to be better known as commentaries on and correctives to such circulation.

"The Last of the Bohemians Is Dead"

Like Kupferberg, Jack Micheline was a fixture on the Village Beat scene throughout the 1950s, and he was considered a "street poet" as his work was known largely through his performances. When Micheline published his first book, *River of Red Wine* (1958), he was given a Beat imprimatur by Kerouac, who agreed to write a short introduction invoking Micheline's expressly nonacademic aesthetic lineage: "Doctor William Carlos Williams I think would like him, if he heard him read aloud."[5] Kerouac goes on to praise Micheline's work for not being "premediated and crafted and revised" and compares him to other "swinging" writers including Ginsberg, William S. Burroughs, Gregory Corso, Michael McClure, Robert Duncan, Robert Creeley, Philip Whalen, and Gary Snyder (7), a comparison group that also implies the outlines of a loosely affiliated Beat canon circa 1958–59. *River of Red Wine* was thus packaged as a Beat book for its first printing (and the 1986 reprint redoubles this effort, proclaiming Micheline a "major, if not understood, voice of the BEAT GENERATION" and including a blurb from Gerald Nicosia placing the book among "the best work of the Beat Generation"). Indeed, Fred McDarrah's 1960 essay "Anatomy of a Beatnik" singles out Micheline as a poet "associated with the Beat Movement" and quotes him saying: "I might have been politically active but it's all corrupt. I want to see better things happen that would help this country ... I've been told that the vitality of my work is identified with the Beat Generation. I'm anti-materialistic, the way I love, the way I feel, the way I think."[6] As with the self-identified Beats interviewed in Lawrence Lipton's widely read treatment of the Beat phenomenon, *The Holy Barbarians* (1959), Micheline pointedly exempts himself from engaging in politics narrowly conceived, but nonetheless claims his work is making a social intervention (he was also careful to distinguish the "Beat Generation" from the Beatnik, whom he defines as "somebody running away from himself ["Anatomy" 7]).[7]

As for the poems themselves: they seem with Kupferberg's work to posit a teasing connection with the scene, even in the use of the word "beat" or "beating," which recurs numerous times across a range of poems. The first poem in *River of Red Wine*, for example, "Lets Sing a Song," ends

> and they took me away
> away
> away
> from the roar
> and the beat
> and the beat
> the beat.[8]

It is as though Micheline is daring readers not to associate the repetition of the word with the so-called Beat Generation, especially given Kerouac's introduction. Beyond the use of the perhaps-incidental word "beat," *River of Red Wine* shares some formal and thematic characteristics of other poetry of the scene, as well as moral indictments familiar to readers of "Howl" or Ray Smith's musings in Kerouac's *The Dharma Bums* (1958). As Micheline writes:

> Machine man blinded
> and binded to the
> comforts
> of their laziness.
> Fear ruled, the universe

of the alcohol drugged
and stuffed on T.V.
commercial madness. (20)

This sort of social criticism underlies the collection as a whole, even as it is written in the seemingly nonpremeditated style of which Kerouac approves. The lengthiest poem in the collection, "The Last of the Bohemians," is notable not so much because it yields original insights into contemporary problems ("The politicians have / fed you with promises / and left you with doubts" [42]) but because it picks up on and makes its own the basic antiestablishment critique that seemed a foundational element of Beat writing:

America
I see
your
millions
of walking dead wobbly
streets.
You are
the wealthiest
the richest
the sickest.
...
When will
you ever
wake up?
Greenwich Village your Sicilian streets are not as wild as
they used to be. The last of the Bohemians is dead. (45)

Taking a somewhat banal critique and extending it to the reputedly countercultural sensibility of the Village – a technique that Gregory Corso, for example, would use in *Gasoline* (1958) and elsewhere – Micheline refuses the distinct binary between mainstream and counterculture on which the Beatnik caricature insisted. To declare "the last of the Bohemians is dead" laments the loss of the bohemian era of the 1920s but leaves it ultimately ambiguous as to whether it is "America" to blame for killing the spirit of bohemianism or the Village's "Sicilian streets" themselves, which, the poem suggests, may have willingly bought in to the sickness of mid-century America.

"You Should Never Be Chips Off the Old Square Blocks"

The master of teasingly associating himself with the Beat Generation was Ted Joans, who by the late 1950s had made his name by performing the most caricatured aspects of the Beatnik. A key African American member of the Beat movement, Joans was canny about exploiting his position as such to claim an authenticity as an actual hipster – in the terms set forth in Norman Mailer's incendiary essay "The White Negro" (1957), or by his friend Kerouac, whose Sal Paradise in *On the Road* notoriously wished to be "a Negro." For Joans, race informed his Beatnik shtick, which he promoted to comic effect both in his poetry and in cultural happenings such as his "bi-annual" birthday party, a flier for which featured a cartoon of Joans in a beret, sunglasses, and goatee holding a briefcase labeled "Beat Poetry" and encouraging the "girls of the Beat Generation [to] bring other chicklets – chicks – and even hip hens."[9] This sort of half-ironic performance reached its most famous heights in November 1959 when Fred McDarrah placed an ad in the *Village Voice* reading: "ADD ZEST TO YOUR TUXEDO PARK PARTY ... RENT A BEATNIK Completely equipped: Beard, eye shades, old Army jacket" (*Beat Generation* 211). Although McDarrah intended mainly to generate interest in the forthcoming book *The Beat Scene* (1960)—which prominently featured his photographs—instead he got an "overwhelming" response to the ad, soon placed others, and wound up creating a small enterprise "renting genuine Beatniks." Unsurprisingly, Joans was a perfect fit for such an undertaking, and *The Beat Scene* has a photograph of him at a Rent-a-Beatnik party paid for by wealthy suburbanites in Scarsdale. As A. Robert Lee has argued, Joans can therefore be understood as "Beat playing Beat, Joans playing himself, offers a simulation, its own kind of performance loop."[10]

Due in large part to this "performance loop," Joans was so well known in the Greenwich scene throughout the late 1950s that in subsequent years his persona has sometimes eclipsed discussions of his work, which detractors have wrongly assumed was mere accompaniment to the Beatnik shtick. By 1959, when he published *Jazz Poems*, Joans was famous enough to the hip crowd that music critic Robert Reisner (who would go on to write the first biography of Charlie Parker) claimed that "In Greenwich Village you can't walk a block with him but that you have to stop while he receives the big hello. If he was walking with Eisenhower, the beats in the Village would say 'Who's that guy with Ted?' "[11] In many ways, then, Joans's image was circulated far more than his actual poetry, as in the well-known color photograph of a beret-clad Joans reading poetry in Café Bizarre, a Village coffeehouse, reproduced in the cover artwork for the softcore porn Beatnik exploitation novel *Like Crazy, Man* (1960).[12] The original photograph appeared in an article on the "Roaming Beatniks" that Kerouac wrote for a special New York-themed issue of *Holiday* magazine, and even in that piece Joans's poetry is not discussed or named except for the caption to the photograph: "Here, before an interested but informal audience, Ted Joans offers one of his creations."[13] It is thus tempting to say that Joans was a victim of his own simultaneous impersonation and undermining of the Beatnik persona, and the fact that he is less read than many of his counterparts speaks to what one observer dubbed his "literary non-career."[14] This is a shame because Joans's poetry is often razor-sharp social commentary about not only the Beat scene but also the political, cultural, and especially racial matters of his times. And, as Kupferberg and Micheline would make the bohemian scene subjects of their work, so too did Joans write explicitly about this scene in order to offer a sly analysis of it. So, while Reisner's introduction to *Jazz Poems* insists that "Ted Joans is a phoney. He is no beatnik. He is no Negro," the poetry that follows nonetheless projects a black Beat sensibility that toys with the perceived distinctions between and expectations of both the "mainstream" and "counterculture."

Like Kupferberg and Micheline, Joans advertises his bohemian bona fides by displaying his knowledge of the "inner circle" of Beat writers, ironically questioning what such writers are understood to represent. In his poem "The Sermon" from *Jazz Poems* – which extends the elaborate play of his birthday party advertisement – Joans seems to offer practical advice for those who want to be "hip little girls":

> You must own a copy of HOWL You must have a copy of on the road
> Kerouac on your shelf and know thou self by reading Norman Mailers
> 'WHITE NEGRO' ... you should read [...]
> Gregory Corso's poem Marriage before ever doing that bit.[15]

But it is not merely reading these most visible of Beat texts that will make the girls "hip," for they are also urged to adopt the attitudes espoused in such work. Joans therefore counsels would-be Beat chicks to

> get rid of that UMBILICAL CORD
> that your dragassed prejudice parents have around your neck,
> [...]
>   if your
> neighborhood aint hip ... SPLIT [...]
>   SLEEP with
> everybody but don't MAKE IT with nobody but Santa Claus [...]
>   DON'T GET HUNG UP!! like your parents...
> You should never be chips off the old square blocks. (np; unbracketed
>   ellipses in original)

This is exactly the sort of advice that in 1959 any writer for *Time* or *Life* or the *Partisan Review* would have seized on to prove the vacuity and immorality of the Beat lifestyle. And yet the specifics of the advice are hard to take seriously. When Joans urges his audience of "sweet angelic CHICKLETS" to embrace all the cartoon aspects of the Beatnik counterculture, he is not so much endorsing a lifestyle as he is mocking those who imagine these features as the substance and totality of the bohemian scene. In this way, "The Sermon" is reminiscent of a work such as Bob Kaufman's "The Abomunist Manifesto" (1959), a half-serious statement about what bohemianism entails: just as Joans absurdly cautions girls to "MAKE IT with nobody but Santa Claus," so does Kaufman assure his readers that "ABOMUNISTS REJECT EVERYTHING EXCEPT SNOWMEN."[16] To take either statement at face value is to misread their ironic play that skewers mainstream perceptions of the Beat scene by seeming to confirm them: like the Dada art that inspired Joans (one poem proclaims "I am a ... graduate of Dada University in Zurich"), the poetry in *Jazz Poems* ought to be taken as sincere and joking at the same time, a put-on with a serious claim about the way the Beats have been packaged and thereby dismissed. In "Howl," the best minds of Ginsberg's generation "threw potato salad at CCNY lecturers on Dadism" (*Howl* 5), a very Dadaesque protest the poem connects to its vision of social and political critique. Likewise, in "The Sermon," the piling up of these Beatnik precepts points to Joans's excoriation of establishment values, as aspiring hipsters also "must free the people behind the Cotten Curtain as well as / those unfortunates behind the Iron one you must not live in Greenwich / Village and pay high ass rent to greedy landlords" (np). It is no more that Joans's imagined audience will participate in direct action in the Jim Crow South or materially assist potential defectors from the Soviet Union than they will make love to Santa Claus, but the mental attitude associated with being hip nevertheless helps one to "SEE THE TRUTH" behind the various instantiations of what Kenneth Rexroth called the "social lie" (quoted in *Holy Barbarians* 294).

As a collection, *Jazz Poems* aims to "SEE THE TRUTH" both in the content of the poems and in their visual arrangement on the page. This is an aspect of Joans's work that is lost when it is read in anthologies or even later collections such as *Teducation* (1999), and yet it is important to read the individual poems in the context of the collection as a whole, which is arranged as a kind of Dada-inspired collage. In *Jazz Poems*, the text of "The Sermon" is juxtaposed against images such as a quaint, old-fashioned drawing of a little girl that reminds one that the imagined recipients of Joans's advice have not yet transformed into "hip little girls," and an illustration taken from a medical textbook showing a human cheek in mid-dissection, suggesting that the poem is similarly dissecting the social mores that regulate human bodies. Likewise, in the poem "Uh Huh," an illustration of a dissected human hand accompanies text comprised of supposedly noncommunicative hipster slang:

> uh huh
> that's it
> yes siree
> Man this is it
> the real thing. (np)

Readers don't know what "it" or "the real thing" refers to, and the poem continues in this chatty vein ("yep yep" and "no shit"), until the final lines: "Well I be damn / here now this is it Uh Huh uh huhuh huh uh huh uh huh / THE COLORED WAITING ROOM" (np).[17] The final line recontextualizes the fragmented slang before it as stunned reactions to the fact of segregation, implying legalized inequality is a far greater moral crime than the perceived degradation of the English language. This claim in turn suggests that the hipsters standing outside "mainstream" culture looking in actually occupy a moral high ground, and the illustration of a dissected hand stands as both a metaphor for the poet's work in dissecting culture and a reminder that the guts of all human beings are the same, regardless of race. Thus while *Jazz Poems* appears to be an indiscriminate celebration of all things Beatnik, in fact in its elaborate play on mainstream expectations about the Beats, the book levels an ironic political critique of phenomena such as de facto and institutionalized racism (see "Why Hurry?"), which is after all a result of the same confident misapprehensions that assume all Beat-associated folk were accurately captured in the pages of *Life* magazine.

"Like That's Uncool"

By 1958, poet and City Lights Books owner Lawrence Ferlinghetti was revered enough as a bohemian figure that Diane di Prima contacted him to write an introduction to her first book of poetry, *This Kind of Bird Flies Backward*. As suggested by her involvement in the little magazine *Yugen* (1958–1962) and later as co-editor (with LeRoi Jones) of *The Floating Bear* (1961–1971), di Prima was active in the Greenwich Village scene in the 1950s, and would add a powerful female voice to the Beat Movement in the well over twenty books she came to publish after *This Kind of Bird Flies Backward*. As was the case with the male "inner circle," who legitimated and mythologized themselves by constantly cross-referencing one another's work, with her first book of poetry, di Prima was canny about linking her work to Ferlinghetti as a way to demonstrate her Beat insiderness, just as a male poet like Micheline had. Even though Ferlinghetti's introduction is only six sentences and begins "I don't know her, never saw her, never heard her," merely carrying his name on the book's cover did the work of letting hip readers know di Prima's work was worthwhile.[18] And yet, one hallmark of *This Kind of Bird Flies Backward* is di Prima's undermining of what readers think they know about "coolness" and the scene. She includes work from as far back as 1953 (the titles of the poems in this section are specific dates), which has the simultaneous effect of establishing di Prima as an "authentic" – that is, pre-*On the Road* and "Howl" – Beat, and allowing her to criticize certain aspects of the supposed Beat lifestyle. Many of the poems are centered around relationships and love, and in them one finds what became a signature of di Prima's sensibility over the next several decades: her ability to skewer self-identified bohemian, progressive men who nonetheless behave in conventionally boorish ways when it comes to women or sexual relationships. This is the case, for example, in "August 1955," which ends with the stanza "Like man don't flip, I'm hip you cooled / this scene. But you can hock the jazz / guitar, in limbo they play ballads."[19] Here di Prima reproduces cartoon Beat slang, what she later called "street language," but she does so self-reflexively: it is a performance of such slang interested in what this language might cover up.[20] In "August 1955," the speaker resorts to slangy jargon to assure the man who has "cooled the scene" that everything is fine, that as a "hip chick" she would never hold him to square standards like commitment. But even as the speaker makes this declaration, the poem is ambivalent about its virtue as readers are left with the sense of callousness with which the man splits, thereby implying that, far from rendering men and women sexual equals, bohemian fantasies of free love can actually enforce conventional gender norms as men flee from genuine connection.

Di Prima explores this theory throughout *This Kind of Bird Flies Backward* (and develops it to greater effect in her next book, *Dinners and Nightmares* [1961]). In a pair of "Poems for Bret," for example, she inverts what later theorists would call the "male gaze" by proclaiming "I've got my eye on you" (34), an assertion of the power of female subjectivity that runs through much writing by Beat-associated women writers. The poem ends by framing such power in terms of the norms of the scene:

> it's nice
> to run a pad
> where both of us
> are cool enough
> to know we're both
> uncool. (34)

As in many other poems in the book, di Prima demonstrates her fluency with Beat slang, but does so in order to dismantle and indeed dispatch such coolness as an affected veneer that only occludes true connection. Thus this poem – and the collection as a whole – relishes being "uncool" if it spells true connection. As di Prima writes in the untitled opening poem:

> I don't forget things
> fast enough, I sing
> last summer's ballads
>
> winter long
> like that's uncool. (2)

This poem suggests that the bohemian ideal of "cool" is as normative as the square injunction to monogamy. If to linger over human connection too long is to be "uncool," then the speaker embraces such uncoolness, however antithetical it may be to what dutiful Beat chicks were supposed to do according to what di Prima later called "our eternal, tiresome rule of Cool."[21] Ronna C. Johnson has explained the Beat rule of cool as "a set of rules for comportment that mandates terse expression and withheld emotion ... it is a social code ... that makes women de facto collaborators with their own oppression, because the essence of cool is the appearance of passivity, indifference, and lack of emotion."[22] A critique of this "social code" is evident throughout *This Kind of Bird Flies Backward*, in which di Prima stakes her claim on her own idiosyncratic visions of love and relationships loosed from both mainstream *and* bohemian values. This is perhaps most evident in the way di Prima conceptualizes her "Love Poems," not as starry-eyed odes to abdominal fluttering or the transformative joys of sex, but rather as hard-nosed inversions of such clichés: "you are not quite / the air I breathe / thank god. / so go" (27). Such inversions are informed throughout the book by a wry assessment of the power dynamics that accompany romantic relationships, even in a bohemian milieu: "In case you put me down I put you down / already, doll / I know the games you play" (24). *This Kind of Bird Flies Backward* is thus a noteworthy moment in Beat publishing because it represents a female critique of Beat gender norms that appeared earlier than the work in the 1960s, 1970s, and beyond with which most students of Beat literature are familiar (perhaps the most well-known example of such a critique being di Prima's own *Memoirs of a Beatnik* [1969]).

Although many accounts of the Beat movement reinforce the general impression that di Prima was the lone woman on the scene publishing in the late 1950s, this is not exactly true. In saying this I don't mean to deny that male voices dominated the scene as they certainly did, but I do think we ought to be careful not to allow such dominance to erase from literary history books such as *This Kind of Bird Flies Backward*, so I want to turn now to a writer who tends to be studied largely in terms of her later work – from the 1960s and after: Lenore Kandel.

"Bored With Sitting Wisely"

When Kandel is mentioned in histories of the Beats, it is usually in connection to *The Love Book* (1966), or to the fact that in *Big Sur* (1962) Kerouac imagined her as Romana Swartz, a "monster beauty … intelligent, well read, writes poetry, is a Zen student, knows everything."[23] But Kandel was long known in Beat or bohemian circles as a prolific and powerful poet who preferred to read her work in coffeehouses rather than attempt to get it published. This changed in 1959 when Grover and Rosie Haynes founded the Three Penny Press out of their apartment in Studio City, California. With this tiny press, the Hayneses were expressly interested in publishing work by those whom they called "local barefoot bards." "Our main sources," wrote Grover Haynes in 1959, "are the poetry readings that are conducted at coffee houses in Los Angeles, Venice West, and San Francisco … Our booklets of poetry are experiments. They are NOT safe and tested literature. They do not have the GOOD HOUSEKEEPING SEAL OF APPROVAL. They have NOT, as yet, found a niche on the bookshelf of every suburban home."[24] With this stance, Three Penny Press was aligned with the Beat literary ethos that explicitly defined itself against literature "safe and tested" for middlebrow readers. As a small, two-person operation aiming to bring alternative voices in contemporary letters to slightly larger audiences, the press drew a direct line to the Beats with titles such as *Beards and Brown Bags* (1959) and *Beat and Beatific II* (1959), collections that included poetry by Kandel and others. Kandel was indeed an ideal writer for the press's list as she was already a force on the coffeehouse circuit but had devoted little energy to bringing her work to print. To remedy this situation, in 1959, the Hayneses published three chapbooks by Kandel: *A Passing Dragon*, *A Passing Dragon Seen Again*, and *An Exquisite Navel*.[25] As Grover Haynes informed readers in his "About the Author" statement in *A Passing Dragon*: "If you are more than a casual visitor to Los Angeles coffee houses, you are probably well acquainted with Lenore Kandel. Her poetry is inextricably tied in with coffee houses and the mood that pervades them."[26] This "mood" characterized the local scene at LA's Unicorn Coffee House and elsewhere, but also the wider Beat scene that sutured New York City, Southern California, and San Francisco, all places in which Kandel had lived as she moved from her birthplace of New York

City to the Los Angeles area and finally to San Francisco, where she would become a fixture of the flourishing 1960s counterculture.

Like *This Kind of Bird Flies Backward*, Kandel's early poetry is pointedly set in bohemia. The opening poem in *A Passing Dragon* announces "All my pockets have holes in the bottoms / and everything I own slides away ... / sooner or later," a passage that denies the importance of material possessions when one appreciates instead the resources of the natural world.[27] The poem concludes: "I filled my pockets with nothing and started again / me and the gray wind." If there is an abiding sensibility of *A Passing Dragon*, it is Kandel's imagining how she might better understand herself through nature, an understanding that her speaker's constitutional impecuniousness only promotes. In this way, Kandel shares with Gary Snyder, Lew Welch, and the Kerouac of *The Dharma Bums* an interest in how the resources of nature can offer better ways of knowing ourselves and our realities. The poetry in *A Passing Dragon* uses varied strategies for exploring this connection, including the playful figurations of men as animals that allow her to poke fun at male-centered "preening," as when she writes

> You are like a lion
> crashing the bars of your cage
> And I am an idiot
> Trying to stay you
> with
> peanuts

or

> Such a tomcat then
> sitting there preening his belly fur ...
> (so infuriating to a she-cat). (np)

Also characteristic of the volume are the moments when Kandel expresses desire for a mystical connection between her speakers and nature, as in the lines "The hot wind blows and / I wish I could blow with it" and "I have fallen in love with the wind / I know I can't catch it" (np).

If *A Passing Dragon* plays with the connectedness of women and the natural world, *An Exquisite Navel* enacts a more familiar Beat quibble with a mainstream culture that was perceived to foreclose individual expression. The opening poem is in the tradition of the "oral messages" of Ferlinghetti, Kenneth Rexroth, and Bob Kaufman, and, in his preface to the volume, Grover Haynes emphasized that, because the work in *An Exquisite Navel* was solicited after being heard aloud in coffeehouses, "the comparative merits of a poem may be ascertained more certainly when it is heard read aloud" (np). In this way, "All I have in the world" explores Beat subjectivity in the face of a hostile mainstream culture in ways reminiscent of work such as Ferlinghetti's "Autobiography" in *A Coney Island of the Mind* (1958). For example, "All I have in the world" contains the lines:

> All I have in the world
> Dark brown hair and a restless mind
> I can feel the earthquakes underneath my feet
> waiting to explode, to erupt, to go boom!

The poem continues to proclaim that the speaker feels straightjacketed by the "shibboleths and syllogisms" underwriting "the nausea of the age." Against such generalized dissatisfaction with the norms of contemporary culture, Kandel ends with a feminist take on the Beat desire to burn brightly:

> And if something doesn't happen
> I'll go
> stark
> staring
> BOOM![28]

This poem offers a portrait of a speaker paralyzed by expectations of complacency. Her navel, which gives the book its title, has tripartite significance as the source of child-bearing, an object of male desire (in his preface, Haynes approvingly notes that "Lenore worked her way through college as a belly dancer in a Turkish cabaret in New York" [np]), and as a site of self-paralysis in the form of navel-gazing. Her body, from her "dark brown hair" to her exquisite navel, is a both a resource and a hindrance to being recognized for her "restless mind." This poem – and the collection as a whole – can be read as a Beat version of what Betty Friedan called "the problem that has no name" in *The Feminine Mystique* (1963).[29] Friedan was describing the inexplicable unhappiness of middle-class housewives who were expected to define themselves in terms of their devotion to their husbands and children.[30] While Kandel was no middle-class housewife, she identified a similar malaise connected even to Beat-approved activities such as Buddhist meditation: "I am bored with sitting wisely / I am tired of being calm" (np). The poem identifies the source of such discontent not only in her being valued only for the exquisiteness of her navel but also in those "shibboleths and syllogisms" of social regulation that demand fairly narrow ideas of cleanliness or virtue. So many lollypops stuffed in the mouths of teeny-boppers are only the most accessible of symbolic pacifiers that would delight in silent women either vacuuming their suburban homes or quietly meditating in bohemia. "All I have in the world" explores the turmoil beneath the veneer of acceptable society, but it does so from a decidedly female perspective, which, like di Prima's work, is not too sure about the distinctions between mainstream and Beat when it comes to gender norms. The poem is representative of the work in *An Exquisite Navel* in that a witty female sensibility takes on both mainstream culture and its supposed inverse in ways that would be elaborated with even more complexity in the coming years.

When read against one another, the works of Kupferberg, Micheline, Joans, di Prima, and Kandel demonstrate a vital Beat poetry scene circa 1958–1959 that is aware of and responsive to the growing fame of figures such as Kerouac or Ginsberg, but crucially not defined by them or their work. These five are in fact a small sampling of writers on the scene, but considering them together reminds us of the extent to which such writers were invested in criticizing the "social lie," whether with respect to the mandates of bohemian versus mainstream cultures or in connection to questions of racial or gender norms. Such critique suggests that Beat writers, even circa 1958–59, were much more slyly political than even their most admiring readers tend to remember.

NOTES

1 Bill Morgan, *The Typewriter Is Holy: The Complete, Uncensored History of the Beat Generation* (New York: Free Press, 2010), 228.

2 Allen Ginsberg, *Howl: Original Draft Facsimile*, ed. Barry Miles (New York: Harper Perennial, 2006), 5.

3 Tuli Kupferberg, *Beating* (New York: Birth Press, 1959), np.

4 Tuli Kupferberg, *Snow Job* (New York: Birth Press, 1959), np.

5 Jack Kerouac, "Introduction," Jack Micheline, *River of Red Wine* (1958; Sudbury, MA: Water Row Press, 1986), 7.

6 Micheline quoted in Fred McDarrah, "Antaomy of a Beatnik," McDarrah and Gloria McDarrah, *Beat Generation: Glory Days in Greenwich Village* (New York: Schirmer Books, 1996), 6–7. The essay was originally published in *Saga* (August 1960).

7 Lawrence Lipton, *The Holy Barbarians* (New York: Julian Messner, 1959).

8 Jack Micheline, *River of Red Wine* (1958; Sudbury, MA: Water Row Press, 1986), 10.

9 This flier is reproduced in McDarrah and McDarrah, *Beat Generation*, 94.

10 A. Robert Lee, *Modern American Counter Writing* (New York: Routledge, 2010), 62.

11 Robert Reisner, "Intro," Ted Joans, *Jazz Poems* (New York: Rhino Review, 1959), np.

12 For a reproduction of this photograph, see Martin McIntosh, ed., *Beatsville* (Melbourne: Outré Gallery Press, 2003), 53.

13 Jack Kerouac, "The Roaming Beatniks," *Holiday* (October 1959), 82.

14 See Gerald Nicosia, "A Lifelong Commitment to Change: The Literary Non-Career of Ted Joans," Ted Joans, *Teducation: Selected Poems* (Minneapolis: Coffee House Press, 1999), i–vii.

15 Ted Joans, *Jazz Poems* (New York: Rhino Review, 1959), np (unbracketed ellipses in original).

16 Bob Kaufman, *Abomunist Manifesto* (San Francisco: City Lights, 1959), np.

17 In the version of this poem printed in *Teducation* (Minnesota: Coffee House Press, 1999), Joans tagged it with "Pulaski, TN 1949" (107).

18 Lawrence Ferlinghetti, "A Non-introduction by Way of Introduction," Diane di Prima, *This Kind of Bird Flies Backward* (1958; New York: Paper Book Gallery, 1963), np.

19 Diane di Prima, *This Kind of Bird Flies Backward* (1958; New York: Paper Book Gallery, 1963), 10.

20 "Pieces of a Song [interview with Diane di Prima]," *Breaking the Rule of Cool*, ed. Nancy M. Grace and Ronna C. Johnson (Jackson: University Press of Mississippi, 2004), 97.

21 Diane di Prima, *Memoirs of a Beatnik* (1969; New York: Penguin, 1988), 133.

22 Ronna C. Johnson, "Mapping the Women Writers of the Beat Generation," *Breaking the Rule of Cool*, 38.

23 Jack Kerouac, *Big Sur* (1962; New York: Bantam, 1963), 61.

24 Grover Haynes, untitled afterword, in Lenore Kandel, *A Passing Dragon* (Studio City: Three Penny Press, 1959), np.

25 *A Passing Dragon* and *A Passing Dragon Seen Again* are essentially the same book but with a few minor changes: Grover Haynes slightly revised his introductory statement (from "About the Poet" in *A Passing Dragon* to "Preface" in *A Passing Dragon Seen Again*), and there are a couple more poems in *A Passing Dragon Seen Again*. The poetry from these hard-to-find chapbooks is collected in *Collected Poems of Lenore Kandel* (Berkeley: North Atlantic Books, 2012).

26 Grover Haynes, "About the Poet," Kandel, *A Passing Dragon*, np.

27 Kandel, "I have chosen for my guide the gray wind," *A Passing Dragon*, np. Unless otherwise noted, the poems in Kandel's early books are untitled, so I refer to them by their first lines.

28 Lenore Kandel, "All I Have in the World," *An Exquisite Navel* (Studio City: Three Penny Press, 1959), np.

29 Betty Friedan, *The Feminine Mystique* (1963; New York: W. W. Norton, 2013), 57–78.

30 For more on the connection between Beat women and *The Feminine Mystique*, see Johnson, "Mapping," 13.

7

KURT HEMMER

Jack Kerouac and the Beat Novel

Is There a Beat Text in This Classroom?

Jack Kerouac is the archetypal Beat novelist, and any discussion of defining the Beat novel must address his aesthetic sensibilities, as varied as they may be. But what exactly is a "Beat" novel? Determining this is deceptively difficult. Many scholars tend to think of the Beat Movement more in terms of a revolution in poetry than in prose. Beat poems and novels share the same characteristics: radical politics and political activism; spiritualism, especially Buddhism and Eastern philosophy; attempts to capture drug-induced and visionary states; a connection to geography; a celebration and rediscovery of the body; antiwar sentiments; ecological and environmental awareness; and rejection of middle-class mores and materialism.[1] Discussions of Beat novelists have included, but by no means have been restricted to, the works of such proto-Beats, semi-Beats, and post-Beats as Kathy Acker, Nelson Algren, Paul Bowles, Richard Brautigan, Charles Bukowski, William S. Burroughs Jr., Edward Dahlberg, J. P. Donleavey, Lawrence Durrell, John Fante, Richard Fariña, William Gaddis, Jan Kerouac, Norman Mailer, Henry Miller, John Rechy, Tom Robbins, Michael Rumaker, Hubert Selby Jr., Gilbert Sorrentino, Terry Southern, Robert Stone, Hunter S. Thompson, Alexander Trocchi, and Colin Wilson. Sarah Schulman's novel *Girls, Visions and Everything* (1986), in which a lesbian protagonist is in dialogue with Kerouac's Sal Paradise, is certainly a valuable work to be treated in a discussion of the Beat novel. Maxine Hong Kingston's *Tripmaster Monkey: His Fake Book* (1989), about a Beat named Wittman Ah Sing, based on the Beat playwright Frank Chin, can even be considered a Beat novel on some level. Though these authors will not be discussed here, some, if not all, deserve more attention within the purview of a longer treatment of the Beat novel. There are other novelists who belong more firmly in the category of Beat, and each has some connection to or owes at least some debt to the work of Kerouac. One of the major problems in establishing *who* is a "Beat" novelist is that each of the major Beat novelists, at one time or another, rejected the appellation "Beat" – including Jack Kerouac and William S. Burroughs. After all, "Beat," like any other literary classification, is foisted on artists by critics. What self-respecting outlaw novelist would want to be confined to any category? To make matters worse, the tag "Beat" has become a marketing tool, especially after the success of the Whitney Museum of American Art's exhibition "Beat Culture and the New America: 1950–1965" in 1996. The backs of novels are now covered with the word "Beat" in order to increase sales for authors who would have avoided such a distinction in the past as much as they would have recoiled from a smelly sandal or a garish beret. So what exactly is at stake in categorizing a novel as "Beat"?

As it has been since the first days in the garden of Plato's Akadēmeia, what is taught by scholars has the privilege of survival, albeit in some cases for an ephemeral survival. In an increasingly illiterate culture, the role of the scholar as caretaker and recoverer of the past has become even more important in literature classes. For most students, the only Beat novels they will ever see will be the ones assigned to them.

So let us begin by defining a Beat novel. There are at least three legitimate ways of approaching this highly contentious topic (and let it be acknowledged from the start that this fluid debate will necessarily be repeated ad nauseam, or in barroom joy, for however long there is interest in the Beat Generation). A Beat novel could be a novel about Beats, or a novel that shares aesthetic qualities recognized as Beat. Perhaps a Beat novel is simply a novel by an author generally acknowledged as Beat. In this case it would include novelists that had at least some intellectual dealings with Jack Kerouac, the only novelist everyone agrees is Beat. This group would include, but would not be limited to, William S. Burroughs, Gregory Corso, Lawrence Ferlinghetti, John Clellon Holmes, Joyce Johnson, and Michael McClure. Under this definition, every novel these authors wrote would be considered Beat. Thus it would include Corso's often neglected *The American Express* (1961), a surreal novel with characters based on Alan Ansen, William S. Burroughs, Jack Kerouac, and Peter Orlovsky. Michael Skau characterizes this daring novel as a portrayal and critique of "the ideals and tactics of exactly such a set of self-proclaimed saviors [as the Beats], providing parallels both to the dangers inherent in the approaches of the rebels and to the concerns of the Beats about how to use their talents to improve humanity."[2] But should the novels of Burroughs's Cut-Up Trilogy (*The Soft Machine* [1961, 1966, 1968], *The Ticket That Exploded* [1962, 1967], and *Nova Express* [1964]) – works of great complexity and cultural significance that have only recently started to be disclosed by the introductions written by Oliver Harris in 2013–14 – be categorized as Beat? And what of Burroughs's great Red Night Trilogy: *Cities of the Red Night* (1981), *The Place of Dead Roads* (1983), and *The Western Lands* (1987)? Are these works as equally "Beat" as *Junky* (1953), *Queer* (written 1951–53, published 1985), and *Naked Lunch* (1959)? And are Kerouac's so-called "Lowell novels" – *Visions of Gerard* (1963), *Doctor Sax* (1959), and *Maggie Cassidy* (1959) – not truly "Beat" novels? To what degree should scholars take into account the time period during which the novel was written or when it was published? The beginning and ending dates of the Beat Movement are contentious. Perhaps the Beat Movement started on October 1, 1944, when Allen Ginsberg started writing notes for the first Beat novella – the unpublished "The Bloodsong" (inspired by the Lucien Carr and Dave Kammerer affair), which can be found in *The Book of Martyrdom and Artifice: First Journals and Poems, 1937–1952* (2006). Ginsberg's novella, which he referred to as a "novel" in his journal, was a precursor to a work inspired by the same horrific events, written in 1945 and not published until 2008, called *And the Hippos Were Boiled in Their Tanks* and co-authored by Jack Kerouac and William S. Burroughs. As the bookend of the Beat Movement, which morphed into the hippie movement, maybe one could use January 14, 1967 – the Human Be-In in San Francisco with Lawrence Ferlinghetti, Allen Ginsberg, Lenore Kandel, Timothy Leary, Michael McClure, and Gary Snyder on the stage. Beat poet Ed Sanders claims that, before this "gathering of the tribes," the Beats were called "Beatniks," but after they were called "hippies."[3] The beginning and ending dates of the Beat Movement are amorphous, but are the novels written by Beats but published after the end of the movement, whichever date you arbitrarily choose, still Beat novels?

If we are going to say that a Beat novel is simply a novel written by a Beat author, then the first published Beat novel is Jack Kerouac's *The Town and the City* (1950), despite the debt it owes to Thomas Wolfe for its style and the fact that it is the most conventional, least experimental of Kerouac's books – to such a degree as to be seen as an anomaly in his oeuvre. John Clellon Holmes considered his own novel *Go* (1952) the first "Beat" novel because it was the first novel to focus entirely on characters based on Beats, and it used the phrase "beat generation." Yet *The Town and the City* has depictions of characters based on Burroughs, Carr, Ginsberg, and Herbert Huncke. It may not display a Beat aesthetic, but neither does the conventionally written *Go*. Steven Moore suggests that Chandler Brossard's *Who Walk in Darkness* (1952) might be the first Beat novel (or perhaps George Mandel's *Flee the Angry Strangers* [1952]), but Moore also calls *Who Walk in Darkness* "American literature's first existential novel."[4] Yet certainly some readers of Paul Bowles's *The Sheltering Sky* (1949) would argue that this proto-Beat novel is the first American existential novel. Brossard's book, like many Beat novels, is a first-person *roman à clef*, with characters based on Anatole Broyard, William Gaddis, and Stanley Gould. What it lacks, like Bowles's *The Sheltering Sky*, is the spirituality that characterizes and separates other Beat novels from the pack.

The Spiritual Outlaw Trope

The essential trope of the Beat novel is the outlaw undergoing a spiritual crisis. According to Nancy M. Grace, "At the forefront of [Kerouac's] thinking were always questions about the existence of God, the Creator's purpose for all forms of life, the concept of mind, the nature of sin, the existence of evil, a hostile/indifferent/benign cosmos, self and other, the definition and function of time, care and compassion, and salvation."[5] At the beginning of *On the Road*, Sal Paradise tells his readers, "Somewhere along the line I knew there'd be girls, visions, everything; somewhere along the line the pearl would be handed to me."[6] Grace calls *On the Road* "a narrative that is just as much about finding God as it is about finding freedom and America" (2–3). The spiritual quest pervades all of Kerouac's major novels. In the most stirring passage in *The Dharma Bums* (1958), Japhy Ryder prophesizes:

> see the whole thing is a world full of rucksack wanderers, Dharma Bums refusing to subscribe to the general demand that they consume production and therefore have to work for the privilege of consuming, all that crap they didn't really want anyway such as refrigerators, TV sets, cars, at least new fancy cars, certain hair oils and deodorants and general junk you finally always see a week later in the garbage anyway, all of them imprisoned in a system of work, produce, consume, work, produce, consume, I see a vision of a great rucksack revolution thousands or even millions of young Americans wandering around with rucksacks, going up to mountains to pray, making children laugh and old men glad, making young girls happy and old girls happier, all of 'em Zen Lunatics who go about writing poems that happen to appear in their heads for no reason and also by being kind and also by strange unexpected acts keep giving visions of eternal freedom to everybody and to all living creatures.[7]

Certainly there are exceptions, novels that some would call Beat that are not spiritually driven, such as Edward Dorn's *By the Sound* (1971), a materialist novel that is a straightforward call for social action in defense of marginalized, unskilled workers in Washington State who have been abandoned by their country and the unions. What Dorn's work has in common with most Beat novels is that it is autobiographical. Another anti-union Beat novel, Ken Kesey's *Sometimes a Great Notion* (1964), is arguably the greatest single novel to emerge from the Beat era. Kesey's *One Flew Over the Cuckoo's Nest* (1962), whose protagonist Randle Patrick McMurphy owes something to *On the Road*'s Dean Moriarty, is also a classic. Though based on some personal experiences, neither of Kesey's novels is an autobiographical *roman à clef*, though *Sometimes a Great Notion*'s protagonists, Hank and Leland, can be seen as two competing sides of Kesey's psyche. Though Kesey claims to have been influenced by Burroughs while writing *Sometimes a Great Notion*, the dozen points of view in the book owe more to William Faulkner.

The point of view in many Beat novels is first person, and these novels often take the form of a *roman à clef*. Kerouac was partially inspired to embrace this style of narrative after reading what we now know as William S. Burroughs's *Junky*. Thomas Newhouse describes what he calls the "underground narrative" – a liberation from the American spiritual wasteland – shared by Beat novels:

> What seemed to set the Beats – Ginsberg, Burroughs, and Kerouac – apart from their peers was a deep, disturbing alienation that transcended their identities as artists and extended to personal idiosyncrasy and a self-destructive bent. Such tendencies were captured in an intellectual fascination, perhaps even an identification, with outcasts and criminals. To be sure, their project was in large part an attempt to reveal, in the most intimate detail, the world of the outcast.[8]

What is crucial to remember is the spirituality in the outlaw narratives of the Beat novels, which is often overlooked due to the presence of sex, violence, and drug use. The biggest failure of Walter Salles's film adaptation of *On the Road* (2012) was its lack of spiritual yearning. Salles featured the speed, sex, and drug use of his characters, but completely missed their spiritual quest.

This quest can be found in Joyce Glassman's (later Johnson's) *Come Join the Dance* (1961), the first novel by a Beat woman. The main characters are based on Johnson and Elise Cowen, young women who have just dropped out of college, as they negotiate the spiritual wasteland of 1950s New York. Susan, the protagonist, has "begun to think like a criminal" and longs to join the community of "outlaws" forging the new bohemia.[9] When Susan decides to reject the traditional path set out for her and instead chooses to take on a new spiritual quest, she tells us, "The outlaws were about to welcome another member" (84). Once she has made her move into bohemia, Susan reflects, "But all the way down Broadway she had had the oddest feeling that when she walked into the Southwick Arms Hotel this time, she wouldn't ever leave; it would really be possible to rent a little room there, find some sort of job – better than going blindly, mean-inglessly to Paris. Instead she could enter the Outlaws' world" (111). As Ronna C. Johnson has recognized, "the novel's valorization of dropping out defines it as Beat."[10]

There are other neglected Beat novels worth mentioning in this con-text. Alan Harrington, who was the model for Hal Hingham in *On the Road*, published *The Secret Swinger* in 1966, dedicated to John Clellon Holmes, which included characters based on Bill Cannastra, Ginsberg, Holmes, and Kerouac. The novel focuses on George Pectin's midlife cri-sis as he searches to reconnect with the spiritual freedom of his lost Beat days. Irving Rosenthal, who had edited the *Chicago Review*, a position he resigned in the face of censorship concerning Beat material in the journal, went on to create the literary review *Big Table*, named by Kerouac, which published material the University of Chicago found offensive. Rosenthal's novel–memoir hybrid *Sheeper* (1967) includes characters based on Burroughs, Cowen, Huncke, and Trocchi. It is about a homosexual try-ing to negotiate a spiritual identity within a heterosexual Beat milieu. Leo Skir's *Boychick* (1971), another neglected work, has characters based on Cowen, Ginsberg, Orlovsky, and Janine Pommy Vega, and depicts the vul-nerability of a male homosexual even within the confines of the homo-sexual environment that had been built in New York City. Both *Sheeper* and *Boychick*, like Johnson's *Come Join the Dance*, deal with the com-plex interplay between sexuality and individual enlightenment. Michael McClure's *Bildungsroman* of heterosexual sex-cum-enlightenment, *The Mad Cub* (1970), claims to have been written in a "spontaneous bop" style reminiscent of Kerouac's. McClure's persona exclaims, "What does matter are the truly religious feelings and visions and the knowledge that life is a spiritual chase in the mystic sense – a grail-search for honesty and beauty."[11] McClure, who was the model for Pat McLear in Kerouac's *Big Sur* (1962), also wrote the psychedelic thriller *The Adept* (1971). Both *The Mad Cub* and *The Adept* are first-person narratives whose protagonist is based on the author himself depicted as an outlaw dealing with a spiritual crisis. The protagonist of *The Adept* separates his Beat outlaw identity from the revolutionary:

> I despise the radical and social Left which would poison me and put me in a prison of Society – leaving me no pleasures but those of happy work, and mar-riage, and perhaps finally automation so that there would be nothing for me to do but watch state-owned television and pursue crafts and cultural events until the utopia breaks up in sheer boredom and one man commits hari kiri upon another with the boredom of existence.[12]

The way toward enlightenment for the Beat novelist is not through new politics but through new aesthetics.

"But It Ain't Whatcha Write, It's the Way Atcha Write It"

There is a discernible Beat aesthetic – a way of writing, a rhythm, influenced by jazz – that can be found in the works of several Beat novelists and that links their works in an artistic manner in ways that go well beyond the content, themes, and characters these novels share. In his seminal study *Naked Angels* (1976), John Tytell rearranges a prose passage from Kerouac's *Visions of Cody* to emphasize the use of rhythmic anaphora and the catalog, which highlights the debt Ginsberg owed to Kerouac as such features are prominent in "Howl."[13] I would like to reverse this process and add a passage from Burroughs's *Naked Lunch* to make my point about a shared aesthetic sensibility of rhythm. Here is the passage by Kerouac:

> I've pressed up girls in Asheville saloons, danced with them in roadhouses where mad heroes stomp one another to death in tragic driveways by the moon: I've laid whores on the strip of grass runs along a cornfield outside Durham, North Carolina, and applied bay rum in the highway lights; I've thrown empty whiskeybottles clear over the trees in Maryland copses on soft nights when Roosevelt was President; I've knocked down fifths in trans-state trucks as the Wyo. road unreeled; I've jammed home shots of whiskey on Sixth Avenue, in Frisco, in the Londons of the prime, in Florida, in L.A. I've made soup my chaser in forty-seven states; I've passed off the back of cabooses, Mexican buses and bows of ships in midwinter tempests (piss to you); I've laid woman on coalpiles, in the snow, on fences, in beds and up against suburban garage walls from Massachusetts to the tip of San Joaquin. Cody me no Codys about America, I've drunk with his brother in a thousand bars, I've had hangovers with old sewing machine whores that were twice his mother twelve years ago when his heart was dewy. I learned how to smoke cigars in madhouses; and hopped boxcars in NOrleans; I've driven on Sunday afternoon across the lemon fields with Indians and their sisters; and I sat at the inauguration of. Tennessee me no Tennessees, Memphis; aim me no Montanas, Three Forks; I'll still sock me a North Atlantic Territory in the free. That's how I feel. I've heard guitars tinkling sadly across hillbilly hollows in the mist of the Great Smokies of night long ago.[14]

Here is part of "Howl" transformed into prose:

> who loned it through street of Idaho seeking visionary indian angels who were visionary indian angels, who thought they were only mad when Baltimore gleamed in supernatural ecstasy, who jumped in limousines with the Chinaman of Oklahoma on the impulse of winter midnight streetlight smalltown rain,

who lounged hungry and lonesome through Houston seeking jazz or sex or soup, and followed the brilliant Spaniard to converse about America and Eternity, a hopeless task, and so took ship to Africa.[15]

Now a passage from Burroughs's *Naked Lunch*:

Followers of obsolete unthinkable trades, doodling in Etruscan, addicts of drugs not yet synthesized, black marketeers of World War III, excisors of telepathic sensitivity, osteopaths of the spirit, investigators of infractions denounced by bland paranoid chess players, servers of fragmentary warrants taken down in hebephrenic shorthand charging unspeakable mutilations of the spirit, officials of unconstituted police states, brokers of exquisite dreams and nostalgias tested on the sensitized cells of junk sickness and bartered for raw materials of the will, drinkers of the Heavy Fluid sealed in translucent amber of dreams.[16]

This passage is so reminiscent of Ginsberg's poetry that it was recited by the Ginsberg character in David Cronenberg's 1991 film *Naked Lunch*.

Even in John Clellon Holmes's novel *The Horn*, dedicated to and admired by Kerouac, can be found traces of the Kerouac sound:

And so he fled down the Great Brown Snake that made the entire continent one vast watershed to it, and that from deepest, woodsy north at its trickling beginnings over smooth Canadian pebbles, to its final, timeless spending in the Gulf, drained out of the heart of America, melling Pittsburgh slag from the Monongahela with dust that blew across the faceless Badlands to the Milk, gathering as the rivers, tributary to it, met (the Platte, the Kansas, the Missouri; the Minnesota, the Chippewa, the Illinois; the Little Sandy, the Cumberland, and the Ohio) to flow, terrific, widening and assuageless, ever south, where still others emptied into it (the White, the Big Black, and the Red), until in huge, instinctive death beyond the last bayous, it joined the other waters of the world.[17]

According to Cynthia S. Hamilton:

The Horn is Holmes' most original and most significant experiment with the novel form. It is a jazz novel not just because jazz musicians are the protagonists and the jazz scene its setting, nor because it deals with the development of jazz, but because it is built from the formal structures of jazz, the riff and the chorus. The riff sections provide the underlying structure, giving the novel continuity ... The chorus sections contain the reactions, reminiscences, and feelings of musicians.[18]

The Horn has characters based on Thelonious Monk, Billie Holiday, Dizzy Gillespie, Lester Young, Charlie Parker, Holmes, and Kerouac. The jazz musicians are also infused with the spirits of Emily Dickinson, Herman

Melville, Edgar Allan Poe, Mark Twain, and Walt Whitman. The jazz into-
nations of the prose show that Holmes and Kerouac shared a similar sound
they both derived from the bebop clubs of New York. This jazz sound can
also be heard in Ferlinghetti's *Her* (1960) as he imagines the great takeover
of the denizens of the Beat Hotel in Paris:

> a wailing wild ragged band of American poets from the Rue Git-le-Coeur
> rushed out of a side street into the middle of the boulevard and fell into the
> winding line, jumping onto the shoulders of the dancers and hanging onto
> the necks of the women, singing and shouting that the Poetry Police were
> coming to save them, the Poetry Police were coming to save them all from
> death, Captain Poetry was coming to save the world from itself, to make the
> world safe for beauty and love, the Poetry Police had arrived to clean up the
> mass mess, the Poetry Police were about to descend in parachutes made from
> the pages of obscene dictionaries, the Poetry Police were about to land simul-
> taneously in the central squares of forty-two major cities, having chartered
> all the planes in the world and being furnished with free seats for an endless
> passage since all were *poids net*, the Poetry Police were about to land on the
> tops of the tallest buildings and bridges and monuments and fortifications
> of the world and take complete command of the rapidly deteriorating world
> situation, the Poetry Police were about to invade Geneva and decide once
> and for all what the shape of the table should be at all future peace confer-
> ences, the Poetry Police were about to consolidate their positions simulta-
> neously in all parts of the world by climbing onto the backs and hanging
> onto the necks of everyone and shouting true profound wiggy formulas for
> eternal mad salvation, the Poetry Police were about to capture all libraries,
> newspapers, printing presses, and automats, and force their proprietors at
> pen's point to print nothing henceforth but headlines of pure poetry.[19]

Just as Picasso and Braque independently studied Cézanne yet found their
canvases reflecting one another, so did Kerouac and Ferlinghetti study the
bebop night and have it reflected in their prose (for more on the specific
ways Beat writers used jazz idioms in their writing, see Chapter 17).

The Duluoz Legend

Jack Kerouac's "The Duluoz Legend" is the crowning achievement of Beat
fiction because of its sustained depiction of an outlaw artist's life in the
midst of a series of spiritual crises for seven novels and its development
of a new form of writing – spontaneous prose – a style partially inspired
by the letters Kerouac received from Neal Cassady. Some scholars, such
as Nancy M. Grace, in her groundbreaking work *Jack Kerouac and the
Literary Imagination* (2007), recognize the Duluoz Legend as the corpus of
Kerouac's work. "The Duluoz Legend," as it is being discussed here, consists

of the seven novels in which Kerouac's protagonist is named Jack Duluoz. There is little agreement about what constitutes "The Duluoz Legend" proper, even among the most genial Beat scholars, but here is a rationale to add to the mix. Kerouac himself obfuscated the structure of his masterpiece when he wrote as a note to *Big Sur*:

> My work comprises one vast book like Proust's except that my remembrances are written on the run instead of afterwards in a sick bed. Because of the objections of my early publishers I was not allowed to use the same personae names in each work. *On the Road, The Subterraneans, The Dharma Bums, Doctor Sax, Maggie Cassidy, Tristessa, Desolation Angels, Visions of Cody* and the others including this book *Big Sur* are just chapters in the whole work which I call *The Duluoz Legend*. In my old age I intend to collect all my work and re-insert my pantheon of uniform names, leave the long shelf full of books there, and die happy. The whole thing forms one enormous comedy, seen through the eyes of poor Ti Jean (me), otherwise known as Jack Duluoz, the world of raging action and folly and also of gentle sweetness seen through the keyhole of his eye.[20]

A reestablishment of which works make up "The Duluoz Legend" proper is crucial to an appreciation of Kerouac's work.

The suggestion put forward by some to reinstate the "real" names on which Kerouac's characters were based is fundamentally at odds with the fact that "The Duluoz Legend" is a work of fiction, not autobiography. Without question *On the Road* is the most read and appreciated work of the Beat Generation. Yet *On the Road* should be removed from "The Duluoz Legend," not only because its protagonist is named Sal Paradise and because Kerouac viewed *Visions of Cody* as the novel he intended to supersede *On the Road* but also because, more importantly, as Tim Hunt astutely explains in his excellent *Kerouac's Crooked Road: The Development of a Fiction* (1981), it is not a work of spontaneous prose: "*On the Road*, in spite of its very substantial achievement, is Kerouac's last apprentice work. *Visions of Cody* is his first mature text and the paradigmatic text for his career."[21] In 1959, Warren Tallman accurately viewed *The Subterraneans* as one of Kerouac's most important novels, yet Warren French argues, based on the facts that the protagonist is symbolically named Leo Percepied and that Kerouac was pressured to change the setting of the novel from New York to San Francisco, that "it would take very extensive revision to fit this nearly hysterical tale into the [Duluoz Legend]."[22] *The Dharma Bums*, Kerouac's second most popular novel and perhaps his work with the greatest cultural impact for its creation of a rucksack revolution, also should not be placed within "The Duluoz Legend," not only because its protagonist is named Ray Smith and because Kerouac was pressured into producing this work (his most conventional novel since *The Town and the City*) for commercial reasons but also and more specifically because it, too, is not an experimental work of spontaneous prose. The same can be said of *Vanity of Duluoz* (1968), which is not part of Kerouac's spontaneous prose project and which, despite the interesting autobiographical information it provides, was written in an effort to secure money for his family after he had largely burned out as a writer. It also, despite the title of the book, refers to the protagonist at times as "Jack Kerouac"; it is the closest Kerouac would come to writing a straightforward autobiography.

"The Duluoz Legend" proper therefore consists of *Doctor Sax* (1959), *Maggie Cassidy* (1959), *Tristessa* (1960), *Big Sur* (1962), *Visions of Gerard* (1963), *Desolation Angels* (1965), and *Visions of Cody* (1973). Some scholars approach these works in the chronological order of Kerouac's life: *Visions of Gerard, Doctor Sax, Maggie Cassidy, Visions of Cody, Tristessa, Desolation Angels,* and *Big Sur*. Both Edward Halsey Foster in *Understanding the Beats* (1992) and Matt Theado in *Understanding Jack Kerouac* (2000) suggest that a more fruitful examination of the texts could be had by examining them in the order of their composition: *Visions of Cody* (1951–52), *Doctor Sax* (1952), *Maggie Cassidy* (1953), *Tristessa* (1955–56), *Visions of Gerard* (1956), *Desolation Angels* (1956, 1961), and *Big Sur* (1961).

Tim Hunt, in the groundbreaking *The Textuality of Soulwork: Jack Kerouac's Quest for Spontaneous Prose* (2014), has begun the serious work of analyzing the various aspects of Kerouac's spontaneous prose, which is a new practice of language as speaking, both verbally and in the mind, not to be confused with undisciplined "spontaneity" or the craftsmanship of manufactured stream-of-consciousness:

> [Kerouac] was probing the nature of language and the nature of writing as a mode of language, and therefore, as well, interrogating the nature and dynamics of textuality. Moreover, his desire to recuperate the dynamics of speech and speaking and enact them within the process of writing – to reimagine writing in the image of speaking – needs to be recognized as nothing less than an attempt to subvert his era's paradigm for textuality and reinvent the category of literature as an expression of what might be termed secondary literacy.[23]

Visions of Cody is the first successful attempt at the "wild form" experiment known as spontaneous prose. Kerouac's next successful experimental effort, *Doctor Sax*, as Grace says, "is a tour de force of language and genre – rich religious symbolism, camera shots, poetry, myths, parodies, and, as Gerald Nicosia observes, 'a mixture of modern American idioms, traditional Yankeeisms, and Shakespearean grandiloquence, of neologisms and puns'" (101). Oliver Harris reminds us:

That Kerouac wrote *Sax* during his two-month stay with Burroughs is well known, but what's been overlooked is the profound and precise influence the writers had on each other during this crucial period in their careers, Kerouac's novel reveals multiple traces – in theme, allusion, and specific phrasings – of his reading of Burroughs' manuscript [*Queer*]. Burroughs, for his part, reported to Ginsberg in mid-May that Kerouac "has developed unbelievably," and while it's unclear whether Burroughs read any of *Doctor Sax*, we do know that he had been reading, and was "very much impressed by," the just-finished manuscript Kerouac brought with him to Mexico: *Visions of Cody*.[24]

Though not as adventurous as *Visions of Cody* or *Doctor Sax*, *Maggie Cassidy*, as Matt Theado observes, is a book that takes a look back at Duluoz trading "his track star hero and local good-boy status for the world of gritty, beat reality."[25] Michael McClure has often cited *Tristessa*, the next work of wild form, which also focuses on a woman, as Kerouac's most moving piece of mystical writing. *Visions of Gerard*, a return to Kerouac's earliest memories, influenced by amphetamine and the spirit of Shakespeare, with its reliance on stories not his own, is according to Theado "the most 'fictional' or 'creative' book in the Duluoz Legend" (135). Kerouac's next work would be another major triumph; Dan Wakefield, reviewing the book for *The Atlantic*, wrote, "If the Pulitzer Prize in fiction were given for the book that is most representative of American life, I would nominate *Desolation Angels*."[26] From there "The Duluoz Legend" ends with the alcoholic collapse and harrowing spiritual struggle of its protagonist. Theado accurately states, "In *Big Sur* Kerouac probes deeper and more dangerous depths than in previous work" (170). A broken Duluoz releases his Buddhist aspirations and finds respite in the womb of Christianity (see Chapter 16).

All other Beat novels must be evaluated beside these novels of "The Duluoz Legend" in terms of experimental composition and spiritual disclosure. The varying degrees to which other writers followed or rejected Kerouac's breakthroughs will need a new appraisal. The place of the Beat novel in the canon of twentieth-century American literature will only be accurately assessed if Kerouac's challenge of developing a new kind of spiritual communication is accurately gauged within his own terms. The Beat novel will not survive the winds of time based on its often sordid content but on its innovative style. As Kerouac put it, "But it ain't whatcha write, it's the way atcha write it."[27]

NOTES

1 Kurt Hemmer, "The Beats," *A History of California Literature*, ed. Blake Allmendinger (New York: Cambridge University Press, 2015), 244.
2 Michael Skau, *"A Clown in a Grave": Complexities and Tensions in the Works of Gregory Corso* (Carbondale: Southern Illinois University Press, 1999), 50.
3 Chuck Workman, dir. *The Source* (Calliope, 2000).

4 Steven Moore, "Foreword," Chandler Brossard, *Who Walk in Darkness* (1952; New York: Herodias, 2000), vi.

5 Nancy M. Grace, *Jack Kerouac and the Literary Imagination* (New York: Palgrave Macmillan, 2007), 2.

6 Jack Kerouac, *On the Road* (1957; New York: Penguin, 1991), 8.

7 Jack Kerouac, *The Dharma Bums* (1958; New York: Penguin, 2006), 73–74.

8 Thomas Newhouse, *The Beat Generation and the Popular Novel in the United States, 1945–1970* (Jefferson, NC: McFarland, 2000), 3.

9 Joyce Johnson (writing as Joyce Glassman), *Come Join the Dance* (1961; New York: Open Road, 2014), 63–64.

10 Ronna C. Johnson, "'And Then She Went': Beat Departures and Feminine Transgressions in Joyce Johnson's *Come and Join the Dance*," *Girls Who Wore Black: Women Writing the Beat Generation*, ed. Johnson and Nancy M. Grace (New Brunswick, NJ: Rutgers University Press, 2002), 77.

11 Michael McClure, *The Mad Cub* (1970; New York: Blue Moon Books, 1995), 172.

12 Michael McClure, *The Adept* (New York: Delacorte Press, 1971), 8.

13 John Tytell, *Naked Angels: Kerouac, Ginsberg, Burroughs* (New York: Grove Weidenfeld, 1991), 216–17.

14 Jack Kerouac, *Visions of Cody* (New York: Penguin, 1993), 367.

15 Allen Ginsberg, "Howl," *Howl and Other Poems* (San Francisco: City Lights, 1993), 11–12.

16 William S. Burroughs, *Naked Lunch: The Restored Text*, ed. James Grauerholz and Barry Miles (New York: Grove, 2001), 45–46.

17 John Clellon Holmes, *The Horn* (1958; New York: Thunder's Mouth Press, 1988), 41–42.

18 Cynthia S. Hamilton, "The Prisoner of Self: The Work of John Clellon Holmes," *The Beat Generation Writers*, ed. A. Robert Lee (East Haven, CT: Pluto Press, 1996), 123.

19 Lawrence Ferlinghetti, *Her* (New York: New Directions, 1960), 42–44.

20 Jack Kerouac, *Big Sur* (New York: Penguin, 1992), iii.

21 Tim Hunt, *Kerouac's Crooked Road: The Development of a Fiction* (1981; Berkeley: University of California Press, 2010), lix.

22 Warren French, *Jack Kerouac: Novelist of the Beat Generation* (Boston: Twayne, 1986), 46.

23 Tim Hunt, *The Textuality of Soulwork: Jack Kerouac's Quest for Spontaneous Prose* (Ann Arbor: University of Michigan Press, 2014), 10.

24 Oliver Harris, "Introduction," William S. Burroughs, *Queer: 25th Anniversary Edition*, ed. Harris (New York: Penguin, 2010), xviii–xix.

25 Matt Theado, *Understanding Jack Kerouac* (Columbia: University of South Carolina Press, 2000), 110.

26 Wakefield quoted in Dennis McNally, *Desolate Angel: Jack Kerouac, the Beat Generation, and America* (Cambridge, MA: Da Capo Press, 2003), 317.

27 Jack Kerouac, "Are Writers Made or Born?" *The Portable Jack Kerouac*, ed. Ann Charters (New York: Viking, 1995), 490.

8

OLIVER HARRIS

William S. Burroughs
Beating Postmodernism

"Something Out of an Old Evil Dream"

When elected to the American Academy and Institute of Arts and Letters in May 1983, William Burroughs responded to the honor with defiant indifference: "Twenty years ago they were saying I belonged in jail. Now they're saying I belong in their club. I didn't listen to them then, and I don't listen to them now."[1] This is typical Burroughs: refusing to accept the official version – what "they" say – and turning it upside down by equating apparent opposites. When is a prestigious club a kind of jail? When being a member gives the impression of being known and therefore safe. If the American Academy is such a club, then so too are the canons of literature and such classifications as "Beat" or "Postmodern" – and even books such as *The Cambridge Companion to the Beats*.

The "they" who said Burroughs belonged in jail also attacked the other Beat writers from the late 1950s onwards, and it is hard to overstate the media vilification and misrepresentation they endured. Such negative coverage ironically helped to promote the Beats, intriguing a young generation of Americans not seduced by television sitcoms and home appliances. But, while Kerouac and Ginsberg were mocked and patronized in the media and likewise marginalized for years by the critical academy, Burroughs was always singled out for special treatment: "For sheer horror no member of the Beat Generation has achieved effects to compare with William S. Burroughs," declared a major feature on the Beats for *Life* magazine in 1959, noting the "hideous preoccupation with man's lowest appetites" in his recently published *Naked Lunch* and describing its author as "cadaverous," as if barely living, hardly human.[2] Burroughs' first public image as a writer, this tabloid typecasting of the man and his work as beyond the pale would never go away. Who is William Burroughs? Not a "Beat writer" nor a "postmodern artist" but a homosexual heroin addict who shot his wife and wrote obscene books with a pair of scissors. Such a mockery stands in the way of recognizing one of the most influential, visionary, and original oeuvres of modern times.

In the 1980s, Burroughs saw official acceptance on the horizon and rightly mistrusted it, but he was wrong about it then and remains so in the twenty-first century. For his place in the canon is still highly equivocal: acclaimed by some, overlooked by many more. Cultural conservatives continue to trash and traduce Burroughs, such as the reviewer for *The New Criterion*, who in 2006 saw his work "as a case history of psychopathology" and therefore not "worthy of serious consideration."[3] Such extreme hostility to Burroughs is a good measure of his enduring influence, which has made him the patron saint of new creative generations and genres from punk to cyberpunk and mashup video, and has quite literally inspired an A to Z of radical writers, artists, musicians, and filmmakers from Kathy Acker to John Zorn and back again, from Frank Zappa to Laurie Anderson. Burroughs' cultural reach is unique and turns up in unsuspected places, so that anyone who has heard "Lust for Life" knows, whether they know it or not, bits of *The Ticket That Exploded* (1967), one of Burroughs' cut-up novels that Iggy Pop and David Bowie cut up to make the lyrics of the song. On the one hand, the extent of Burroughs' cultural presence makes nonsense of the label "Beat writer," which would limit his relevance, historically fixing him in the postwar era. On the other hand, to call him a postmodernist might make Burroughs more our contemporary only at the price of enrolling him in an equally unsuitable club.

Before considering the merits and effects of preferring one label over another, we should recognize the most ironic point of intersection between the Beat Burroughs and the postmodern Burroughs: his mythologization as a Beat. For the creation of Burroughs as an iconic figure could be said to inaugurate the postmodern world of mediated realities, celebrities, and free-floating signs, the society of the spectacle and simulacra. To borrow one of his own key terms, Burroughs went "viral" as copies of his image began to replicate independently in the culture. The Beats were the first generation of writers to emerge through the modern mass media, and Kerouac appeared on television the same month that *Life* poured scorn on them all, November 1959; but the projection of Burroughs was always different. To begin with, he had an image whose attraction was almost the opposite to that of Kerouac – cold, sinister, and dangerous rather than soulful and rebellious – so that it appealed to quite different people. Just as importantly, the Burroughsian identity was created and circulated in unique ways.

The sensationalized image of Burroughs distributed by the mass media only spread more widely the shadowy, legendary figure already fabricated by his fellow Beats. Before readers had a chance to encounter Burroughs' *Naked Lunch* in 1959, they knew from Ginsberg's dedication to "Howl" (1956) that it was "an endless novel which will drive everybody mad" and from Kerouac's *On the Road* (1957) that Burroughs, thinly fictionalized as "old Bull Lee," radiated "phenomenal fires and mysteries" like "something out of an old evil dream."[4] Such fantasy visions became lenses for reading *Naked Lunch* or – since the book is a challenge for most readers – replaced the need to read it at all. This ironic triumph of the image was always one of Burroughs' central subjects and it made *Naked Lunch* the first plausibly postmodern novel. And so, when Brian Nicol asserts in his *Cambridge Introduction to Postmodern Fiction* that "Burroughs is significant to postmodernism not just as a literary influence but as an iconic cultural figure," he implicitly backdates postmodernity to the iconographic images of Burroughs projected by his fellow Beats.[5]

Does this make Burroughs the first postmodernist or a postmodern Beat? No answer can resolve the problem of definition. "Beat" was a loose term, an adjective rather than a noun, so that, even if it least fitted Burroughs, in a sense none of the Beat writers were Beat. As for "postmodern," it is probably the most contested term in cultural history. But, broadly speaking, the labels denote incompatible if not mutually exclusive realities. Historically, "Beat" corresponds to the America of the 1940s and 1950s, when the major authors first met and then published their most famous works. In contrast, "postmodernism" is usually dated from the 1960s and is identified far more globally as the cultural logic of late capitalism (to use Fredric Jameson's terms).[6] Aesthetically, the labels likewise seem to be worlds apart: whereas "Beat" is shorthand for relatively straightforward, autobiographically based writing that resists social authority, "postmodern" is shorthand for complex, language-based fiction that questions its own status as literature and mirrors back a fragmented, relativistic world. Put in such reductive terms, Burroughs is too Beat to be postmodern (too autobiographical, too political) and too postmodern to be Beat (too complex, too experimental).

The result of thinking through these labels is to make clear why the binaries they produce exist but do not hold, why they are more apparent than real. For example, there were direct points of contact and inspiration between Beats and postmodernists: Burroughs and William Gaddis knew and admired one another's work; Thomas Pynchon acknowledged his debts to Kerouac. Above all, there was a strong experimental strain in Beat writing that was hidden by the very level of popular success that particular works achieved. This is the case with Ginsberg's "Howl," whose fame as a generational "protest poem" eclipsed the sophisticated and rigorous poetics that informed it. Likewise, Kerouac's *On the Road* was destined to totally overshadow its aesthetically more challenging sequel, which went unpublished for two decades, *Visions of Cody* (1972). Perceptions are slow to change, but scholars like Tim Hunt have demonstrated that both novels are advanced experiments in literary form,[7] and Kerouac's work was indeed, in Robert Holton's phrase, "on the road to the postmodern."[8] Then again, as we will see, Burroughs's extreme experimentalism does not necessarily make him a postmodernist, any more than his role in the Beat Generation makes him a Beat.

"Jesus Christ, Get Him Out of Here"

Burroughs appears absolutely central to Beat history, one of its three major literary figures, who mentored the other two in New York during the mid-1940s, giving Kerouac and Ginsberg esoteric reading lists and subversive direction to their desires as fledgling writers. The same facts can support an entirely different reading, however, one where Burroughs is not central but marginal. He played the role of mentor because he came from *another* generation, being a decade older than Ginsberg and Kerouac, and was equally set apart by his class background, which connected him on both sides of his family to institutions in American business and public relations. He didn't *look* like a Beat, and when, in 1944, he first turned up in his Chesterfield overcoat and snap-brim fedora to sell a sawed-off shotgun and some morphine, Herbert Huncke thought Burroughs must be the FBI: "Jesus Christ, get him out of here, man. This guy is heat."[9] The irony is that, as a gay man and a drug user, Burroughs was doubly criminalized, and by the end of the decade he had to get himself out of America, to begin twenty-five years as a writer-in-exile. While the Beat Generation spread from East Coast to West throughout the 1950s, Burroughs was living and writing thousands of miles away in Latin and Central America, North Africa, and Europe. He then spent the 1960s in Paris and London developing the Cut-Up Project, a radical multimedia experiment with collage-based methods (of which more below) that was as far removed aesthetically and politically from the Beat scene as it was geographically.

By the time he returned to New York in the mid-1970s, to be received as a counterculture hero by a new generation of post-Beat artists and writers from Patti Smith to Anne Waldman, Burroughs had created an oeuvre and established a reputation that existed quite independently of Beat history. To be sure, his name was essential to the academic field of Beat Studies that began to emerge at this time, but this reveals less about his work than about the politics of canon formation, which needed Burroughs to form with Ginsberg and Kerouac a Beat Holy Trinity. Since the 1990s, as the "major authors" approach declined and new critical agendas massively expanded the Beat field in terms of race and gender, the centrality of Burroughs has no longer been necessary or even seemed so desirable. A similar situation applies within Burroughs criticism: most studies have followed the example of Robin Lydenberg's *Word Cultures* (1987), which did not even mention Kerouac and related Burroughs's experimental work to critical theory and by association postmodernism, rather than that of Jennie Skerl's *William S. Burroughs* (1985), for which "Burroughs's aesthetic – the Beat aesthetic – is one that defines art as consciousness."[10] Just as Beat Studies no longer needs Burroughs to firm up its legitimacy, so too Burroughs' reputation is such that his scholars can now ignore a field of dubious relevance. It is only in the more general cultural and biopic narratives, which continue to inform the way both are popularly understood, that Burroughs and the Beats still belong inseparably together, as in films based on their lives and works such as *Naked Lunch* (1991), *On the Road* (2012), and *Kill Your Darlings* (2013).

If Burroughs seems to exist in parallel universes as a Beat – now central, now marginal – so does he as a postmodernist. Again, this curious position has much to do with the politics of canon formation. Most Burroughs critics recognize the relevance of postmodernism as a context, but many have distanced him in one way or another: from Jamie Russell, who sees Burroughs as "a writer whose inherent essentialism has always made him a poor postmodernist at the best of times" to Timothy Murphy, who theorized "Amodernism" in order to separate Burroughs from the self-reflexive language experiments of postmodernism and better argue for his work's political power.[11] As for the critical field of postmodernism itself, Burroughs was named in the second paragraph of one of its founding texts, Jameson's "Postmodernism, or The Cultural Logic of Late Capitalism" (1984); however, appearing alongside Thomas Pynchon and Ishmael Reed may have been less recognition of Burroughs than a sign of how few major writers could then be labeled postmodern. Once postmodernism began to flourish, with very few exceptions critics and theorists mainly name-checked Burroughs or avoided him.[12] The indifference, and even outright hostility, of much postmodern criticism toward Burroughs accounts for the prevalence of barely credible thumbnail sketches in many introductions to the field: "This rigmarole," declares one of them, when describing Burroughs' cut-up methods, "has prompted skeptical critics to make unflattering comparisons between Burroughs and monkeys with typewriters."[13] It is as though Burroughs remains trapped in the early 1960s, when *Time* magazine mocked his cut-up novels as "utter babble" in a review so malicious that he was forced to sue.[14] We are left to wonder why, in the twenty-first century, so many critics still fail to take seriously Burroughs' experiments with collage – the central aesthetic of postmodernism – and prefer to exclude or ridicule him, as if to say, "Jesus Christ, get him out of here!"

"A Good Bedside Manner"

If we turn from the popular and critical reception of Burroughs to his actual work, at first it looks surprisingly simple to divide his oeuvre into decades and map these along a Beat–postmodern axis. Everything in the 1950s seems to bear the Beat stamp: from his debut novels, *Junky* (1953) and *Queer* (1985; but written in 1952), and *The Yage Letters*, which he co-authored with Ginsberg (1963; but partly published in the mid-1950s), up to *Naked Lunch*, whose title Burroughs credited to Kerouac in the book's de facto introduction. The first works have always been seen as by far Burroughs' most conventionally realist and autobiographical narratives, while *Naked Lunch* is hailed as the third of the three great Beat works, after "Howl" and *On the Road*. What followed, the Cut-Up Project of the 1960s, separates Burroughs from Beat literature and brings him closer to postmodernism, as does later work such as his final trilogy of novels concluding with *The Western Lands* (1989), which has been described as "an exemplary text of postmodern subversion."[15] However, there is both more and less to Burroughs' Beat decade than first appears.

Certainly, the 1950s was the one period when Burroughs' personal and creative relationships with Ginsberg and Kerouac were of material textual importance, and to the above sketch we can add that Ginsberg played a vital role promoting Burroughs' writing, serving as his amateur agent by tirelessly lobbying magazine editors and publishing houses. Ginsberg was also actively involved in editing Burroughs' manuscripts, most famously in Tangier in 1957 along with Kerouac and others, helping to turn his fragments into "Interzone," a first draft of *Naked Lunch*. Above all, Burroughs' dependence on Ginsberg had been essential to his writing after he moved to Tangier in 1954. Four thousand miles away, Burroughs invested desire and dark creative energy in an intense long-distance epistolary relationship with Ginsberg that, as I have shown elsewhere, generated many of the comic-grotesque routines that give *Naked Lunch* its mosaic structure and the corrosive force of its political critique.[16] But do such material connections make the resulting work "Beat"? Where are the hallmarks of Beat literature in Burroughs' writing of the 1950s?

Junky is often read as one of the first Beat books because of its assumed basis in autobiography. And yet, on this very ground, Burroughs' debut novel actually stands apart. Its minimal plot does derive from the facts of Burroughs's experience, which is what makes the first-person narration of William Lee an authentic first-hand piece of reportage, documenting the addict's view of how early postwar America looked behind the billboards. But to read Lee's narrative as a *roman à clef* only draws attention to the conspicuous exclusion of scenes involving versions of Kerouac or Ginsberg in a narrative that begins in New York in the mid-1940s, the precise time and place the three met and formed the original Beat circle. In striking contrast, Kerouac and Ginsberg consistently mythologized both Burroughs and each other in their work as a commitment to narrowing the gap between art and life. Likewise, if there is a Beat aesthetic of spontaneity that embodies a utopian desire for self-expression and spiritual community, it is not there in the cold, solitary, and grimly affectless world of *Junky*.

Queer and *The Yage Letters* (specifically the "In Search of Yage" section dated 1953) were again drawn from Burroughs' immediate experience, but the dramatic change in writing style and persona signal the dangers of reading this early trilogy as autobiography. In *Junky*, William Lee is an ironically deadpan narrator, slyly trapping the reader into taking his advice about how to become a heroin addict: "You need a good bedside manner with doctors or you will get nowhere."[17] In *Queer* and *The Yage Letters*, both set in Central and Latin America, Lee transforms into a manic, monstrous character who takes on the burden of his national identity to perform the role of the Ugly American. Lee therefore becomes the vehicle for an entirely different type of political critique: as an American abroad, he exercises a fascistic racism and colonialist elitism that invert his own demonized status as a homosexual at home. The result of baring the contradictions in American national identity seems designed to insult and alienate the reader, whose discomfort in *The Yage Letters* is only increased by uncertainty about the status of the text: is Lee a satirical fictional character or is this Burroughs' own voice? The epistolary form invites us to take the 1953 letters at face value, but they are signed five different ways (Bill, William, Willy Lee, W. Lee, William Lee), hinting at both the confusion of and gap between the author and his persona. That appearances are deceptive is confirmed by the complex manuscript backstory, which reveals how carefully Burroughs fabricated its epistolary structure out of notes and real letters. For Burroughs, the safety of "fiction" lets the reader off too lightly, and we begin to see how disturbingly his work undercuts the expectations we bring to literature.

To speak of the "manuscript backstory" to Burroughs' early writing might seem a secondary issue, a digression, but it actually brings to the foreground one of the unique features of all his work: its extreme *materiality*, from a physical manipulation of text to its dependence on contingency and collaboration. While these factors long went unnoticed in his early writing, in the case of *Naked Lunch*, a mythologized version of its materiality is only too well known: after the novel was assembled by Kerouac and Ginsberg from notes written while Burroughs was out of his mind on drugs, "the shape of the rat-gnawed typescript of *The Naked Lunch* was determined by the random order in which its sections happened to fall into place as the final draft went to the printer" (*Introduction to Postmodern Fiction* 66). Such glibly inaccurate accounts focus attention in the right place – the agency of factors other than the author's intentions – but only to trivialize the important point: Burroughs embraced contingencies as part of his working methods. His goal was to short-circuit a determinism within, a terrifying force inside himself that corresponded to the controlling power of external determinisms. That force was language, and he wasn't lazily surrendering control but fighting it.

The material dimensions to Burroughs' texts matter because they clarify why the singularity of his oeuvre is so easily misrecognized: critical interpretations that assume a self-reflexive literary purpose stand Burroughs on his head. Ironically enough, those postmodern critics who attack him may actually get the point: he is *not* a writer of metafiction playing sophisticated philosophical games with words. *Naked Lunch* materializes dark traumas of determinism and exercises power in order to exorcise it, and so, while it subverts realism and is highly self-conscious, it is no more adequate to call it the first novel of postmodernism than it is to call it the third of the three great works of Beat literature.

"So Long Flatfoot!"

Consider the opening scene of *Naked Lunch*, set on a New York subway:

> Young, good looking, crew cut, Ivy League, advertising exec type fruit holds the door back for me. I am evidently his idea of a character. You know the type: comes on with bartenders and cab drivers, talking about right hooks and the Dodgers, calls the counterman in Nedick's by his first name. A real asshole. And right on time this narcotics dick in a white trench coat (imagine tailing somebody in a white trench coat. Trying to pass as a fag I guess) hit the platform.

I can hear the way he would say it holding my outfit in his left hand, right hand on his piece: "I think you dropped something, fella."

But the subway is moving.

"So long flatfoot!" I yell, giving the fruit his B production.[18]

Although we start reading as invisible spectators, we quickly find ourselves included in the scene, directly addressed by a narrator who presumes not only that we know what he knows ("You know the type") but also that we agree with him ("A real asshole"). We are therefore forced to identify with him, even though his performance is a cheap fiction, a "B production." If we don't immediately recognize that *we* are the ones being taken for a ride, it is made clear soon after when the narrator confides in us his plan to con his victim, arranging "to sell him some 'pod' as he calls it, thinking, 'I'll catnip the jerk.' (Note: Catnip smells like marijuana when it burns. Frequently passed on the incautious or uninstructed.)" (5). The note presumes we know no more about catnip than the jerk who is about to be catnipped, revealing us as potential prey for the narrator rather than his trusted confidant. Since the jerk works for the desire factory that drives consumer capitalism – advertising – it is entirely fitting payback that he should be lost in a world of fake drugs and false images; but then so are we. As *Naked Lunch* goes on, the images get uglier and uglier, testing our stomach in line with Burroughs' definition of the book's title as "a frozen moment when everyone sees what is on the end of every fork" (199). The strategy is to make the lunch hard to swallow, forcing us to *see* what we eat, to *look* before we buy.

On this reading, Burroughs' text appears as postmodern in its self-reflexive playfulness as in its mosaic assemblage of every literary style from hard-boiled pulp fiction to surrealist prose poetry. However, such a reading fails to take into account the level of affective experience. For, while often very funny and highly literary, displaying Burroughs' dazzling mastery of idiom and a memorable phrase, *Naked Lunch* does not feel like a clever critique of political and aesthetic norms; reading it mainly feels like being physically assaulted. One of Burroughs' running jokes is to address us as the "Gentle Reader," as if this were a nineteenth-century novel on friendly, helpful terms with its audience: a kind of *companion*, indeed. The gag is played most fully in the "Atrophied Preface," the book's final section, which seems to belatedly offer an explanation for the text's disorientating disarray. "Why all this waste paper getting The People from one place to another? Perhaps to spare The Reader stress of sudden space shifts and keep him Gentle?" (182). Although Murphy claims that here "Burroughs himself offers a straightforward, practical pedagogy of his writing," the exact opposite is just as plausible: that Burroughs gives us only more of what we *want.*[19] Playing on our desire to grasp the rules of the literary game and our dependence on others to guide us, it's just another B production, more catnip.

In fact, *Naked Lunch* is so relentlessly hostile to interpretation that we must invert the standard question "How can a critical guide help to understand it?" for that can only explain the text *away*. With Burroughs, the question is always: "How can we preserve what is most difficult and distinctive?" We have to learn how to read a Burroughs text without turning it into something it is not, even while being led to question what "reading" is. Like any other label, once we apply "postmodern" to it, *Naked Lunch* becomes less confusing, less shocking, less alien and alienating – robbing us of precisely the reading experience unique to it. And so, if *Naked Lunch* is postmodern, it is a virulently aggressive and utterly nihilistic form of it, as if the so-called first postmodern novel were also its self-negating terminal point. "So long flatfoot!"

"Is Burroughs *Serious?*"

As the title of Fred Kaplan's cultural history puts it, 1959 was "the year everything changed," and, in ways that help to clarify his relationship with the Beat Generation and postmodernism, this could not have been more true than for William Burroughs.[20] That July *Naked Lunch* was published, and three months later Burroughs was introduced to what became known as the cut-up method. Both these events took place in Paris and helped seal to the fame of a shabby thirteenth-class establishment in the Latin Quarter at 9 rue Gît-le-Coeur. Indeed, no other locations achieved for the American writers what Ginsberg later claimed for the Beat Hotel in Paris: "our coming together at the hotel   allowed us to spark each other. That was its contribution: getting us all under the same roof at the same time so we could hit off each other's energy day and night."[21] However, this site of Beat rendezvous, which in 1958 brought Burroughs together with Ginsberg and Corso, was also a point of rupture and radical new beginnings.

Between 1957 and 1963, the Beat Hotel was the base for two separate, almost antagonistic periods: the nine months to July 1958 when Ginsberg lived there, and the remaining four and a half years when Burroughs stayed on and off, working with his new creative partner, the painter Brion Gysin. During that time, Burroughs completed *Naked Lunch*, began the cut-up collaborations with Gysin that resulted in the manifestos *Minutes to Go* and *The Exterminator* (both 1960), and composed two volumes of the Cut-Up Trilogy, *The Soft Machine* (1961) and *The Ticket That Exploded* (1962).

Therefore, 9 rue Gît-le-Coeur ought to go down in cultural history not as "the Beat Hotel" but as "Burroughs's Cut-Up Headquarters."

The story of Gysin's discovery has often been retold, but it has been easy to miss both the materially precise and the broadly historical significance of what happened that day in October 1959 when his Stanley knife accidentally sliced through magazines to create surprisingly meaningful results. Materially, it was crucial that Gysin happened to cut up copies of *Life*, because the very next month the magazine's vicious attack on Burroughs and the Beats appeared. Turning the coincidence into a meaningful connection, Burroughs realized that chance operations and collage techniques applied to printed materials offered a practical response to the media's falsification of reality by the manipulation of words and images. That is to say, he recognized the methods of the media as forms of black magic and decided to fight fire with fire. Accordingly, the first cut-up text in *Minutes to Go* was entitled "OPEN LETTER TO LIFE MAGAZINE" and was a scrambled collage of the *Life* article that made a mockery of the magazine's own effort to mock Burroughs and the Beats.

What does this material scenario reveal about the bigger historical picture for Burroughs, the Beats, and postmodernism? First, it confirms that in 1959 Burroughs effectively cut up the Beat Hotel, splitting himself off from his Beat associations. Corso, Ginsberg, and Kerouac were all mystified and appalled by his new methods. For Burroughs took literally the military metaphor of the avant-garde, announced in a wraparound band issued with *Minutes to Go* that declared "un règlement de comptes avec la Littérature." This "settling of scores" against not only political enemies, such as Henry Luce, the media magnate behind *Life* magazine, but also literature itself inevitably alienated Burroughs' former literary allies. Indeed, while Corso had been one of the four contributors to *Minutes to Go* (with Burroughs, Gysin, and Sinclair Beiles), he withdrew his support and the pamphlet included a retraction in which he dismissed cut-ups as an old Dada trick: "Tzara did it all before."[22] Cut-up methods actually had little in common with Tristan Tzara's notorious stunt for making poems by randomly pulling words out of a hat (actually, a bag), and over the years Burroughs would prove Corso wrong with extraordinary rigor and creativity. More immediately, Corso's retraction helped to draw battle lines and made clearer Burroughs' plan to mobilize others to join a cut-up revolution. His cut-up texts did not address the traditional reader of fiction, of course, but nor did they solicit the "active co-creator of meaning" valorized by postmodern criticism (*Introduction to Postmodern Fiction* xiv). As radical acts of *détournement* – turning received texts against themselves – cut-up methods sought to sabotage lines of power, create new possibilities, and recruit allies in a war, as Burroughs insisted: "The cut ups are not for artistic purposes. The cut ups are a weapon."[23]

In fact, it was more a case of both/and rather than either/or, since there would be many versions of the method, with various aims and results. Working empirically rather than from a coherent theory, Burroughs developed cut-up techniques for political warfare, scientific research, personal therapy, magical divination, and conjuration as well as for artistic purposes. And so, while 1959 may have been the high-water mark of Beat literature and media coverage involving Burroughs, it was also a switch point, the year that everything changed for him. Up until the publication of *Naked Lunch* it is still possible to call Burroughs a writer, even possibly a "Beat writer." But, from this point on, he was no more a writer than his texts were novels, and the phrase "experimental writing" seems hopelessly metaphorical for work that literally conducts experiments on language, and indeed on the reader. From 1959 onwards, writing was one technology in an ever-larger experiment involving a series of collaborators applied to tape recordings, film, photography, collage, and photomontage. Even the most stable textual results, such as the novel-length Cut-Up Trilogy, *The Soft Machine, The Ticket That Exploded*, and *Nova Express* are highly *un*-stable, disorientating texts that exist in multiple revised editions. Combining manuals for political revolution with instructions for time travel while creating highly disturbing poetic effects, they defy classification and fiercely resist being confined in the category of the "literary."

It is possible to see the cut-up method as simultaneously the end of the Beat road for Burroughs and the ground zero of postmodernity, and indeed for David Banash the discovery of the cut-up method "has become a kind of myth about the origins of postmodernism itself."[24] However, the Cut-Up Trilogy should not be mistaken for early postmodern science-fiction novels, ludic meta-fictional literature that plays on the equation of word with world. Burroughs wasn't playing the literary game. On the contrary, he believed he had *weaponized* writing. To ask the question, "Is Burroughs *serious?*" (as Frederic Dolan has done) is reasonable, even if it is not strictly answerable (545). In the end, the undecidability of his work is itself part of the challenge it poses, and we have to accept the paradoxical situation in which Burroughs exists in parallel universes, both highly literary and absolutely literal, at the heart of movements and at the edges of them, a Beat, a postmodernist, and entirely *sui generis*, in a club all his own.

"You Are Reading the Future"

In their early anthology of criticism, Skerl and Lydenberg noted that, just as Burroughs was "the quintessential postwar or Beat writer to critics in the 1960s, he was now [in the 1980s] perceived as an exemplary model of postmodernism."[25] In the twenty-first century, perceptions should change again, in part because the Beat and postmodern fields have been dramatically redefined and in part because our understanding of Burroughs's oeuvre has begun to alter quite radically. He appears less and less Beat not only because his work developed over time but also, just as importantly, because his oeuvre has enlarged so much since his death in 1997. Now that it is far more widely available, his enormous body of cut-up work beyond the book form and in multiple media has become increasingly central. As a result, it's clear how far Burroughs's experiments left behind the Beat 1950s, and it's also clear how distinct these works were from other 1960s work labeled postmodern. To some contemporaries, Burroughs appeared to be going back to the future, rehashing the avant-gardism of the Dadaists and Surrealists.[26] Now we can see that what looked like old hat or utter babble was in fact a scissors-and-paste prophetic preview of the digital age. And, whereas postmodernism is often seen to uncritically reflect that age, years in advance of it Burroughs offered visionary tools for resistance and rewriting. Burroughs was one step ahead, and still is. And so, to update Barry Miles's claim that "each Beat had his own decade"[27] – Kerouac the 1950s, Ginsberg the 1960s, Burroughs the 1970s – we might conclude by identifying the distinctive relationship to time in each of their oeuvres and say that, if Kerouac's time was the past and Ginsberg's the present, then with Burroughs, as he put it in a collage for *Nova Express*, "you are reading the future."[28]

NOTES

1 Quoted in Ted Morgan, *Literary Outlaw: The Life and Times of William S. Burroughs* (New York: Henry Holt, 1988), 13.
2 Paul O'Neil, "The Only Rebellion Around," *Life* (November 30, 1959), 123, 126.
3 Anthony Daniels, "All Bark, No Bite [review of *The Yage Letters Redux*]," *New Criterion* (November 2006), 77.
4 Allen Ginsberg, *Howl and Other Poems* (San Francisco: City Lights, 1956), 3; Jack Kerouac, *On the Road* (1957; Harmondsworth: Penguin, 2000), 129, 135.
5 Brian Nicol, *The Cambridge Introduction to Postmodern Fiction* (Cambridge: Cambridge University Press, 2009), 65.
6 See Fredric Jameson, "Postmodernism, or The Cultural Logic of Late Capitalism," *New Left Review* 146 (July/August 1984).
7 See Tim Hunt, *The Textuality of Soulwork: Jack Kerouac's Quest for Spontaneous Prose* (Ann Arbor: University of Michigan Press, 2014).

8 See Robert Holton, "Kerouac Among the Fellahin: *On the Road* to the Postmodern," *Modern Fiction Studies* 41.2 (1995).

9 Benjamin Schafer, ed., *The Herbert Huncke Reader* (London: Bloomsbury, 1998), 247.

10 Robin Lydenberg, *Word Cultures: Radical Theory and Practice in William S. Burroughs' Fiction* (Urbana: University of Illinois Press, 1987); Jennie Skerl, *William S. Burroughs* (Boston: Twayne, 1985), 18.

11 Jamie Russell, *Queer Burroughs* (New York: Palgrave, 2001), 163; Timothy Murphy, *Wising Up the Marks: The Amodern William Burroughs* (Berkeley: University of California Press, 1997).

12 Among the most important exceptions is Marianne DeKoven, *Utopia Limited: The Sixties and the Emergence of the Postmodern* (Durham, NC: Duke University Press, 2004).

13 Stuart Sim, *The Routledge Companion to Postmodernism* (London: Routledge, 2001), 129.

14 "King of the YADS," *Time* (November 30, 1962), 97.

15 Frederick M. Dolan, "The Poetics of Postmodern Subversion: The Politics of Writing in William S. Burroughs's *The Western Lands*," *Contemporary Literature* 32.4 (1991), 535.

16 See Oliver Harris, *William Burroughs and the Secret of Fascination* (Carbondale: Southern Illinois University Press, 2003).

17 William S. Burroughs, *Junky: the Definitive Text of "Junk,"* ed. Oliver Harris (New York: Grove, 2003), 18.

18 William S. Burroughs, *Naked Lunch: The Restored Text*, ed. James Grauerholz and Barry Miles (New York: Grove, 2003), 2.

19 Timothy Murphy, "Intersection Points: Teaching William Burroughs's *Naked Lunch*," *College Literature* 27.1 (2000), 84.

20 See Fred Kaplan, *1959: The Year Everything Changed* (Hoboken, NJ: John Wiley & Sons, 2009).

21 Ginsberg quoted in Christopher Sawyer-Laucano, *The Continual Pilgrimage: American Writers in Paris 1944–1960* (London: Bloomsbury, 1992), 287.

22 William S. Burroughs, Brion Gysin, Gregory Corso and Sinclair Beiles, *Minutes to Go* (Paris: Two Cities, 1960), 63.

23 William S. Burroughs, unpublished typescript cited in *Nova Express: The Restored Text*, ed. Oliver Harris (New York: Grove, 2014), xx.

24 David Banash, "From Advertising to the Avant-Garde: Re-thinking the Invention of Collage," *Postmodern Culture* 14.2 (2004).

25 Jennie Skerl and Robin Lydenberg, eds., *William S. Burroughs at the Front: Critical Reception, 1959–1989* (Carbondale: Southern Illinois University Press, 1991), 11.

26 On postmodernism and the avant-garde, see Andreas Huyssen, *After the Great Divide: Modernism, Mass Culture, Postmodernism* (Bloomington: Indiana University Press, 1986).

27 Barry Miles, *William Burroughs, El Hombre Invisible* (London: Virgin, 1992), 7.

28 Burroughs, untitled collage, cited in *Nova Express*, xl.

9

BRENDA KNIGHT

Memory Babes

Joyce Johnson and Beat Memoir

"Damn the pain; it must be written."
–Brenda Frazer/Bonnie Bremser, from the
epigraph to *Troia: Mexican Memoirs*

Beat writers are some of the most confessional in their work, whether it be poetry, haiku, novels, short stories, or prose conceived as life chronicles. The Beats had an extraordinary impact upon literature, creating a postwar shock wave of sound – the stream-of-consciousness rants of Allen Ginsberg, the polemics of Diane di Prima, the Holocaust haiku of survivor ruth weiss, the altered statements of William S. Burroughs, and the jazz-infused bop prosody of Jack Kerouac. With the publication of *On the Road* in 1957, Kerouac broke literature wide open when he abandoned formalism and wrote like his friend Neal Cassady sounded. He recorded in words this messy, confounding – but wholly exhilarating – zeitgeist as he and his compadres were living it. On the simplest level, this is what memoirists attempt: to convey the spirit of the times. In the case of Beat writers, their sensibility was additionally informed by Buddhism, antiwar sentiments, homosexuality, polyamory, and a strong reaction to the commercial urges of postwar America. These writers came of age, for the most part, before World War II and before the hippie generation who opposed the Vietnam War. The Beat writers, in their search for the new, forever marked the mid-twentieth century with their intense desire to differentiate themselves from everything that came before in art, literature, film, politics, and lifestyle.

A True Good Heart: Joyce Johnson

Joyce Johnson's *Minor Characters* (1983) was a breakthrough work that revived interest in the Beats as a whole. Johnson's memoir fleshed out the narrative of the Beat Generation with the stories of the women who were there all along. With its nuanced depictions, *Minor Characters* challenged the conventional notion that the "Beat boys" were the main attraction. Johnson, born Joyce Glassman, wrote her story and that of her women friends on a human scale. What Johnson accomplished in her book was quietly momentous. In contrast to the caricatures that had become commonplace about Jack Kerouac, her truthful remembrances of the man behind the myth revealed how uncomfortable the glare of the spotlight was for him. Johnson believed that a good memoir relies on the power of observation. "It's in my nature to be a watcher. That was something I shared with Jack ... [And in memoir] I'm looking for the truth of what happened – I don't want to fictionalize it. I want to find out, what was it really?"[1]

Through the eyes of young Joyce Glassman, we can understand how Kerouac's fame felt close to accidental. Then, as today, a review in the *New York Times* could make or break a book. The main reviewer was a rigorous traditionalist for whom rave reviews were few and altogether unlikely for "wild form." Luckily, *On the Road* went to younger fill-in reviewer, Gilbert Millstein, who had reviewed John Clellon Holmes's *roman à clef*, *Go* (1952). Kerouac was staying with Johnson the day the review came out. They waited until midnight and then headed to a newsstand at 66th Street and Broadway to collect the first of the reviews. Millstein proclaimed it "the most beautifully executed, the clearest and most important utterance yet made by the generation Kerouac himself named years ago as 'beat,' and whose principal avatar he is" (thus even the *New York Times* rendered him superhuman whereas Johnson reminds us he was very much just a man).[2] In *Minor Characters*, later readers get to relive that watershed moment for *On the Road* – Ginsberg was not there, nor Burroughs and not even Cassady. Johnson brings us into the fold to experience it with her and Kerouac.

We also see that the younger Glassman had literary ambitions the equal of Kerouac and was able to accomplish something he was never able to – truly autobiographical work. Kerouac drank as much as he could to get back to the ecstatic excess that drove the Beat machine, and both the success and the alcohol got in the way of his writing. Johnson noted that he was trying to write a chronicle of his childhood, titled *Memory Babe*, "But he was too demoralized by his experiences following the publication of *On the Road*, and by the increasing alcohol, to ever complete it. It was the first time that it happened to him, that he had to abandon a project. It was very upsetting to him" ("I Never Met").

Johnson needed to tell the stories that had been untold, those of her generation of young women. As she says in the memoir, "In the late 1950s, young women – not very many at first – left home rather violently ... they, too, came from nice families, and their parents could never understand why the daughters they had raised so carefully suddenly chose precarious lives."[3] Through the power of Johnson's telling, we are able to understand how the trappings of a safe and comfortable middle-class life could feel like a prison sentence to some young women and drive them to extremes. This was the case for poet Elise Cowen, an important part of *Minor Characters* and a person for whom defenestration and suicide followed after stints in Bellevue and rejection by her homophobic family. *Minor Characters* fomented a thirst for more writing from the women Beats, whose work, in many cases, finally saw print after decades of rejection and indifference. The memoirs, travelogues, and autobiographical works from the female perspective were tantamount to a secret history of the Beat Generation.

Before They Were Famous: Elizabeth Von Vogt

If Kerouac was "the principal avatar" of the Beats, the man who paved the way for all Beat writing was John Clellon Holmes. He was the author of the 1952 social realism novel *Go*, with jazz-infused sketches of private lives that became very public – Burroughs, Lucien Carr, Cassady, Ginsberg, Herbert Huncke, and Kerouac. In one of his funnier stories, Holmes's mother looked askance at the human hurricane Neal Cassady, fearing that he might steal something after he showed up uninvited at her apartment with a skinny Lu Anne Henderson in tow. Later, Elizabeth, a curious bobby soxer and Holmes's sister, encountered Huncke shooting up at a druggie party. It seemed too Beat even for John Clellon Holmes, who spirited Liz away and was infuriated by the whole situation. Holmes became a mentor to Liz and taught her about music, politics, and literature by introducing her to his friends at the nearly nonstop party at his place upstairs.

Elizabeth Von Vogt's memoir *681 Lexington Avenue: A Beat Education in New York City, 1947–1954* (2008) is a bookend to her brother John's first novel. It is a rarity, a coming-of-age story from a young girl's perspective in post-World War II Manhattan as the conformity of the 1950s gave way to a cohort of people who wanted to live outside the conventions of society. Holmes's flat was akin to a laboratory where the thought experiment of the Beat Generation was conceived, researched, and refined. Elizabeth was an eyewitness to it all. Von Vogt's vivid memories capture a snapshot of the Beats that no other writer could supply: because she was an adolescent, the players were not "on" – they didn't try to impress her and didn't notice her hanging around the sidelines. This comes across very clearly in a scene with Jack Kerouac, Liz, and her older sister, Lila, a head-turning beauty. Jack behaved differently around Lila; as Liz so perceptively phrased it, he "metamorphosed into a presence."[4] Von Vogt's memoir most successfully depicted the genius loci, the spirit of the place, both at 681 Lexington Avenue and in New York City; she captured the fleeting atmosphere of these years when Beat was born.

Honest Criminals and American Hipsters: Herbert Huncke and Harold Norse

Herbert Huncke not only introduced a group of aspiring writers to the concept of Beat world-weariness but also contributed one of the earliest short-form Beat memoirs: *Huncke's Journal* (1965). A small, mixed-media volume of his recollections, poems, and stories accompanied by drawings, it was published by Diane di Prima's Poets Press. Huncke, ostensibly the most Beat of the entire group, wrote with no ambition to see print. Huncke the junkie thief was poignantly the real innocent in terms of writing; inclusive and unrepentant, he simply shared his life as he lived it – his dark urges, petty crimes, sexual shenanigans, lustful longings, even thoughts of suicide. Although Huncke was a crook and a liar in his daily dealings, he knew the value of honesty in his writing. *Huncke's Journal* was published with modest aims but sold out and got reprinted. When di Prima moved to San Francisco, she took cases of his book and distributed them in the Haight-Ashbury.

Years later, Huncke's prison journals became his "get-out-of-jail-free card." In a literary legal twist, he recalled in *Guilty of Everything* (1990),

> Jail in the beginning was an experience and then gradually it became a way of living for me which took up long periods of time. I developed a prayer system wherein I kept asking for God's help and, at one point, requested a miracle ... What happened was exactly this. My lawyer advised me, because I told him I was compiling my writings presently into a journal to be published the following year, to make a statement to the effect that the purpose of my book was to have it act as a warning against using drugs ... I made the statement and apparently delivered the goods since the judge passed sentence of six months – suspended the sentence – and I walked out of the courtroom.[5]

Fellow heroin addict William S. Burroughs contributed a foreword, citing *Guilty of Everything* as "an honest book" and "never more entertaining than when recounting some horrific misadventure."[6]

While these two Beat characters appear to have much in common on the surface, their backgrounds could not have been more different: one cadging for every dime he can beg, borrow, or steal, and the other heir to a Midwestern manufacturing empire, the Burroughs Corporation. Huncke suspected Burroughs of being a federal agent but eventually learned of their shared love of the needle. A look at the bigger picture reveals that Huncke was more akin to Neal Cassady, since they initially viewed their writer pals as marks. In a beautiful irony, these two thieves and brothers-in-crime ended up inspiring a literary juggernaut and giving so much more than they took.

Harold Norse's *Memoirs of a Bastard Angel* (1989) is often linked to Herbert Huncke's personal chronicles but the two men are another study in contrasts. Huncke's associates were dope fiends, thieves, carnival hucksters, and Elsie John, the gender illusionist and sideshow performer who purposefully skewed the data when interviewed for inclusion in Alfred Kinsey's seminal *Sexual Behavior in the Human Male* (1948). Norse befriended the poet W. H. Auden, for whom he worked as a secretary, as well as James Baldwin, Dylan Thomas, and Allen Ginsberg. He even spent a summer in a fisherman's shack with playwright Tennessee Williams in Provincetown as *The Glass Menagerie* (1944) was being completed. William Carlos Williams urged Norse to "break free from academic poetry," suggesting he write the way he talked: Brooklynese. Williams also wrote a letter that declared "you are the best poet of your generation."[7] Norse followed his mentor's advice and his body of work packs a punch as result.

Norse took pride in being a literary renegade and became close with Charles Bukowski, a fellow proponent of writing in the common idiom. Norse had the courage to be an openly gay artist when so many others did not. The child of an illiterate Lithuanian mother, he also experienced anti-Semitism. *Memoirs of a Bastard Angel* is a story of a life of extremes – from childhood poverty and hunger in the immigrant ghetto of Brooklyn to hobnobbing with the most highly regarded writers in America, Norse's is a life writ large. James Baldwin penned an introduction to Norse's memoirs, which he felt groundbreaking, particularly for a gay readership: "If light ever enters the hearts of men, Harold Norse will be one of those who have helped to set it there" (*Memoirs of a Bastard Angel* 10). Norse came to the attention of Anaïs Nin, who was fascinated by his sexual candor in his memoirs. While Carolyn Cassady and Joyce Johnson address sexuality at a distance, both landing glancingly on the topic by describing Jack Kerouac as "brotherly" in bed, Norse joined Diane di Prima and Lenore Kandel as Beat writers whose work is fueled by the explicitly erotic.

Memory as Love: Carolyn Cassady, Joan Haverty Kerouac, and Edie Parker Kerouac

To examine the literary form of memoir is to consider the very nature of memory, to "re-member," or piece back together that which has passed on. Memoir is beautifully democratic; anyone can write one. The very best are set apart by the honesty the author brings to bear. How many of us are able to pour the unvarnished truth about ourselves onto the page? Are you willing to include all the ugly bits and raw moments that comprise every life but are required for a work of integrity? The British have a saying, "Who is she when she's at home?" Indeed, representing the person behind the social façade, with no protective veneer, is the only way to make a memoir that will ring true. Carolyn Cassady's memoir *Off the Road* (1990) shared many intimate moments, but her portrayal of her husband Neal revealed a different kind of man from what anyone familiar with Beat history knows. Her book serves as a sort of apologia for the wayward and wild Neal Cassady; in the book, she defends him as a husband and defends the legacies of Neal and of Jack Kerouac. As a young art student, Carolyn's first sighting of Neal was mesmerizing. She saw him as someone with "a Runyonesque flavor" and like a kinetic sculpture; this first enthrallment would connect them for the rest of their lives together. Carolyn viewed Neal as the living embodiment of art, as did Jack Kerouac and countless others who were captivated by Dean Moriarty and the man who inspired *On the Road*.[8]

If readers were eager to hear about Carolyn Cassady's side of the story, Joan Haverty Kerouac's *Nobody's Wife: The Smart Aleck and the King of the Beats* (2000) took over thirty years to find a publisher. Her memoir is an illuminating chronicle of the time in which she came of age and moved to New York, where she got involved with neurasthenics, intellectuals, and ne'er-do-wells. A self-described "smart aleck," she was not a sentimental soul, which placed her in contrast to the man who would become the father of her daughter, Jan. The Jack she portrays through memory is a man-child, impulsive and not entirely formed. Elsewhere in the annals of Beat writing, we only get glimpses of Memère, Kerouac's mother Gabrielle. The scarce mentions made her seem like a shadowy figure hovering in the background. Thanks to Haverty's unvarnished sensibility, Memère emerges as flesh and blood, chiding Joan for being too young to be away from her own mother. She also revealed something that only Kerouac's mother could ever say: "He loves ze cheeldren and to chase ze girls. Some day he make good money."[9] Memère made sure Jack's sister, already a mother, joined the circle of Beat women. The shock that reverberated through Joan Haverty Kerouac's life was Jack's denial of his paternity of his daughter Jan: the mama's boy denied being a father. The titular disavowal of her memoir serves as her response to his repudiation.

When *On the Road* became the handbook for the Beat Generation, Kerouac received thousands of fan letters in large postal sacks all filled with hails to the King of the Beats. In 1958, one of the big US Post Office bags spilled a letter from Edie Parker Kerouac. She was Jack's ex-wife, from whom he had amicably split thirteen years prior. Her written appeal asked for a reconciliation and for her to join him on a world book tour. Edie was a girl from a nice family in the swank suburb of Grosse Point, Michigan. Back in the early 1940s, Edie's parents had secured admission to Columbia University for their daughter and made it no secret they wanted her to find a suitable husband there. Edie did find a circle of intellectuals to stimulate her mind at the venerable institution, but they were hardly what her parents had in mind.

In 1944, Edie met Joan Vollmer Adams and the two got an apartment on 118th Street, which became a kind of salon featuring a passing parade of intellectuals, drug addicts, bums, posers, collegians, and petty criminals, with William S. Burroughs, Lucien Carr, Allen Ginsberg, and David Kammerer as some of the regular guests. A boyfriend, Henry Cru, introduced Edie to fellow merchant seaman Jack Kerouac, and they became intimate while Cru was working the boats. She realized she was pregnant while both were out to sea but she did not know which man was the father. Edie decided to not have the baby. Jack was irate when he came back to town and learned what had happened. He left embittered and angry but returned out of "Catholic guilt" and said they should be together. Jack moved in with Edie and they maintained a happily open relationship for a time.

This came to an abrupt end due to the stabbing of David Kammerer by Lucien Carr after an alcohol-fueled evening at the West End Bar. Carr was infuriated by the older man's advances and knifed him, then dumped the body in the Hudson. Burroughs and Kerouac got rid of evidence, including a pair of spectacles and the Boy Scout blade used to kill Kammerer. Carr turned himself in to the police two days later. Burroughs and Kerouac were picked up by the police as material witnesses. Burroughs's wealthy father bailed him out but Kerouac's father judged that his son should rot in a cell. Kerouac turned to Edie, who had expressed the desire to marry, and proposed a deal: if her well-off parents would put up bail, he would agree to marry her. In this way, though certainly not as planned, the Parkers got their wish that their daughter Edie would find a husband who had attended Columbia University. The 1944 marriage was very short-lived; they split in 1946 and the marriage was legally annulled soon after, but they remained friendly. Edie Parker Kerouac never let go of her feelings for Jack and always hoped they might reunite some day. Edie took up writing and it was a source of great frustration to her that she couldn't find a publisher: "Why don't people want to read about my great love affair with Jack Kerouac?" she asked. At Jack's funeral in 1969, Edie exclaimed loudly to all in attendance, "I'm Mrs. Jack Kerouac!"[10]

Fifteen years after her death, City Lights published her memoir *You'll Be Okay: My Life With Jack Kerouac* (2007), wherein she was finally able to tell her side of the story. Had Edie Parker followed her family's prompting, she would have been a debutante and socialite. Her memoirs depict one party after another along with many trips and adventures. While all this socializing with her Beat friends takes place on a wholly different side of the tracks from the wealthy suburbs, her sweet voice and perky, determined cheer shine through. The high points of her personal chronicle are when she takes pride in her own achievements – working on the docks beside the men, and making her own way through her wits. Edie Parker Kerouac accomplished much more than just being the wife of Jack Kerouac, but it remains unclear whether she acknowledged this. Joyce Johnson understood Edie's unrequited point of view:

> This is something Edie knows, an unarticulated sadness. That Jack, despite the "Oh, we'll have our Bohemian period and then we'll settle down and he'll write his books and we'll love each other forever," is unpossessable. But Edie's got her resourceful spirit, working as a longshoreman while Jack's at sea and as a cigarette girl on Forty-second Street. You can weave such an exciting ambience around a man he'll hardly know he's being held by it. (*Minor Characters* 9)

A Life in Words: Hettie Jones

Anne Waldman has cited the memoir form as "the strongest literary genre by the women of the so-called Beat generation" and Hettie Jones proved this.[11] Her *How I Became Hettie Jones* (1990) explicates exactly how a nice Jewish girl from Long Island can become an underground publisher of radical literature and half of a biracial marriage with co-editor at *Yugen*, LeRoi Jones (later known as Amiri Baraka). Jones opens her memoir with an epigraph from Jane Bowles: "The idea … is to change first of our own volition and according to our own inner promptings before they impose completely arbitrary changes on us."[12] By the end of *How I Became Hettie Jones*, Hettie herself states it more plainly when she decides to put own writing first: "Without a *him* in the house, there was of course more space/time for *her*, and I tried to redefine the way a woman might use it" (233–4). *How I Became Hettie Jones* is a testament to living against the grain – Hettie endured much bigotry during her marriage to an intensely outspoken artist who later joined the Black Power Movement; she also faced the brunt of ill-treatment from her family when her biracial children were bullied and shunned. Hettie Jones's personal writing is part of the body of work that subverts the memoir form, unafraid of the day-to-day aspects of life, even domesticity. Her chosen genre may have been ignored by the Beat men in favor of poetry and fiction, but Jones was an artist in her own right and her own creativity shines off the page of her book.

The Road Is Home: Janine Pommy Vega and Brenda Frazer/Bonnie Bremser

Other Beats also took to the road, leaving home far behind. Janine Pommy Vega traversed the globe. Hers was not a booze-fueled wilding, however, but a holy quest to cross four continents in search of the kundalini energy of the sacred feminine. Vega had been an adventurer since her New Jersey teen years, when she read about the Beats and hitchhiked to the Cedar Tavern in Manhattan. There, she met Gregory Corso and Peter Orlovsky, the latter of whom became her first lover. She covered the early part of her life in her journal, "Seeds of Travel," which was later published in *Tracking the Serpent* (1997). Her writing was the truth of her experience, threaded through with mysticism and her search for the extraordinary.

In midlife, Vega suffered a serious accident, which made travel more difficult. But the indefatigable Vega went to the sacred ground of Glastonbury, where she experienced a life-changing epiphany at the site of ancient mound earthworks in the shape of a snake. She recalled, "Threading the maze meant snaking your way through the passageways of a wide expanse before reaching the core. It meant touching down and covering every inch of it, over and over in diminishing circles until you reached the heart."[13] Vega resolved to make pilgrimages to all the ancient temples dedicated to the sacred feminine, which became the basis for *Tracking the Serpent*, her spiritual and feminist manifesto. Vega took more risks than Neal Cassady, Lu Anne Henderson, or Jack Kerouac, despite all the carousing described in the picaresque adventures of *On the Road*. She walked the labyrinths in France's Chartres Cathedral, went upriver into the Peruvian Amazon, lived as a hermit on an island in the middle of Lake Titicaca, and headed north to Kathmandu in Nepal. Here, she faced true danger, going alone to tiny outcroppings high in the Himalayas, trekking in blinding snowstorms, and ceaselessly searching both within and without. As she explains her impetus:

> I had to give up everything to find my way back to who I was. I hiked the cordilleras, I lived with somebody, I got pregnant, I had a miscarriage. And still, I didn't go far enough. By which I mean, I wanted to have no one. What I was asking for I was not yet big enough to contain. The divinity in yourself requires a certain discipline on your part. We practice until we get it perfect. (177)

Brenda Frazer/Bonnie Bremser and Janine Pommy Vega became part of
Allen Ginsberg's larger orbit. They also shared a love of travel and sought
to find their place in the world far away from the safety of suburban, white
America. Raised by her unhappily married parents, Frazer grew up in
Washington, DC. Her mother's despair was palpable, and, as a teenager,
she sensed she could not escape the pervasive sadness of the household. She
felt like a misfit, marked and different from everyone else in her neighborhood and school. She made her big break as a nineteen-year-old Sweetbriar
College co-ed. There she met Ray Bremser, a hipster and self-proclaimed
renegade who introduced her to drugs, everything from marijuana to psych-
edelics. They married immediately and she changed her life completely, even
renaming herself Bonnie Bremser to express the intensity of her love for
Ray. They had a daughter, Rachel, who was born two months premature. As
soon as the baby was released from the hospital, they moved to Mexico to
help Ray avoid a prison stint.

Despite the depth and intensity of feeling between the newlywed parents, life was much harder in Mexico and it was brutally difficult to make
ends meet. Bremser related their travails in *Troia: Mexican Memoirs* (1969).
Hunger, their drug habits, and a lack of money drove the couple to the
brink. They decided that Ray would act as Bonnie's pimp and she would
make money through prostitution. Bonnie's life reads as a series of metamorphoses, and the phase as a sex worker on the streets of Mexico took her
from a lovely and lithe young woman to a drug-addicted wraith, bone thin
and bleached out. While many other writers would have shied away from
the truth of selling their body on the street, Bonnie was unexpurgatedly honest about her day-to-day life, as well as what she saw going on around her
in what was then a third-world country. *Troia* revealed that Bonnie shared
some of Jack Kerouac's views of the "fellaheen," an idealistic notion of the
locals as other. They desired a close connection to what they viewed as the
oppressed indigenous population. In what she referred to as her "romantic
primitivism," Bonnie and Kerouac overlooked the misery and poverty of the
Mexican fellaheens by portraying them in a generalized way as authentic,
primitive, joyful, and living in harmony with nature.

Bremser went further to embrace the fellaheen – literally – than Kerouac,
whose writing she greatly admired. She decided to brown herself in the sun,
reveling in her changed appearance and showing her body in a dress sewn
by a neighbor to make it clear she was a prostitute available to any man. She
wore skirts slit all the way to reveal the bikini underneath, and loved the way
her dark skin looked "so impressive in contrast to the yellow sheets" as she
conducted her trade.[14] In the end, the life of courtesan, a *troia*, took too much
of a toll and Bonnie feared she might not survive Mexico. She escaped again,

leaving Ray and Rachel behind; adoption to a good home offered the promise of a better life for her daughter. She also left the name Bonnie Bremser behind. It could be argued that this woman's "beaten" condition, as first defined by Herbert Huncke, transcended any of the other Beat writers, man or woman.

Eventually, Brenda Frazer got herself to Allen Ginsberg's farm in Cherry Valley, where she became healthy and worked the land successfully. Vega and she became fast friends during the farm era and Vega was astounded by what she described as Frazer's brilliance tending the land while studying and conducting experiments in organic farming. Frazer got several master's degrees, including one in biochemistry, which led to her working for the US Department of Agriculture. Chameleon-like, she reinvented herself completely, shedding her Beatnik skin, putting down the pen, and taking up the ploughshare. She renamed herself to work on technical articles on cultivation science, remarking that she had "left her Beat life far behind" (*Women of the Beat Generation* 270). Sadly, she experienced financial setbacks late in life, enduring poverty and homelessness. She regarded the process of writing her memoir with a refreshing candor and had no sentimentality regarding being part of a movement:

> I defined myself when I sat down to write. It was a rebellion against my most immediate authority figure, my husband, who was once again in jail. Writing was a therapy I could afford. It was exciting then and still is to give myself that freedom. Alone I evolved my personal story. There is no mentor or male muse to be a live-in example for me. I have more faith in my creativity. Creativity is in the middle, at the turning point of gender, either, neither, not. (Bremser quoted in *Women of the Beat Generation* 271)

Ann Charters places this work in the proper context: "With *Troia*, Bonnie became the only woman on the Beat scene who actually lived on the edge and came back to write a heartfelt book about it."[15]

The Ecstatic Truth: Neal Cassady, Diane di Prima, and Jack Kerouac

Why is it that the literature of the Beat Generation still compels? It has been sixty years since the oeuvre made its mark, yet the body of work of these writers continues to fascinate, and, more importantly, to move. Perhaps it is because the writers themselves were moved. And deeply. From Kerouac to Hettie Jones to Janine Pommy Vega and Harold Norse, these and other poets and scribes sought to express, to vent, to reveal fully. These memoirs were a thing apart and something new – raw and confessional. In the case of the women, who often went unpublished and stood in the shadow of the men, they needed to bear witness to what went on during the Beat age.

They were often the most present, observant, and sober witnesses. There is no sense of shame anywhere in the Beat chronicle; a truth and retina-searing heat rolls off the page, in effect ripping twentieth-century American literature out of the safe zone and away from academic formalism with finality.

It is one of the great losses to Beat scholars that Neal Cassady was unable to complete his memoirs. In 1971, City Lights published Cassady's *The First Third*, a memoir that, as Carolyn explains, Neal "worked on ... in erratic spurts of intensity over a six-year period between 1948–1954."[16] The result is uneven and fragmentary, only a faint echo of the stylistic verve of Cassady's famed "Joan Anderson Letter," said to have inspired Kerouac to change his writing style. Indeed, on one such trip during which Kerouac looked to Cassady for inspiration, he accepted the Cassadys' invitation to stay with them in San Francisco. The domesticated Neal presented the converse of Kerouac's free-spirited wild man: he was jobless, depressed, and carless, caring for his children while Carolyn supported the family. Kerouac tape-recorded long drunken and high dialogues with Neal and typed them up, as reproduced in *Visions of Cody*. This process became an inspiration for Kerouac's writing. It became the foundation of *On the Road*. Neal received much encouragement from Ginsberg and Kerouac to get his words on paper, to join them in the ranks of writers. All this reinforcement and well-intended support from two men who wrote so passionately as though their lives depended upon it served to stop Neal; he was utterly paralyzed and filled with a sense of inadequacy, as is clear from what we do have of *The First Third*. He confessed to Carolyn that the more he thought of himself as a writer, the more blocked he became. The total lack of inhibition, of self-consciousness that informed his full-throttle style was now hindered by being "a writer" and points to why some people can write a compelling memoir and others simply cannot. Writers must be able to turn an unflinchingly honest eye upon themselves as subjects, the same as if they were to write a biography of another. Personal writing should be honest and readers exult in these all-too-rare truths.

Meta-memoir joins the Beat canon in Diane di Prima's sensual work *Memoirs of a Beatnik* (1969). Her underground classic is a counterpart of *On the Road* as well as its opposite, a fictionalized memoir of experience gained. At age eighteen, di Prima elected to stop studying physics at Swarthmore and dedicated herself to writing full time. She moved to the West Village, where the jazz clubs and cafés were as abuzz with ideas and deep discourse as were the bookstores di Prima worked in so she could read the books on the shelves. These new bohemians suited her pursuit of total freedom and she lived in several pads that became stages for her exploits as described in *Memoirs of a Beatnik*, which was, at the request of her publisher, erotica for a new readership. In *Memoirs*, di Prima deliberately seeks to shock her reader in the first few pages with an eighteen-year-old female narrator awakening after a seeming orgy. She used her very real memories and the account is redolent of the real; you smell the wax in the homemade candles, the naked bodies, the wine, and the smoke of the joints passing around – and yet these memories were played for lurid effect. Hers is an authentic voice and, even in discussing the work, di Prima made no attempt to hide that *Memoirs* was written, as Connie Lauerman reports it, "because she needed money badly – and quickly. It is mostly accurate, she said, except for the sex parts."[17]

Although some critics assert that the male Beat writers repudiated the memoir as a lesser literature, even Kerouac, nicknamed "Memory Babe" for his feats of total recall, intended all his works as a "*roman fleuve,* a memoir cycle woven into the mythic, wondrous tapestry of his life."[18] Kerouac loved Marcel Proust's model of high literature through remembrance. Many of his books were written years before *On the Road,* evincing this planned long history, the Duluoz Legend (see Chapter 7). Biographer Gerald Nicosia explains when that inspiration struck on a stint as a merchant seaman: "On his last morning in Liverpool that vision of 'beatness' as he later called it, prompted him to conceive of 'the Duluoz Legend.' Sitting at his typewriter in the purser's office, he suddenly foresaw as his life's work the creation of a 'contemporary history record.'"[19] In 1955, Kerouac explained to his editor Malcolm Cowley, "everything from now on belongs to *The Duluoz Legend* ... when I'm done, in about 10, 15 years, it will cover all the years of my life, like Proust, but done on the run, a Running Proust" ("Visions"). Despite Kerouac's idea here, his publisher insisted he change the names of all his friends in because of possible legal consequences. And, when a box of the first printed copies of *On the Road* arrived at his house, he kicked it under a table to hide the books from Neal Cassady after Neal seemed embarrassed and unnerved at their friends' reactions to seeing their portrayal (*Memory Babe* 554). Cassady was, at first, deeply unhappy at seeing some of his antics in print – until the aura of fame eased the pain. Carolyn, fictionalized as Camille, also stated that Neal's name was the last one to be changed as the scroll was edited into a fiction.

John Clellon Holmes described how Kerouac felt that he had "lied so far" up to the novel *The Town and the City* (1950), and that he wanted to finally reveal the truth through remembrance.[20] It is hard to know whether Gilbert Millstein would have announced a nonfiction version of *On the Road* as the epochal book that sparked a new generation. Given the subjugation of the genre, it is doubtful. It is fitting and fateful that Kerouac's partner at the time, Joyce Glassman (later Johnson), would elevate the memoir to a higher form and bring forward a chorus of voices previously unheard, the women of the Beat Generation.

NOTES

1 Laura Barton, "I Never Met Anyone Else Like Jack Kerouac [interview with Joyce Johnson]," *The Guardian* (11 October 2007), www.theguardian.com/books/2007/oct/12/fiction.jackkerouac (accessed September 9, 2016).

2 Gilbert Millstein, "Book of the Times [review of *On the Road*]," *New York Times* (September 5, 1957), 27.

3 Joyce Johnson, *Minor Characters: A Beat Memoir* (1983; New York: Penguin 1989), xxxii.

4 Elizabeth von Vogt, *681 Lexington Avenue* (Wooster, OH: Ten O'Clock Press, 2008), 35.

5 Herbert Huncke, *Guilty of Everything* (New York: Paragon House, 1990), 179.

6 William S. Burroughs, "Foreword," Herbert Huncke, *Guilty of Everything*, ix.

7 Harold Norse, *Memoirs of a Bastard Angel* (New York: William Morrow, 1989), 191.

8 Carolyn Cassady, *Off the Road* (New York: William Morrow, 1990), 2.

9 Joan Haverty Kerouac, *Nobody's Wife: The Smart Aleck and the King of the Beats* (Berkeley: Creative Arts Book Company, 2000), 127.

10 Brenda Knight, *Women of the Beat Generation* (San Francisco: Conari Press, 1996), 79.

11 Brenda Knight and Debra Winger, *Women of the Beat Generation: The Writers and Muses at the Heart of a Revolution* [audio cassette] (San Bruno, CA: Audio Literature, 1996).

12 Hettie Jones, *How I Became Hettie Jones* (New York: Grove Press, 1990), 3.

13 Janine Pommy Vega, *Tracking the Serpent* (San Francisco: City Lights, 1997), 21.

14 Bonnie Bremser, *Troia: Mexican Memoirs* (1969; Champaign, IL: Dalkey Archive Press, 2007), 167.

15 Ann Charters, "Introduction," Bremser, *Troia*, 4.

16 Carolyn Cassady, "After-word," Neal Cassady, *The First Third* (1971; San Francisco: City Lights, 1981), 140.

17 Connie Lauerman, "Beat Poet Diane Di Prima Reflects On Life Outside The Mainstream," *The Chicago Tribune* (April 19, 2000), http://articles.chicagotribune.com/2000-04-19/features/0004190043_1_beat-generation-jack-kerouac-di-prima (accessed October 17, 2016).

18 David Barnett, "Visions of Jack Kerouac ... in an Epic 13 Volumes," *The Guardian* (July 24, 2013), www.theguardian.com/books/2013/jul/24/jack-kerouac-13-volume-memoir (accessed February 22, 2016).

19 Gerald Nicosia, *Memory Babe* (1983; Berkeley: University of California Press, 1994), 109.

20 John Clellon Holmes, *Nothing More to Declare* (New York: E. P. Dutton, 1967), 80.

10

HILARY HOLLADAY

Beat Writers and Criticism

In studying and writing about the Beats, we would do well to step back in time and revisit T. S. Eliot's "Tradition and the Individual Talent" (1921). In that important essay that helped to define the critical approach known as formalism or New Criticism, Eliot wrote, "No poet, no artist of any art, has his complete meaning alone."[1] By this he meant that individual poets do not exist in a vacuum; they are best understood in the context of a poetic tradition that includes the epoch-making poems that came before and after their own. If they are truly great poets, their poems will not only influence the shape and meaning of those written after theirs but will also subtly alter the meanings of poems already recognized as central to the tradition. Poems enter into a continuum, according to Eliot's thinking, and converse with one another across time and space. Readers who know the continuum can appreciate the complexity of the conversation and see how different poems accrue meaning in response to one another. Applying Eliot's ideas to Allen Ginsberg, for instance, we might say that, just as he was influenced by William Carlos Williams, Walt Whitman, and the Old Testament, so are they influenced by him.

It is likewise true that no literary movement has its meaning wholly apart from movements coming before, during, or after its time. Thus, although experimental writing of the Beats represented a tectonic shift in American poetry, it cannot be totally teased apart from the San Francisco Poetry Renaissance, which was already in progress when Ginsberg and Jack Kerouac made their westward journeys in the early 1950s. It is useful, further, to acknowledge the Beat overlap with the writings of the Black Mountain poets, the Confessional poets, the Black Arts poets, and the New York School poets. Beat precursors Whitman and Williams, among others, and the feminist, gay, and lesbian poets of the 1970s and 1980s are also part of the continuum in which the Beats have a significant place.

To truly grasp the significance of the Beat writers, further, one should realize that, for all that has been said and written about their drug use, sexual experimentation, and rebellious tendencies, the Beats were deadly earnest about the study and writing of literature. They were well read and fully aware of their precursors and peers (for further discussion of the Beats and literary history, see Chapter 4). Poetry was more important to them than any kind of social movement. They wanted to be seen as part of the immortal tradition that Eliot described, and they intuitively understood, as Eliot made clear, that poets need to be deeply aware of the past and open to all knowledge coming their way: "What happens is a continual surrender of [the artist] as he is at the moment to something which is more valuable. The progress of an artist is a continual self-sacrifice, a continual extinction of personality" ("Tradition"). The Beats' penchant for writing out of their life experiences has obscured this point, which is nevertheless demonstrated time and again in their best works.

Although their biographies are important to the study of the Beats as a cultural phenomenon, one need not know Kerouac's life story to understand what he called his spontaneous prose in books such as *The Subterraneans* (1958) or *Maggie Cassidy* (1959). Nor does one need to know Ginsberg's biography to make sense of "Howl" or "Sunflower Sutra" (both 1956). The biographical approach can in fact create impediments, because one starts compulsively looking for the authors within their works and paying less attention to the works themselves. This would seem to be the opposite of what Kerouac and Ginsberg wanted, even though they never hid the auto-biographical bases for their writings. Both writers were trying very hard, in their art and their energetic study of Buddhism, to slip the yoke of personality and move into something larger, less limiting, and ultimately more meaningful to them and their readers. Kerouac especially was consumed by the tragic limitations of personality: in the books comprising his Duluoz Legend (see Chapter 7), he shows how the individual self (modeled after himself) wounds, destroys, and repeatedly fails. Only occasional moments of joy – like those roman candles he wrote about in *On the Road* (1957) – illuminate the long dark road of life. The mortal author, no matter whether he or she is closely allied to his or her persona or not, will pass from the earth. The writing, an entity apart from the hands that typed it, is what lasts. Those were Kerouac's great insights, though rather familiar ones for anyone who has read Eliot or Shakespeare or the biblical Psalms.

Beat Criticism

Students looking to learn about the Beats will find a great deal of material in print and online about the movement and the lives of the most prominent male authors. They will not find a wealth of substantive literary criticism.

Even now, sixty years after the publication of his *Howl and Other Poems* (1956), there are few book-length studies of Allen Ginsberg's poetry.[2] The critical surface of Beat poetry has barely been scratched.

The roots of the problem are fairly easy to trace. First of all, the initial skepticism about the Beats during the 1950s calcified into received wisdom among many scholars and teachers of modern poetry schooled in the New Criticism (careful examinations of word choice, imagery, metaphor, symbolism, meter, rhyme, and form) that Eliot, among others, promoted. They didn't necessarily dislike Ginsberg's "Howl," whose declamatory power and wondrous imagery could hardly be denied. Yet they hadn't been trained in college or graduate school to understand what was interesting and important about the rest of Beat literature – the seemingly artless, unconventionally spiritual poems – and they were put off by the cult of personality that had grown up around the Beats. With so much popular emphasis on the writers' rebellious ways and the lackadaisical Beatnik lifestyle, it was hard to imagine applying the tools of New Criticism to poems such as Ginsberg's "America" (1956) or Corso's "Marriage" (1959). Graduate students seeking degrees and jobs and faculty members up for tenure and promotion opted to specialize in the great white male Modernists – W. H. Auden, T. S. Eliot, Robert Frost, Wallace Stevens, and William Butler Yeats – whose intricate and gorgeous poems responded well to New Criticism, which in its purest form steers clear of biographical insights. And, since the Modernists' work responded well to protracted scrutiny, the detailed scholarship done on them was hardly time wasted.

Then, when critical theory came into vogue in the 1970s and 1980s, young scholars began applying the principles of deconstruction, poststructuralism, new historicism, reader-response theory, Marxist theory, and feminist theory to works of literature, primarily fiction. These wide-angle lenses gave new direction to the writing of countless graduate students who embraced theory wholeheartedly, but the concentrated study of poetry fell by the wayside.[3] Beat poetry had not gained critical traction anyway, so its absence from undergraduate syllabi and grad school reading lists was hardly noticed. Once the theoretical approaches began to wear thin and some people started complaining that the language of critical theory was opaque to the point of meaninglessness, many scholars, and whole English departments, gradually moved toward a hybrid, cultural studies approach emphasizing the study of race, gender, sexuality, and class.

These days, the study of poetry continues to languish. In undergraduate literature surveys, students whose grandparents were taught prosody in high school know little or nothing of scansion or poetic form. They quake through Sylvia Plath's "Lady Lazarus" (1965) in search of all things gendered and suicidal. As much as they may feel its jagged power, they don't understand how or why the poem works, and they can think of little to write about Plath that hasn't already been said in class or doesn't appear in their anthology's headnote about her. The critical pendulum thus swings perilously close to the biographical approach of centuries long past, with all its limitations.

The implications of this for Beat literature are significant. We have a plethora of biographies of Kerouac and a few biographies of the other prominent male Beats;[4] an assortment of very interesting anthologies and overviews of the movement; and a few good documentaries and distressingly inadequate film adaptations of Kerouac's novels.[5] There are biographical websites and an archive of little magazines, mostly out of print.[6] There are some fine multiauthor essay collections on the Beats and imaginative cultural studies.[7] We are fortunate to have Tim Hunt's *The Textuality of Soulwork: Jack Kerouac's Quest for Spontaneous Prose* (2014) and Michael Skau's *"A Clown in a Grave": Complexities and Tensions in the Works of Gregory Corso* (1999).

The bulk of critical attention to date has gone to Kerouac.[8] It seems he really was, and is, King of the Beats. Not coincidentally, Kerouac is the one, though long dead, still publishing the most books. Penguin and a couple of other presses continue to print virtually every apprentice effort that the Kerouac literary estate pulls out of its stash of previously unpublished works. These books have a built-in audience of fans who might enjoy a book by or about some other Beat writer if only they knew what to look for, but Kerouac is the one who keeps popping up in hardback at Barnes & Noble. Forever replicating himself, like Henrietta Lacks's cancerous cells, Kerouac keeps going and growing, a phenomenon unto himself. Publishers like him because he sells; he sells because he is familiar to readers; he's familiar because he remains part of the cultural zeitgeist; he's part of the zeitgeist because so many different people, upon reading a great book such as *On the Road* or *The Dharma Bums* (1958), feel a visceral, personal connection with him. All of that aside, he is not the only Beat writer of interest, and the commodification of Kerouac in print and on film, which sends a strong message to the public that he is the Beat author who really counts, is not healthy for the broader aims of Beat literary studies.

The Beat writers' rebellious ways have always been part of their charm and part of the problem with their critical reception. In *Unpacking the Boxes: A Memoir of a Life in Poetry* (2008), poet Donald Hall confesses that, in the early years, he was less than thrilled about the Beats: "when *Howl* came out I felt attacked, not liberated – my castle razed by barbarian hordes – and for a couple of years I denounced the Beats," writes Hall, a Harvard-educated contemporary of Ginsberg who had published two books of verse by 1955. "I rejected Ginsberg's 'Sunflower Sutra' for the *Paris Review* – whereupon Ginsberg told [editor-in-chief] George Plimpton that I wouldn't know a poem if it buggered me in broad daylight."[9] Hall went on to change his mind about the barbarians storming the castle. He was too deeply engaged by the world of contemporary poetry to hold a grudge.[10]

Ginsberg, it turns out, was the intractable one. For a poet who made not just a persona but also a career out of railing against the establishment, the young Ginsberg had a rather conventional definition of literary success. As his disparaging remark about Hall ironically demonstrates, Ginsberg longed to have "Sunflower Sutra" appear in the elite *Paris Review* (which had in its winter 1955 issue published "The Mexican Girl," an excerpt from Kerouac's as-yet-unpublished *On the Road*). Denied the *Paris Review* imprimatur and perhaps jealous that Kerouac had made the cut while he had not, Ginsberg recycled his insult of Hall in the liner notes accompanying the 1957 Fantasy record of his poems. This time he took aim at a larger group: "A word on the Academies: poetry has been attacked by an ignorant and frightened bunch of bores who don't understand how it's made, & the trouble with these creeps is they wouldn't know poetry if it came up and buggered them in broad daylight."[11] What had before been a witty insult aimed at a specific person was now a churlish generality, a small rock thrown at the departing backs of the lumberingly pluralized "Academies."

It is no wonder that so many of the best minds of the literary establishment of their generation derided the Beats. Corso, Ginsberg, and Kerouac resented anyone they deemed unreceptive to their ideas. Their irreverence was sometimes a matter of pure ego. For all their excited talk of angels, they were not terrific at being beatific. What saved them from the shunning they courted, or pretended to court, was the darkly shining merit of their signal works. The 1957 censorship trial that took up the question of the alleged obscenity of *Howl and Other Poems* shows just how seriously the establishment on both sides of the case took Ginsberg and his chosen art form. Of the nine expert witnesses speaking in support of *Howl*, six were English professors. It hardly needs saying that the publicity that the trial generated made Ginsberg much more famous than he would have been otherwise.

Outgoing, full of himself, and possessed of a beautiful, resonant voice, Ginsberg emerged as a public figure just as poetry readings were coming into vogue in San Francisco and elsewhere. His performances drew crowds. On one early occasion, in response to a heckler, he stripped naked on stage to show he didn't mind being vulnerable. That sort of exhibitionism, plus the discursive brilliance of "Howl," got people talking. So it was with the whole Beat Movement, which has always provoked the taking of sides.

Love them or hate them, one can't deny that the Beat authors have maintained a stubborn hold on the public imagination. Early on, a few perceptive critics understood why that was. "For all the indignation the Beat writers have aroused," John P. Sisk wrote in 1959, "I think it must be admitted that the general reading public is remarkably permissive towards them, as it has learned to be towards all writers in the subversive tradition – as if it is a part of a developing national awareness of that tradition's function as the hypersensitive, if often quite fantastic, conscience of America."[12] Such a comment usefully categorizes the Beats without denying what is special about them.

The Case of Thomas Parkinson

Sisk's essay "Beatniks and Tradition" was reprinted in *A Casebook on the Beat*, a 1961 anthology edited by Thomas Parkinson. One of the first books devoted to the study of Beat literature, this fine collection delivers, as its cover blurb promises, "The pros and cons of the beat movement – with 39 pieces of beat writing." The first half includes selections by William S. Burroughs, Corso, Lawrence Ferlinghetti, Ginsberg, Kerouac, Michael McClure, Gary Snyder, Philip Whalen, and John Wieners. The second half, "Criticism and Commentary," is a singularly well-balanced reckoning of the male Beats in their own time. Kenneth Rexroth, Warren Tallman, and Dorothy Van Ghent are among those providing incisive analyses of Beat culture, writing, and individual authors. (In her very brief essay, Van Ghent outlines the mythic qualities of Beat literature; Tallman writes in inspired detail of jazz influences in "Kerouac's Sound" in a piece originally published in 1959.) Energetic naysayers include John Ciardi, Herbert Gold, and Norman Podhoretz; Ciardi, a poet and poetry editor for *The Saturday Review*, lambasts Kerouac as "basically a high school athlete who went from Lowell, Massachusetts, to Skid Row, losing his eraser en route."[13] Adding further interest to the volume, the secondary bibliography lists a hundred essays, reviews, and articles about the Beats that appeared in books and periodicals from 1956 to 1960. *A Casebook on the Beat* is, in short, an excellent resource for anyone interested in the critical reception of the Beats in their own time.

The volume's editor, Thomas Parkinson, was a heroic figure whose name is little remembered today. A prominent authority on Yeats, a well-published poet, and an English professor at the University of California – Berkeley, he grew up poor in San Francisco's Haight-Ashbury district. After being discharged from the army for being unusually tall, he worked in the shipbuilding and logging industries before eventually earning three degrees from Berkeley.[14] He was part of the San Francisco Poetry Renaissance, which he preferred to call an "awakening," and became friends with the Beat authors, his contemporaries. Ginsberg, in his opinion, was "the genuine article," and he wrote eloquently in support of *Howl*'s literary merit at the time of the obscenity trial.[15]

Around the time he was compiling and editing *A Casebook on the Beat*, Parkinson vocally supported student protesters at Berkeley. A slanderous rightwing broadside soon appeared that denounced him as "a Stalinist and homosexual" and precipitated a hideous foreshadowing of today's rash of campus shootings. According to a memorial tribute to Parkinson, who died in 1992, "an insane former student, who, commanded by God, and wanting, he said, 'to get someone associated with Communism,' walked into Tom's office with a sawed-off shotgun under his coat and fired it point-blank. The student with Tom was killed; half of Tom's face was wrecked, and vertebrae in his neck were fused" ("English: Berkeley"). Parkinson somehow managed to get on with his life, his activism, his writing, and his teaching. In 1967, he defended the merits of *The Love Book* (1966), a poetry collection in the Beat tradition by Lenore Kandel, in yet another obscenity trial in San Francisco ("English: Berkeley").

An astute critic, Parkinson was able to step back from his friendships and assess the Beats with grace and wisdom. In "Phenomenon or Generation," he exposes a salient truth that has eluded many of today's chroniclers of the milieu that the Beat writers claimed as their own. In his view, "American Bohemia in reacting against suburbia tends to produce a reverse image of the society that makes the hydrogen bomb, throws its money around in idiot frenzy, and refuses to vote for school bonds; the same moral flaccidity, the same social irresponsibility, the same intellectual fraudulence operate throughout the two worlds that are, finally, not opposed" (278). With such thoughts in mind, the conundrum of Kerouac's Dean Moriarty begins to come into new focus: driven by lust, unable to see beyond his immediate needs, and only superficially interested in anyone besides himself, the whirling dervish of Dean is at bottom perhaps not so different from the most craven of his suburban brethren.

Parkinson realized that the Beats and many of the critics of their day were at an impasse that made both sides look bad: "it was possible to talk their work to death by considering only their odd habits, and since their contempt for the intellect preserved them from any rational critical self-defense, they could become figures of derisive fun," he writes. "The fact that Gregory Corso publicly boasted that he has never combed his hair has led to the belief that he could not then have taken much care with his poetry. The quality of the work could then remain unexamined" (286–87). Leaving the plethora of Beat works unexamined would have been a huge mistake, given all that was interesting and new about them, and Parkinson's further reflections reveal how much thought he had given to Beat poetic technique. Arguing that "The primary problem of poetry is notation," and "A poem is a score," he observes that idiosyncratic punctuation and "the shift from vernacular idiom to lofty rhetoric," among other things, are valid innovations in poetic notation. "The beat poet is best considered as a voice, the beat prose writer as an active reverie," he continues, surely placing Kerouac in the latter category, though he does not name him. "Into this reverie come past and present, but the reverie is chiefly preoccupied with keeping up with the process unfolding outside and inside the narrator" (288). One wonders how much Parkinson knew of Kerouac's typewriting experiments when he remarks, "The ideal book by a writer of beat prose would be written on a single string of paper, printed on a roll, and moving endlessly from right to left, like a typewriter ribbon" (288). Such an attempt, though stupefying for author and reader alike, would build on the aesthetic principle behind the scroll manuscripts that Kerouac created by feeding long strips of paper into his typewriter and then taping them together.

The choosing of authors and their works for an anthology is a form of literary criticism, and it is interesting to note that the exemplars of Beat writing in *Casebook* are all poets except for Burroughs and Kerouac. However, these two are perhaps better understood if we approach them as if they *were* poets, and Parkinson's selections of Kerouac's "October in the Railroad Earth" and Burroughs's "The Cut Up Method of Brion Gysin" and "A Newspeak Précis of the Article Made in Its Image With Its Materials" point us in that direction. Kerouac, of course, wrote poems and thought of himself as a poet, but that is not the issue. What is significant here is that it is nearly impossible to analyze the experimental writing of either Kerouac or Burroughs the way one would analyze conventional prose (Herbert Huncke's meandering dreamlike sketches present the same difficulty). Even *On the Road* invites the close attention that verse demands. Like James Joyce (a precursor Kerouac claimed for himself) and Toni Morrison (coming along later), Kerouac has a way of dropping poems into his novels. To cite two familiar examples, the much-loved passage early in *On the Road* ("The only ones for me are the mad ones") and the concluding paragraph ("So in America when the sun goes down") evince the intuitive logic and graceful rhythms of poetry.[16] So much of Kerouac invites a formal close reading – the scrutiny of imagery, word choice, symbolism, and even the meter. This is the sort of thing undergraduates can do with guidance in class and later, on their own, in papers that challenge them to think hard about the words, and the works, rather than getting sidetracked by the authors' personalities.

Close reading, central to New Criticism, remains the most effective way to get inside a poem or a poetic work of prose. Done right, it is not a tedious act of "over-analyzing," as some students over the years have grumbled. Nor is it a door slammed in the face of critical theory or cultural studies. So much that we have learned as scholars and teachers from feminist theory, African American literary theory, and queer studies (to name just a handful of critical approaches) and from brilliant theorists such as Mikhail Bakhtin and Hélène Cixous can be applied to the Beats. But, in my view, any meaningful study of the Beats must begin with acknowledging that they were primarily poets. Understanding what they wrote in the 1950s depends on our knowledge of poetry that came before and during their time and an intelligent awareness of the important poetry written since then. To grasp what is truly Beat about them means, further, reading what they wrote before and especially after the period when they became known as Beat authors. That is the way to isolate the Beat essence, however one might define that.

Kerouac, Corso, Huncke, and Elise Cowen are perhaps the only ones who stayed definitively Beat in ethos and worldview. Many of the others went on to other things: witness the subject matter and literary accomplishments of Amiri Baraka, Burroughs, Diane di Prima, and Snyder.[17] Ginsberg also grew and changed. If we insist on making him a brash young Howler for all time, we miss out on a great deal.

Seeing it as a cultural phenomenon of the 1950s, we can point pretty easily to what Burroughs, Ginsberg, Kerouac, and others of the Beat Movement were reacting against – the stifling social mores and governmental preoccupation with war, money, and power, for starters. It's a lot harder to say what the Beats were aiming for. They were individuals with individual talents contributing as best they could to a literary tradition they honored and believed in. They were, as Thomas Parkinson so eloquently put it, voices and reveries. The challenge before us today is to study and teach them as poets rather than mere personalities.

NOTES

1   T. S. Eliot, "Tradition and the Individual Talent" (1921), www.bartleby.com/200/sw4.html (accessed September 9, 2016).
2   For two such works, see Lewis Hyde, ed., *On the Poetry of Allen Ginsberg* (Ann Arbor: University of Michigan Press, 1985) and Tony Trigilio, *Allen Ginsberg's Buddhist Poetics* (Carbondale: Southern Illinois University Press, 2007).
3   Harold Bloom, Marjorie Perloff, Helen Vendler, and Linda Wagner-Martin are among the prominent poetry critics who have insisted modern and contemporary poetry is important *as* poetry. They continue to be vitally important voices in the critical discourse. Among younger scholars, Amanda Golden is doing the innovative and in-depth writing about poets and poetry that is very much needed.

4 I recommend Dennis McNally, *Desolate Angel: Jack Kerouac, the Beat Generation, and America* (1981; New York: Da Capo Press, 2003). Though not the newest or most detailed of the many Kerouac biographies, it is fair-minded, eloquent, and manageable in length. For the other male Beats, see Barry Miles, *Ginsberg: A Biography* (New York: Harper Collins, 1990) and Bill Morgan, *I Celebrate Myself: The Somewhat Private Life of Allen Ginsberg* (New York: Viking, 2006). For Burroughs, see Barry Miles, *Call Me Burroughs: A Life* (New York: Twelve, 2014). For Huncke, see Hilary Holladay, *Herbert Huncke: The Times Square Hustler Who Inspired Jack Kerouac and the Beat Generation* (Tucson: Schaffner Press, 2015).

5 Ann Charters's *The Portable Beat Reader* (New York: Penguin, 1992) is the standard-bearer among Beat anthologies. Two others I recommend both for their subject matter and the editors' cogent commentaries are Brenda Knight, *Women of the Beat Generation: The Writers, Artists and Muses at the Heart of a Revolution* (Berkeley: Conari Press, 1996) and Regina Marler, *Queer Beats: How the Beats Turned America On to Sex* (Berkeley: Cleis Press, 2004). Although not limited to the Beats, Lawrence Ferlinghetti, ed., *City Lights Pocket Poets Anthology* (San Francisco: City Lights, 2015) is also valuable. Of the general-interest overviews, I recommend Steven Watson, *The Birth of the Beat Generation: Visionaries, Rebels, and Hipsters, 1944–1960* (New York: Pantheon, 1995). Kurt Hemmer, *Encyclopedia of Beat Literature* (New York: Facts on File, 2007) is an excellent reference book with an admirable focus on the writings. Matt Theado, *The Beats: A Literary Reference* (New York: Carroll & Graf, 2002) is an extraordinarily useful compendium of historical material, including excerpts from early reviews of the Beat authors' works. Of the Beat documentaries, *Original Beats* (1996) and *Burroughs: The Movie* (1983) are especially good.

6 See Allenginsberg.org, Beatstudies.org, Huncketeacompany.com, Jackkerouac.com, and Litkicks.com. For the journals, see *Beat Scene, Dharma Beat, The Evergreen Review, Journal of Beat Studies, Moody Street Irregulars: A Jack Kerouac Magazine,* and *The Unspeakable Visions of the Individual.*

7 See, for instance, A. Robert Lee, ed., *The Beat Generation Writers* (East Haven, CT: Pluto Press, 1996); Daniel Belgrad, *The Culture of Spontaneity: Improvisation and the Arts in Postwar America* (Chicago: University of Chicago Press, 1998); Cornelius A. van Minnen, Jaap van der Bent and Mel van Elteren, eds., *Beat Culture: The 1950s and Beyond* (Amsterdam: VU University Press, 1999); and Erik Mortenson, *Capturing the Beat Moment: Cultural Politics and the Poetics of Presence* (Carbondale: Southern Illinois University Press, 2010).

8 See Tim Hunt, *Kerouac's Crooked Road* (1981; Berkeley: University of California Press, 1996); Regina Weinreich, *Kerouac's Spontaneous Poetics: A Study of the Fiction* (1987; New York: Thunder's Mouth Press, 2002); James T. Jones, *A Map of Mexico City Blues: Jack Kerouac as Poet* (Carbondale: Southern Illinois University Press, 1992); Robert Holton, *On the Road: Kerouac's Ragged American Journey* (New York: Twayne, 1999); James T. Jones, *Jack Kerouac's Duluoz Legend: The Mythic Form of an Autobiographical Fiction* (Carbondale: Southern Illinois University Press, 1999); Matt Theado, *Understanding Jack Kerouac* (Columbia: University of South Carolina Press, 2000); Hilary Holladay and Robert Holton, eds., *What's Your Road, Man? Critical Essays on Jack Kerouac's On the Road* (Carbondale: Southern Illinois University Press, 2009); and Hassan

Melehy, *Kerouac: Language, Poetics, and Territory* (London: Bloomsbury, 2015). Although more of a personal narrative than formal criticism, Clark Coolidge, *Now It's Jazz: Writings on Kerouac and the Sounds* (Albuquerque: Living Batch Press, 1999) is also valuable.

9   Donald Hall, *Unpacking the Boxes: A Memoir of a Life in Poetry* (Boston: Houghton Mifflin, 2008), 122.

10 In the mid-1980s, as an editor at the University of Michigan Press, Hall encouraged Lewis Hyde to compile and publish a volume of essays on Ginsberg's poetry.

11 Allen Ginsberg, "Notes Written on Finally Recording 'Howl' [LP liner notes]" (Fantasy, Spoken Word Series, 7006, 1959), reprinted in *A Casebook on the Beat*, ed. Thomas Parkinson (New York: Crowell, 1961), 30.

12 John P. Sisk, "Beatniks and Tradition," *Casebook*, ed. Parkinson, 198.

13 John Ciardi, "Epitaph for the Dead Beats," *Casebook*, ed. Parkinson, 262.

14 "Thomas F. Parkinson, English: Berkeley," University of California: In Memoriam (1992), http://texts.cdlib.org/view?docId=hb7c6007sj&doc.view=frames&chunk.id=div00047&toc.depth=1&toc.id= (accessed September 9, 2016).

15 Thomas Parkinson, "Phenomenon or Generation," *A Casebook on the Beat*, ed. Parkinson (New York: Thomas Crowell, 1961), 280, 287.

16 Jack Kerouac, *On the Road* (1957; New York: Penguin, 1991), 8, 309–310.

17 Scholarship on the Beat women, many of whom outlived their male counterparts, is a rich field of inquiry. See Ronna C. Johnson and Nancy M. Grace, *Women Writing the Beat Generation* (New Brunswick: Rutgers University Press, 2002); Grace and Johnson, *Breaking the Rule of Cool: Interviewing and Reading Beat Women Writers* (Oxford, MS: University Press of Mississippi, 2004); and Tony Trigilio, ed., *Elise Cowen: Poems and Fragments* (Boise, ID: Ahsahta Press, 2014).

11

RONNA C. JOHNSON

The Beats and Gender

The Beat Generation of hipsters, bohemians, and outriders, and the literary movement of experimental writers and artists formed under its name, straddles the Modern–postmodern "great divide" of the postwar mid-twentieth century.[1] This era of civil rights and counterculture movements, as well as women's and gay liberation, had pronounced theoretical and sociocultural implications for Beat poetics and gender formations. Derived from Dada and Surrealism, and influenced by nineteenth- and twentieth-century poets from Walt Whitman to Charles Olson, Beat poetics were expressed in signature themes of literary and existential freedom of expression that resonated with the 1960s sexual revolution and catalyzed censorship attacks on published and performed works.[2] The subtitle to *Howl and Other Poems* (1956) from Whitman – "Unscrew the locks from the doors! / Unscrew the doors themselves from their jambs!" – articulates the Beat vow to assail literary repression and restraints imposed on art and experience.[3] Avant-garde Beat writing by both women and men elaborated this manifesto often in gender-specific ways, challenging postwar limits on sex, sexual orientation, speech expression, and, notably, gender roles themselves. Gender and a gendered system of themes and existential convictions are vital to Beat literature and poetics and to constructions of the Beat writer, and were often contentious issues within the movement and its works. Immersed in patriarchal discourses, the Beat Generation elevated male over female writers, supporting a reactionary feminine–masculine gender disparity at odds with the movement's open, improvisational poetics and colloquial hipster style. Thus, however radical in poetics, politics, and sexuality, with regard to gender – the system of cultural meanings ascribed to sex – the Beat movement's canonical male artists were confounded in their counterculturalism, even as their experimental writing manifested transformations that were afforded by their dissenting poetics and biographical chronicles of profligacy and that were promoted by the growing contingent of female bohemian writers.

The Beat movement formed a hierarchical, generational succession stamped by gender. Four white male writers, two openly homosexual – William S. Burroughs, Gregory Corso, Allen Ginsberg, and Jack Kerouac – are the canonized founders of a classic strain of Beat literature, the masculine Romantic protest against restraint, convention, and law;[4] they are the self-proclaimed "daddies" of Beat poetry, a trope of hipster slang that reifies the contradiction of a movement that is dedicated to challenging the patriarchal while being itself a patriarchy.[5] With the exception of Diane di Prima, who came to voice with the male Beat progenitors, the cohort of women Beat writers influenced by their groundbreaking forerunners emerged in the second and third generations of the movement.[6] Including artists such as Sheri Martinelli, Brenda Frazer/Bonnie Bremser, Joanne Kyger, Lenore Kandel, and Anne Waldman, white women writers informed Beat literature with salient dimensions of female sexuality and feminine cultural subjectivity; however, consigned to a periphery, these writers were not assimilated to the movement until recently. Crystallizing the sexual politics of this exclusion is Joyce Johnson's sardonic appellation "minor characters," her "girl gang" rebuke to Ginsberg's 1954 "dream letter" that "the social organization ... most true of itself to the artist is the boy gang," an elect closed to women.[7] As this declaration suggests, gender in Beat Generation literature was complacently sexist, marked by traditional binary oppositions of female and male, feminine and masculine, hetero- and homosexual that were preserved mostly by the male writers in their ostensibly radical stances. Women Beat writers challenged these constraining stances in a proto-feminist push-back; a performed insistence on female agency, gender equality, and gender refusal characterized their Beat rebellion and expanded the literary movement that contained it.

This chapter explores femininity and masculinity in the movement, and foregrounds women Beat writers and their literature of protest and critique. The female–male Beat binary etymologizes gender as a bivalent system, a dimorphic construction of complementary but opposing female and male positions aligned with nominal sex identity, dependent on differentiation, but also subject to postwar transformations that rendered homogeneous binary roles into heterogeneous hybrid ones.[8] Beat gender codes are manifested in discourses and rhetorical events that trace a continuum from high Modern templates to postmodern neologies, suggesting evolutions in Beat Generation sexual politics. The movement commenced in a dogmatic universalized masculinity (Ginsberg's "Howl" [1956]) that colonized a black feminine (Kerouac's *The Subterraneans* [1958; written in 1953]), which a corresponding white femininity parodied (Sheri Martinelli's "Duties of a Lady Female" [1959]), graphically challenged (Bonnie Bremser's *Troia: Mexican Memoirs* [1969]), and outflanked (Lenore Kandel's *The Love Book* [1966]), and which a recuperated masculinity misogynistically eradicated (Burroughs's *The Wild Boys* [1971]).[9] Transformations in gender subjectivities in Beat writing have correlation and cause in the postwar cultural and political dislocation famously formulated by Fredric Jameson as "a shift in the dynamics of culture pathology ... in which the alienation of the [modern] subject is displaced by the fragmentation of the [postmodern] subject."[10] The postmodern condition of fragmentation of the subject is synchronous with the Beat hipster, who is seen as "a hybridized subject, a product of cultural miscegenation, a cross-dresser, neither completely white nor black, masculine nor feminine, heterosexual nor homosexual, working class nor bourgeois" (*Taking It Like a Man* 52). This theory of the male Beat subject – whom David Savran terms the postwar "white rebel male" (52) –equally fits conditions of the female Beat subject. The instability, contingency, and erosion of boundaries between and within sex roles, sexualities, and gender constructions in the paradigm-shifting postwar era mark the postmodernity that historicizes Beat Generation subjects and the movement's immanence (1944–1965).

Postmodern hipster indeterminacy and contingency struggle against binary gender roles in Kerouac's novel *The Subterraneans*, which figures the Modernism/postmodernism divide as a generational conflict of hipsters – "me hot, them cool" – stamped by subjectivities of race.[11] The narrator, Leo, confesses to "white ambition thoughts or white daydreams" (62) and the "crudely malely sexual ... lecherous and so on propensities" (5) of an "adolescent cocksman" (25) in his desire for the hipster paradigm Mardou, a "black Cherokee" "Negro" (62) and fetishized object of his lust, "her feet in thongs of sandals of such sexuality-looking greatness" (4). But it is Mardou's linguistic hybridity, correlated to her mixed-race and ethnic heritage, that epitomizes the new subterraneans who displaced the 1940s white male hipster. She has "cultured funny tones of part Beach, part I. Magnin model, part Berkeley, part Negro highclass, something, a mixture of langue and style of talking and use of words ... [Leo] never heard before" (10), a composite, linguistically crossbred speech that unfixes binary race categories and prophesies American multiculturalism. On the brink of the classic phase of the Civil Rights Movement, before *Brown v. Board of Education* in 1954 and the 1955 murder of Emmett Till (for speaking to a white woman), *The Subterraneans* depicts what Savran calls the "cultural miscegenation" (52) that undergirds movements for racial justice and women's liberation. Both are embodied in Mardou who "from the first" is "self-dependent and independent announcing she wanted no one" (13), while her "story of spiritual suffering" (50) is equal to those of "the great men ... [the] great heroes of America" (49) who inspire Leo and Beat Generation romantic narratives.

She is like a hipster man. Her literary-cool letter to Leo is undermined by his deconstruction and critique of it; the heroine's text is fractured by the narrative authority of the male (75–84), whose persistence depends on restoring her to inferiority, a sex object, so that the narrative author(ity) can "go home ... And write this book" (152), reinstating male power and thus male literary subjectivity. As this rescripting of racial and female status suggests, Beat gender codes are manifested in discourses and rhetorical events that oscillate from reductive binary constructions of female and male, feminine and masculine, hetero- and homosexual, colored and white, as decreed by Leo, to bold blurrings of binary distinctions in a mixed-race femininity of the postwar postmodern fragmentation and hybridity as represented by Mardou. The oscillation of these tendencies reflects the continuous struggle with gender that marks Beat Generation sexual politics and literature.

Other male writers, such as Ginsberg and Gary Snyder, resisted the postmodern undermining of binary polarities, defending codes of male superiority and female inferiority that encoded misogyny and privileged their own maverick sexual beliefs and orientations. Ginsberg disputed the movement's disregard of women writers but accepted "blame ... for exploiting the women ... the men didn't push the women literally or celebrate them." Yet he also defended this lapse, contending that "among the group of people we knew at the time," there were no women "writers of such power as Kerouac or Burroughs"; thus the men were not really "responsible for the lack of outstanding genius in the women we knew" because the women did not measure up.[12] In Ginsberg's formulation it is female literary inferiority – the failure of women writers to meet the genius bar, to be "a strong woman writer who could hold her own, like Diane di Prima," and therefore enjoin the men to "work with her and recognize her" – rather than misogyny, or the dependence on and entitlement to women's subordination, that accounts for the historical exclusion of women from the Beat canon (*Sunday Camera* quoted in Peabody, 1). Women Beat writers were marginalized by such assumptions and by poetics of female silence (Kerouac's hipster "girls [who] say nothing and wear black"), centerlessness (John Clellon Holmes), and essentialized Freudian darkness (Snyder).[13] At best, women Beats are figured as complements to male preeminence, as in John Wieners's "poets with pale faces, girls dressed in black beside them," a binary of "poets" and "girls," visual ciphers who ensure male subjectivity.[14]

But, when this binary occurs in Beat literature, its female writers deconstruct it. Diane di Prima's poem "The Quarrel" (1961) depicts hipster sexual politics as a woman's fight against male entitlement and patriarchal complicity. The poem's cryptic direct address replicates strategies of the oppressed who critique by indirect and "unspoken" ways, in order to contend with the

trope of female bohemian inferiority. The poem's subversiveness comes from
its poetics of thoughts that are unsaid in the dialogue yet spoken textually
to express objections to the double standard that makes men artists and
women housekeepers. It performs the expected female compliance of the
"chick" in ways that lay waste to the category and expose the fatuousness
of male hegemony, embodied by "Mark." The female speaker addresses this
boyfriend directly only twice; all other talk is presented as the unspoken
("I didn't say it out loud") or as words addressed to inanimate objects. The
poem begins:

> You know I said to Mark that I'm furious at you.
> No he said are you bugged. He was drawing Brad who was asleep on the bed...
> Jesus I thought you think it's so easy. There you sit innocence personified. I didn't
>   say anything else to him.
> You know I thought I've got work to do too sometimes. In fact I
> probably have just as fucking much work to do as you do...
> I am sick I said to the woodpile of doing dishes...
> Just because I happen to be a chick I thought. ("The Quarrel" in *Different* 46;
>   ellipses mine)

The poem continues: "And what a god damned concession it was for me
to bother to tell you that I was bugged at all I said to the back of his
neck. I didn't say it out loud." With its textual indicators of speech and
thought, the unspoken is spoken, a literary irony that exposes the folly of
male confidence in female silence and subordination. Gender inequity is
clear: the speaker's automatic consignment to dishwashing rather than to
making art "Just because I happen to be a chick" exemplifies a biological
determinism that abets silence over confrontation because "it's so fucking uncool to talk about it," a hipster code that complements and con-
veniently reinforces the incommensurate roles assigned by gender. As if in
answer to Ginsberg, critic Helen McNeil concluded that "there were no
female Kerouacs because external social controls of the women functioned
as silencer."[15] The poem's bitter review of sexism and the hipster hegemony
of cool denounces women's silenced omission from considerations of Beat
art and creativity, refuting contentions of female artistic inferiority such
as Ginsberg's even when that poet is, as in the case of "The Quarrel," the
named exception to the rule.

Joanne Kyger extends the poetic protest strike against direct speech
and confrontation, rendering visible the male hegemony that erases her as
a poet. Many years after the 1962 "trip to India" specified, Kyger's 1996
poem "Poison Oak for Allen" (evidently for Ginsberg) deconstructed gender
inequity and crystallized the paradox of women Beats' erased presence in
legends of Beat history:

Here I am reading about your trip to India again with Gary Snyder and Peter
Orlovsky. Period. Who took the picture of you three

With smart Himalayan backdrop

The bear?[16]

The poem is discursively ordered on Kyger's (non)absence and makes use
of the exasperating invisibility assigned her by Beat Generation masculinity; its witty coherence contradicts male Beat myths of self-generation
and female wordlessness and centerlessness, paradoxically foreground-
ing the ineradicable inconspicuousness of the poet's presence.[17] The poem
embodies the Beat manifesto to "unscrew the doors from their jambs" to
reveal what has been hidden; but here the revelation is directed by the
woman poet to the radical Beat agenda that suppresses the feminine and
the female, not to the mainstream culture that destroys the "best minds"
(*Howl*, 9). Claiming authorial literary status, women Beat poets such
as Kyger protested the explicit sexism and misogyny of male-centered,
male-authored Beat writing, resisting their exclusion from cultural and
literary salience in the movement and in the global literary history it
charted.[18]

The Beat literary assumption of male priority, a tendency universalizing
the masculine, is evident throughout the canon, commencing with "Howl,"
a poem commemorating men: it is not about the "generation" of best minds
but about the best male minds. Avant-garde Beat discourses and culture promoted a near-homogeneity through poetics and thematics that minimized
gender differentiation while still being implicated in gender dimorphism. In
"Howl," the stanzas of "the best minds of my generation" promise in theory
equal-opportunity destruction in madness, but that abstraction is disproved
by reinstated gendered antitheses: those "angelheaded hipsters" "waving
genitals and manuscripts / who let themselves be fucked in the ass by saintly
motorcyclists" and by "N. C., secret hero of these poems, cocksman and /
Adonis of Denver" are joyful male hedonists who fall to the witches of
womankind; in one of the long poem's only references to women, the male
hipsters "los[e] their loveboys to the three old shrews of fate the one eyed
/ shrew of the heterosexual dollar the one eyed shrew that / winks out of
the womb and the one eyed shrew that does nothing but sit on her ass"
(12), and with that the poem reveals its unabated gender segregation and
exclusion.

The redundant identification of female occupation with gender and the
consciousness of female invisibility that are cursed by di Prima and mocked
by Kyger are parodied by Sheri Martinelli in "Duties of a Lady Female."
Martinelli is less well known than even other women Beat writers such as

di Prima,[19] but her long poem, composed in 1959 for Ezra Pound, resonates with and rescripts "Howl," listing aspirations and obstacles but for adventurous hipster women.[20] The poem advises aspiring female lovers of men on how to keep them and how to repel female rivals. In this way, the poem appears to accommodate the gender binary and male supremacy, but it sardonically undercuts that impression with advice that infantilizes men: "No high or harsh tones of voice. He is more sensitive than you, to them. He's got a better sense of hearing & smell. Dont cry for yourself except by yourself. It acts on his nerves like a rockdrill. If you GOT to cry, do it for him" or "Dont talk too much ... Dont talk to him about anything but himself" (*Different* 154, 155). Midway through, the poem becomes a manifesto for female solidarity, but again sardonically, advising combat over men: "If another female even EYE BALLS your male, do this: ... Always go out prepared to fight for your male or stay home with him" (156). Playing on stereotypes of female duplicity, the parodic verses attack yet also inscribe antiwoman impulses, reinstating patriarchal dicta of female competitiveness for men, the "duties" that reduce women to the insulting redundant rank of "lady females," in a disproof of stereotype by its proof that is similar to di Prima's indirect strategy in "The Quarrel."

The long-line imperative verse form and style of "Duties of a Lady Female" evoke "Howl," though the former's analogous gender focus deploys satire to raise and rouse warrior women to "duties" that reconstruct the lived world: through matrilineage ("Children are a female responsibility & should descend through her"); through transcendence of postmodern multiplicity ("To SEE beyond local things like race, age, sex, class or religions"); and through female solidarity ("Fraternise with other females. Build a code of behaviour") (*Different* 157, 155). The poem figures a Cartesian gender existentialism, a mind–matter dualism of a "female code" that allocates to the "male ... what ... bodies can do" and to the female putting "ideas into ... minds" (157). This reverses gender-binary attributes that align female with body and male with mind, thus elevating the male, by this reversal enacting a Beat Generation resistance to conformity but against its constitutional sexism. In a last dictate, the "duties" of the "lady female" are to "redeem our race of women" against the "renegade" or antifeminist "female ... [who] puts her vanity before the honor of the race of females," deploying gender essentialism to challenge gender constructionism and exposing the meaninglessness to women of "the word 'illegitimate' ... NO such thing as an illegitimate child" (157–158). Martinelli's poem is a revisionary counterpart to "Howl" that purports to lionize the male while iconographizing the female, just as "Howl" purports a universality that is in actuality male precedence. Martinelli's under-recognized work merits prominence in Beat poetry; it contributes to the counternarrative of female writers' expansion of the movement and relevance to its impact on the postmodern emergence.

Steered by fixities of the heteronormative gender binary, Beat literature reduces to a point–counterpoint dialogue – a martial stand-off in which heterosexual "love is a duel."[21] The love duel puts in dramatic narrative form rules of "sexual politics," the dynamic recognized by Kate Millett in her book of that name. A pair of late 1950s Beat poems by combatant poets playing the dozens dramatizes this analysis of gender formation and its adversarial politics. The infamous Snyder poem "Praise for Sick Women," first published in 1958, instigated a counternarrative from di Prima in her parrying poem, "The Practice of Magical Evocation."[22] These dueling poems of hostile poetics enact misogynist patriarchy's recourse to biological essentialism, even in ostensibly antideterminist Beat writing.

Flashing a derisive gynophobia, Snyder's poem opens by patronizingly congratulating "sick" females on their biological infirmity of menses:

> The female is fertile, and discipline
> (contra naturam) only
> confuses her ...
> All women are wounded ...
>   you young girls
> First caught with the gut-cramp ...
> Sick women ...
> in the change of the moon:
> In a bark shack
> Crouched from sun, five days,
> Blood dripping through crusted thighs. (*Riprap* 6–7)

Western misogynist clichés abound in Snyder's verses: the essentialized incompatibility of female fertility and discipline, female mental inferiority and confusion, and female genitalia and bloody wound. The "menstrual hut" of sequestration itself signifies the essential impurity and contaminating touch ascribed to the female beyond five menstrual days. All the gynophobia of patriarchal tradition is distilled into a handful of slicing lines.

Di Prima's "The Practice of Magical Evocation" is designated as a retort to Snyder by its epigraph of the first three lines of "Praise for Sick Women." A raid on patriarchy, it is the counter-punch to the male Beat poet's rampant and willful misogyny. In a defusing move the di Prima poem lays claim to the

essentialism that the Snyder poem deploys to wound women by reminding
them of their "wound"; the di Prima poem reverses the stigma, deploying
essentialism to praise:

> I am a woman and my poems
> are woman's: easy to say
> this. The female is ductile
> and
> (stroke after stroke)
> built for masochistic
> calm.[23]

The speaker's untroubled identification of woman poet with "woman's"
poems – with woman's body, in turn – disputes male condescension ("discipline ... only / confuses her") and leads to the stronger rejoinder, pairing but
opposing the Snyder poem's retiring "fertile" with the nearly homonymous,
dauntlessly malleable "ductile" in a pointed rebuke. "The Practice of Magical
Evocation" pushes alleged female pliancy forward into what in Snyder is an
anatomical mire, answering his "wounded" female genitalia with the bold
"cunt gets wide / and relatively sloppy," evoking the outcome of female fertility in human infant delivery. Not just for male sexual pleasure, to be "assailed
inside & out," female genitalia are both agents and portals of female creativity. Though childbirth has consequences for the texture of female "pelvic
architecture," (124) female genitalia are for di Prima the sanctified origins of
life.

Insofar as Beat poetics and aesthetics foreground, perform, engage, and
advance postmodernism's flexibilities and hybridities, the movement's variations are wrung by its subaltern practitioners: women and writers of color.
For example, LeRoi Jones/Amiri Baraka's statement of poetics, "How You
Sound??" (1959), mobilizes the poet's freedom of composition and linguistic emancipation to a comprehensive creation: "There cannot be anything
I must fit the poem into. Everything must be made to fit into the poem. There
must not be any preconceived notion or design for what the poem ought to
be."[24] Influenced by Charles Olson's ideas of open field composition, this
poetics entirely disallows gender and hails the disparate and the discon-
nected, a nod to the abstract personism of Frank O'Hara's "Everything is in
the poems ... You just go on your nerve."[25] Di Prima's poetic formulations
meet those of Jones, her *Floating Bear* co-editor: Jones's "MY POETRY
is whatever I think I am" ("How You Sound??") is evoked in her poem
"Rant" (1985), which conceptualizes poetics grounded not in literary history or iconography but by dismissing boundaries dividing poetry making
from the quotidian – from the poet's existence and identity ("Mapping" 30).

Ratifying Jones in a Beat poetics of expansive conception, di Prima magisterially stipulates the poet's totality of resources:

> there is no part of yourself you can separate out
> saying, this is memory, this is sensation
> this is the work I care about, this is how I
> make a living
> it is whole.[26]

Her neo-Beat poetics defies any segregating tendencies of literary theory:

> There is no way you can not have a poetics
> no matter what you do: plumber, baker, teacher you do it in
>   the consciousness of making
> or not making yr world. ("Rant" 160–161)

This, as in much writing by women Beats, effects the erosion of gender categories, disrupting and displacing ascriptions of identity by sex with anarchic interventions of race and desire. In her 1967 book *Word Alchemy*, Lenore Kandel avoids gendered positions altogether and pronounces "Poetry is never compromise. It is the manifestation / translation of a vision, an illumination, an experience," a Beat poetics of idealistic insight and blank candor.[27] Like di Prima and Jones, Kandel endorses an opened-out art: "whatever is language is poetic language" with the "only proviso ... that the word be the correct word as demanded by the poem and only the poet can be ultimate judge of that" (vi). This declaration fastidiously avoids or transcends gender as such, as well as postmodern hybridity, for a neutral poetry authority residing in the demands of a poem, as if it were an autonomous, undifferentiated formal entity detached from both poet and culture, a retreat from postwar fragmentation.

This poetics of gender neutrality is in distinct contrast to the highly gendered strategy of Kandel's most well-known work, *The Love Book* (1966). The map of gender discourse in Beat poetry takes emphatic shape with this collection, whose confessional sexual appetite and unvarnished colloquial language describing heterosexual intercourse and erotica caused it to be impounded for obscenity in San Francisco. Although the charges against Kandel's book were dropped, this seizure repeated the 1957 obscenity trial for "Howl" in the same city. Now it was a female Beat poet wielding the patriarchal language of sex to affirm subjectivity, a language usually allocated to male Beat objectifications of women and homosexual celebrations of same-sex desire. This shift to female literary empowerment in the middle of the Beat era – the shift from Ginsberg to Kandel as the poets of gender hegemony censored and condemned by law – corresponds with the postmodern investiture and its mass culture correlative in the 1960s counterculture, of which Kandel, like Ginsberg, was a prominent exemplar. *The Love Book* recasts Beat literary discourses by focusing on women and gender, augmenting, revitalizing, and reinventing the Beat female poet as a subject in poetry:

> there are no ways of love but / beautiful
> I love you all of them
> I love you / your cock in my hand stirs like a bird
> in my fingers
> as you swell and grow hard in my hand forcing my fingers open
> with your rigid strength
> you are beautiful / you are beautiful. (1–2)

Intercourse here issues from fantasies of sexual caress. The speaker describes her literal possession of the "cock"; she speaks about holding in her hand in ecstatic foreplay the virtual stylus-signifier of literary subjectivity. Even so, the gender binary has mysteriously disappeared in this song, not to be replaced by postmodern hybridity but by an equality of pleasure giving and receiving.

In a turn from that intimacy, Kandel looks to the gendered world of the classic Beat Generation, annexing the male Beat canon for women, manifesting descent from and allegiance to the movement's predecessors. "Blues for Sister Sally" (1967) interpolates women into Ginsberg's "holy litany" of "best minds":

> she bears the stigma (holy holy) of the raving christ
> (holy holy)
> holy needle
> holy powder
> holy vein. (*Word Alchemy* 62)

Kandel aligns with proto-feminist "sister" Beat poets in this same poem, which appropriates images and discourses from "Howl" by centering on the connection between the female poet and the poem's female subject, who would be installed in a pantheon: "how shall we canonize our sister who is not quite dead / who fornicates with strangers / who masturbates with needles," a female iteration of "best minds" (62).

But it is the erotic and (hetero)sexually radiant Dionysian sex poems of *The Love Book* that evince the postmodern transformation from the gender binary to the hybridity and dissipation of gender categories, ironically so since in this book Kandel writes about uninhibited intercourse between women and men, with each partner graphically occupying divergent, asymmetrical physical roles reflective of the sex–gender materiality of vagina and penis. This fragment from "To Fuck With Love, Phase II" authorizes the woman Beat poet in the autonomous, uncompromised power of her text:

> fuck – the fuck of love-fuck – the yes entire – love out of ours – the cock
> in the cunt fuck – the fuck of pore into pore – the smell of fuck taste it –
> love dripping from skin to skin – ... – I / you
> pure love-lust of godhead beauty unbearable
>   carnal incarnate. (*Love Book* 4)

Kandel was wary of free poetics' tendency toward self-referentiality: "when it becomes enamored of itself it [craft] produces word masturbation" (*Word Alchemy* v), an ironic metaphor given the onanistic invitation of *The Love Book*, the tumescence the text elicits. But the erotic self-focus of this poem is overridden by a poetics of multiplicity, eroded distinctions, and expanded vision; as she writes, "[t]here are no barriers to poetry or prophecy; by their nature they are barrier breakers, bursts of perception, lines into infinity" (*Word Alchemy* vii). The transition from canonical male Beat poets such as Ginsberg to outsider female claimants such as Kandel refreshes and alters Beat Generation radical sexual politics. Both the gender binary and its dissipation in hybridity are engulfed in the free language of sex-love that Kandel brandishes in *The Love Book*, pointing to the possibility of gender transcendence.

Anne Waldman's list-poem "Fast Speaking Woman" (1975), a late Beat work over thirty pages long, embraces gender transcendence while paradoxically being in substance entirely about gender.[28] The emblematic simultaneity of the postmodern ethos is conveyed in the poem's incantatory inclusiveness; every kind of woman and femininity is invoked in "vibrating incantory repetitions of the declarative enunciation 'I am,' an anaphoric proliferation of limitless claims for women" (*Breaking the Rule of Cool*, 257), as in these opening lines:

> I'm a shouting woman
> I'm a speech woman
> I'm an atmosphere woman
> I'm an airtight woman
> I'm a flesh woman
> I'm a flexible woman
> I'm a high-heeled woman
> I'm a high-styled woman ("Fast Speaking Woman" 3)

"Fast Speaking Woman" chants a hybridity of its postmodern moment that typifies Waldman's work: the urgent exclamatory poem places her as a gender-feminist radical of the "hot" school of Beat writing. The poem's composite of the feminine and masculine Beat literary impulses preserves gender in its Whitmanic/Ginsbergian style while nevertheless obliterating it in the visceral rush of its female enumerations. In "Feminafesto" (1994), Waldman transmutes Beat's poetics into "an enlightened poetic" that spurns gender subordinations and exclusions, advocating "a poetics defined by your primal energy not by a heterosexist world ... a poetics of transformation beyond gender."[29] This post-Beat exhortation surpasses atavistic gender divisions by enlisting materialistic sexualities to rescript poetics in a postmodern proliferation of "transsexual ... [and] transvestite literature" (145).

The gender bivalence resisted by women Beat writers is modified by imperatives of genre. As opposed to Waldman's epiphanic poetics "beyond gender," aesthetics of Beat prose narratives disrupt or eradicate gender binarism through stories that attain a radical sexual politics of subjectivity. Joyce Glassman's (later Johnson) *Come and Join the Dance* (1962), the under-studied first Beat Generation novel by and about a Beat woman, warily approaches the Cold War gender binary as an obstacle to female self-realization that can be thwarted by its roles' reversals.[30] The narrative consigns the Beat antihero Peter to domestic detention: "wak[ing] up in his apartment each day ... go[ing] out for breakfast because there weren't any clean cups ... drift[ing] up and down Broadway" (162), landlocked without his smashed-up car and emasculated in the private sphere traditionally assigned to women, while the heroine Susan breaks free of the feminine sentence to silence and sexual compliance, dropping out of college and sailing into the world, a gender defiance patriarchy reserves for men, as narrativized in *On the Road* (90–91, 175–176).[31]

Brenda Frazer/Bonnie Bremser's transnational Beat road tale *Troia: Mexican Memoirs* (1969) is a fiercely female-centered account of the travel adventures and existential transformations of classic Beat literature that amplifies Glassman's fledgling Beat female subjectivity. Empowered by the road's displacements of gender expectations and its geographic alienation, Bremser's memoir disperses the purdah of the female position in the gender binary with a radical, public multiplicity. The protagonist Bonnie Bremser embodies simultaneously patriarchal roles for women of "matron" *and* "whore," which, like the feminine and the masculine of the gender binary, are traditionally mutually exclusive. Forced by her impecunious poet husband to become a streetwalker, Bonnie, wife and mother, grudgingly also becomes the family provider; in a "horror of being the breadwinner" (33), her femininity is conscripted into the masculine. To be a wife who is also a "whore" is a paradox of the feminine that unmakes gender binary divisions, albeit within the feminine position alone. In the collapse of gender polarities that devolves when the Madonna is literally the whore, the radical sexual aesthetics of the narrative transform the female Beat abject. As subjugated wife, desperate mother, and ambivalent prostitute, Bonnie achieves subject status by her narrativized, aestheticized integration of these simultaneous selves, troped in her *cri de guerre*, "I embrace my prostitution."[32]

Kate Millett observes that "misogynist literature" is "frankly propagandistic" in its aim to keep "both sexual factions" separate and unequal (45). Just so *The Subterraneans* constructs female sexuality as castrating: Mardou "intend[ed] to bust us [men] in half" through her orgasmic "contraction and great-strength of womb" (104). In William S. Burroughs's *The Wild Boys: A Book of the Dead* (1971), men are *sui generis* as well as misogynistic: a "[l]ittle boy without a navel ... places an apple on a teacher's desk ... rolls over to the blackboard and rubs out the word MOTHER" (155). The gynophobia in male-authored Beat writing favors the gender binary, for its segregations mollify misogynist fears. In Burroughs the female threat of vagina dentate is less a social-sexual fear than an existential liability unmitigated by postmodern tendencies to hybridity: preserving the binary distinctions, women are apologists for the thought police, while queer men like the wild boys are rebels and outlaws. In the novel's sensational cinematic discourses, the young guerilla fighters who "take no prisoners" (148) engage in tumultuously choreographed group rituals of homoerotic gratification. Renouncing women, the fantasied wild boys continue their kind among themselves:

> a baby and semen black market flourished ... we recruited male infants from birth. You could take your boyfriend's sperm ... [and] arrange to inseminate medically inspected females. Nine months later the male crop was taken to one of the remote peaceful communes ... A whole generation arose that had never seen a woman's face nor heard a woman's voice. (153–154)

In *The Wild Boys*, women are monstrous errors of creation, a biological snare for male homosocial freedom; not the gender binary but the entire gender is eliminated in this hallucinated vision.

The mutually exclusive female–male poles of patriarchy's binary gender codes influenced Beat literature's experimental tropes and tainted its radical sexual politics and poetics, calling into question the depth and extent of Beat counterculturalism. But its many practitioners, major and "minor" characters both, struggled with the binary and often found compromises, transcendences, and evolutions that sometimes surmounted gender altogether. In contrast to Burroughs, Ginsberg, and Kerouac, for example, Corso obscured binary gender distinctions, reducing them to the inclusively human, if only in ruminations found in his letters. For instance, he radically problematized the Beat trope "angel," which is used by (mostly male) Beat writers and typically signifies exaltation, sanctity, abjectness. His meditations on both female and male "angel" writers eroded gendered distinctions that the trope might carry.[33] For Corso, the poet Hope Savage, a.k.a. Sura, a "beautiful Shelley with a cunt," is "truly an angel," "the best" of "all the wise heads ... in the early 50s" (*Accidental* 406), among whom Corso found "Too many angels with cocks" (6). Extending the gender deconstruction of the Beat "angel," Corso also appointed Joyce Johnson to be "Jack [Kerouac]'s angel with a cunt" (102). Beat poetics of uninhibited confession effected transcendence of the gender binary by anatomical fiat, the slang for genitalia that renders "angel" omni-gendered: embodied, occupied, and defined equally by women and men, evoking and contending cultural beliefs about difference expressed in the dubious theory of female "penis envy." Postmodern contingencies that are in play in Beat writing and poetics subvert the Cartesian split that renders the male as mind and the female as body, reflecting through women Beat writers the emergence of second-wave feminism in the postmodern era that Beat literature itself helped to delineate. As their works evince, it might be said that the existence of the very cohort of women Beat writers is itself a disruption of Beat Generation gender codes; certainly that is the thesis of *The Wild Boys*. When gender is anarchically unfixed from sex, Beat writing's liberated postmodern forms broaden the generation's rebel discourse by defying reactionary gender differentiations essential to hierarchies and hegemonies of patriarchal sexual politics. This shift from Modernist alienation to the fragmentation and hybridity of the postmodern is the Beat Movement revolution: it is the shift, at its best and too rarely realized, to gender transcendence.

NOTES

1 See Andreas Huyssen, *After the Great Divide: Modernism, Mass Culture, Postmodernism* (Bloomington: Indiana University Press, 1987).
2 See Alan Nadel, *Containment Culture: American Narratives, Postmodernism, and the Atomic Age* (Durham, NC: Duke University Press, 1995) and David Savran, *Taking It Like a Man: White Masculinity, Masochism, and Contemporary American Culture* (Princeton: Princeton University Press, 1998).
3 Allen Ginsberg, *Howl and Other Poems* (San Francisco: City Lights, 1956), np.
4 The Beat movement is an avant-garde analogous to the contemporaneous New York School, San Francisco Renaissance, and Black Mountain movements or "schools," which, reflecting Cold War culture, also marginalized or dismissed female practitioners.
5 William S. Burroughs, in "Introductory Notes," Gregory Corso, *Mindfield: New and Selected Poems* (New York: Thunder's Mouth Press, 1989), xix.
6 See Ronna C. Johnson and Nancy M. Grace, eds., *Girls Who Wore Black: Women Writing the Beat Generation* (New Brunswick: Rutgers University Press, 2002).
7 Joyce Johnson, *Minor Characters* (New York: Houghton Mifflin, 1983), 83–84.
8 See Kate Millett, *Sexual Politics* (1969; New York: Ballantine, 1970).

9 See Ginsberg, *Howl and Other Poems*; Jack Kerouac, *The Subterraneans* (New York: Grove Press, 1958); Lenore Kandel, *The Love Book* (San Francisco: Stolen Paper Review Editions, 1966); Bonnie Bremser, *Troia: Mexican Memoirs* (New York: Croton Press, 1969); William S. Burroughs, *The Wild Boys: A Book of the Dead* (New York: Grove Press, 1971); and Sheri Martinelli, "Duties of a Lady Female," *A Different Beat: Writings by Women of the Beat Generation*, ed. Richard Peabody (London: Serpent's Tail, 1997).

10 Fredric Jameson, "Postmodernism, or The Cultural Logic of Late Capitalism," *Postmodernism: A Reader*, ed. Thomas Docherty (New York: Columbia University Press, 1993), 71.

11 Kerouac, *The Subterraneans*, 11.

12 Allen Ginsberg, *Boulder Sunday Camera Magazine*, quoted in Peabody, ed., *Different*, 1.

13 See Jack Kerouac, "The Origins of the Beat Generation," *On the Road*, ed. Scott Donaldson (New York: Penguin, 1979), 362; John Clellon Holmes, *Go* (1952; New York: New American Library, 1980), xvii; and Gary Snyder, "The Real Work: Interview with Gary Snyder [with Paul Geneson]," *The Real Work: Interviews and Talks 1964–1979*, ed. William Scott McLean (New York: New Directions, 1980), 80.

14 John Wieners, *707 Scott Street* (Los Angeles: Sun and Moon Press, 1996), 10. See also Barbara Ehrenreich, *The Hearts of Men* (New York: Anchor Books), 49.

15 Helen McNeil, "The Archeology of Gender in the Beat Movement," *The Beat Generation Writers*, ed. A. Robert Lee (London: Pluto Press, 1996), 193.

16 Joanne Kyger, *Again: Poems 1989–2000* (Albuquerque: La Alameda Press, 2001), 102.

17 Ronna C. Johnson, "Mapping Women Writers of the Beat Generation," *Breaking the Rule of Cool*, ed. Nancy M. Grace and Ronna C. Johnson (Jackson: University of Mississippi Press, 2004), 20.

18 See Kyger, "A Brisk Wind is Blowing," *Again*, 156.

19 As if anticipating a school of women Beat writers, the poem resonated with di Prima, who met Martinelli when she visited Pound in 1959, and she published "Duties of a Lady Female" later in *The Floating Bear* 32 (1966).

20 See Johnson, "Mapping," 10–11 and Steven Moore, "Sheri Martinelli: A Modernist Muse," *Gargoyle* 41 (summer 1998), 28–54.

21 Jack Kerouac, *On the Road* (New York: Viking, 1957), 85.

22 Gary Snyder, "Praise for Sick Women," *Riprap and Cold Mountain Poems* (Berkeley: Counterpoint, 2009), 6–7; Diane di Prima, "The Practice of Magical Evocation," *Selected Poems 1956–1975* (Plainfield, VT: North Atlantic Press, 1975), 39. It is not clear where the poem was first published; possibly the epigraph quoting Snyder's poem did not appear until the poem was printed in *Selected Poems*.

23 "The Practice of Magical Evocation," *The Beat Book*, ed. Anne Waldman (Boston: Shambala, 1999), 124.

24 LeRoi Jones, "How You Sound??" *New American Poetry 1945–1960*, ed. Donald Allen (New York: Grove, 1960), 424.

25 Frank O'Hara, "Personism: A Manifesto," *The Collected Poems of Frank O'Hara*, ed. Donald Allen (Berkeley: University of California Press, 1995), 498.

26 Diane di Prima, "Rant," *Pieces of a Song: Selected Poems* (San Francisco: City Lights, 1990), 159–161.

27 Lenore Kandel, *Word Alchemy* (New York: Grove, 1967), v.

28 Anne Waldman, "Fast Speaking Woman," *Fast Speaking Woman* (San Francisco: City Lights, 1996).

29 Anne Waldman, "Feminafesto," *Kill or Cure* (New York: Penguin, 1994), 145.

30 Joyce Johnson (writing as Joyce Glassman), *Come and Join the Dance* (New York: Atheneum, 1962).

31 See Ronna C. Johnson, "'And Then She Went': Beat Departures and Feminine Transgressions in Joyce Johnson's *Come and Join the Dance*," *Breaking the Rule of Cool*, 69–95.

32 See Ronna C. Johnson, "Beat Transnationalism Under Gender: Brenda Frazer's *Troia: Mexican Memoirs*," *The Transnational Beat Generation*, ed. Nancy M. Grace and Jennie Skerl (New York: Palgrave, 2012), 51.

33 Gregory Corso, *An Accidental Autobiography*, ed. Bill Morgan (New York: New Directions, 2003).

12

POLINA MACKAY

The Beats and Sexuality

The Beats were notorious nonconformist postmodernists who sought what seemed in their heyday (1950–1969) to be a distinctly non-American form of self-fulfillment, which they proposed might come from alternative ways of being: perpetual travelers, spiritualists, or literary experimentalists. Much of this notoriety for the wider public, however, does not originate from the Beats' nuanced philosophy of being; instead it comes from myths about their sexual behaviors and from the treatment of sexuality in their works. For a start, the Beats rose to fame through two obscenity charges that took issue with the treatment of sexual content in their works: these were the prosecutions of two seminal Beat texts, Allen Ginsberg's *Howl and Other Poems* (1956) and William S. Burroughs's *Naked Lunch* (1959), the trials of which concluded that the literary merit of the works outweighed any offense that might be caused through their content. Nevertheless, Beat writing is often seen exclusively as propounding sexual experimentation, a precedent of the sexual revolutions of free love that ensued in the 1960s, whether expressed in Ginsberg's explicit references to homosexuality or Jack Kerouac's tendency to give his principal characters multiple sexual partners. Adding significantly to the myth of the Beats as exponents of free love and casual sex is Diane di Prima's widely read *Memoirs of a Beatnik* (1969), a semifictional memoir about the author's involvement with well-known figures from Beat circles, written as pornography for money in the 1960s. Perhaps one of the most well-known instances of Beat Generation history is a scene from that book in which the author-protagonist has an orgy with a group of people that includes Ginsberg and Kerouac.[1] *Memoirs of a Beatnik* seems to confirm that the Beats were indeed experimenting with sexual behaviors of all kinds; to the most conservative members of the public, the book paints these writers as lacking a sense of sexual morality in what appears an outright rejection of fidelity and monogamy. Yet, at the same time, *Memoirs of a Beatnik* is an excellent example of the Beats' treatment of sexuality: for Beats like Ginsberg, Burroughs, Kerouac, di Prima, and many others whom I discuss below, one's sexual preferences do not point to one's ethical choices; rather, sexuality is celebrated as a fluid concept tied always to political or social commentary.

In one of the first studies of sexuality in Beat literature, Catharine Stimpson argues that Beat writers perpetuate an "unfettered, uncensored, regenerative" sexuality.[2] There are indeed many examples in Beat texts of such fluidity. Ginsberg's early poetry offers an in-depth exploration of (homo)sexuality in late 1940s and early 1950s America, a time of predominantly conformist tendencies in mainstream American culture. As Nick Selby notes, however, this conformist public was simultaneously fascinated by sexual behaviors, which might explain why the two Kinsey reports into sexual practices became bestsellers in the 1950s.[3] Many of Ginsberg's poems published near this time are prime examples of the "unfettered sexuality" Stimpson describes; the earliest instance is the poem "In Society," from *Empty Mirror: Gates of Wrath* (1961), which contains the lines "I ate a sandwich of pure meat; an / enormous sandwich of human flesh, / I noticed, while I was chewing on it, it also included a dirty asshole."[4] Many of Ginsberg's poems are likewise explicit, offering images of homosexual sex, including "Please Master" (1968), which features the lines "please master can I lick your groin curled with blond soft fur ... please master grab my thighs and lift my ass to your waist ... please master make me go moan on the table" (502–503), or the poem "Sphincter" (1986), which announces

> I hope my good old asshole holds out ...
> active, eager, receptive to phallus
> coke bottle, candle, carrot
> banana & fingers –
> Now AIDS makes it shy, but still
> eager to serve. (950)

Ginsberg's use of the confessional mode in both these poems, evident not only in the abundant use of the pronoun "I" but also in the focus on personal and private experience, suggests a significant link between the author's sexuality and his poetics.[5]

The world that emerges out of a lifestyle immersed in promiscuous gay love in Ginsberg's early poetry could be deemed primarily "queertopian" (queer + utopian). This is evident in one of his most well-known poems from this early period, "The Green Automobile" (1953), where the poet presents male homosexuality as an idealized alternative to the conformity of marriage and offspring. The poem alludes to the real-life sexual relationship between Ginsberg and Neal Cassady, who at the time was married with three children. The two men's relationship effectively unleashes the poem, later described by Ginsberg as "a big, long, beautiful love poem to Neal Cassady," which charts what the poet sees as a kind of elevated "tenderness, kneeling together, holding on, traveling together, and then ultimate separation."[6] The poet describes here a queertopia where homosexual love is an expression of spiritual devotion and companionship in both pleasure and hardship. Opposing this utopian fantasy are the home, wife, and children. This opposition is apparent at the very beginning of the poem, when the speaker says that, if he had the magical green automobile, he would go to his friend's house and

> [H]onk [his] horn at his manly gate,
>   inside his wife and three
>   children sprawl naked
>   on the living room floor.
> He'd come running out
>   to my car full of heroic beer
>   and jump screaming at the wheel
>   for he is the greater driver. (*Collected* 91)

Ginsberg builds on the image of his lover abandoning his family to offer a fantasy of simultaneous beauty and recklessness, which exists exclusively in the world of the moving green automobile. We see the two lovers "bounding toward the snowy horizon / blasting the dashboard with original bop ... where angels of anxiety / careen through the trees," and together they see "the beauty of souls / hidden like diamonds / in the clock of the world" (91–92). This idealized universe, where nature fuels the lovers' love and devotion for each other, is clearly meant to be perceived as the opposite of the suburban home, a fantasy of free homosexual love.[7]

Ginsberg's most celebrated poem, "Howl," offers a similar veneration of homosexuality: "The tongue and cock and hand and asshole holy," an image followed by a parade of lovers (*Collected* 142). It should be noted, however, that, despite this glorification of one form of sexuality that is obvious in "Howl," Ginsberg's poetry exposes oppositional thinking (the tendency to see oneself as not the other) as a construction of capitalism. The voice that speaks in "Howl" arises out of the need to speak of/for an entire generation of others who have very little in common other than their ability to see the source of their problems for what it truly is: Moloch, a false God, a demonic figure that arose out of capitalism and other systems of control (e.g. government) to spread fear, conflict, and injustice. The poet of "Howl" has seen – and, Whitman-like, contains within himself – those who refuse to be consumed by this capitalist machine. Such a containment of otherness within oneself can be defined in the same terms as bisexuality. Nick Selby has argued of this feature of Ginsberg's poetry that it matches Martin Duberman's conceptualization of bisexuality as ironically signifying that "each one of us may contain within ourselves all of those supposed opposites we've been taught to divide humanity into," creating a model of sexual identity similar to Camille Paglia's definition of bisexuality as fluid sexuality (quoted in "Queer Shoulders" 128). Ginsberg's poetry is by no means openly bisexual, but it does champion a subjectivity without clear boundaries evident mostly in his work's privileging of movement over stasis: note, for instance, the way the poet of a younger, modern generation keeps shifting from one site of inspiration to the next in "A Supermarket in California" (1955), "wander[ing] in and out" of spaces half real and half imagined as he appropriates Walt Whitman, his inspiration and the author of the book he is holding, for postmodern America (Collected 144). Note also the equally dreamlike quality of "Howl," which becomes symbolic of a universe that constantly changes, a world reflective perhaps of the constant movement of capital in societies such as modern America; or the poems of transformation that Ginsberg wrote toward the end of his life in which the poet, at death's door, seeks transcendence (see "Death & Fame," "Dream," and "Things I'll Not Do (Nostalgias)" [all 1997]: Collected 1130–32, 1159, 1160–61).

Even more notorious are the sexual escapades of Jack Kerouac and his literary creations. One of the most attractive attributes of Kerouac as a modern author is the fact that, as Matt Theado has rightly noted, he "takes himself to the edge of experience, whether that experience is sexuality, drugs, fast cars, bop jazz, religious and spiritual epiphanies, or madness, and he records the sensations that he feels."[8] Most biographies of Kerouac, of which there are many precisely because of the subject's potential for such thrills, offer vivid and detailed accounts of his sexual relationships.[9] However, while the details of Kerouac's sexual relationships are interesting in their own right, they tell us very little about the author's treatment of sexuality in his works. On the Road, Kerouac's most famous novel, which propelled him into stardom when it was first published in 1957, is filled with descriptions of sexual encounters of the narrator-protagonist, Sal Paradise, and his hero, Dean Moriarty, with various partners. Sex in the book becomes as fluid as the moving geographies the constant travelers pass through. Most often Sal's first thought when he meets a woman is sex, though just as often he is shown to be shy and hesitant around potential partners. As the book progresses, however, it becomes apparent that Sal prefers talking to sex:

> I had to support her on the stool; she kept slipping off. I've never seen a drunker
> woman, and only eighteen. I bought her another drink; she was tugging at my

pants for mercy. She gulped it up. I didn't have the heart to try her. My own girl was about thirty and took care of herself better. With Venezuela writhing and suffering in my arms, I had a longing to take her in the back and undress her and only talk to her.[10]

Sal's desire to connect with those he has sex with on some spiritual level differentiates him from other male characters in the novel, principally from his hero, Dean. While it is obvious that sex is the main motivation behind most of Dean's actions, Sal's comments are designed to offer the reader a more nuanced understanding of sexual desire. Rather than seeing Dean's constant want of sex as at best a distraction and at worst derogatory to young women, Sal presents it as a desire for holiness.

Eventually, one of Sal's own sexual encounters seems to him something a lot more than casual sex on the road; in his eyes, sex with Terry is a holy deed, a brief encounter with the sublime:

Terry came out with tears of sorriness in her eyes. In her simple and funny little mind had been decided the fact that a pimp does not throw a woman's shoes against the door and does not tell her to get out. In reverent and sweet little silence she took all her clothes off and slipped her tiny body into the sheets with me. It was brown as grapes. I saw her poor belly where there was a Caesarian scar; her hips were so narrow she couldn't bear a child without getting gashed open. Her legs were like little sticks. She was only four foot ten. I made love to her in the sweetness of the weary morning. Then, two tired angels of some kind, hung-up forlornly in an LA shelf, having found the closest and most delicious thing in life together, we fell asleep and slept till late afternoon. (85)

It becomes clear here that in *On the Road* sex is a gateway into spiritual fulfillment, itself made apparent symbolically in the body of Terry, which is transformed from a body with a "poor belly," a "Caesarian scar," narrow hips, and legs that looked like sticks into, alongside her lover, an angel who found peace. In this regard Terry resembles the beatified suffering brother of *Visions of Gerard* (1963) and is depicted with just as much sentimentality.

Kerouac's link between sexuality and spirituality may not come as a surprise to those familiar with Buddhist teachings. Kerouac's Catholicism, his Buddhism, and the ways in which he may have tried to reconcile the two in his works have been a subject of much debate, which I have no space to go into.[11] However, it is worth noting that, in the context of the discussion of sexuality in Kerouac, the connection between sexual pleasure and spiritual fulfillment is predicated on the idea that mindfulness is a direct result of bodily awareness. As Albert Gelpi has pointed out in his analysis of incarnational poetics in the Beats, here lies the paradox embraced by many religions (but principally Buddhism and Christianity): "the body as the locus at once of mortality and immortality, of death and transcendence, of sexuality and spirit."[12] Sal and Terry in the example above become somewhat enlightened through sex as they find "the most delicious thing in life," a thing that is appropriately never named, left as an aporia for the reader to seek and find. In such a state, their sexual bodies are no longer suffering; in this union of mind and body, sex transforms them from tormented souls to peaceful angels (at least from Sal's point of view).

For Burroughs, the third writer most often associated with the Beat Generation, sex is the opposite of fulfillment; in Burroughs's work, sex is some sort of an emptying out of an inconsistent, inefficient body. In one of the most puzzling extracts from *Naked Lunch* (1959), the narrator suddenly bursts into a speech about the organs of the human body and puts forward the theory that "no organ is constant as regards either function or position ... sex organs sprout everywhere ... rectums open, defecate and close ... the entire organism changes color and consistency in split-second adjustments."[13] This description of the human body intrigued the philosophers Gilles Deleuze and Félix Guattari, who cite Burroughs in their own work to illustrate the meaning of a revolutionary concept, the "body without organs." Like the Burroughsian body of sprouting sexual organs, Deleuze and Guattari's body without organs is not static but a continuous process, as "the organ changes when it crosses a threshold, when it changes gradient."[14] For Deleuze and Guattari, the Burroughsian body eradicates clear distinctions and is thus relevant to the postmodern cultures of the late twentieth century, which have increasingly become more diverse yet also blur into one another. Burroughs's work has therefore been frequently read in light of Deleuze and Guattari's theories. For instance, Timothy S. Murphy's landmark work of Burroughs scholarship, *Wising Up the Marks* (1997), shows that Burroughs's work is illustrative of the world the philosophers envision, a world of constant fluidity with no clear binaries.[15] Similarly, Robin Lydenberg notes that the philosophers "coincide with Burroughs in their perception of the gradual degeneration of the procreative principle in the restricted arenas of sexual dualism, family, and society."[16]

While noting Burroughs's resistance to any form of organization, including sexual identity, is significant, it only tells half of the story. The first sustained scholarship on Burroughs fell into the trap of assuming that, because Burroughs seems to privilege fluidity and inconsistency, for him sexuality is irrelevant. Lydenberg, for example, argues that sexuality in Burroughs's work is merely an undesirable consequence of repression in a network of authoritarian systems designed to suppress individuality (109–113). She goes on to suggest that his novels are rather of "a new pansexuality," of a suspended and impersonal form of sexuality that is as monotonous as the drug addict's need (109), a necessity Burroughs also documents and fictionalizes extensively in *Naked Lunch* and elsewhere (e.g. his first novel *Junky* [1953]). This reading excludes Burroughs's *Queer*, a novel he wrote in 1952 but did not publish until 1985.

The book is semiautobiographical, referring to real-life events that took place in Mexico between 1949 and 1952 and chronicling William Lee's unrequited, obsessive love for Eugene Allerton. Allerton is based on Lewis Marker, a man Burroughs was in love with and who accompanied him to Ecuador in 1951 in search of the hallucinogenic drug yage. Once ignored in the Burroughs canon, largely because of the fact that it remained unpublished for decades, *Queer* has now rightly taken a central position in Burroughs Studies.[17] Moreover, the text has been somewhat further "restored" in the Burroughs canon in a new edition published in 2010 to commemorate the twenty-five-year anniversary of its first publication. Edited and with a new introduction by Oliver Harris, this new *Queer* is framed differently. The 1985 edition starts with Burroughs's introduction, in which he sketches the events surrounding the accidental death of his common-law wife, Joan Vollmer, in 1951, following a drunken game with a gun. In this introduction, he explains his reluctance to publish *Queer* as a direct result of these painful memories, claiming that "the book is motivated and formed by an event which is never mentioned, in fact is carefully avoided: the accidental shooting of my wife, Joan, in September 1951."[18] The 1985 introduction ends with a much larger claim: that the death of Joan motivated him to write as killing her brought him into contact with an Ugly Spirit who had possessed him, with his writing being the only way out of this possession. In other words, Burroughs sees *Queer* as a kind of therapeutic emptying out of traumatic memories. Moreover, as Harris argues elsewhere, "What is more obviously concealed in Burroughs's introduction to *Queer* is his homosexual identity, the very subject of the text itself. This is a kind of *open secret*, in the sense that it is entirely obvious and yet almost always overlooked."[19] Harris's 2010 edition places this introduction at the end as an appendix and in so doing severs the text from Burroughs's original narrative. Without Burroughs's introduction as a frame, then, the book is less a reaction to personal circumstances and more a response (resistance even) to attempts at regulating the homosexual subject by heterosexual/heteronormative society.[20]

It is clear from the discussion above of the three most well-known Beat writers, Burroughs, Ginsberg, and Kerouac, that sexuality – their sexual behaviors and relationships, the representation of sexual identity, and depictions of sex – play a significant role in their works. We can make a similar observation of other male authors associated with the Beat movement. Examples include the work of sexual outlaw Gregory Corso in poems such as "God is a Masturbator" (1970), which shows God's transformation into a sexual being; Gary Snyder's orgasmic depictions of sexuality as the work of the sacred in poems such as "Fear Not," "The Manichaeans," and "Song of the Taste"; and Amiri Baraka's *Preface to a Twenty Volume Suicide Note* (1961), replete with sexual imagery.

But it is the work of female authors associated with the Beat Generation that turns sexuality and its potential for breaking the rule of gender conformity into a significant trope of Beat writing. Sexuality as a theme features particularly highly in the work of di Prima, Lenore Kandel, Brenda Frazer/Bonnie Bremser, and Anne Waldman, four major women of the Beat Generation. Di Prima's *Memoirs of a Beatnik* (1969) is one of the most sexually explicit texts ever to have been published by a Beat-associated author. The book is a creative memoir of sorts: on the one hand, many of the sexual encounters di Prima describes did take place in the 1950s in and around New York where she was living; on the other hand, these were much exaggerated for effect. As the author explains in the afterword that accompanies the 1988 edition, when she was asked to write erotica by Maurice Girodias, notorious publisher of texts such as *Naked Lunch* and Vladimir Nabokov's *Lolita* (1955), she went down memory lane and started to recall sexual encounters that she would rework into pornographic writing (*Memoirs* 135–38). She writes of having several lovers, both men and women, and living in a New York pad where these lovers would come and go continuously; "I thought of it as fucking my comrades," the narrator remarks (123). Even sexual violence and rape become scenes of erotica (39, 48) in the context of the "rule of cool," which requires that a Beatnik accepts whatever life throws at her. Besides this fusion of fact, memory, and fiction, *Memoirs of a Beatnik* is an in-depth look at sexual mores and models of sexuality of the 1950s. Pillars of human relationships, such as the figure of the good father who takes an interest in his children or the bond of sibling love, are turned on their head: the friend's father rapes the young Diane (48–50) and the brother, who had been abused by their uncle, rapes his sister after they have consensual sex (39–40). A far cry from the middle-class nuclear families often associated with the 1950s, family units in *Memoirs of a Beatnik* turn out to be sexually deviant in ways that are unlawful, a fact that makes the groups of emancipated Beatniks in the book a viable new model of community.

The book is also one of the first writings about the Beatnik era that is told entirely from the perspective of female desire. The opening pages are filled with sensual language from the woman's point of view, leading gradually to a scene where the male body is beautified. The narrator describes the body of her first lover in great detail, talking of his "beautiful cock," "the fine bones of his pelvis," and "the smooth skin between his navel and groin" (4). Sexual scenes toward the start of the book, as the narrator loses her virginity and then starts to become a more experienced lover, are presented as acts in the protagonist's sexual awakening as she becomes more aware and accepting of her desire. This state of mind eventually leads to sexual experimentation with multiple partners, then to bisexuality and orgies. It has to be noted, however, that these scenes are written for men as male fantasies. This is particularly evident in the scenes of lesbian sex as the narrator lingers on the young girls' skin, breasts, and underwear (28–31) and in the odd sexual politics, which become more noticeable as the book progresses. While the narrator seems to find pleasure in all sex – controversially even in being raped – the infamous orgy with Ginsberg and Kerouac toward the end of the book does not seem to subscribe to the rules of pornography: di Prima initially plans to sleep as she has her period; Kerouac is depicted as not a brilliant lover; and one of the men who has sex with Ginsberg, Benny, begins to cry in the middle of it. The narrator's comments are designed to make the scene anything other than arousing: "It was a strange, nondescript kind of orgy," she begins, and later interjects to explain, "It was very boring" (181, 184). Even the comment "Allen by this time was reciting Whitman and rubbing Leslie's cock with his feet" (185) seems designed to cause laughter rather than sexual arousal. Rather than erotica, then, *Memoirs of a Beatnik* is a satire of pornography for men.

Although not intended as a serious exploration of women's sexuality of the 1950s in the Beat circles, *Memoirs of a Beatnik* does draw attention to female desire, even if it is produced primarily for men. A similar work from a female author associated with the Beat Generation is Brenda Frazer/ Bonnie Bremser's *Troia: Mexican Memoirs*, also first published in 1969. Like *Memoirs of a Beatnik*, Bremser's book is written for the male gaze – in Bremser's case, specifically for the gaze of her then-husband, poet Ray Bremser, who was in prison. A fictionalized autobiography documenting a year Bremser spent in Mexico, the narrative mirrors Kerouac's *On the Road* in its depiction of travel as a quest. But unlike *On the Road*, whose narrator, Sal Paradise, has very little responsibility to others, *Troia* is written from the perspective of a single mother who has to fend for herself and ends up working as a prostitute. In constituting Ray as the intended erotic gaze, the narrative muddies the waters surrounding the problematic issue of romanticizing the figure of the nomadic prostitute, and glosses over the real dangers of life on the street for young women. Of course the book is not intended as a sociological study of female prostitution in Mexico in the 1960s but is rather an exploration of female desire and sexuality at that time. In a telling incident, the narrator is transformed from an object to a subject of desire: "Me, in my new bikini lolling around by the windowsill ... I come onto Ray in my new bikini."[21] Bremser's depiction of the prostitute's want serves to empower her, for in the fulfillment of her own desire she is shown to be in control of both her image and her sexuality. As the book continues to offer eroticized images of the Beat prostitute on the road, the reader is once again made aware of the narrator's authorial control, until in the final pages the prostitute discovers a self-reliance in the control of her own story:

> Now I have no muse to resort to, no sun to proclaim, no babies to worship, no steadfast love to defend myself with, no roads and mountains to climb with my eyes seeing freely, nothing but my own heart to search out in cold Mexcity ... and saw things I hoped never to experience, the loneliness of a street corner, the self-reliance of staying out all night because there is no place and nobody to go home to, and no expectation of it. I was alone in the world, and why not, why not? (187)

The act of speaking alone in this creative memoir is a performance of self-reliance of sorts, as Kurt Hemmer has suggested, but, as the book's ending implies in its treatment of authorial identity as a fusion ground for public and private (the roads, mountains, the street corner vs love, a baby, loneliness, the lack of a home), identifying the place from which Bremser speaks is a complex task.[22] As Ronna C. Johnson has argued, *Troia: Mexican Memoirs* is situated in the minor spaces of a marginal literature, a road novel by a Beat woman. As such "It conveys traditional Beat movement discourses of free sex, visionary enunciation, and existential adventure, but its experimental hybrid narrative form of gender and alterity – the protagonist's female subjectivity – deconstruct 'beat.' "[23] Bremser's various female identities – mother, wife, whore, etc. – mold her depictions of sex, motherhood, travel, disappointment, and fulfillment. What is more, as Johnson rightfully points out (referencing Judith Butler's theory of gender performativity), *Troia* "performs, rather than represents, sexuality and gender" (55). Her prostitution and the subsequent narrativization of it in the book is a spectacle of sex for Ray Bremser; the narrative's depiction of pros-titution as display – "I put on a good enough show so that none would ever know" (quoted in "Beat Transnationalism" 56) – reveals "a transactional sexuality legible only in performance" ("Beat Transnationalism" 56) and hence the difficulty of reading the prostitute's final proclamation of freedom and self-reliance. These are not the words of a sexually emancipated Beat woman but those of a mirror image of patriarchal culture's conceptualiza-tion of the transnational prostitute, distorted in Bremser to engender the Beat narrative of the road tale and sexual liberation.

The final example I would like to discuss is the poetry of Lenore Kandel, another female author associated with the Beat movement whose major works were written during the Beats' heyday. Like the writers discussed above, Kandel's poetry depicts sexuality as malleable. It also shares a sig-nificant similarity with Kerouac in its link between sexuality and spirituality. The difference is that Kandel makes a conscious decision to speak from the perspective of a liberated woman who, as her collection *The Love Book* (1966) controversially announced in a series of interlinked poems, likes to "Fuck with Love."[24] *The Love Book* must have been such a surprise to con-formist culture in the 1960s (like *Howl and Other Poems* and *Naked Lunch*, it was subject to legal action due to obscenity); the four poems comprising the short collection speak predominantly of cocks, cunts, and fucking, occa-sionally bursting into chant-like invocations of sex-worship: "fuck – the fuck of love-fuck – the yes entire – / love out of ours – the cock in the cunt fuck –" (6). However, anyone surprised by this kind of explicit language would have missed the central point of Kandel's work: physical pleasure through sex is the first step toward spiritual fulfillment. The poems in *The Love Book*, sexually explicit language and imagery aside, also depict sex as a sacred act:

> sacred the sacred cunt!
> sacred the sacred cock!
> miracle!   miracle!   sacred the primal miracle!
>   sacred the god-animal, twisting and wailing
>   sacred the beautiful fuck. (6)

Kandel repeats and expands the connection between sexuality and spiritu-ality in subsequent work. In *Word Alchemy* (1967), the poet moves from depicting spiritual fulfillment through sex as a desire to articulating it as a need and a demand. She writes in "Age of Consent," "I cannot be satis-fied until I speak with angels … I demand the access of enlightenment" (24), which she eventually finds in the image of a Greek deity, Eros. In "Eros/Poem," also in *Word Alchemy*, the poet praises Eros for illuminat-ing that *eros* – to love and desire – is truth and sexuality is beauty (33).

For Kandel, beauty offers not just pleasure but also a spiritual awakening and awareness of humanity's holiness. As Kandel puts it in a previously unpublished poem,

> if I am holy
> – and I am –
> then you are holy
> – and you are –
> then all of us are holy. (200)

Kandel's connection of sexuality to holiness and spirituality invokes Ginsberg's and Kerouac's descriptions of sex; as we have seen, their works depict sex as a gateway to not just varied forms of holiness but also transcendence. Thus it makes sense that sexuality appears in these authors as fluid, capable of changing shape and purpose as it reacts to and against cultural norms of the time.

Other female Beat writers of later generations, who started to write their major works from the 1970s onwards, continue to position sexuality as an important feature of identity. For example, Anne Waldman's three-volume epic *The Iovis Trilogy* (first published in one book in 2011) conceptualizes female sexuality as the manifestation of a pansexual androgyne. To achieve this, the poet draws on multiple sources, both male and female: Burroughs, Ginsberg, H.D., Kerouac, Charles Olson, Sappho, and many others. In Waldman's responses, hermeneutic gender stereotypes are challenged, discarded, and replaced with transgendered models as the narrative works toward the achievement of a world beyond engendered sexualities. She presents this vision clearly in *Vow to Poetry* (2001) when she writes: "I want here to declare an enlightened poetics, an androgynous poetics … I propose a transsexual literature, a transgendered literature, a hermaphroditic literature, a transvestite literature, and finally a poetics of transformation beyond gender."[25] A similar vision appears in the later work of di Prima. Her two-volume epic, *Loba* (1976, 1978, 1998), features pansexual deities and the woman as loba, a she-wolf, who continuously changes shape; a mythical creature, a hyperactive sex Goddess, a lesbian, a primitive dancer, the Virgin Mary, Eve; and, in Book II, a kind of spirit of all things as she is transformed into the eternal feminine until this essentialism is negated in the final poem. In "Persephone: Reprise," like Brenda Frazer/Bonnie Bremser before her, di Prima suggests that women's sexuality is the axis of a performative female identity – a reprise as the title implies – which, much like Persephone (also known as Kore, the maiden), has been played out in patriarchal culture as a narrative of first possession and then loss of virginity. Di Prima writes in *Loba*'s last poem "not in 'deflowering' do we come / into bloom; we have been always / there at the fluid boundary of Hades."[26]

As the various writers explored here suggest, the boundaries of Beat sexual identity are fluid and, as such, changeable and adaptable. But, far from merely engaging in heterodox or fluid sexualities as empty self-indulgences or affected postures meant to shock the middle-class or conformist America of the 1950s and 1960s, such fluidity was always connected in Beat writing to social and political critique. Whether Ginsberg's resistance to heteronormativity, which he viewed as inextricably bound to capitalism, or Kerouac's depiction of sexuality as a form of spiritual fulfillment, or Burroughs's refusal to be labeled at all as a way to highlight the complex systems of control inherent in the postmodern moment, or di Prima's playful exploitation of a Beatnik "rule of cool" that could be as retrograde in its gender expectations as mainstream culture, or Kandel's linking of sexuality to spirituality in order to confirm the validity of female sexual desire, what is finally perhaps most valuable when exploring the varieties of Beat sexual experience is the way in which it also represented social and political engagements that are still being recognized.

NOTES

1 Diane di Prima, *Memoirs of a Beatnik* (1969; San Francisco: Last Gasp, 1988), 130–33.
2 Catharine Stimpson, "The Beat Generation and the Trials of Homosexual Liberation," *Salamagundi* 58 (fall/winter 1982–1983), 374.
3 Nick Selby, "'Queer Shoulders to the Wheel': Whitman, Ginsberg and a Bisexual Poetics," *The Bisexual Imaginary: Representation, Identity and Desire*, ed. Phoebe Davidson, Clare Hemmings, Ann Kaloski and Merl Storr (London and Washington: Cassell, 1997), 132.
4 Allen Ginsberg, *Collected Poems, 1947–1997* (New York: HarperCollins, 2006), 11.
5 See Glen Burns, *Great Poets Howl: A Study of Allen Ginsberg's Poetry, 1943–1955* (New York: Lang, 1983) and Michael Schumacher, *Dharma Lion: A Critical Biography of Allen Ginsberg* (New York: St. Martin's, 1992).
6 Allen Ginsberg with Allen Young, *Gay Sunshine Interview* (Bolinas, CA: Grey Fox, 1974), 394.
7 In this vein, see also Ginsberg, "The Homosexual Imagination," *College English* 36.3 (November 1974).
8 Matt Theado, *Understanding Jack Kerouac* (Columbia: University of South Carolina Press, 2000), 170.
9 Recent examples include Jim Jones, *Use My Name: Jack Kerouac's Forgotten Families* (Ontario: ECW Press, 1999) and Paul Maher, *Kerouac: The Definitive Biography* (New York: Taylor Trade, 2004).
10 Jack Kerouac, *On the Road* (1957; New York: Viking, 2007), 288.

11 For a good analysis of Buddhism and Catholicism in Kerouac's *Tristessa* and *Visions of Gerard*, see *Understanding Jack Kerouac* 123–140.

12 Albert Gelpi, *American Poetry After Modernism: The Power of the Word* (New York: Cambridge University Press, 2015), 101.

13 William S. Burroughs, *Naked Lunch* (1959; London: Flamingo, 1993), 22.

14 Giles Deleuze and Félix Guattari, *A Thousand Plateaus: Capitalism and Schizophrenia*, trans. Brian Massumi (1980; London: Athlone Press, 1988), 153.

15 Timothy S. Murphy, *Wising Up the Marks: The Amodern William Burroughs* (Berkeley: University of California Press, 1998), 35–45.

16 Robin Lydenberg, *Word Cultures: Radical Theory and Practice in William S. Burroughs' Fiction* (Urbana: University of Illinois Press, 1987), 156.

17 See, for example, David Savran, *Taking It Like a Man: White Masculinity, Masochism, and Contemporary American Culture* (Princeton: Princeton University Press, 1998), 88–99; Timothy S. Murphy, *Wising Up*, 57–66; and Oliver Harris, "Can You See a Virus? The Queer Cold War of William Burroughs," *Journal of American Studies* 33.2 (1999), 258–264.

18 William S. Burroughs, *Queer: 25th Anniversary Edition*, ed. Oliver Harris (London: Penguin, 2010), 131.

19 Oliver Harris, *William Burroughs and the Secret of Fascination* (Carbondale: Southern Illinois University Press, 2003), 42.

20 See Jamie Russell, *Queer Burroughs* (Basingstoke: Palgrave, 2001), 13.

21 Bonnie Bremser, *Troia: Mexican Memoirs* (1969; Champaign, IL: Dalkey Archive Press, 2007), 146.

22 Kurt Hemmer, "The Prostitute Speaks: Brenda Frazer's *Troia: Mexican Memoirs*," *Paradoxa* 18 (2003).

23 Ronna C. Johnson, "Beat Transnationalism Under Gender: Brenda Frazer's *Troia: Mexican Memoirs*," *The Transnational Beat Generation*, ed. Nancy M. Grace and Jennie Skerl (Palgrave: New York, 2012), 53.

24 Lenore Kandel, *Collected Poems of Lenore Kandel* (Berkeley: North Atlantic Books, 2012), 5–7.

25 Anne Waldman, *Vow to Poetry: Essays, Interviews, & Manifestos* (Minneapolis: Coffee House Press, 2001), 24.

26 Diane di Prima, *Loba* (London: Penguin, 1998), 314.

13

A. ROBERT LEE

The Beats and Race

Few race markers in Beat authorship have attracted greater attention, and on occasion controversy, than those met with in "Howl" (1956), Ginsberg's visionary poem-epic, and *On the Road* (1957), Kerouac's totemic life chronicle. As Ginsberg writes: "I saw the best minds of my generation destroyed by madness, starving hysterical naked, / dragging themselves through the negro streets at dawn looking for an angry fix."[1] And as Kerouac's Sal Paradise muses:

> At lilac evening I walked with every muscle aching among the lights of 27th and Welton in the Denver colored section, wishing I were a Negro, feeling that the best the white world had offered was not enough ecstasy for me ... I wished I were a Denver Mexican, or even a poor overworked Jap, anything but what I was so drearily, a "white man" disillusioned.[2]

Despite such vivid and potentially problematic moments across the best-known canon of Beat authorship, to include the companion writing of William S. Burroughs, Gregory Corso, and Lawrence Ferlinghetti, race has tended to get underplayed as a contributing feature. If *Howl and Other Poems*, along with *Kaddish* (1961), bespeaks Jewish Ginsberg, or *On The Road*, and more explicitly *The Subterraneans* (1958) and *Pic* (published posthumously in 1971), summon Kerouac's interracial as well as sexual and jazz interests, they have understandably won greater reckoning for their overall plies of dissent.[3] But, if indeed race does not hold preemptive sway in canonical Beat culture and writing, it can hardly be said not to have come into imaginative view, whether out front or in a variety of local seams and threads.

Any map dealing with the Beats and race needs to steer carefully between text and context, both the connections and the gaps. Of necessity there arise conceptual issues. In Beat, as in other cultural practice, is race – or raciality as it has sometimes been termed – to be differentiated from ethnicity, the former with its often troubling connection to supremacist genetics and the latter usually construed more in terms of performed identity? Can Beat, both its leading and ancillary names and in common with virtually all Atlantic and Western customs of its time, be exempted from temptations to exoticize or stereotype? How, too, does nationality enter the frame? Whichever the designation, there can be no doubt that from the outset Beat drew from a lattice of multicultural geographies. These, for sure, span North America. But they also range more inclusively to Latin America, Europe, the Greco-Italian and other Mediterranean sites, the Hebraic world, the Maghreb, Africa, the Sino-Japanese East, and India from the Ganges to the Himalayas. For all the vex of definition, and in common with Beat issues of, say, self-authenticity or spirituality, race ought not to be denied due acknowledgment. That holds with quite unique force for those Beat-connected writers, notably African American, whose origins and experience of America lie outside cultural whiteness as assumed norm.

Historical and Cultural Contexts

The Beats and their writings are far from alone in reminding one how racial the 1950s and 1960s were as an era of change. Civil rights and Black Power, color-line Dixie and Harlem – each march and killing became a necessary headline. King's "I Have a Dream" speech (1963) gave enduring public eloquence to the call for change. The 1965–67 riots in Watts, Detroit, and other cities, together with the rise of the Student Nonviolent Coordinating Committee, the Black Panthers, and the Nation of Islam, underscored the emerging new politics of race. Yet it has to be said that, both in life and writing, Beat literary players do not in any conspicuous way intersect with the racial upheavals of the 1950s and 1960s. The *Brown v. Board of Education* decision (1954) outlawing segregated schooling and the white-supremacist reaction it sparked across the South seem a long way away from the kind of "protest" associated with the Beats. The brutal murder of the fourteen-year-old black youth Emmett Till in 1955 in Mississippi took place a year before the publication of *Howl*, again a different kind of history from that being forged by Ginsberg and Kerouac in Greenwich Village.

The activism of César Chávez and the United Farm Workers drew attention to Brown Power born of Chicano/a and Filipino/a agricultural labor exploitation in California and the southwest. The Asian American Movement, mindful of Yellow Peril, linked community memory of China, Hiroshima, and the Mekong, as well as the Chinatowns and World War II Japanese American internment, to the protests against the Vietnam War. The American Indian Movement (Red Power) emphasized sovereignty along with ecology or coyote myth of the kind notably engaged by Gary

Snyder. Lines like "Negro streets at dawn" and "Wishing I were a Negro ... a Denver Mexican ... a poor overworked Jap," however contentiously, give Beat particularization to this changing awareness of American demography and its cultures.

Popular culture adds a key measure. The young, from white middle America for the most part, who gathered for Haight-Ashbury's Summer of Love in 1967 and New York State's Woodstock Festival in 1969, celebrated Jimi Hendrix, Afro-Beat troubadour, as headliner. If many of the Beats' acolytes came out of city and suburban white culture from Manhattan to the beaches of California, they at the same time found a musical sound-wrap not only in rock-pop but also in black soul, Latin rhythm, and the folk music of Jewish-born Bob Dylan and Hispanic-heritaged Joan Baez. The couture may have been one of flares and shades, but it was also one of afros, Mao jackets, Asian sarongs, and Native American beads and headbands. Sports celebrity looked to the glamorous athleticism of Muhammad Ali but found itself challenged by his Black Muslim conversion. The taste for transcendental meditation, Tai-chi, and Eastern martial arts became widespread. Ethnic Studies syllabi entered the colleges with black and Asian shelves equally to be found in the malls and airports. Drugs, marijuana to LSD, may have become de rigueur, but so also did foodways: black–Southern, Mexican, and Asian. Each played its part in helping to situate the Beats' own racial compass, poetry, and fiction; eventually the life writings and memoirs; and the bodies of theatre, photography, and film.

More exact contextual hallmarks can readily be summoned. Interracial Beat relationships pass into legend, be they Kerouac's personal and jazz friendship with Ted Joans or the LeRoi Jones/Imamu Amiri Baraka marriage to Hettie Cohen and the former's affair with Diane di Prima. Beat intimacy with Afro-jazz, and the profound racial history within its fashioning, connects to a galaxy from Charlie Parker to Miles Davis to John Coltrane. The Beats' eclectic Buddhist borrowings draw from the Zen of Kyoto and temple Japan and the spirituality of India's city of Benares along with the vedas and sutras. Ginsberg's public chanting of the mantras and the Hindu-Sanskrit *Om*, his *India Journals* (1970), and great long poems "Angkor Wat" (1963) and "Wichita Vortex Sutra" (1966) are all especially apropos, as are Subcontinent diary-memoirs such as Snyder's *Passage Through India* (1983) and Joanne Kyger's *Strange Big Moon: The Japan and India Journals, 1960–1964* (1981).[4] Beat invocations of Mexico and other aspects of Latin America – the metro-cities, the indigenous life, and, never least, the drug routes – run through not only *On the Road* but also Kerouac's spontaneous jazz poetry in *Mexico City Blues* (1959).[5] They likewise enseam the Burroughs–Ginsberg yage correspondence, Neal Cassady's sorties and even death near San Miguel de Allende in 1968, and Bonnie Bremser's on-the-run, frequently harrowing, and yet for many proto-feminist life writing of *Troia: Mexican Memoirs* (1969).[6]

Magreb and Arab culture at large make for any number of "inter-zone" racial and irreverent black-humor allusions throughout Burroughs's *Naked Lunch* (1959), as when he writes: "I am working for an outfit known as Islam Inc." and "*Mohammed?* ... He was dreamed up by the Mecca Chamber of Commerce."[7] His fiction joins the considerable Beat-inflected North African literary roster for whom race, or silhouetted versions of it, supplies a reference point. Kerouac's *Desolation Angels* (1965) alights briefly upon Burroughs's Tangier of writer outposts, kif and hashish, "Mohammedan cafés," and "fine Arabs."[8] Paul Bowles's *The Sheltering Sky* (1949) transposes desert culture and its people into a hallucinatory back-drop to the collapsing Moresby marriage.[9] Brion Gysin, painter-poet, uses his visual and word cut-ups to limn a Morocco of contrasting populations, Berber to European. Others with Beat credentials found themselves equally drawn to Mediterranean Arab demography. Alan Ansen, whom Kerouac made over into Rollo Greb in *On the Road* and Corso into Dad Deform in *The American Express* (1961), brought scholarship and a body of poetry and playwriting to bear. Ira Cohen, Tangier-based, edited the avant-garde journal *GNAOUA* (the name taken from a Berber trance-sect), whose contributors included Burroughs, Ginsberg, Gysin, Michael McClure, Harold Norse, and Ian Sommerville.[10]

Varieties of Beat Racial Experience

The Pocket Books series from Ferlinghetti's City Lights, under whose auspices Beat writing found historic publication, yields another context. One line of American influence, poetics and visual art, was to be found in Frank O'Hara, Kenneth Patchen, and Kenneth Rexroth. A more transnational impact lay in the work of luminaries such as Antonin Artaud, Denise Levertov, Fernando Pessoa, and Jacques Prévert. Norman Mailer, however, in "The White Negro" (1957), originally published in *Dissent* and then as a City Lights pamphlet, turned to quite explicit racial fare.[11] He argues, from within an America beset by Main Street conformism and Cold War anxiety, for the bravura example of the black American as hipster/existentialist. In Mailer's figuring here was to be found authenticity, the dare of identity in the face of frequent life-on-the-line racial violence, in which jazz was a veritable encoding of sexuality. Notwithstanding charges of exoticization, Mailer's heady version of blackness touched a nerve, the would-be paradigm for a white countercultural politics of self. Chandler Brossard, a key progenitor both of Mailer and the Beats – and himself of Creole mixed race – can be said to anticipate these equations in the Greenwich bohemia and Harlem scenes of his novel *Who Walk in Darkness* (1952).

Ginsberg and Kerouac, Beat progenitors, supply the contours. To re-encounter "Howl" six decades on from its shock-horror court case and publication can leave little doubt that the call to awareness possesses a highly eclectic racial-cultural input that crosses borders and countries. The poem's New York of Brooklyn Bridge, Staten Island Ferry, Union Square, Harlem, Woodlawn, the Hudson, Madison Avenue, Rockland Asylum, and Pilgrim State Hospital aggregates into an accusing city of night. Its aegis, repeated lines insist, belongs to Moloch, predatory Canaanite fire-idol, "whose blood is running money" and whom Ginsberg also knew from Fritz Lang's *Metropolis* (1927). "Uncle Max" from Russia ("America," *Howl*, 40) joins company with Carl Solomon and Naomi Ginsberg to underscore Jewish legacy both of the Torah and of secular radicalism. These allusions, bridging the "poles" of Kerouac's New England, French Canadian upbringing and Ginsberg's own Paterson upbringing, with Manhattan as midway, and also bridging Middle Eastern deity and Viennese-born film genius, even so suggest only a portion of the poem's cultural reach.

If "Howl" begins in New York's "negro streets" it equally invokes a wider panoply. The Qur'an's "Mohammedan angels" feature, as does "Zen New Jersey" and the drug withdrawal learned from Burroughs of "Eastern sweats and Tangerian bone-grindings and migraines of China" (11). A seagoing homocentrism finds expression in "the caresses of Atlantic and Caribbean love." "German jazz" of the 1930s wins reference. Asian landscape transfers to North Carolina's Rocky Mount, where Kerouac and others sought "to tender Buddha." The will to transcendence enlists the Egyptian-born Plotinus, whose doctrine of One greatly attracted Ginsberg, and joins the poem's gallery of Poe and St. John of the Cross under the rubric of "bop kab-ballah." Cézanne enters in the allusion to the Latin of a universalist "Pater Omnipotens Aeterna Deus" as does biblical supplication in the Greek of "eli eli lamma lamma sabacthani" with its Hebrew and Christly origins. The term "racial" might have to do elastic duty to cover all these elements, but it serves as working gloss (12, 20).

On the Road likewise moves in and through various racial intertexts. No doubt an author baptized Jean-Louis Lebris de Kerouac of Québécois-Catholic – and, however distant, of Mohawk lineage – and raised a *joual*-speaker in foundationally Protestant Lowell, Massachusetts, would inherit a special sensitivity to race and ethnicity. Sal Paradise's volatile male comrade-ship with Dean Moriarty is quick to extend to Ginsberg as Jewish-surreal Carlo Marx and Burroughs as WASP-dissident Old Bull Lee. His *campesina* lover Terry and her son in the San Joaquín Valley embody the migrant-worker fusion of Mexico and California. The Cajuns near Lee's Louisiana marijuana farm recall past Acadian history. The black bar clients in Detroit underline a major jazz city and historic African American south-to-north migration. The Minnesota farm-youth truckers point back to Scandinavia's settlement of the Midwest. The figure of Remi Boncoeur as buccaneer French thief links to Kerouac's personal ancestry. The Pan-American Highway avails itself of south-of-the-border marijuana and sex but also Mexican family hospitality. Sal's close encounters with small-trade Native Indian populations compare with the Mazatlán Indians called "Mexico Fellaheen" in *Visions of Cody* (1972), who, as if to anticipate Native American Leslie Marmon Silko's *Almanac of the Dead* (1991), it is averred will one day reclaim all the Americas.[12]

The Subterraneans (1958) assumes a more distinct centering in race, not to say Kerouac's celebrated "bop prosody" with its spontaneous run-on style. The complexities of sex, jealousy, and, given the era, racial transgression run thick and fast throughout San Francisco in the interethnic love of Leo Percepied, self-nominated Canuck, and Mardou Fox, Cherokee-black young woman bohemian. But, if race inevitably weighs (Mardou "part Negro highclass" with "near-Indian eyes," Leo's "white man heart"), it does so amid other kinds of focus (7, 49). The pathology of both lovers plays its role, with Mardou having been in therapy from early orphaning and Leo having a knot of Oedipal attraction to his mother. The city, its subterranean-inhabited bars and cellars and its gay salons, serves also as jazz and literary fiefdom – one, symptomatically, of Charlie Parker and City Lights. But an indicative reference back to *On the Road* is to be heard in Leo's "wanting to be vital, alive like a Negro or an Indian or a Denver Jap or a New York Puerto Rican" (70). Critique, in kind with that stirred by the race-discussion sequences in John Clellon Holmes's novel *Get Home Free* (1964), has taken opposing turns: a novel of persuasive confessional verve or a novel loaded in race-cliché and chauvinism.[13] Kerouac's later novella *Pic* is written in the colloquial voice of a North Carolina black boy who steps north to the New York of Harlem and jazz in the late 1940s with his brother and then across the country to California, and might be thought a coda, Kerouac's scaled-down and as it were "racial" *Huckleberry Finn*. Assuming this racial-ized idiom could easily have opened Kerouac to suspicions of appropriation, a borrowed tongue. But the consensus has been that it more or less works – a venture, however unexpected, fashioned in general good faith.

Other major Beat names add their own particularities. Burroughs's laconic assaults on Anglo-white power structures can be found in *Junky* (1953), with its plethora of race-marked monikers ("George the Greek" and the "young Italian hipster named Ray").[14] These amplify in *Naked Lunch* and texts such as *The Soft Machine* (1961) and *Nova Express* (1964) through to the late writings of *The Western Lands* (1987) and *My Education: A Book of Dreams* (1995).[15] "No glot ... C'lom Fliday," Burroughs's famous parody-phrase in *Naked Lunch* with its allusion to Chinese heroin dealers, under-lines his own considerable sense of race as width and contradiction (184). *Italianità*, the memory of passed-down custom, makes not a few entrances. A Corso poem such as "Uccello" (1958) summons the painter's canvases of Florentine warriors. Ferlinghetti's "Old Italians Dying" (1979) offers a Little Italy picturing of "the Piedmontesi the Genovese the Siciliani" (220). Di Prima's "Backyard" uses its Brooklyn setting and a ply of allusions to opera and Mediterranean cuisine to invoke Italian immigrant dynasty.[16]

Jewish literary Beat runs considerably beyond Ginsberg. This "whiteness of a different color" looks early to Elise Cowen and her scant, dark-shadowed elliptical poetry, as much as her love affair with Ginsberg and her Washington Heights suicide. Barbara Probst Solomon's *The Beat of Life* (1960) delivers Manhattan bohemia and blighted Jewish-Gentile coupledom.[17] Carl Solomon, illustrious dedicatee of "Howl," contributes the Dada but politically aware chapbook *Mishaps, Perhaps* (1966).[18] In the follow-up, *More Mishaps* (1968), he is to be heard observing, "They want me to be just a good Jewish boy oth-erwise they'll hit me in the belly again."[19] Jack Micheline, who made his bow with *Rivers of Red Wine* (1958), speaks of himself as "the crazy Jew" in the poem "Chasing Kerouac's Shadow," which was written "on a bus from San Francisco to Santa Rosa, March 1987."[20] David Meltzer, author of *Beat Thing* (2004), with its range from Auschwitz to California's North Beach, and editor of *The Secret Garden: An Anthology in the Kaballah* (1976), gives a Jewish patina to his myriad Beat verses and music compositions. Wallace Berman contributed yet another direction of voice, the image-and-word assemblages often also with Kaballah implications published in mail-package folios under the auspices of his journal *Semina* (1957–64).[21]

Joyce Johnson's Beat connection, that of a bookish daughter whose rebel-lion against staid Jewish parents led on to the Village and her legendary love affair with Kerouac, is to be met in the adeptly styled reminiscence of *Minor Characters* (1983), *Door Wide Open: A Beat Love Affair in Letters, 1957–1958* (2000), and *The Voice Is All: The Lonely Victory of Jack Kerouac* (2012).[22] Her world notably extends to a Beat women's circle of Joan Vollmer Adams, Elise Cowen, Hettie Jones, and Edie Parker. For her part, in *How I Became Hettie Jones* (1990), Jones (née Cohen) engag-ingly recapitulates her closeted Jewish upbringing in Queens, New York; her literary and jazz life in Greenwich Village; and her Beat-era cross-racial marriage and children with Jones/Baraka through to her divorce in 1965. She speaks, tellingly, of the frequent perception of her as "one-half of the blackman/whitewoman couple, that stereotype of lady and stud."[23] In ruth weiss, Berlin-born Holocaust survivor who became a major figure in North Beach art circles, Beat has long had a sympathetic co-spirit, as borne out in the eclectically international and Kerouac-esque blues writings of *Desert Journal* (1977) and the autobiography of *Can't Stop the Beat: The Life and Words of a Beat Poet* (2011).[24] Irving Rosenthal's *Sheeper* (1968) operates as homocentric *vita sexualis* replete with commanding Jewish mother, and is also a chronicle of Morocco and other travel in which the footfalls not only of Burroughs but also the Kafka of *The Metamorphosis* as Jewish literary mentor are unmistakable.[25]

Three Black Beats: Jones, Joans, and Kaufman

The conjunction of Beat and race can yield no keener register than in African American authorship. LeRoi Jones, before his Black Nationalist turn and Islamizing of his name to Baraka and then subsequent move into third-world Marxism, holds early status. His Beat phase, the Village years of "hip bohemianism" during 1957–62 according to the *LeRoi Jones/Amiri Baraka Reader* (1991), inaugurated this serial career.[26] Like other black Beats, Jones/Baraka paid respects to Burroughs, Ginsberg, and Kerouac as much as to Charles Olson and Frank O'Hara, and not least in the avant-garde journals *Yugen* (1958–62) and *Floating Bear* (1961–71), co-edited respectively with Hettie Jones and Diane di Prima. Likewise he gave them due in "How You Sound" (1959), his statement on open poetics in Donald Allen's seminal *The New American Poetry 1945–1960* (1960), and the collection Jones himself edited, *The Moderns: An Anthology of New Writing in America* (1963).[27] But at the same time he tactically kept his imaginative distance. How could a writer steeped in Afro-America truly accommodate the ways of white bohemians, whose lives were drawn so far from the black pulse of Mississippi or even his own Newark?

Jones's slim first collection, *Preface to a Twenty Volume Suicide Note* (1961), published by the Totem Press he co-founded, warily explores questions of race.[28] The long poem "Hymn for Lanie Poo," titled from his pet name for his show-business sister Sandra Elaine and written as though jazz line and counterpoint, plays Beat and black several ways at once. The circuits of talk, drink, coffee shops, partying, Zen, sex, and even protest may all exert their allure for its speaker. But the opening citation from Rimbaud regarding "*faux Nègres*" points to a sense of betrayal. "Beat," for all its countercultural impulses, is sedimented in whiteness, so is he not at risk of selling out? "The god I pray to / got black boobies / got steatopygia" reads a deliberate, insistently "black" reprimand (*Baraka Reader* 5). Coltrane, with his sax virtuosity, is to set the standard as much as Tchaikovsky. The sister becomes the figure of accommodation who dislikes teaching in Newark "because there are too many coloured children in her classes" ("Hymn for Lanie Poo" 10). The world at hand exists under a

> huge & loveless
> white-anglo sun/of
> benevolent step
> mother America. (10)

If this is Beat writing, it also points toward a quite contrasting American life realm, the historic experience of blackness, which now runs close to playing false to itself.

A shared perspective no doubt lies behind Jones's several teasings, and indeed self-teasings, at Beat's proclamation of New Bohemia. Jones's "One Night Stand," written for Ginsberg, not untypically toys with triumphalism ("We entered the city at noon! the radio on ... We *are* foreign seeming persons ... uncertain which of the masks is cool" [21]). "Looked for You Yesterday, Here You Come Today," which uses a blues line for its title, mixes nostalgia for the radio and comic-book world of Tom Mix, Dickie Dare, Captain Midnight, Superman, and the Lone Ranger, and nods also to Jones's present Beat self-absorption. My "silver bullets" and "black masks," he laments, are "trampled in the dust." "I try to hum lines from 'The Poet in New York,'" the poem's voice discloses in mock anxiety. "Terrible poems come in the mail" is said in ironic editorial lament. Most apposite, perhaps, are the closing lines ("& Tonto way off in the hills / moaning like Bessie Smith" [11–14]). Long-ago radio so loops into the South's blackest of black Empress of the Blues. For Jones/Baraka, the connection could not hold greater significance. The move out of the comforting terrain of boyhood acts as a kind of self-haunting. In shared manner, his adult life as an African American has ambiguously folded into Beat white bohemia, exhilarating, even fun, but, as in most of the writing in *Preface to a Twenty Volume Suicide Note*, not without acknowledgment of inner cost.

"Notes for a Speech" puts the point even more explicitly. "African blues / does not know me" (*Baraka Reader* 14). But, if this is heritage left behind, the speaker yet again cannot be at home amid "white man / talk" (14). A state of things so half in, half out, however, would meet its comeuppance in Jones/Baraka's radicalizing visit to Cuba in 1960 and move to Harlem in 1967 after the death of Malcolm X. Beat, for him, yielded to the era's Black Nationalist ethos and clenched-fist militancy. The evidence becomes clear in the collection *The Dead Lecturer* (1964), nowhere more so than in "BLACK DADA NIHILISMUS," Jones/Baraka's "blacker art" poem of race division and insurrectionary redress.[29] The landmark stage-play *Dutchman* (1964) culminated with a white woman murdering a black man, a physical manifestation of a warring colloquy, intransigently sexual, set in the New York subway as emblematic of deeper subways within the racial psyche.[30] *Home: Social Essays* (1966) lays down the new dictum: "A Negro literature, to be a legitimate product of the Negro experience in America, must get at that experience ... in its most ruthless identity."[31]

In the wake of black nationalism there ensued the Marxist–Leninist mantle of Jones/Baraka's essay work such as *Daggers and Javelins* (1982) through to the accusing query and recognition of Islamic grievance in "Someone Blew Up America" (2001), written in the wake of 9/11.[32] The Beat phase in which *Preface to a Twenty Volume Suicide Note* was written increasingly takes on the look of interlude, temporary creative mooring. This is not to deny the Afro-America in view throughout the poetry's riffs of voicing and image. But it is also to recognize how it presages the altogether more unyielding "racial" Jones/Baraka to follow.

In "I, Too, at the Beginning" (1996), wryly echoing "Howl," Ted Joans offers a typical show of his Beat affiliations:

> I am the early Black Beat
> I read with some of the
> Best Beat minds
> When the Apple was Beat Generating.[33]

This sense of himself as Afro-Beat in a near thirty-volume career was to be indicated in collections such as *Black Pow-Wow: Jazz Poems* (1969) and *Afrodisia: Old and New Poems* (1969) and given retrospect in *Teducation: Selected Poems 1949–1999* (1999).[34] Joans's ruling passions of jazz ("a unique musical religion," he calls it in "Jazz Is My Religion") and Surrealism (rhinos and aardvarks especially serve as totems) have from the outset assumed a Beat styling.[35] The same holds for the verse tributes he pays to each great jazz and blues virtuoso, a Mingus or Bessie Smith, along with Breton, Dalí, Magritte, Wilfredo Lam, Basquiat ("a Black Positive Power" [85]), the Martinique writer Etienne Léro, and Langston Hughes ("Passed on Blues: Homage to a Poet" speaks of Hughes's "Harlem sonata" and his Afro-world of "ROUND ABOUT MIDNIGHT"). "A Few Blue Words to the Wise" combines relish of the creative wellsprings within black life and a Joans manifesto of sorts:

> We must write poems black brothers about our own black relations
> We must fall in love and glorify our beautiful black nation
> We must create black images   give the world
>   a black education. (1)

Openness, wit, and skeins of wordplay have rightly been the watchwords associated with Joans. That holds throughout his career as performance poet in café and gallery, as a painter greatly familiar with MoMA and the Guggenheim, and as a trumpeter and one-time roommate of Charlie Parker. It was he who on the jazzman's death created the memorial graffiti "Bird Lives." His characteristic spontaneity is to be met with in the work that reflects not only the Village's Macdougal and Bleeker Street circuits, or Paris, or in his last years Vancouver, but also, of equal importance to him, Mali and other areas of sub-Saharan Africa. In "Afrique Accidentale," using argot that overlaps black and Beat, he writes of reaching "Timbuctoo / Yeah!!" and "I have traveled a long way on the Beat Bread I made / now I'm deep in the heart of Africa, the only Afroamerican spade."[36] Yet, whatever his companionability of page and life, Joans exhibits no illusions about the misdemeanors of race. Notwithstanding interracial Beat friendships, or those with Jackson Pollock and Frank O'Hara and his marriage to Laura Corsiglia, his poetry was clearly underwritten by familiarity with the longstanding historic fault lines whereby race acts to divide or injure. "The Nice Colored Man" can be said to deploy Beat counter-voice in the form of a detoxifying paradigm of the N-word beginning from "Nice Nigger Educated Nigger Never Nigger" and eventuating in: "Eeny Meeny Minee Mo / Catch Whitey by His Throat / If he says – Nigger CUT IT!" (*Teducation* 90). Beat always summoned Joans, with his dissent and performative verve. But there is no mistaking the seasoned racial memory he brought to bear.

Beat and race spiral throughout almost all his work. "The Sermon," a mock-counseling to would-be Beat women, lists as desiderata "LISTEN to Jazz ... own a copy of *Howl*, ... [read] Norman Mailer's 'White Negro'" (*Teducation* 94) and "be hip be happy be cool" (96). "The Wild Spirit of Kicks," his memorial to Kerouac, sees the author of *On the Road* as "Ole Angel Midnight singing Mexico City Blues / In the midst of Black hipsters and musicians" (97). In "Why Try," a light-of-touch rhapsody, Joans juxtaposes a beauteous brown woman seated "in the Beat Café" with a white girl obliged to throw away her "brand new jar/ of suntan lotion" (115). In "Him the Bird," his lyric requiem for Charlie Parker as "café-au-lait colored bird" who "blew his horn in the Village and wailed for the world" (167), Joans again takes blackness into Beat. The upshot makes for a rare, certainly memorable, fusion.

Bob Kaufman's notoriety did not always do him favors, not least his adult years as street and drink rowdy in California's North Beach counterculture haunts. New Orleans-born of a Catholic mother and Pullman-porter father, one-time Marine Union activist, Greenwich Village denizen, jailee, addict, and taker of a decade-long Buddhist vow of silence on John F. Kennedy's assassination, Kaufman has every claim to serious standing as a Beat presence. The poetry of *Solitudes Crowded With Loneliness* (1965), *Golden Sardine* (1967), and *The Ancient Rain: Poems 1956–1978* (1981) gives abundant proof, three volumes of Beat-inflected voice.[37] African American life does not always assume the forefront in his writing, though it can be explicit, as in the untitled "THE SUN IS A NEGRO / THE MOTHER OF THE SUN IS A NEGRO ... HEAVEN IS NEGRO" (*Ancient Rain* 59). His various jazz and jail compositions and the Dada-Abomunist telegrams, with their flights of anarchist inventive wit, work to more tacit racial effect. They assume blackness carried into a yet wider girth of racial-cultural allusion, his insistence on human variety and width.

Kaufman's Beat signature can be met with as readily as anywhere in "West Coast Sounds –1956." He invokes San Francisco as "hipster land," its *dramatis personae* to include "Allen on Chestnut Street / giving poetry to squares," "Corso on knees, pleading, / God eyes," and "Kerouac at Locke's / writing Neil." Rexroth and Ferlinghetti get their mentions, as does Mexico as Beat road-destination (*Solitudes* 11). Similarly, in "Ginsberg (for Allen)," Kaufman pays tribute to Beat's poet laureate for both his challenges to the establishment ("Ginsberg won't stop tossing lions to martyrs") and his compassion ("I love him because his eyes leak") (23). In "Benediction," the compassion belongs to the poem's Beat speaker ("America I forgive you"); invoking the Goyaesque horror of the South's treatment of black citizenry, the speaker makes an extraordinary statement:

> I forgive you
> Nailing black Jesus to an imported cross
> in Dawson, Georgia... I forgive you
> Eating black children. (*Solitudes* 9)

As to African American identity, "I, Too, Know What I Am Not" gives a rich imagist repudiation of myths attributed to it: the country's bastard child, the rapist, the assumed African, the blues or jail victim. "No," runs the finely caught paradox of the concluding line, "I am not anything that I am not" (*Solitudes* 28). Prompted by his horror at Hiroshima ("War Memoir" alludes to Japanese "stereophonic screaming" [52]) and at the electric chair (the untitled opening poem of *Golden Sardine* centered on the execution of Caryl Chessman), much of Kaufman's poetry displays a utopian vein with jazz as healing musical balm. Work set to Beat measure such as "Bagel Shop Jazz" ("Talking of Bird and Diz and Miles" [15]), "Blues Note" as encomium to Ray Charles, and "*Jazz Te Deum* for Inhaling at Mexican Bonfires," in which "African jazz" is to be blown "in Alabama jungles," all underline the point (32–33).

Kaufman's vision of a postracial world, his sense of Beat as rooted in beatific, is rarely bettered than in "Like Father, Like Sun" with its appeal for redemption born variously of "Apache, Kiowa, and Sioux ranges," "Muddy Mississippi," and "Africa's Black Handkerchief" (*Ancient Rain* 35–36). This is to hold America to transcendence indeed beyond all the fissures of race, "triumph" over "loss":

> America is a promised land, a garden torn from naked stone,
> A place where the losers in earth's conflicts can enjoy
> their triumph.
> All losers, brown, red, black and white; the colors from the
> Master Palette. (37)

Kaufman's ending lines amount to visionary Beat, nothing short of the imagining of multicultural apotheosis.

Further Perspectives

Both in the United States and beyond, Beat and race can be pursued into yet other strings. One adds the Afrocentricity woven into the Beat verse of A. B. Spellman and the tenor saxophonist Archie Shepp. Is there not an Asian American consortium of Beat in the fiction of Frank Chin and in the transposed portrait of him as Wittman Ah Sing in Maxine Hong Kingston's *Tripmaster Monkey* (1989)?[38] Among contributing Beat players are Albert Saijo of *Trip Trap* (1973) (a road haiku written with Jack Kerouac and Lew Welch) and the memoir *Outspeaks: A Rhapsody* (1997), and Shig Murao, celebrated City Lights Bookstore manager and editor of *Shig's Magazine* (1960–69).[39] Latino/a names with a claim to Beat connection include Oscar Zeta Acosta; the Dr. Gonzo of Hunter Thompson's *Fear and Loathing in Las Vegas* (1972), even if his autobiographies excoriate City Lights as "a hangout for sniveling intellectuals" yet have him referring to himself as "a faded beatnik"; and Lorna Dee Cervantes, who for all her poetry of *la raza* and California blue-collar life also avers that "I know that my roots come out of the Beat movement."[40] The bilingual journal *El Corno Emplumado / The Plumed Horn*, begun in 1962 under the co-editorship of Margaret Randall and Sergio Mondragon, would publish Ginsberg and other Beats along with a host of Spanish-language and multicultural poets: step beyond America and there is what might be designated

Beat international. Outriders born of other national cultural histories include England's Michael Horovitz, Russia's Andrei Voznesensky, the Netherlands's Jan Kramer and Simon Vinkenoog (translator of "Howl"), and Japan's Nanao Sakaki and Kazuko Shiraishi.[41] In their multiple international voicing Beat, these and other writers find in the broad category of race various wellsprings and conjunctions. Together with well-known Beat writers and those racially marked in obvious ways, these figures suggest that what we consider Beat lies far beyond white Americans writing about alienation from mainstream culture.

NOTES

1   Allen Ginsberg, *Howl and Other Poems* (San Francisco: City Lights, 1956), 9.
2   Jack Kerouac, *On the Road* (New York: Viking, 1957), 163–64.
3   Allen Ginsberg, *Kaddish and Other Poems: 1958–1960* (San Francisco: City Light, 1961); Jack Kerouac, *The Subterraneans* (New York: Grove, 1958); Jack Kerouac, *Pic* (New York: Grove Press, 1971).
4   Allen Ginsberg, "Wichita Vortex Sutra," *Planet News 1961–1967* (San Francisco: City Lights Books, 1968), 110–32; Allen Ginsberg, *Angkor Wat* (New York: Fulcrum Press, 1968); Gary Snyder, *Passage Through India* (San Francisco: Grey Fox, 1983); Joanne Kyger, *The Japan and India Journals, 1960–1964* (Bolinas, CA: Tombouctou Books, 1981).
5   Jack Kerouac, *Mexico City Blues* (New York: Grove Press, 1959).
6   Bonnie Bremser, *Troia: Mexican Memoirs* (New York: Croton Press, 1969), reprinted as *For Love of Ray* (London: Tandem Press, 1971).
7   William S. Burroughs, *Naked Lunch* (1959; New York: Harper Collins, 1993), 119, 97.
8   Jack Kerouac, *Desolation Angels* (New York: Coward, 1965).
9   Paul Bowles, *The Sheltering Sky* (London: John Lehmann, 1949).
10 Gregory Corso, *The American Express* (Paris: Olympia Press, 1961).
11 Norman Mailer, *The White Negro* (San Francisco: City Lights Books, 1958). The essay first appeared in *Dissent* (fall 1957).
12 Jack Kerouac, *Visions of Cody* (New York: McGraw-Hill, 1972); Leslie Marmon Silko, *Almanac of the Dead* (New York: Simon & Schuster, 1991).
13 John Clellon Holmes, *Get Home Free* (New York: E. P. Dutton, 1964).
14 William S. Burroughs, *Junky*, ed. and intro. Oliver Harris (1953; New York: Grove, 2003), 33, 47.
15 William S. Burroughs, *The Soft Machine* (Paris: Olympia Press, 1961), *Nova Express* (New York: Grove Press, 1964), *The Western Lands* (New York: Viking/Penguin, 1987), and *My Education: A Book of Dreams* (New York: Viking, 1995).
16 Gregory Corso, "Uccello," *Gasoline* (San Francisco: City Lights, 1958); Diane di Prima, "Backyard," *Pieces of a Song: Selected Poems* (San Francisco: City Lights, 1990); Lawrence Ferlinghetti, "Old Italians Dying," *These Are My Rivers: New and Selected Poems* (New York: New Directions, 1993).

17 Barbara Probst Solomon, *The Beat of Life* (New York: J. B. Lippincott, 1960).

18 Carl Solomon, *Mishaps, Perhaps* (San Francisco: City Lights, 1966).

19 Carl Solomon, *More Mishaps* (San Francisco: City Lights, 1968), 56.

20 Jack Micheline, "Chasing Kerouac's Shadow," www.jack-micheline.com/chasing_kerouac.htm (accessed September 9, 2016).

21 David Meltzer, *Beat Thing* (Albuquerque: La Alameda Press, 2004).

22 Joyce Johnson, *Minor Characters: A Young Woman's Coming-of-Age in the Beat Orbit of Jack Kerouac* (Boston: Houghton, 1983), *Door Wide Open: A Beat Love Affair in Letters, 1957–58* (New York: Viking: 2000), and *The Voice Is All: The Lonely Victory of Jack Kerouac* (New York: Viking, 2012).

23 Hettie Jones, *How I Became Hettie Jones* (New York: E. P. Dutton, 1990), 35.

24 ruth weiss, *Desert Journal* (Boston: Good Day Poets, 1977) and *Can't Stop the Beat: The Life and Words of a Beat Poet* (Studio City, CA: Divine Arts, 2001).

25 Irving Rosenthal, *Sheeper* (New York: Grove Press, 1968).

26 Imamu Amiri Baraka, *The Autobiography of LeRoi Jones/Amiri Baraka* (New York: Freundlich Books, 1984).

27 Donald M. Allen, *The New American Poetry 1945–1960* (New York: Grove Press, 1960); LeRoi Jones, *The Moderns: An Anthology of New Writing in America* (New York: Corinth Books, 1963).

28 LeRoi Jones, *Preface to a Twenty Volume Suicide Note* (New York: Totem Press/Corinth, 1961).

29 Amiri Baraka, "BLACK DADA NIHILISMUS," *The Dead Lecturer* (New York: Grove Press, 1984).

30 LeRoi Jones, *Dutchman* and *The Slave* (New York: William Morrow, 1964).

31 LeRoi Jones, *Home: Social Essays* (New York: William Morrow, 1966), 119.

32 Amiri Baraka, *Daggers and Javelins: Essays 1974–1979* (New York: William Morrow, 1984) and *Someone Blew Up America and Other Poems* (Saint Martin: House of Nehesi, 2003).

33 Ted Joans, "I, Too, at the Beginning," *Contemporary Authors Autobiography Series*, Vol. XXV (Detroit: Gale, 1996).

34 Ted Joans, *Black Pow Wow: Jazz Poems* (New York: Hill & Wang, 1969); *Afrodisia: New and Selected Poems* (New York: Hill & Wang, 1979); *Teducation: Selected Poems 1949–1999* (Minneapolis: Coffee House Press, 1999).

35 Joans, *Teducation*, 49. Unless otherwise specified, all further quotations from Joans's poetry are from *Teducation*.

36 Ted Joans, *Afrodisia: New & Old Poems* (New York: Hill & Wang, 1970), 8.

37 Bob Kaufman, *Solitudes Crowded With Loneliness* (New York: New Directions, 1965); *Golden Sardine* (San Francisco: City Lights, 1967); *The Ancient Rain: Poems 1956–1978* (New York: New Directions, 1981).

38 Maxine Hong Kingston, *Tripmaster Monkey: His Fake Book* (New York: Knopf, 1989).

39 Albert Saijo, with Jack Kerouac and Lew Welch, *Trip Trap: Haiku Along the Road from San Francisco to New York* (1959; Bolinas, CA: Grey Fox Press, 1973); Albert Saijo, *Outspeaks: A Rhapsody* (Honolulu: Bamboo Ridge Press, 1997).

40 Oscar Zeta Acosta, *The Autobiography of a Brown Buffalo* (San Francisco: Straight Arrow, 1972), 26, and *The Revolt of the Cockroach People* (San Francisco: Straight Arrow, 1973), 43. Lorna Dee Cervantes, "The Beats and Beyond," *Beats at Naropa*, ed. Anne Waldman and Laura Wright (Minneapolis: Coffee House Press, 2009), 113.

41 For an account of these different Beat traditions, see A. Robert Lee, "Beat International: Michael Horovitz, Andrei Voznesensky, Kazuko Shiraishi," *Modern American Counter Writing* (New York: Routledge, 2010), 70–83.

14

TODD F. TIETCHEN

Ethnographies and Networks
On Beat Transnationalism

Beat literature serves as a testimony to travel and migration, an ambitious criss-crossing of territories mapped in volume upon volume of narrative and poetry. Within those volumes, going "on the road" is most often offered as an antidote to the stultifying demands of Cold War nationalism, as Beat writers (and their questing avatars) seek out social arrangements more robust and liberating than those being offered within postwar containment culture. During an era of rampant patriotism and militarized political rhetoric, the Beat movement refused to accept nationality or the nation-form as the most natural (or normative) container for one's social and political commitments. Since the 1990s, increased critical attention has been paid to the transnational imagination of the Beat writers, as the movement's willingness to call nation-bound assumptions regarding collective life into question has made its writers' work newly relevant to scholars invested in the cultural analysis of globalization and consequent transnational phenomena. Embodying a rich variety of perspectives, transnational Beat scholarship reveals Beat literature as a repository for both the colonial attitudes and the attendant histories of resistance that presaged the world-ordering ambitions we continue to live through in our neoliberal era.

Much of the transnational scholarship on the Beats has focused upon what should be called Beat ethnography, in which writers such as William S. Burroughs and Jack Kerouac render their experiences of cultures other than their own. In his 1998 essay "With Imperious Eyes," Manuel Martinez argues that, while the Beat movement might have fashioned itself as iconoclastic, its quest for alternative modes of sociality beyond US borders most often relied upon the precincts and byways of postwar privilege and imperial power. As a result, Latin America often became figured as "a sort of Club Med" offering exhausted Westerners such as Burroughs and Kerouac a licentious retreat into drug use and promiscuity, which both likened to spiritual renewal.[1] Other scholars, such as Allen Hibbard, Oliver Harris, Rachel Adams, and Hassan Melehy, have since attempted to render the social and political stakes of Beat travel writing in more nuanced ways. In "William Burroughs and US Empire," Hibbard has argued that the transnational imagination of the Beats is irreducibly dualistic; while offering migration and travel as an escape from the stultifying conditions of social belonging as offered in the Cold War United States, much Beat writing remains "entangled with the operating conditions of empire, as both an enabling condition for travel and the potential for radical critique of the construction and effects of American Empire."[2] Harris largely concurs, as in his introduction to *The Yage Letters Redux* he admits that Burroughs's travel aesthetic remains "anomalous and enigmatic," balancing between tales of "colonial appropriation" and parodies of the Ugly American.[3] In *Continental Divides: Remapping the Cultures of North America*, Rachel Adams offers a similar take on Kerouac, documenting his attempts at highlighting the affinities between Mexico's mestizo population and the Canadian Metís, whom the Kerouacs claimed within their lineage, while arguing that "Kerouac is also aware that such cross-cultural recognition can only go so far."[4] Melehy's approach to Kerouac in "Jack Kerouac and the Nomadic Cartographies of Exile" builds upon that of Adams in that Melehy presents a challenge to critics such as Martinez who "have accused Kerouac of exoticizing marginalized populations ... of writing the dreams of a white boy out slumming."[5] Melehy additionally attempts to overturn these characterizations by insisting upon Kerouac's own standing as a postcolonial author with roots in Québécois culture and the French Canadian diaspora in New England.

To quote Harris, when Beat narrative turns its attention to "foreign lands – mapping tropical jungles rather than mainly North American urban underworlds," it simultaneously lays bare the close relationship of travel writing to "its scientific double, ethnography," which usually comes entangled with tales of imperial adventuring of one sort or another (*Yage Letters* xxvi). Scholarly analyses of Beat ethnography have emerged alongside a historiographical tradition focused more upon the extent to which the perspectives and concerns of the Beat movement were embedded in transnational networks – or on those historical instances in which Beat aesthetics and outlooks became catalyzed or mobilized by other aesthetic and political movements operating within transnational scales. What we encounter in this tradition of transnational scholarship is a more developed treatment of the Beat movement as a repository for social and political concerns that are simultaneously part of and excessive to the movement itself, which is to say that the depths of Beat cosmopolitanism or worldliness become most evident when Beat writers assume, and collaborate upon, the concerns of other political and aesthetic movements – or when they participate in networked, border-crossing interactions preserved in archives waiting to be mined. As

such, the methodologies favored by such scholars tend to be less hermen-
eutical on the whole, as research remains more clearly bent on recovering
transnational genealogies of interaction that had been long concealed within
the rigidities of nation-bound literary, historical, and cultural study.

Daniel Belgrad's "The Transnational Counterculture: Beat–Mexican
Intersections" (2004) remains a signal moment within this second tradition
of transnational Beat scholarship. In arguing that a number of Beat writers
were moved by a conception of Mexico as home to values and perspectives oppositional to the Cold War corporate order – a conception that they
shared with their Mexican contemporaries working in magical realism –
Belgrad provides a more complicated vision of the Beats' Latin American
interactions than can be discovered in Martinez.[6] In *The Cubalogues: Beat
Writers in Revolutionary Havana* (2010), I followed Belgrad's lead,
reconstructing Beat entanglements within the early culture of the Cuban
Revolution while arguing that what might be found in those interactions
with Caribbean revolutionaries, French existentialists, and central figures
of the Latin American Boom was a more socially and politically sophisticated mode of transnational longing than might be discovered in the eth-
nographical work of Burroughs and Kerouac. The Cuban writings of Amiri
Baraka, Lawrence Ferlinghetti, and others are presented in that study as "a
quite different manifestation of inter-American contact," as models of transnational loyalties allied more explicitly with progressive social and political ends.[7] Similarly, Michele Hardesty's "'If the Writers of the World Get
Together': Allen Ginsberg, Lawrence Ferlinghetti, and Literary Solidarity
in Sandinista Nicaragua" (2012), employs Ferlinghetti's *Seven Days in
Nicaragua Libre* (1984) and Allen Ginsberg's "Statement on Nicaragua"
(1986) to explore the transnational literary solidarities that formed around
Sandinista Nicaragua, where Ginsberg and Ferlinghetti were joined by other
world-famous literary figures, such as Julio Cortázar and Salman Rushdie,
in participating in the Sandinistas' commitments to mass literacy as a political and developmental strategy.[8]

Also driven by the desire to reveal long obfuscated genealogies of collaboration and influence, Robin Kelley's work on Surrealism contextualizes
Beat literature within a more sweeping history of twentieth-century oppositional culture, as in *Freedom Dreams: The Black Radical Imagination*
(2002), where he convincingly renders Surrealism as a transnational and
intergenerational revolutionary movement offering "a vision of freedom far
deeper and more expansive" than a majority of the other social justice movements to emerge across the twentieth century and into the twenty-first.[9]
Moreover, Surrealism wrote its concerns into Beat writing and Beat perspectives in significant ways through the oft-overlooked work of artists such as

Ted Joans, Bob Kaufmann, and Philip Lamantia, each of whom extended the leftist political motivations of André Breton – friend to both Joans and Lamantia – in order to reflect upon the legacies of colonialism and imperialism as they unfolded during the decades following World War II. In "The Beat Manifesto: Avant-Garde Poetics and the Worlded Circuits of African American Beat Surrealism" (2012), Jimmy Fazzino extends the concerns of Kelley's work, offering highly contextualized analyses of Amiri Baraka's "BLACK DADA NIHILISMUS," Ted Joans's "Proposition for a Black Power Manifesto," and Bob Kaufman's *Abomunist Manifesto*, all of which lay bare the commitments of these writers to achieving a "worlded" perspective bent on revealing the contributions that Africa and African-derived peoples have made to planetary culture – including to the political and cultural concerns of the past century's avant-gardes.[10]

Beat Ethnography

In what follows, I will further explore the orienting claims of ethnographic and networked approaches to Beat literature in relation to representative writings by Burroughs, Kerouac, and Joans. I have chosen these writings with the hope that they might elucidate the overriding concerns and contradictions of Beat transnationalism in ways that help to guide further study in the area of transnationalism. Let me start my consideration of these texts by echoing Harris's observation that travel writing has been intrinsic to the historical development of colonial ethnography and imperial adventuring for quite some time (one need only consider, for instance, the writings of Christopher Columbus or William Bradford) and that transnational Beat writing helps to make those connections legible.

Drawing on Ali Behdad's work in *Belated Travelers: Orientalism in the Age of Colonial Dissolution* (1994), Hibbard has helpfully asserted that Beat travel writing dramatizes sympathies "with the colonial subject and, at the same time, a residual alliance with the power structures of societies from which they traveled – a foot in both camps, if you will" (17). Burroughs's *Yage Letters* (1963) perfectly encapsulate this duality: his letters to Allen Ginsberg chronicle his journeys (during the 1950s) through the Amazonian jungles searching for yage (or ayahuasca), a psychotropic botanical drug of great hallucinogenic potency. Over the course of those letters, however, Burroughs's professed antiauthoritarianism remains inconsistent in its thought, ultimately incapable of remedying the Western and/or American "systems of control" it seeks to oppose. This is not to say that Burroughs lacks sincere and tangible motivations. As Harris points out, "Demonized as an addict and homosexual, Burroughs simply could not have written his first two titles, *Junkie* and *Queer,* inside the disciplinary straightjacket of Cold War America" (*Yage Letters* xii). His global questing does in fact represent a grappling with that straightjacket, an attempt at breaking free from the containment culture of Cold War America and its stifling morality. Indeed, this is a stock Beat theme, in which nomadic life choices are equated with principled marginality and self-exile, catalyzed by a professed disdain for American authority and lifeways as expressed domestically and abroad. Nevertheless, these attempts to access a greater degree of moral license via transnational travel often lead to behavior that not only dissipates cosmo-politan ideals but also at times degenerates into wantonness and the victimi-zation of others.

Burroughs's disdain for nationalism and what he viewed as its overreach-ing modes of policing and surveillance is on explicit display throughout *Yage Letters.* At one point he encounters a member of Colombia's Policia Nacional who boasts of fighting alongside US troops in the Korean War. Burroughs not only identifies the officer as an "unappetizing person" but also admits that "I never feel flattered by this promiscuous liking for Americans. It is insulting to individual dignity, and no good ever comes from these America lovers" (11). The level of Burroughs's disdain for US hemispheric influence is also made quite evident by his open criticism of the Point Four Program throughout *Yage Letters.* Established by Harry Truman in 1949, Point Four offered US assistance to nations throughout the devel-oping world in an attempt at establishing and maintaining international political influence. It was a program designed primarily to demonstrate that democracy and capitalistic economics were superior modes of governance and development to Soviet-style communism.[11]

As openly critical as he may be of US world-ordering ambition, Burroughs nevertheless benefits from the efforts of Western corporations and govern-mental agencies jockeying for influence in the developing world. He con-fesses, for instance, that he is able to find passage into the Amazonian rainforest by attaching himself "to an expedition – in a somewhat vague capacity to be sure – consisting of Doc Schindler, two Colombian Botanists, two English Broom Rot specialists from the Cocoa Commission" (*Yage Letters* 23). Schindler is a pseudonym for the founder of ethnobotany, Richard Evans Schultes, who spent years studying the medicinal and cer-emonial use of plants by indigenous populations throughout the Americas. Burroughs further admits his great joy at in turn being "treated like visiting royalty under the misapprehension I was a representative of the Texas Oil Company traveling incognito. (Free boat rides, free plane rides, free chow; eating in the officers' mess, sleeping in the governor's house)" (24). His delight over his access to influence is often accompanied by his pretensions over what he views as a lack of administrative acumen and governmental competency across Latin America, as when he complains to Ginsberg from Colombia: "Will leave here in the next few days for Mocoa and the Putumayo. Won't write from there since mail service beyond Pasto is extremely unreliable depending on volunteer carrier-bus and truck drivers mostly. More letters are lost than delivered. These people do not have even the concept of responsibility" (16).

More troubling is Burroughs's fascination with sexual slavery and his persistent fantasies of kidnapping an indigenous boy to serve in just that capacity. Writing from Peru, Burroughs informs Ginsberg that he would like to capture an Auca boy, explaining that he would simply block both exits of the boy's home and murder everyone he did not "wanna fuck" (35). Harris has argued that in such instances Burroughs is merely putting the reader on, donning the persona of the Ugly American in order to parody the modes of imperial privilege he explicitly criticizes. Ultimately, though, Burroughs's intentions remain murky in such instances, leaving scholars such as Martinez to view him as a predatory, hedonistic imperialist. The most conclusive thing that might be said regarding this murkiness or ambiguity – which Burroughs never took the time to clarify – is that it continues to clear a space in Burroughs's work for different interpretative framings ranging from literalism to parody. Regardless of where one ultimately falls within this interpretative spectrum, it remains undeniable that Burroughs possessed a penchant for sexual tourism and was able to leverage his Western privilege into numerous encounters with boy prostitutes over a great many years of living outside the United States.

Such possibilities, along with the promise of exotic drugs in more licentious environments, largely explain Burroughs's decision to make Tangier his home beginning in 1954. Tangier's longstanding status as an international zone – a French colony run collaboratively by eight separate nations – had transformed it into a loosely governed site of permissiveness that greatly appealed to Burroughs (and fellow Americans Jane and Paul Bowles). Western sexual imperialism had been practiced in Morocco since the early seventeenth century, and Burroughs especially appreciated being able to pay impoverished street boys to have sex with each other in public, bragging that "they will do it anytime for forty cents."[12] Burroughs further elaborates on this appeal in "International Zone," admitting that "The special attraction of Tangier can be put in one word: exemption. Exemption from interference, legal or otherwise. Your private life is your own, to act exactly as you please ... It is a sanctuary of noninterference."[13] Burroughs's outlook in this instance appears libertarian rather than cosmopolitan, and, as Barry Miles has pointed out, comes animated by the orientalism characterizing so much of Burroughs's writings on Tangier and Latin America (*Call Me* 265). When the anticolonial Istiqlal Revolution arrived in 1956, Burroughs rather predictably remained ambivalent, tending to worry more about his supply of drugs than the possibilities of Moroccan self-determination.

Global Slumming?

Two of the major objectives of the Istiqlal Revolution were to curb drug use and prostitution, as those practices had helped to transform the region into a den of Western vice. Adhering to an anticolonial, and hence anti-Western, agenda, the Revolution declared the use of kif, a highly resinous and potent cannabis derivative, illegal – though the drug's new illegal status did not stop Kerouac from imbibing prodigious amounts of kif while visiting Burroughs in Tangier in February 1957. Kerouac's kif use in Tangier would later be memorialized in *Desolation Angels* (1965), as would his fondness for veiled prostitutes. These admissions highlight the extent to which Beat explorations of the transnational peripheries so often degenerated into modes of global predation, difficult to decouple from imperial and racial privilege, which is to say that their liberation (or "exemption" as Burroughs puts it) cannot help but stand upon the backs of others.

The term "slumming" is often employed as shorthand for just this sort of arrangement, in which one travels through geographies below one's economic standing as a form of sensual and experiential adventuring thought to provide access to authenticity. A characteristic example can be found in *On the Road* (1957), in which Sal Paradise strolls through "the Denver colored section, wishing I were a Negro, feeling that the best the white world had offered was not enough ecstasy for me, not enough life, joy, kicks, darkness, music, not enough night."[14] Bemoaning the vacuity of "white ambitions," Kerouac wishes he could switch places with the people of color he encounters in Denver's impoverished neighborhoods. Responding to Kerouac's ruminations in "The Black Boy Looks at the White Boy" (1961), James Baldwin declared them "absolute nonsense, of course, objectively considered, and offensive nonsense at that: I would hate to be in Kerouac's shoes if he should ever be mad enough to read this aloud from the stage of Harlem's Apollo Theater."[15] Baldwin's offense stems primarily from the fact that Kerouac romanticizes impoverished conditions to which he is not ultimately subject; he has access to "Denver's colored section" as a privileged tourist, a privilege that cannot be reciprocated to the marginalized subjects of his reverie. Baldwin's ruminations on Kerouac align with Martinez's critique of the Beats and find further justification in Kerouac's description of crossing the US border into Mexico in his sketch "Mexico Fellaheen," in which he declares "the moment you cross the little wire gate and you're in Mexico, you feel like you just sneaked out of school when you told the teacher you were sick and she told you you could go home, 2 o'clock in the afternoon."[16]

Melehy has argued that accusing Kerouac of "slumming" misses the mark for he is himself a postcolonial writer, who in works such as *Visions of Gerard* (1963) and *Dr. Sax* (1959) crafted an ethnographic literature of the Québécois diaspora in New England. Moreover, Melehy suggests that Kerouac's adoption of the term "fellaheen" speaks to the author's sense that his family history is compatible with that of other colonized populations, that Kerouac

> sketches the genealogy of the Duluoz family, referring to his Québécois lineage as fellaheen, the Arabic word he frequently uses for Mexican and other peasants. Kerouac adapts this term from Oswald Spengler, who in *The Decline of the West* uses it to designate the peoples who precede and follow the organization of civilization – hence, those who stand outside it and effectively offer nothing to it. (43)

Melehy's observation is indeed useful for it points out that Kerouac was perhaps not as "Anglo" as Martinez imagines, and might at times have been guided by a conscious and principled desire to ally himself with marginalized groups on the other side of World War II.

Whereas Spengler identified the fellaheen with the eventual dissipation of Western civilizations as the result of the historical rise of what he viewed as lesser, equatorial peoples, Kerouac at times hoped to align his experiences of American marginality with Spengler's inhabitants of the planetary margins. Consider the following selection from *Book of Sketches*:

> Get rid of *pride*
> Get rid of *sorrow*
> Mix with the People
> Go with the People,
> the Fellaheen not the
> American Bourgeois Middle
> class World of neurosis
> nor the Catholic French
> Canadian European World
> – the People –
> Indians, Arabs, the
> Fellaheen in country, village,
> of City Slums[17]

While Kerouac does not in this passage collapse his experience as a French Canadian into that of the fellaheen, he clearly (as Melehy suggests) extends Spengler's category into a cartography of anticolonial and intercultural resistance spanning the developing world to the impoverished inhabitants of American cities. In instances such as this, Kerouac voices an allegiance with these groups as a transnational alternative to American bourgeois striving and the legacies of European culture.

Moreover, the work of Melehy and Adams asks us to reconsider Kerouac's denunciation of "white ambitions" in postwar America as perhaps more historically complex than scholars such as Martinez have imagined. The complexity of Kerouac's position comes into sharper view when we consider the extent to which World War II had served as a defining moment – or perhaps redefining moment – in US cultural representations of race, especially in terms of the nation's conceptions of whiteness, or of who might be counted or understood as white. While engaged in a militarized and ideological struggle against the explicitly racist fascism of Nazi Germany, the United States nevertheless maintained a segregated military that forbade black and Asian-derived citizens from serving in white regiments. However, as Gary Gerstle points out, Hollywood studios at the same time colluded with the US Office of War Information on propagating the notion of a newly integrated military through "multicultural platoon films," featuring fighting units "made up of Protestants, Catholics, Jews, southerners, westerners, and easterners, all of whom were white."[18] In films such as *Sahara* (1943), *Gung-Ho* (1943), and *The Fighting Seabees* (1944), "the diverse backgrounds of platoon and crew members" were foregrounded early on, though the "diversity roster varied from one film to another" across white ethnicities (25). In retrospect these films, despite their ideological intentions, speak to a new elasticity in American conceptions of whiteness, which had become pliable enough to accommodate ethnicities in addition to Martinez's "Anglos."[19]

Many of the Beat writers lived through this mid-century transition as white ethnics. Aside from Kerouac (as discussed by Adams and Melehy), Gregory Corso, Diane di Prima, Lawrence Ferlinghetti, and Allen Ginsberg – all among the movement's most influential figures – experienced a new relationship to whiteness and access to "white ambitions" in the decade following World War II, so that the movement's interests in global marginality and people of color appears at times to be invested in an oppositional sociality. That is to say, the Beat reaction against postwar middle-class and consumerist culture in the United States might actually, in a sense, be read as a rejection of whiteness in favor of an alternative intercultural imaginary viewed as antithetical to the continuance of social dominance and imperium into the Cold War era. Indeed, even Baldwin, despite his explicit criticism of Kerouac, seemed to notice the complexities surrounding race and ethnicity in Cold War bohemia. Baldwin's awareness is made quite evident in his novel *Another Country* (1962), much of which is set in Greenwich Village during the 1950s. A major tension in *Another Country* stems from the efforts of Vivaldo, a young and struggling Italian American novelist, to empathize with his best friend, the black saxophonist Rufus Scott, whose suicide Vivaldo failed to foresee and prevent. Vivaldo's predicament becomes even more complicated when he finds himself romantically involved with Rufus's sister, the aspiring jazz vocalist Ida. On one hand, Baldwin wrestles with the attempt by white ethnics and black artists inhabiting postwar bohemia to imagine "Another Country," a more cosmopolitan and intimate milieu beyond the strictures of racialized nationalism in the United States. On the other hand, Baldwin remains pessimistic about the possibility of a new social paradigm of inclusion emerging out of the contact between American blacks and white ethnics in postwar bohemia, for no structure of empathy can be said to exist between groups whose historical relationship to whiteness has been so dissimilar. As traditions of marginality and oppression are not homologous in structure, boundaries between those differences are not as easily surmountable as Kerouac tends to imagine throughout his poetry and novels (as in *On the Road*, where Sal claims to have been easily integrated into the Mexican community of agricultural workers). This realization goes a long way toward explaining Baldwin's reaction to Kerouac in "The Black Boy Looks at the White Boy," in which he admits that, while there "is real pain in" Kerouac's alienation from white ambitions, that pain is ultimately too "diluted" and "thin" to communicate its concerns with an audience at the Apollo (278).

Oppositional Networks

While Melehy's work asks us to reassess scholarly accusations of Beat slumming in a more nuanced fashion – as perhaps an attempt at articulating new political and social alliances within transnational or subnational scales – completely overturning such accusations shall always remain a herculean task. In spite of Kerouac's attempts to align his experience with that of the fellaheen, his writings consistently associate slumming with the quest for spiritual enlightenment and hipster visions of authenticity, validating Martinez's characterization. Moreover, Kerouac's indifference to events such as the Istiqlal Revolution relegate his transnational narratives to the perspective of the *flâneur*, a footloose observer seeking out bliss in this or that contact zone (those places where cultures touch). The same can of course be said of Burroughs, and it is this proclivity toward indifference – or apolitical "coolness" – that differentiates so much of transnational Beat ethnography from the networked transnational histories in which we sometimes find Beat writers enmeshed. Further, those histories of transnational alliance and collaboration are often explicitly interested in global revolutionary and anticolonial politics – which is to say that they do not fall prey to either the ambiguities of parody or the ultimately noncommittal empathy of the ethnographic tradition.

In *The Cubalogues*, for instance, I explored the Beat Movement's involvement in Cuban revolutionary culture during the late 1950s and early 1960s, a historical instance in which certain Beats found themselves in Cuba alongside Harold Cruse, Simone de Beauvoir, Maya Deren, the Maysles brothers, Jean-Paul Sartre, and C. Wright Mills. All traveled to Cuba hoping to foment a new transnational arena of alternative thinking and oppositional sociality within Fidel Castro's unfolding revolution; that is to say, this impressive cast of thinkers and artists hoped that they might collaborate with native artists such as Guillermo Cabrera Infante and the editorial board of the Cuban literary journal *Lunes de Revolución* in transforming Cuba into a third space for thinking through pressing political and social concerns foreclosed from the era's paranoid nationalisms as articulated across the US–Soviet ideological divide. Resulting works of autobiographical reportage such as Amiri Baraka's "Cuba Libre," Ferlinghetti's "Poet's Notes on Cuba," and Ginsberg's "Prose Contribution to Cuban Revolution" recast Beat road narratives and ethnography as political quests. Cuban political events came to anchor a critique of Cold War US militarism and world-ordering ambition, while calling for modes of expressive freedom and racial and sexual justice forestalled within US containment culture. Baraka's Cuba encounter is particularly notable as it catalyzed his life-altering political transformation of the 1960s. That transformation involved his abandonment of what he had come to view as the incoherent political commitments of the New York Beats such as Burroughs and Kerouac for Black Power, which Baraka situated within global anticolonial struggles throughout Africa and Asia, a transformation also explored by Fazzino and in Van Gosse's *Where the Boys Are: Cuba, Cold War, and the Making of a New Left* (1993).

Similar commitments to anti-imperialism and planetary egalitarianism are evident in the Beat Movement's involvements with Surrealism. Robin Kelley has made clear that Surrealism's debts to global anticolonialism remain irrefutable, traceable as they are to the longtime relationship between Breton and the architects of Négritude – Aimé Césaire and Léopold Senghor. All three, for instance, published in *Tropiques*, a Martinique surrealist journal

guided by antiessentialist and antinationalist commitments to cosmopolitanism or to world citizenship. Suzanne Césaire summed up the mission
of *Tropiques* in 1943, declaring that "surrealism will enable us to finally
transcend the sordid antinomies of the present: whites/Blacks, Europeans/
Africans, civilized/savages" (*Freedom Dreams* 171). Ted Joans, a painter
and poet who came of artistic age alongside Ginsberg and Kerouac within
the New York branch of the Beat Movement, also occupies a central place
within the radical transnational history of Surrealism as preserved in journals such as *Tropiques*. Like other Beat writers, Joans traveled the globe,
living in various locations throughout Europe and Mexico and maintaining
a home in Timbuktu from the 1960s until the end of his life in 2003. Along
with the roots he established in Mali, Joans resided for extended periods
in Paris, as he also was a close friend of Breton and a member of the Paris
Surrealist Group.[20]

Joans's dedication to Surrealist values and perspectives is on full display
in "Eternal Lamp of Lam" (1979), an incantatory elegy to Cuban artist
Wifredo Lam that concludes: "AFRO / CHINO / CUBANO / WIFREDO /
AFRO / CHINO/ CUBANO / WIFREDO WIFREDO WIFREDO LAM!"[21]
These lines clearly offer Lam's life and art as refutations of the "sordid
antinomies" identified by Suzanne Césaire. Born in Cuba to a Chinese father
and Afro-Cuban mother (capable of tracing her roots through slavery back
to the Congo), Lam remained interested in Afro-Cuban culture for much
of his life, though he was also a student of Salvador Dalí in Madrid and a
lifelong friend of Pablo Picasso. Immersed in both Caribbean art and the
European avant-garde, Lam became known for paintings that fused surrealist techniques with Afro-Cuban iconography, resulting in the prominence of
hybrid figures across his vast body of work.

The hybrid nature of Joans's own work as a painter and poet explains
his admiration for Lam. Joans not only helped to write the concerns
of Surrealism into Beat poetry but also remained ever cognizant of the
ways in which Beat literature extended the perspectives and aesthetic philosophies of the European avant-garde. In a letter to André Breton, for
example, Joans exclaims that the "Beat Generation owes practically everything to surrealism. I have discussed this subject with Kerouac, Corso,
and Ginsberg" (*Black, Brown* 230). Though often unacknowledged, Beat
writing was significantly indebted to Surrealist automatism, an aesthetic
precursor to spontaneous prose and the improvisational mastery of the
modern jazz artists so adored by the New York Beats. Indeed, in poems
such as "Jazzemblage," Joans creates Surrealist imagery via spontaneous
poetics, his poem referencing Surrealists such as De Chirico alongside jazz
pianist Bud Powell, suggesting that both Joans's own Beat aesthetic and

modern jazz are extensions of Surrealist thought and creativity that transcend nationalist boundaries.

Joans's outlooks on the geopolitical stakes of that transnational genealogy become more evident in his 1981 essay "Bird and the Beats." During the early 1950s, Joans became known for throwing costume balls in order to raise the rent money for his Greenwich Village apartment. Joans tells us that Charlie Parker (known as "Bird" or "Yardbird") attended one of these rent parties that was specifically "dedicated to surrealism, Dada, and the Mau Mau. Bird arrived late but he hastily improvised his own Mau Mau [costume] plus aided other hipsters [in assembling their own]."[22] The Mau Mau Rebellion was an anticolonial uprising in British-controlled Kenya from 1952 to 1960, and in Joans's recollection of this particular rent party he identifies Parker (as he identifies Lam) as a composite symbol of improvisational aesthetics, Surrealist playfulness, and anticolonial politics. Particularly telling is the fact that, as the essay develops, Joans begins to refer to the Beat Generation as instead the Bird Generation. In Joans's words, Parker "understood what the Bird G. was about at the core, that we wanted to be a swinging group of NEW people, like his music, intent on international joy. We broke out of America's squareness just as Bird had done" ("Bird and the Beats"). Implicit in Joans's commemoration of Parker as a cosmopolitan or world citizen for whom the Beat Generation should be retroactively renamed is a critique of his fellow New York Beats as lacking in their political devotions to anticolonialism, a critique that seemingly echoes Baldwin's criticism of postwar white bohemia.

Transnational Humanities and the Specter of the Beats

Cosmopolitanism is often proffered as the philosophical basis for world citizenship, or for conceptions of social belonging that refuse to be nation bound. Bruce Robbins defines cosmopolitanism as a "fundamental devotion to the interests of humanity as a whole," and there are aspects of the Beat literary and cultural enterprise that certainly resonate with his definition, aimed as they are at exploring transnational and subnational forms of sociality.[23] As Robbins has explained, however, cosmopolitanism has often seemed "to claim universality by virtue of its independence, its detachment from the bonds, commitments, and affiliations that constrain ordinary nation-bound lives. It has seemed to be a luxuriously free-floating view from above" or to have been marked by a tacit assumption of privilege (1). The cosmopolitan ethos, as embodied in the work of American writers ranging from Henry James to Gertrude Stein to Paul Bowles, is most often based in a conscious decision to declare oneself a world citizen, a declaration of affiliation that other planetary subjects simply cannot afford; many people, including those born in the impoverished areas of the world, have traditionally migrated from place to place in order to alleviate their poverty, and have not (and still do not) invest their migratory needs with ethical devotions to humanity as a whole – or to forms of sociality that are consciously opposed to the conventional forms of political and social alignment. Robbins claims that theories of cosmopolitanism, or Western notions regarding world citizenship, have long been blind to coerced migration and that scholars should be more attentive to the fact that there are multiple cosmopolitanisms circulating through our contemporary world. Beat literature does not ultimately provide us with access to narratives from the impoverished inhabitants of the global margins, though many Beat writers certainly passed through and engaged those margins from a multiplicity of perspectives. As a result, Beat literature continues to open a useful window upon the multiple ways in which writers and artists have rendered the stakes of inhabiting an increasingly interconnected, though far from egalitarian, world.

Ultimately, one of the most important things that transnational Beat narrative powerfully dramatizes is the fact that world travel – or intercultural interaction within contact zones such as Burroughs's interzone – can at times generate the opposite of tolerance and acceptance toward those deemed different from ourselves, even as we might be explicitly engaged in acknowledging the limitations of nationalism and national belonging. On the other hand, the work of figures such as Joans models the extent to which a dedication to migratory ways and transnational seeking might indeed foment new modes of empathy and collaboration. Remaining open to the inherent complexities and paradoxes animating Beat transnationalism as a whole requires that we remain vigilantly suspicious of the political value of transgressive literature. That is to say, we should never assume that transgressive or iconoclastic writers, whose work remains invested in challenging social and cultural mores, are simultaneously invested in replacing those mores with socially progressive agendas or perspectives. The range of issues and perspectives comprising Beat literature remains a sobering reminder that transgressive art and literature can often be as socially regressive as it can be socially progressive. By extension, this remains a problem for Beat canonicity given the now longstanding focus in the humanities on progressive political concerns, in which academic work often quite explicitly announces its alignment with a broad spectrum of social justice claims. Over the past several decades humanities scholars have come to see themselves as agents of such changes – and my own work is certainly not immune here – invested in remaking the world in more inclusive and equitable ways. Within that context, transnational Beat narrative remains a cautionary tale, for both scholars and students, that human loyalties and perspectives often remain complex, inconsistent, and contradictory.

NOTES

1   Manuel Martinez, "With Imperious Eyes," *Atzlan* 23.1 (1998), 42.
2   Allen Hibbard, "William Burroughs and US Empire," *The Transnational Beat Generation*, ed. Nancy M. Grace and Jennie Skerl (New York: Palgrave Macmillan, 2012), 15.
3   William S. Burroughs and Allen Ginsberg, *The Yage Letters Redux*, ed. Oliver Harris (San Francisco: City Lights, 2006), ix–xi.
4   Rachel Adams, *Continental Divides: Remapping the Cultures of North America* (Chicago: University of Chicago Press, 2009), 165.
5   Hassan Melehy, "Jack Kerouac and the Nomadic Cartographies of Exile," *Transnational Beat Generation*, 41.
6   Daniel Belgrad, "The Transnational Counterculture: Beat–Mexican Intersections," *Reconstructing the Beats*, ed. Jennie Skerl (New York: Palgrave Macmillan, 2004).
7   Todd F. Tietchen, *The Cubalogues: Beat Writers in Revolutionary Havana* (Gainesville: University Press of Florida, 2010), 9.
8   Michele Hardesty, "'If the Writers of the World Get Together': Allen Ginsberg, Lawrence Ferlinghetti, and Literary Solidarity in Sandinista Nicaragua," *Transnational Beat Generation*.
9   Robin D. G. Kelley, *Freedom Dreams: The Black Radical Imagination* (2002; Boston: Beacon Press, 2009), 159.
10 Jimmy Fazzino, "The Beat Manifesto: Avant-Garde Poetics and the Worlded Circuits of African American Beat Surrealism," *Transnational Beat Generation*, 68.
11 The extent to which Burroughs's work might be read as a critique of globalization in its nascent and more advanced stages is explored in David Scheiderman and Philip Walsh, eds., *Retaking the Universe: William S. Burroughs in the Age of Globalization* (London: Pluto Press, 2004).
12 Barry Miles, *Call Me Burroughs: A Life* (New York: Twelve, 2014), 293.
13 William S. Burroughs, "International Zone," *Interzone*, ed. James Grauerholz (New York: Penguin, 1989), 56.
14 Jack Kerouac, *On the Road* (1957; New York: Penguin, 1991), 179–180.
15 James Baldwin, "The Black Boy Looks at the White Boy," *Collected Essays*, ed. Toni Morrison (New York: Library of America, 1998), 278.
16 Jack Kerouac, *Lonesome Traveler* (New York: Grove, 1960), 21.
17 Jack Kerouac, *Book of Sketches* (New York: Penguin, 2006), 274.
18 Gary Gerstle, *American Crucible: Race and Nation in the Twentieth Century* (Princeton: Princeton University Press, 2001), 204.
19 Also see Matthew Frye Jacobson's *Whiteness of a Different Color* (Cambridge: Harvard University Press, 1999), especially 201–273.

20 See Robin D. G. Kelley and Franklin Rosemont, eds., *Black, Brown & Beige: Surrealist Writings from Africa and the Diaspora* (Austin: University of Texas Press, 2009), 228.

21 Ted Joans, "Eternal Lamp of Lam," *Teducation: Selected Poems* (Saint Paul: Coffee House Press, 1999), 157.

22 Ted Joans, "Bird and the Beats," *Coda* 181 (1981), np.

23 Bruce Robbins, "Introduction Part I: Actually Existing Cosmopolitanisms," *Cosmopolitics: Thinking and Feeling Beyond the Nation*, ed. Pheng Cheah and Robbins (Minneapolis: University of Minnesota Press, 1998), 1.

15

JOHN WHALEN-BRIDGE

Buddhism and the Beats

The writers of the Beat Generation most strongly associated with Buddhism include Allen Ginsberg, Jack Kerouac, Joanne Kyger, Gary Snyder, Anne Waldman, Lew Welch, and Philip Whalen.[1] In this chapter I discuss some high points of Beat Buddhist writings to consider the literary transmission of Buddhist themes, references, and even contemplative practices into American culture as a historical process, one in which Beat writers answered the perception of oddity and foreignness with sometimes self-subverting humor. The "Zen lunacy" praised by Ray Smith, Jack Kerouac's avatar in *The Dharma Bums* (1958), his *roman à clef* about the Beat generation's embrace of Buddhism, has a history. If, as Samuel Johnson has written, nations, like people, have their infancy, then so do literary and cultural formations.[2] In this chapter I focus on Beat Buddhism as the adolescent phase of a larger cultural movement, one in which religious ideas and practices from Asia would come to have a considerable influence on American culture as a whole.

Literature and the Transmission of Religious Ideas

As Thomas Tweed points out in *The American Encounter with Buddhism, 1844–1912: Victorian Culture and the Limits of Dissent* (1992), the traders, missionaries, and diplomats of the century before the Transcendentalist writers "lumped together Confucianism, Taoism, Buddhism, Shinto, Hinduism," and a few other traditions, calling them "heathens" or "pagans," or, when feeling more charitable, "Oriental religion."[3] As for actual Buddhists in North America in the nineteenth century and before, our knowledge is quite sketchy. Tweed notes the existence of Ah Nam (d. 1817), "a cook for the Spanish governor of Monterey, California, as the first Chinese immigrant on record" (34), and he was followed by more Chinese in the 1850s, and then Japanese and Korean Buddhist workers in California and Hawaii. The Japanese sent missionaries with the immigrants to the new world, partly "in response to Christian missionary efforts" at the end of the nineteenth century, but the effects of institutional support on American culture as a whole were negligible, since "Japanese Buddhists were viewed as alien and treated with hostility because of both their race and religion" (36). Beats who would later affiliate themselves with Zen Buddhism were aligning themselves with an enemy the United States had only recently defeated, the Japanese, something we should remember when we consider the too-easy charges of Orientalism.

Much more important to the overall American understanding of Buddhism was the translation and publication of inspiring texts, which began to find their way into American writing in the mid-nineteenth century, especially through the Transcendentalist organ *The Dial*. As can be expected, the first attempts to understand systems of thought so different from one's own were provisional. In *How the Swans Came to the Lake: A Narrative History of Buddhism in America* (1992), Rick Fields described the moment in 1843 when the first copy of the *Bhagavad Gita*, one of the foundational scriptures of Hinduism, made its way to Concord, Massachusetts. Emerson wrote to Elizabeth Hoar to praise "the much renowned book of Buddhism, extracts from which I have often admired but never before held the book in my hands." Fields observes that Emerson's misrecognition of the *Bhagavad Gita* as a Buddhist text was "symptomatic of the confusion that reigned about the differences between Hinduism and Buddhism."[4]

Richard Hughes Seager has complained about the narrative, constructed by Beat writers and historians of the movement such as Fields, in which "a generation of cultural revolutionaries in search of alternative spirituality found their way to Buddhism," a narrative that "never satisfactorily factored in the arrival" of Asian American Buddhists.[5] The transmission of Buddhism as a religion from Asia to America was not accomplished by Transcendentalist and Beat writers alone, however instrumental their writings have been in reorienting Buddhism in the American imagination. The challenges faced by these writers were more than a little daunting, as they saw themselves as heir to a kind of cultural transmission that they knew had taken centuries in some Asian countries. Philip Whalen, classmate of Gary Snyder and Lew Welch at Reed College before becoming part of the San Francisco Renaissance in the 1950s, comically bemoans the size of the job in his seven-line poem "The Dharma Youth League" (1966):

> I went to visit several thousand gold Buddhas
> They sat there all through the war,–
> They didn't appear just now because I happened to be
> > in town
> Sat there six hundred years. Failures.
> Does Buddha fail. Do I.
> Some day I guess I'll never learn.[6]

Part of the humor comes from the ease with which the poet imagines the strangeness of Buddhism. Mahayana Buddhists – at least those like Whalen, who went on to become a Zen priest, head monk for Richard Baker-roshi, and eventually abbot of the Hartford Street Zendo in San Francisco – promise each day to save *all* sentient beings, apparent lack of progress notwithstanding.

Whether or not writers such as Whalen, Snyder, Kerouac, and others would succeed in transplanting Buddhism to America by "holding a lotus to the rock" was an open question at best and a dubious proposition to many onlookers. Even as sympathetic an interpreter as Alan Watts expressed grave doubts about "Beat Zen," which he saw as ranging from a way to justify "sheer caprice in art, literature, and life to a very forceful social criticism and 'digging of the universe' " in the writings of Ginsberg, Snyder, and, "rather unevenly," Kerouac.[7] Zen was popularized by these writers and also by proponents such as Watts, Zen scholars such as D. T. Suzuki, and transplanted Japanese teachers such as Sokei-an (1882–1945, head teacher of the First Zen Institute) and Ngoyen Senzaki (1876–1958, interned during World War II and a Zen teacher in Los Angeles following the war), all of whom delighted in presenting Zen as a very interesting thing that cannot really be conceptualized. Any attempt to do so resulted in a shortcoming, as we see when Watts, in "Beat Zen, Square Zen, and Zen" (1959), discusses a few attempted haiku by Ginsberg, naturally finding the verse "too indirect and didactic for Zen, which would rather hand you *the thing itself* without comment" (611). As Whalen puts it near the end of his long poem "Scenes of Life from the Capital" (1969), "Japan is a civilization based upon / An inarticulate Response to cherry blossoms" (*Collected* 646). Poetic expression, paradox, and comic celebration of the limits of logic have been central features of Zen-inspired writing.

The Comic Mode of Beat Buddhism: Zen Lunacy and Preemptive Parody

In the 1950s and 1960s, Beat writers attempting to present specifically Asian mythologies, philosophies, and literary references faced a huge challenge: while creating entertaining and instructive work that incorporated Buddhist philosophy, history, and aesthetic principles, the writer had to bring along an audience that knew little about it, perhaps having read introductory works by D.T. Suzuki or Alan Watts. This is one of the main reasons that critics of Beat literature often make the mistake of thinking that many of the writers lacked knowledge about Buddhism. The writers had to educate the reader in a pay-as-you-go fashion, and they often did so by freely mixing new ideas with familiar analogs.

Ginsberg's *Howl and Other Poems* (1956), Kerouac's *Scripture of the Golden Eternity* (1960), and Whalen's "Scenes of Life from the Capital" were licensed not only by the increasingly familiar conventions of surrealistic juxtaposition but also by notions of "Zen lunacy" and iconoclasm. J. D. Salinger did not affiliate himself with the Beats in any way, but he also developed the technique of providing the reader with a smorgasbord of Asian and Euro-American philosophical references and literary allusions, a sometimes overwhelming mixture that understandably caused many critics and scholars to assume that the methods and meanings of the Buddhist literary tradition had been misunderstood.[8] In part this syncretism developed from an anti-institutional spirituality in which all roads lead to the same mountaintop – a mish-mash approach that Snyder distains in his brief but definitive essay "Notes on Religious Tendencies" (1959).[9] In that essay, Snyder suggests that a person cannot make it "in his beat life" without developing in the three areas essential to progress on the Buddhist path, namely "contemplation," "morality," and "wisdom" (306). These are the three branches of the Eightfold Path that is pervasive within Buddhism, and it is telling that Snyder organizes his wide-ranging appraisal of possible spiritual disciplines according to the Buddhist division of disciplines. In this suggestive essay, Snyder pulls back from requiring adherence to any particular creeds or disciplines – one could as well experiment with peyote, yoga, Sufism, Quakerism, or Yurok shamanism – but he argues for some form of traditionalism even as he squares off against the world of squares. Even one who fails "may get pretty far out, and that's probably better than moping around classrooms or writing books on Buddhism and Happiness for the masses, as the squares (who will shortly have succeeded in putting us all down) do" (306).

The resentment about squares who wish to "[put] us all down" is one pole, and the confident expression of "beatific" yearnings for (absolute or relative) transcendence is another. This is the meaning that has more or less prevailed in popular understanding, and it is winningly associated with self-deprecation and humorous presentations of spiritual ideals. The middle stanza of Snyder's poem "Tōji" (1958) captures perfectly what is meant by the phrase "Beat Buddhism":

> Peering though chickenwire grates
> At dusty gold-leaf statues
> A cynical curving round-belly
> Cool Bodhisattva – maybe Avalokita –
> Bisexual and tried it all, weight on
> One leg, haloed in snake-hood gold
> Shines through the shadow
> An ancient hip smile
> Tingling of India and Tibet. (*Portable* 305)

First and foremost, this poem is *playful*. The image is a projection of the poet's thoughts and desires, especially the wish to find precedent for the artist's countercultural difference in statues of esoteric heroes carved centuries before, by another generation of backward-looking spiritual revolutionaries. That is, the temple artists who created the statue personifying compassion (if it is indeed Avalokiteshvara) were ornamenting a Japanese Shingon temple, Snyder tells us in the poem, by revivifying the tantric imagery of India and Tibet. The poet peers through the constraining chickenwire, but there is no hindrance, and words such as "cynical," "cool," and "hip" invite identification. This is not the language of an art historian or a scholar, and the anti-institutional attitude has erroneously led to the conclusion that writers such as Snyder misconstrued their direct subjects.

Snyder's work here is juvenile relative to his later work, dated in its condemnation of "squares," but there is benefit to recognizing the effects of youth and neophyte enthusiasm on literary form. If we recognize adolescence as a literary stage of development within this strand of Beat writing, we allow for the possibility of artistic maturation and do not fossilize the writer in the context of the mid-1950s. Kerouac lived a bit more than a dozen years after writing *The Dharma Bums*, but Japhy Ryder's inspiration, Gary Snyder, is still publishing fine work six decades later, and the encounter between American writers and complex Asian philosophical and religious systems needs to be understood as a gradual process.

Even in its beginnings, the Beat encounter with Asian religions had not only historical but also psychological, artistic, and rhetorical dimensions. The intercultural situation is dynamic: the work is not a passive mirror, and the audience may offer considerable resistance. Before we examine novels and poems to see whether they are authentic transmissions of complex religious positions, we need to figure in this resistance and remember what Emily Dickinson wrote about her audience in the previous century: "Tell all the truth, but tell it slant: / success in circuit lies."[10]

In his essay "Hypothesis and Belief" (1948), Christopher Isherwood, an English expatriate who converted to Vedanta, discusses most specifically the motives underlying reticence in relation to what might be called "conversion embarrassment":

> If a member of the so-called intellectual class joins any religious group or openly subscribes to its teaching, he will have to prepare himself for a good deal of criticism from his unconverted and more skeptical friends. Some of these may be sympathetic and genuinely interested; others will be covertly satirical, suspicious, or quite frankly hostile and dismayed ... Henceforward, his conduct will be narrowly watched for symptoms of pretentiousness, priggishness, prudery and other forms of Puritanism.[11]

Isherwood then analyzes possible responses to this hostile reception, and the dual possibilities he describes might be called the convert's dilemma, noting that the convert, feeling "self-conscious and badly rattled," inadvertently confirms the prejudices against him, as he is "almost sure to behave unnaturally," either by preaching at friends in a boring way, "Or he will make desperate attempts to reassure them, by his manner and conversation, that he is still 'one of the gang.'" He will be "the first to blaspheme" (36). "Preaching" and "blasphemy" are the extremes of possible behavior, but what I most wish to describe is not the writer taking one horn of the dilemma or the other but rather the admixtures of these extremes, which have left us with writings we may construe as "parodic preaching."

The writers who experimented with Buddhist sutras and to some degree made light of their own serious efforts, however, worked with cultural strangeness. Strange, from the Latin *extraneus*, means external or foreign, and Buddhism regularly signifies strangeness when references appear in American texts. The Beat writers used humor to make readers familiar with strangeness, and the tonal lightness and surreal juxtapositions in no way meant the writers were not in some sense serious about the subject matter. If the writing is occasionally campy, it is high camp. As Isherwood's character Charles Kennedy says in *The World in the Evening* (1954), camp concerns serious issues even as it revels in flightiness: "you're not making fun of it; you're making fun out of it."[12]

Semisacred Sutras and the Camp Aesthetic

Kerouac, Snyder, and Ginsberg are the three most well-known writers associated with both Beat literature and Buddhism, and all three have written "sutras."[13] Attempts to write "sacred literature" within the secular mode of belletristic writing risk critical attack; the text might involve esoteric ideas, or the attempt to introduce the sacred into secular literature might be considered poor taste.

In response to Snyder's suggestion that he write a sutra, Kerouac composed *The Scripture of the Golden Eternity*, a playful celebration of Buddhist themes that at times reads like a parody of bad Beat habits. Constantly risking absurdity, Beat writers freely mixed Judeo-Christian theology and Buddhist metaphysics, as Kerouac does in Section 22 (of sixty-six fascicles) of *The Scripture of the Golden Eternity*:

> 22: Stare deep into the world before you as if it were the void: innumerable holy ghosts, buddhies, and savior gods there hide, smiling. All the atoms emitting light inside wavehood, there is no personal separation of any of it.

A hummingbird can come into a house and a hawk will not: so rest and be assured. While looking for the light, you may suddenly be devoured by the darkness and find the true light.[14]

Kerouac is sometime criticized for having had a superficial understanding of Buddhism, but volumes published posthumously, such as *Some of the Dharma* (1997) and *Wake Up: A Life of the Buddha* (2008), as well as a number of passages from *The Dharma Bums*, make evident a sophisticated grasp of Buddhist ideas, literary motifs, and practices.[15] The problem with the passage quoted above is that the writer cannot quite make a choice between sublimity and cuteness. There is an unshareable sort of playfulness throughout much of this writing, it seems to me, in which the reader either indulges the author his unearned insights or closes the book. The text has its pleasures, but it also confronts the reader with less successful attempts. The writing is lax; the puns are weak: the pun on Buddha/buddy, which Salinger also makes through his character Buddy Glass, has not aged well.

Whether or not *The Scripture of the Golden Eternity* is a masterpiece, but Kerouac claimed that the writing was especially valuable to him; because it was a "sutra," he would not compose it in a purely spontaneous manner, he told Snyder. Embarrassment arises on a number of different counts – although it is possible that the embarrassment is the result of successful literary design rather than artistic failure. Perhaps it is a mistake to take Kerouac seriously in the "strictly literary" manner of my initial approach. What if "only kidding" is, in this instance, a parodic form of revelation? Susan Sontag's essay "Notes on Camp" (1964) raises the question of intention: "In naïve, or pure, Camp, the essential element is seriousness, a seriousness that fails. Of course, not all seriousness that fails can be redeemed as Camp. Only that which has the proper mixture of the exaggerated, the fantastic, the passionate, and the naïve."[16] One problem with the overly sincere approach is that it does not leave room for the reader or listener whose views differ, but it may not always be clear whether the writer is being serious. Some readers will feel that we are putting too much effort into the rescue mission at this point, that a theoretical recontextualization shouldn't be necessary if the literature is really valuable, but the attempt illustrates one point: the writers were aware that they would be attacked both for being too serious (i.e. they were blinded by religious devotion in ways that badly affected their judgment) and not serious enough (i.e. the particular religious commitments could be construed as quietist or otherwise irresponsible forms of behavior). The camp aesthetic is one solution to this double-bind, and, whether or not reference to camp can reorient our approach in ways that justify much attention to *The Scripture of the Golden Eternity*, we'll see that the strategy was widespread, and often more successful than Kerouac's.

Christopher Isherwood, the disciple of Vedantism who defends the possibility of a passionately serious silliness called "High Camp" in his novel *The World in the Evening*, brings up camp in an interview in which he has been asked about the problem of writing religious fiction. Here Isherwood discusses the embarrassment of proselytizing:

> Every artist does that – they have to, in one way or another. But I just meant that I didn't think that this particular brand of things is important at all. I mean, you have to swallow such a lot with anything you do. There's all the trappings. Hinduism is exceedingly off-putting to a lot of people; it's very alien and odd.[17]

One solution to this embarrassment is to stress something universal about what is supposedly strange, which Isherwood does in the quotation, and another way would be to disown the sentiment expressed in the work through an ironic signal that one had not been "taken in" by the beliefs one is presenting. Isherwood's camp solution backs up a step and argues not that the literature produced is less genuine than the original (meaning, in this case, whatever scriptures or practices from Vedanta provided inspiration for Isherwood's published work), but rather that the original itself was not meant as a sincere expression of a religious piety: "What's great about the Hindu thing is that it's very lively and kind of campy and fun" (130). To treat a religious text or practice as itself campy is to pre-empt the charge that one has diminished the value of the religious experience as a compromise with a resisting or unfamiliar audience.

Camp is, essentially, a sympathetic form of parody.[18] While numerous examples of camp as a form of satirical attack will readily suggest themselves, it is also possible to see camp as "a comic vision of the world. But not a bitter or polemical comedy. If tragedy is an experience of hyperinvolvement, comedy is an experience of underinvolvement, of detachment" ("Notes on Camp" section 44). Camp aims to "dethrone the serious" (section 41), and in doing so it solves the problem of *The Scripture of the Golden Eternity*, a fatal deficit of irony that assumes you shall assume what I assume, when in fact you do not.

Allen Ginsberg exploits the camp solution in a number of poems, especially "Wichita Vortex Sutra" (1966). This poem weaves together Ginsberg's personal mind stream (with references ranging from the "Prajnaparamita Sutra" to Sufi mysticism as well as American historical, political, cultural, and popular references) with news reports about the developing war in Vietnam. Creating a matte painting of the Midwest with a few deft images, Ginsberg also refers directly to camp (although he does not reference Sontag's essay directly):

> Big Dipper leaning above the Nebraska border,
>   handle down to the blackened plains,
> telephone-pole ghosts crossed
>   by roadside, dim headlights –
> dark night, & giant T-bone steaks,
>   and in *The Village Voice*
>   New Frontier Productions present
>   Camp Comedy: *Fairies I have met.*[19]

Camp makes fun of the distinction between the real and the fake by reducing everything to stylization, and so Ginsberg, as a homosexual artist far from bohemian New York, haunted (one might say) by T-bone steaks and other icons of super-macho Americana, draws comfort from an advertisement in a scrap of newspaper – a campy reference that reduces his own isolation. Just as Ginsberg's camp references make room for his homosexuality in a heteronormative landscape, so too do his Orientalist religious references, presented in a thick and thoroughly over-the-top syncretic stew of mysticism, eroticism, and goofy popular culture, make room for his Buddhist commentaries. It could be said that the verses, in presenting Buddhist values and images as part of a stream-of-consciousness hodge-podge, discount the whole field of reference, doing more harm than good (from a would-be Buddhist proselytizer's point of view, that is). But, if the poet and his readers share camp aesthetic values as described by Isherwood and Sontag, then writers and audience commune in shared references that presumably are unwelcome in other parts of America, especially in places such as Wichita. The references may seem jokey or negative, but the fact is that they exist – the values and the identities from which they proceed are speakable rather than unspeakable.

The last ten lines of Ginsberg's "Holy Ghost on the Nod Over the Body of Bliss," written in December 1966, present a number of "gods" in ways that at once cancel them all out but that also, through the double movement I have been describing, make a place for them:

> Chango holds Shiva's prick, Ouroboros eats th'cobalt bomb,
> Parvati on YOD's perfumèd knee cries Aum
> & Santa Barbara rejoices in the alleyways of Brindaban
> *La illaha el (lill) Allah hu – Allah Akbar!*
> Goliath struck down by kidneystone, Golgothas grow old,
> All these wonders are crowded in the Mind's Eye
> Superman & Batman race forward, Zarathustra on Coyote's ass,
> Lao-tze disappearing at the gate, God mocks God,
> Job sits bewildered that Ramakrishna is Satan
> and Bodhidharma forgot to bring Nothing. (*Complete* 475)[20]

Ecstatic relations occur between deities of historically separate religions: as in the yabyum scene of *The Dharma Bums*, transgressive sexuality is a ritual of bohemian empowerment. The orgiastic vision includes not only figures from the conventional religions of East and West but also personifications from popular culture and Nietzschian philosophy – Ginsberg stirs in Superman and Batman, who might be considered deities of the comic-book imagination but who are easily recognized as camp references in the wake of Sontag's essay. Once again, the rudest of rude humor and an utterly blasphemous play with gods of various traditions is entirely successful at distracting the reader from the embarrassment of presenting strange gods and strange beliefs. In "Holy Ghost on the Nod Over the Body of Bliss," the aggressive ridicule of satire and the gentler tug of sympathetic parody merge in a kind of imaginative tantric union of profane and sacred images. A hostile reception would stress the improper adulteration of religious references, but a sympathetic respondent, one who grants the poet his freedom to find similarity in apparently discordant references, will find that writers such as Ginsberg successfully introduce spiritual concerns into the worldliest of conversations.

Play, Not Parody

When the word "camp" is used in relation to Gary Snyder, one thinks more about hiking boots and rucksacks than theatrical self-presentations with homosexual overtones, and yet there are poems in which Snyder, it might be said, camps it up just a bit. Snyder's 1969 "Smokey the Bear Sutra" would be one good example. Snyder uses the Mahayana sutra conventions to present, as a mock-deity or protector figure, the United States Forest Service's heroic fire-fighter, Smokey the Bear:

> Wrathful but Calm. Austere but Comic. Smokey the Bear will illuminate those
> who would help him; but for those who would hinder or slander him,
> HE WILL PUT THEM OUT.[21]

A sutra often goes through several stages. Purification words and imaginary offerings to the personification of a certain value (such as fearlessness or compassion) usually precede the recitation of a sacred mantra, and "Smokey the Bear Sutra" follows these conventions quite carefully, including the creation of a Sanskrit mantra that Snyder translates as follows: "I DEDICATE MYSELF TO THE UNIVERSAL DIAMOND / BE THIS RAGING FURY DESTROYED" (242). The sutra, like a genuine sutra in the Mahayana tradition, designates particular values that it promotes and particular obstacles that it uses to vanquish or limit. Smokey will "protect those who love woods and rivers," including "Gods and animals, hobos and madmen ... playful women, and hopeful children." Anyone "threatened by advertising, air pollution, television / or the police" can chant Smokey the Bear's war spell to confound the enemy: "DROWN THEIR BUTTS / CRUSH THEIR BUTTS / DROWN THEIR BUTTS / CRUSH THEIR BUTTS" (243) – and Smokey will put them out with his Vajra-shovel.

Clearly Snyder is using Smokey the Bear as a kind of joke, as a mock-deity, but it is also clear that Snyder, despite the playfulness of the poem, is seriously committed to the values his imagined deity playfully protects. When he writes in the addendum, "Regarding 'Smokey the Bear Sutra'" that "It's hard not to have a certain devotional feeling for the Large Brown Ones, even if you don't know much about them" (243), he is not using the same jocular tone as when he describes the bear's "left paw in the Mudra of Comradely Display" (242). Snyder tells of evidence in Austrian caves indicating "that our Neanderthal ancestors were practicing a devotional ritual to the Big Fellow about seventy thousand years ago," and also of a particular meditative session in which "it came to me that the Old One was no other than that Auspicious Being described in Buddhist texts as having taught in the unimaginably distant past, the one called 'The Ancient Buddha'" (243). "Smokey the Bear Sutra" straddles preemptive parody and the utterly confident artistic assertions that predominate in Snyder's work.

It would be a mistake to overstate the parodic element in Snyder, although the corrective gesture of playfulness often accompanies even his most pious apprehensions of tranquility, impermanence, and embodied bliss. In subsequent sections of *Mountains and Rivers Without End* (begun 1956 and finished 1996), Snyder continues to find a standpoint somewhere between pious reverence and satirical incredulity, such as in "Circumambulation of Mt. Tamalpais." Snyder, Philip Whalen, and Allen Ginsberg all climbed Mt. Tamalpais on October 22, 1965, and Snyder and Whalen each wrote poems about the hike. These two poems are playful renditions of actual religious disciplines, as Snyder points out in his note to the poem in *Mountains and Rivers Without End*: "Walking meditation, circumambulation, *pradakshina*, is one of the most ancient human spiritual exercises. On such walks one stops at notable spots to sing a song, or to chant invocations and praises, such as mantras, songs, or little sūtras" (*Snyder Reader* 161). The poem, originally published in 1966, has some playful moments, but the poem is not what one would call parodic: "Hazy day, butterflies tan as grass that sits on silver-weathered fenceposts, a gang of crows. 'I can smell fried chicken' Allen says – only the simmering of California laurel leaves. The trail winds crossed and intertwining with the dirt jeep road."[22]

Compare this with a similar moment in Whalen's "Opening the Mountain, Tamalpais: 22:x:65":

> Fourth Shrine: Rifle Camp lunch, natural history:
> Allen: "What do wasps do?"
> Gary: "mess around." (*Collected* 486)

At the height of the ceremony (and the mountain), the poets and friends perform "a Tibetan encore for Tara, / Song against disaster" (486). Calling a religious song an "encore" shows a certain distance between oneself and piety, and yet both of these poems "initiate" American readers and sometimes hikers into an Asian form of walking prayer.

The last poem of *Mountains and Rivers Without End*, the masterpiece of Buddhist Beat writing that Snyder has described as a sutra to the Tibetan Buddhist deity Tara, is "Finding the Space in the Heart," and it contains the sort of pastiche that is more a stylistic imitation than a performance of parodic ridicule. Or perhaps we could say a pastiche is a parody that has fully overcome its original embarrassment. The following verse imitates and echoes the *via negativa* of the "Heart Sutra," which is arguably the central poetic expression of Mahayana Buddhism. The intimations of absence or gap or lack that in other poems give way to parodic joking do not, in this poem, ensue parody of any sort. The verse kicks itself off with a casual allusion to Shakespeare in which the poet is

> Off nowhere, to be or not to be,
> all equal, far reaches, no bounds.
> Sounds swallowed away,
> no waters, no mountains, no
> bush no grass and
>   because no grass
> no shade but your shadow.
> No flatness because no not-flatness.
> No loss, no gain. So –
> nothing in the way! (*Mountains* 151)[23]

The next verse mentions "a far peak called King Lear," and the reference, like "to be or not to be," is incidental and casual. There is no tragic weightiness to the references. "Lear" is the name of a mountain peak but also signifies a man tortured by emptiness and loss, and Hamlet's suicidal worry about whether "to be or not to be" also exists in some relation to all the words and signs in the poem, but they in no way condition the tone of the verses in the expected manner. When Snyder works with the Shakespeare references, it cannot be said that parody is a stylistic deviation from an original, as the verse, alternatively, presents images of dreadful void so as to demarcate difference.

In considering Snyder's expression of Buddhist sentiments and imitations of Buddhist forms in the 1990s and since, we bump into a slight problem: the poet's claim that the word "Beat" never really applied to him. In a 2011 interview with Junior Burke at Naropa University, Snyder tells of a reading with Lawrence Ferlinghetti (the November 7, 2011, reading at the Fugazi Club in San Francisco) at which both men eschewed the term "Beat," so much so on Snyder's part that he "once refused to be included in an anthology with the word in the title."[24] As we have also seen, however, he wrote himself into that literary history when he composed essays such as "Notes on Religious Tendencies" and allowed himself to be included in various other anthologies of Beat literature; so why has Snyder in recent decades been lukewarm or even cold about the term? It could be that the patterns of maturation that this chapter has noted, in which the earlier expressions were conditioned not only by the authors' youth but also by the audience's relative unfamiliarity with the subject, seem much less mature – especially from the perspective of the writers who survived a half-century beyond the 6 Gallery reading – than subsequent expressions. No writer wants to be a fly caught in amber, always seen in relation to what she or he was writing in 1956 or 1959. In studying the Beats in relation to Buddhism (or poetics, or politics, or any number of other contexts), it is helpful to keep in mind the degree to which a very powerful term in literary history can hinder our appreciation of a given writer's sometimes startling development.

NOTES

1 Waldman, born in 1945, is generationally a step behind Philip Whalen (1923–2002), Allen Ginsberg (1926–1997), Gary Snyder (b. 1930), and Joanne Kyger (b. 1934), but she is extremely important to the institutionalization of Beat literature, not only through her own writing and anthologization but also through her work in organizing the Jack Kerouac School of Disembodied Poetics, part of the Naropa Institute (founded in 1974; now Naropa University). Ginsberg and Waldman were both students of Chögyam Trungpa, and Beat writers have been a regular presence at the annual Summer Writing Program hosted by Naropa.

2 Samuel Johnson, "Preface to Shakespeare," www.bartleby.com/39/31.html (accessed October 17, 2016).

3 Thomas Tweed, *The American Encounter with Buddhism, 1844–1912: Victorian Culture and the Limits of Dissent* (Bloomington: Indiana University Press, 1992), xvii–xviii.

4 Rick Fields, *How the Swans Came to the Lake: A Narrative History of Buddhism in America*, 3rd edition (Boston: Shambhala, 1992), 59–60. Emerson and

Thoreau selected and published what they called "Ethnical Scriptures," including the Laws of Manu, the sayings of Confucius, and, in 1844, "The Preaching of the Buddha," which was actually a fragment of the Lotus Sutra (Fields, *How the Swans Came to the Lake*, 61). Fields actually reports that Henry David Thoreau was the translator of the text, 61, but Thomas H. Tweed corrects the record in his preface to the paperback edition of *The American Encounter with Buddhism, 1844–1912: Victorian Culture and the Limits of Dissent* (Berkeley: University of California Press, 2000), xvi. Tweed reports that scholar and special collections librarian Wendell Piaz discovered in 1993 that Elizabeth Palmer Peabody actually translated the first Buddhist text for American readers.

5 Richard Hughes Seager, *Buddhism in America* (New York: Columbia University Press, 1999), x.

6 Philip Whalen, *The Collected Poems of Philip Whalen*, ed. Michael Rothenberg (Middletown, CT: Wesleyan University Press, 2007), 537.

7 Alan Watts, "Beat Zen, Square Zen, and Zen," *The Portable Beat Reader*, ed. Ann Charters (New York: Penguin, 1992), 611.

8 For example, Jennie Skerl mentions in her introduction to *Reconstructing the Beats* (New York: Palgrave Macmillan, 2004) the "dismissive attitude toward the depth and pervasiveness of Buddhism in Kerouac's thought: Either Kerouac has been considered a superficial student of Buddhism or a failed Buddhist unable to overcome his training in Catholicism" (5). The two essays in Skerl's volume that challenge underestimations of this sort are Deshae E. Lott's "'All Things Are Different Appearances of the Same Emptiness': Buddhism and Jack Kerouac's Nature Writings" and Tony Trigilio's "'Will You Please Stop Playing with the Mantra?': The Embodied Poetics of Ginsberg's Later Career'."

9 Gary Snyder, "Notes on Religious Tendencies," *Portable Beat Reader*.

10 Emily Dickinson, *The Complete Poems of Emily Dickinson*, ed. Thomas H. Johnson (New York: Little, Brown, 1960), 504.

11 Christopher Isherwood, "Hypothesis and Belief," *Vendanta for the Western World*, ed. and intro. by Isherwood (London: George Allen & Unwin, 1948), 36–40.

12 Christopher Isherwood, *The World in the Evening* (1954; Minneapolis: University of Minnesota Press, 1999), 110.

13 Sutra is a Sanskrit word meaning "discourse" or "sermon," the equivalent of the Pali Sutta. Strictly speaking, a sutra is the direct speak of the historical Buddha, but, in the Mahayana tradition, starting around the first century AD, hundreds of sutras were composed. It is a convention of these sutras that they were indeed said by the Buddha; see Robert Buswell Jr. and Donald S. Lopez, *The Princeton Dictionary of Buddhism* (Princeton: Princeton University Press, 2014), 875.

14 Jack Kerouac, *The Scripture of the Golden Eternity*, intros. Anne Waldman and Eric Mottram (1960; San Francisco: City Lights, 1994), 32.

15 Jack Kerouac, *Some of the Dharma* (New York: Viking, 1997). For an insightful consideration of the quality of Kerouac's knowledge of Buddhism, see Robert Thurman's introduction to Kerouac, *Wake Up: A Life of the Buddha* (New York: Viking, 2008).

16 Susan Sontag, "Notes on Camp," *A Susan Sontag Reader*, ed. Elizabeth Hardwick (1964; New York: Farrar, Straus & Giroux, 1982), 112.

17 Christopher Isherwood, *The World in the Evening* (London: Methuen, 1954), 130.

18 Sontag's notes have been widely influential and have undergone subsequent modification by queer theorists, but the general sense remains that camp is, first and foremost, a form of sympathetic parody; for example, see Paul Gaita, "Camp Conventions in *Hold Me While I'm Naked*," *Latent Image* (spring 1992).

19 Allen Ginsberg, *Complete Poems, 1947–1980* (New York: Harper and Row, 1984), 396.

20 Ginsberg's *Collected Poems* includes helpful notes, collected during the translations of many individual volumes of poetry. Chango: Afro-Cuban God who is a "phallic creation divinity" comparable to Hindu's Shiva (777). Ouroboros: great cosmic snake (cultural tradition not given) (791). Parvati: consort of Shiva (791). YOD: Hebrew abbreviation of divine unutterable name of God (791). Coyote: Amerindian trickster-hero god (791). Ramakrishna: ecstatic Hindu saint (791). Brindaban: holy town near Delhi where Krishna spent his childhood as a cow herder (779). La illaha etc.: There is no god but God (Allah) – a Sufi chant popular with Bay Area Sufi groups in the mid-1960s (776).

21 Gary Snyder, *The Gary Snyder Reader: Prose, Poetry, and Translations* (Washington, DC: Counterpoint, 1999), 242.

22 Gary Snyder, *Mountains and Rivers Without End* (Berkeley: Counterpoint, 1996), 85.

23 Compare Snyder's mature tone to that of Philip Whalen at the end of his 1956 poem "Sourdough Mountain Lookout": "Gone / Gone / REALLY gone / Into the cool / O MAMA!" (Whalen, *Collected Poems*, 45). Neither version attempts to thrust the reader directly into sublime depths in the way the Heart Sutra does, each, to a different degree, setting the jewel of emptiness within a relatable context.

24 Meredith May, "Lawrence Ferlinghetti, Gary Snyder at Club Fugazi," *SFGate* (November 9, 2011), www.sfgate.com/entertainment/article/Lawrence-Ferlinghetti-Gary-Snyder-at-Club-Fugazi-2323917.php (accessed September 9, 2016).

16

KIRBY OLSON

Beat as Beatific

Gregory Corso's Christian Poetics

Gregory Corso is often considered the second most important Beat poet after Allen Ginsberg. The two poets were friends from their early twenties until Ginsberg's death fifty years later; Ginsberg was four years older. Corso is not, however, only thought of as a successful poet from the perspective of Beat studies, as positive critical appreciations of his poetry have come from luminaries such as Randall Jarrell, Archibald MacLeish, Frank O'Hara, and many others from various traditions inside his native United States and around the world. Ginsberg's poetry is still much better known both inside and outside academia, partly because Ginsberg weighed in during the great debates of the 1960s and 1970s surrounding issues such as atomic power, gay rights, and socialist economics. As Ginsberg said, Corso was more of a "poet's Poet," but some of his most famous poems, such as "Bomb" (1958) and "Marriage" (1959), are well known to most students and practitioners of poetry over the past half-century.[1] Much of his work is more complex than these well known poems, and it references his fascination with Catholic and Surrealist thought and his intense study of the Western literary tradition. Unlike Ginsberg, Corso was not involved in an immersion in Hindu or Buddhist texts, and, also unlike Ginsberg, he was not a traveler to Cambodia, India, or Japan. Corso traveled a lot within the United States and Europe, but he rarely ventured outside those areas. His poetry therefore may seem parochial by comparison to Ginsberg's, but, where it might be lacking in geographical and religious breadth, it is deeper in its use and awareness of Western traditions, particularly Christianity, and as such represents a useful example of Beat writing that seems to challenge reductive notions of the Beats as only interested in Eastern religions such as Buddhism.

Indeed, one of the central themes throughout Corso's work is a constant striving to integrate physical experience back into his version of Christian experience. In his poetry, not only does modern humanity's physicality get resacralized within the Christian tradition but he also goes back to prerecorded history in his poem "In Praise of Neanderthal Man" (1981).[2] This is also the case in many of the animal poems that recur throughout his oeuvre, such as "Seed Journey" (1961) and "A Difference of Zoos"(1961) (*Mindfield* 110, 111). The separation between human beings and other species is a wall he sought to break down. Corso told me in a conversation, in the late 1970s, that he had always loved animals, and he still owned a ferret at that time. His fingers were constantly bandaged because the ferret bit him. We were at Naropa Institute in Colorado, where I was his student as well as the student of many of the other Beats (William S. Burroughs enjoyed feeding squirrels in a park in Boulder, allowing them to climb on his shoulder before offering them a nut; this seemed a Beat endeavor as I never saw anyone else attempting this).

In his fraught relationship with animals – particularly with whether it was ever ethical to eat them – Corso was actually harkening back to issues found in the Old Testament. In the Book of Isaiah, for example, there occurs the famous image of the wolf lying down with the lamb: "The wolf will live with the lamb, the leopard will lie down with the goat, the calf and the lion and the yearling together; and a little child will lead them" (Isaiah 11:6). For Corso, the problems of eating animals and of the human–animal relationship are foregrounded in this utopian image, and yet, paradoxically, central to the Christian experience in the ritualistic recital of Christ's passing out the bread and wine and declaring "This is my body, this is my blood." In his poetry, Corso often depicts eating in a ritualistic fashion reminiscent of the Eucharist, and uses such depictions to ask whether any and all animal life is sacred. In "Youthful Religious Experiences" (1981), for example, he revisits the image of the Eucharist getting stuck in his tooth (*Mindfield* 180). Is this human sacrifice? How is one to assimilate such experience? In my book *Gregory Corso: Doubting Thomist* (2002), I discuss at greater length the problem "of being ethically human within nature," but in this poem Corso asks whether one can be ethical when eating other creatures in order to live.[3] Corso's answer seems to be "no," as eating animals is inherently violent.

However paradoxically, Corso also reverses this claim by turning the entire food chain into God's body, and thus everything we eat is "his body, and his blood." In fact, as he told me in 1977, his heroin use was partly a way to get around food. He thought that heroin was a super-food, and, because it was plant-based, it was ethical. He celebrates traditional nutrition as well as very odd delicacies such as giraffe in his lengthy poem "Food" (1957), but the poem doesn't appear to have a philosophical dimension except to indicate that Corso really liked food and sex. But, reading his collection *The Happy Birthday of Death* (1960), one finds a muted denial as to the goodness in ethical terms of food (he accepts the aesthetics but not the ethics). Food as sacrament bothers him, as it bothers the Jains of India, whose priests starve themselves, since every living thing is considered a saintly being. Heroin, being plant based, was Corso's way around the problem of food, but it's hardly very good as nutrition, and it hurt him badly – his teeth had fallen out by the time he was forty-five. This all suggests that, even though Corso was not necessarily aligned with organized religious practices consistently throughout his life, various Christian values and worldviews mattered very much to him and continually inform his poetry.

Although the Beats tend to be associated in popular imagination with Eastern religions such as Buddhism, forms of Christianity also played a prominent role. Recall, for example, that in the late 1950s, when the media was accusing the Beat Generation of being violent hoodlums, Kerouac connected the word "beat" to beatific, "to be in a state of beatitude, like St. Francis, trying to love all life, trying to be utterly sincere with everyone, practicing endurance, kindness, cultivating joy of heart."[4] Kerouac's friend and fellow poet Philip Lamantia wrote on Catholic themes throughout his lifetime, and his devotion was in fact so intense in the 1950s that it "seemed to inhibit his poetic practice, or, at least, his confidence in its results."[5] By the end of the decade, he was able to manifest this devotion in poetry, and his second collection, *Ekstasis* (1959), is perhaps his deepest exploration of such themes, and contains a number of poems about Christ and Christianity.[6] Perhaps the most avowedly Catholic Beat-associated writer was William Everson, who took the name Brother Antoninus when he joined the Dominican order in the early 1950s. Everson was a longtime pacifist poet from the west coast when he became associated with writers such as Kenneth Rexroth in the 1950s, and he became known in popular depictions as the "Beat Friar." Although less well known than Everson, Brenda Knight includes one-time nun Mary Norbert Körte as a Beat-associated poet in her landmark *Women of the Beat Generation* (1996). According to Knight, Körte joined a convent at age eighteen, but in the mid-1960s she was inspired by writers such as Diane di Prima and Lenore Kandel to undertake poetry activism.[7] As these examples attest, Christianity, and Catholicism in particular, had deep ties to a Beat ethos.

Yet, unlike writers such as Everson and Körte, who wrote from inside the institution of Catholicism, Corso was always on his own, and his discourse community was primarily other Beat writers, or the semiliterate young women whom he seduced and lived with from time to time. Given the nature of his interlocutors, Corso often questioned phenomena such as evil, but remained free from the orthodox understandings of any tradition; in fact, one might ask to what extent Corso viewed sin as an enlightening experience. In asking such questions, we can compare his writing to that of Blake (which had influenced Ginsberg), such as when Blake exhorts us to ride over the bones of the dead on the way to heaven. This has an ancient Gnostic counterpart in the libertine Carpocratian tradition, and yet Corso never completely relinquished his Franciscan version of the world. His attempt to reconcile eating and, say, the hydrogen bomb (both forms of destruction) with the omnipresence of God was never thoroughly successful for him, unlike for thinkers such as St. Francis. Hence the apparent ambivalence in "Bomb": "You Bomb ... I cannot hate you" (*Mindfield* 65). In this well-known meditation on the hydrogen bomb, Corso in fact links it to Christian imagery by asking "hath not St. Michael a burning sword" (65). Indeed, in the poem, the most sublime aspect of the bomb seems almost evidence of God's own sublimity, for Corso declares that "the heavens are with you / hosanna incalescent glorious liaison," a prayer-like invocation that morphs into the suggestion that the godlike power of the bomb might in fact supplant God's power: "A thunderless God A dead God / O Bomb thy BOOM His tomb" (67).

Despite such continual references to Christianity in his poetry, Corso never returned to any kind of orthodox or mainstream religious practice with weekly worship and submersion in a given congregation within a given denomination. He shot off on his own and thought he could explain it all, again using the food chain itself as a symbol of the Eucharist, at least as a young man. Experience did not jibe with this early theory. His theory may have been that to turn everything into the Eucharist was going to work, but did it? In his poem to St. Francis in *Long Live Man* (1962), he has many sad moments, and asks: "What good a proper frame of mind on which foundations rest / When what is built thereon has no permanence?"[8] In this early volume he heralds the coming of a new age in which life sustains itself against death, and he ends his poem with a denunciation of Rikers Island's wardens and executioners, and then briefly says they have nothing to do with Mithras (a Persian god on whose sacred ground the Vatican was apparently built, and who also celebrated a version of the Eucharist): "it's not Mithras kills their eat, / Nor the wine they drink be Bacchus kind" (*Long* 40). In the parts of the poem to St. Francis where he's optimistic, Corso tries to fold not only eating but also sexual life into his poetic thought. In this sense he was a good postmodernist along the lines of Michel Foucault or many other French thinkers, but he was also writing in a lineage that reaches back into Gnostic and ancient Greek libertinism as well.

Like other Beat poets such as Ted Joans, Corso wrote in the Surrealist tradition as well, and somehow also never abandoned the beauty of this world. This world's beauty is something the Gnostics rejected, and thus they never had an artistic tradition, as the Catholics had and have. The Surrealist tradition is replete with figures who attempted to bring art and Christianity alongside one another. Magritte's apple and Dalí's Christ sit alongside each other as figures still not entirely recuperated into an intellectual tradition, but Corso's work surely belongs in that Surrealist lineage, whose members themselves appear to be a kind of heretical offshoot of the Catholic lineage. The Surrealists flirted with all kinds of occult and religious heritages, as did the later Beats, without ever precisely choosing one, but Corso always seems to be aligned in his major works with his juvenile Catholicism, which he never relinquished but which he did not take into his maturity with regular congregational communion.

Corso may finally, to his own satisfaction, have assimilated the food chain within the context of the bread and wine (used as symbols in communion) and also within the context of thankfulness and gratitude (expressed over food and in ceremonies by Catholics); however, if so, he was aware not only of the terror and darkness experienced by animals as they are seized and eaten but also of the ethical problems the Jains and Gnostics experience(d) as they ate. Corso once told me while I was dining with him that he liked to eat the optic nerve of cows and other animals. He was clearly provoking me. He was disturbed and wanted me to share in his disturbance. He may have attempted a way out of these conundrums through a kind of pantheism, but he was only partly successful. Part of Corso's "demolition" is that he broke his teeth on this conundrum, even if he did use almost the entirety of his poetic oeuvre in attempting to resolve it. His massive intake of wine may have been yet another way of overdoing it with the Eucharist, or at least one element of it.

Corso's poetry can be read as the high and low points of his resolve to incorporate the theodicy of eating and drinking with his sacralization of all life via St. Francis, or else indicate that he didn't quite make it, and increasingly turned toward drug usage as a balm for the anxiety he felt. Corso never, however, completely gave up on the beauty of life, as the Gnostics did (they decided this was a prison planet, with no redeeming values). While Jack Spicer and some other contemporary poets studied Gnosticism and used Gnostic imagery in the creation of poetry, Corso seems to have been aware of this tendency and yet did not accept it. He continued to write poetry and to study art. The beauty of life versus the evils that surround us remained a source of lyrical tension throughout his life and are what continued to produce his poems.

From a young age, Corso was a Thomist, meaning that he was influenced by the philosophical school descended from the writings of the Catholic saint Thomas Aquinas. When his mother left and his father abandoned him, Corso became an orphan who was helped through Catholic charities of

New York City, and as such he inherited the sense of their beatitude of this world; however, his own sense of things coming up and out of a dark and often difficult childhood belied this, and gave him much to reconcile. The Catholic nuns and others of his childhood are not always presented as saintly, and the Beat "saints" who surrounded him were often not altogether saintly and, at least at times, were exploitative. Corso was still grateful enough to give us his poetry as evidence that his faith remained central, and the Eucharist was something that may very well have been a sustaining metaphor.

Corso, Kerouac, and Beat Catholicism

While Burroughs and Kerouac were primarily novelists, Corso and Ginsberg were primarily poets. Another way to parse the four is to note that, whereas Burroughs and Ginsberg were refugees from the Judeo-Christian tradition, Corso and Kerouac never completely left, but neither one was exactly what you would call a saint. Even if he was no Mother Theresa, Kerouac was a Catholic from birth, and he never relinquished this religious identity, or its basis in the Sermon on the Mount. Corso also kept his Catholic identity, as a kind of passport that entitled him to permanent residence within at least one healthy institution.

Both writers described Catholic religious visions. In "Youthful Religious Experiences," for example, Corso writes: "When I was five / I saw God in the sky"; later he says he "asked the priest / in the confessional box what it all meant," and the priest explained that the boy ought to do good or "burn forever" in hell (*Mindfield* 179). Although such experiences were perhaps particularly vivid because of the poet's youth, they remained a powerful presence throughout his life, as the poem ends "to this very day / I cannot totally comprehend / what it all meant" (180).

Likewise, near the end of Kerouac's *Big Sur* (1962) – the opposite of a work about "youthful" experiences, as it traces the writer's most bitter engagements with his own middle-aged mortality – Duluoz experiences a Christian vision:

> I see the cross, it's silent, it stays a long time, my heart goes out to it, my whole body fades away to it, I hold out my arms to be taken away to it, by God I am being taken away my body starts dying and swooning out to the Cross standing in a luminous area of the darkness.[9]

If in his work on eating animals and the Eucharist Corso meditates on the ethics of consuming other beings and the body of Christ, here Kerouac imagines being himself consumed by the cross, his body fading away as relief from his alcoholic misery.

But, despite such moments in their writing in which Corso or Kerouac seem to connect with a Christian god, living an ethical life or figuring out what exactly love meant in a Catholic context was a perennially vexed endeavor for both of them. At times, love seemed for Kerouac just to mean that the young and hip could sleep with one another's wives and girlfriends and have this deepen rather than destroy their friendships.

Corso as Obstinate American

Recently, one important turn in Beat studies has been toward multiculturalism or transnationalism. It is true that the Beats spent long periods in India (see Deborah Baker's *A Blue Hand* [2008]); in Mexico (see Juan Garcia-Robles's *At the End of the Road* [2014]); in Cuba (see Todd Tietchen's *The Cubalogues* [2013]); and in Morocco (see Brian T. Edwards *Morocco Bound* [2005]); and spent much time in Paris, back when Paris was still relatively cheap after World War II (see Barry Miles's *The Beat Hotel* [2000]).[10] A few (especially Cid Corman, Joanne Kyger, and Gary Snyder) spent time in Japan. Some, such as Philip Whalen, fully enrolled and became Buddhist monks, renouncing any Christian tradition. Corso was comparatively monocultural, although he did live in Paris and traveled in Amsterdam, and briefly went as far north as Sweden. Much of his time in Paris is documented in *The Beat Hotel*, which refers to a hotel on Paris's Left Bank that Corso had discovered, and that many Beats at one time lived in or visited. And yet, even as he traveled and lived abroad, unlike writers such as Snyder or Whalen, Corso always remained inside the Western tradition. Indeed, his poetry tends to be set in the Western hemisphere and look back to its classical and Judeo-Christian traditions. He once announced to Ginsberg that, while he (Ginsberg) sometimes strayed in favor of other gods, "He was sticking with God" (*Blue Hand* 204), and further insisted that "I was born and raised to die a Catholic."[11] Moreover, Corso continued to believe in America, which he viewed as bound up in Christian tradition. Corso saw his middle name, "Nunzio," as the Italian meaning "messenger," and his message was to tell the world that "Columbus was St. John the Baptist, America Christ" (355).

To Corso, Columbus was a forerunner of America itself, which he saw as godly. Corso felt at home in Western culture and in America, whereas outside that circle he never really felt comfortable. This geographic and religious reading of Corso's oeuvre should now revisit in detail one of his only forays into a third-world country – Mexico. While Burroughs and Kerouac had gone there and stayed for lengthy periods, Corso went briefly, and stayed in a fine hotel in Mexico City. He did not enjoy the visit. He worried that Mexican thieves would steal his new cashmere sweater, given to him by his girlfriend, Hope Savage (*Blue Hand* 52). Ginsberg, in later attempting to lure Corso to India, described the spacious rooms and the luxurious food, and finally said that Savage herself was there, waiting to welcome him home into her arms (*Blue Hand* 138–139). Corso had had enough of the third world after Mexico. He stayed home, trying in his own way to lure Ginsberg and others back. The arc of Baker's book reveals the tension between the West-focused Corso and his globe-trotting multicultural friends, and documents the lifelong romance between Corso and Savage.

In this context, scholar Glenn Sheldon puts Corso on trial for the crime of cultural imperialism toward Mexico and for preferring America to its southern neighbor, but his charges go wildly astray because he does not have his facts straight. Among Corso's few poems that describe Mexico are "Mexican Impressions" and "Puma in Chapultepec Zoo," both found in the early volume *Gasoline* (1958). In "Puma in Chapultepec Zoo," he writes:

> Long smooth slow swift soft cat
> What score, whose choreography did you dance to
> When they pulled the final curtain down?
>
> ...
>
> How sad you seem: looking at you
> I think of Ulanova
> Locked in some small furnished room
> In New York, on East 17th Street
> In the Puerto Rican section. (*Mindfield* 27)

In the poem, he describes the puma as being similar to "Ulanova/ locked in some small furnished room in New York." Sheldon analyzes the passage as if Ulanova were "a Puerto Rican friend who evidently finds New York less than habitable," apparently oblivious to the fact that Ulanova is a Russian name and that she was not Puerto Rican but rather a star of the Bolshoi Ballet.[12] Corso had visited the Bolshoi while in Mexico City, as he mentions in his letters. Sheldon writes, "Ulanova, the Puerto Rican, is 'locked' into her fate like the puma," and argues that Corso's reading of the situation is wrong in that Mexicans have more freedom than Corso's imperialistic American mind can imagine (86). Sheldon's misreading of the poem through his misunderstanding of the personage of Ulanova indicates the paucity of some Beat criticism, which can be impaled on a serious lack of erudition, which many critics assume also to be the case for the Beats themselves. Sheldon rightly indicates that Corso looked down on third-world cultures and preferred his own, but whether he would have had a no-name

Puerto Rican friend is yet another question. If nothing else, Corso was very widely read, and he acquainted himself with the fine arts and history of every Western culture at every opportunity, and he was also more than a bit of a social climber. In "Puma at Chapultepec Zoo," Corso (unlike Sheldon) is not thinking about identity politics; he is thinking about the grace of an animal, comparing it to the finest ballet dancer of modern Russia and arguing for its release (as perhaps he wished to be released on the grounds of his beauty during his own time in prison). For Corso, the puma's beauty is its nature – but it is an elite beauty, like that of a dancer or a poet. It is an angry, restless beauty, and one that could suddenly become ferocious.

Corso's strength as a poet is to find beauty in the Western tradition and to insist on it with all of his characteristic vehemence: "America is the Second Coming because Christopher Columbus means Christ bearer, his ship Santa Maria meant same, angels in his dreams told him to find America" (*Accidental* 351). As Corso asserts this to Ginsberg, he uses a vast lineage of qualitative analysis to play with ideas that have haunted the Catholic Church and American historians for centuries and that will continue to do so. If Corso criticism is to deepen, it will need to revive serious scholarship on the teasing links between the Beats, American Catholicism, and Corso's and Kerouac's idiosyncratic paths – links that remain tenuous but binding.

Insofar as Corso's work points a way out of identity politics and toward reclaiming a basic patriotic belief in God and the United States (in spite of his refusal to take a loyalty oath at the University at Buffalo), he opens the way toward revalorizing the American Christian tradition. "True God can be a plot of land," Corso writes to Ginsberg, urging him to come back from India and take upon himself the United States' messianic mantle, something that both Ginsberg and Kerouac did, wrapping themselves in the nation's history as if they were the lyrical hopes of a generation (*Accidental* 352). At a time when many within the left despaired of the United States and turned against it – including many other Beat and Beat-associated writers – Corso urged the opposite and sought to reawaken the notion of the United States as the world's savior. This position may not seem paradigmatically "Beat," yet it comes from a figure who in many ways embodies the very essence of Beat, a paradox utterly in keeping with Corso's lifelong refusal to fit comfortably into any category.

NOTES

1 Allen Ginsberg, "On Corso's Virtues," Gregory Corso, *Mindfield: New and Selected Poems* (New York: Thunder's Mouth Press, 1989), xii.
2 Gregory Corso, "In Praise of Neanderthal Man," *Mindfield*.

3 Kirby Olson, *Gregory Corso: Doubting Thomist* (Carbondale: Southern Illinois University Press, 2002), 31–32. For a more recent discussion, see Loni Reynolds, "'A Humane Yet Dark Tribute to Life': The Eucharist in the Work of Gregory Corso," *Religion and Literature* 47.1 (spring 2015).

4 Jack Kerouac, "Lamb, No Lion," *The Portable Jack Kerouac*, ed. Ann Charters (New York: Viking, 1995), 562–63.

5 Garrett Caples, Andrew Joron and Nancy Joyce Peters, "High Poet: The Life and Work of Philip Lamantia," *The Collected Poems of Philip Lamantia*, ed. Caples, Joron and Peters (Berkeley: University of California Press, 2013), xxxix.

6 Philip Lamantia, *Ekstatis* (San Francisco: Auerhahn Press, 1959).

7 Brenda Knight, *Women of the Beat Generation* (San Francisco: Conari Press, 1996), 257–58.

8 Gregory Corso, *Long Live Man* (New York: New Directions, 1962), 39.

9 Jack Kerouac, *Big Sur* (1962; New York: Bantam, 1963), 169.

10 See Deborah Baker, *A Blue Hand: The Tragicomic, Mind-Altering Odyssey of Allen Ginsberg, a Holy Fool, a Rebel Muse, a Dharma Bum, and His Prickly Bride in India* (New York: Penguin, 2008); Juan Garcia-Robles, *At the End of the Road: Jack Kerouac in Mexico* (Minneapolis: University of Minnesota Press, 2014); Todd Tietchen, *The Cubalogues: Beat Writers in Revolutionary Havana* (Gainesville: University Press of Florida, 2013); Brian T. Edwards, *Morocco Bound: Disorienting America's Maghreb, From Casablanca to the Marrakech Express* (Durham, NC: Duke University Press, 2005); and Barry Miles, *The Beat Hotel* (New York: Grove, 2000).

11 Gregory Corso, *An Accidental Autobiography* (New York: New Directions, 2003), 357.

12 Glenn Sheldon, *South of Our Selves: Mexico in the Poems of Williams, Kerouac,Corso, Ginsberg, Levertov, and Hayden* (Jefferson, NC: McFarland, 2004), 83.

17

MICHAEL HREBENIAK

Jazz and the Beat Generation

In 1903, W. E. B. Du Bois described African American music as "the singular spiritual heritage of the nation and the greatest gift of the negro people."[1] Since then countless artists have responded to the full range of cultural associations with jazz, its influence transgressing social and disciplinary boundaries. While many proclamations of devotion were modish, if not gauche, numerous writers of significance have acknowledged a rapport with the music and its practitioners. In the case of the most adventurous writing associated with the Beat Generation, this extends to a conscious attempt to emulate its procedures.

Having taken jazz into the realm of the avant-garde, where it would thrive in a refusal of generic conformity, bebop accelerated its influence upon developments across forms.[2] For Beat writers, bop provided a model for registering the rhythms of contemporary American life, much as New Orleans and swing styles had resonated for Langston Hughes, Carl Sandburg, and William Carlos Williams. Gregory Corso's early poem "Requiem for 'Bird' Parker, Musician" (1955), is notable for its use of the framework of dramatic dialogue to register a subterranean demotic that will soon shift into a national idiom:

third voice
yeah, by that time BIRD realized the fake
had come to goof
BIRD was about to split, when all of a sudden
the nowhere bird sunk its beady head
into the barrel of BIRD's horn
bugged, BIRD blew a long crazy note[3]

Corso's conferring of occult status upon bop's ruined genius by provisionally raising his name in the text is amplified across Beat writing. In the case of Jack Kerouac, the recognition of the music's centrality to US culture is achieved not merely through the iteration of hipster expressions but also by using the music to underscore his own poetics. "Bop began with jazz," he declares,

> but one afternoon somewhere on a sidewalk maybe 1939, 1940, Dizzy Gillespie or Charley Parker or Thelonious Monk was walking down past a men's clothing store on 42nd Street or South Main in L.A. and from the loud-speaker they suddenly heard a wild impossible mistake in jazz that could only have been heard inside their own imaginary head, and that is a new art. Bop. The name derives from an accident.[4]

Kerouac's commentary affirms the value of chance in the creative act, permitting freedoms that the careful execution of prior schema might otherwise disallow. "*No revisions*," he insists in "Essentials of Spontaneous Prose" (1958): "not 'selectivity' of expression but following free deviation (association) of mind into limitless blow-on-subject seas of thought" (*Good Blonde* 65–70). "First thought, best thought," Allen Ginsberg is said to have advocated in paraphrase of Blake and in thrall to a libertarian process of discovery through imprecision. "I want to be considered a jazz poet," declares Kerouac in *Mexico City Blues* (1959):

> blowing a long blues in an afternoon jam
> session on Sunday. I take 242 choruses;
> my ideas vary and sometimes roll from
> chorus to chorus or from halfway through
> a chorus to halfway into the next.[5]

As the achievements of scores of soloists working against the force of preconceived intention show, improvisation is not mere expediency in the absence of a viable teleology ("Jazz and Fiction" 195). Through the 1950s, the jazz vanguard catalyzed much activity across the US arts, including the Abstract Expressionist strike against the European tradition of the "well-made" artifact, the jilting of high-finance Broadway values in the Living Theater productions of Julian Beck and Judith Malina, and the repudiation of Hollywood's technical polish in the films of Stan Brackage, John Cassavetes, and Jonas Mekas. The claim here is not that extemporization is without precedent but that the relegation of creativity to market engineering in postwar America heightens the relevance of its procedures.

Moreover, by mid-century, interdisciplinary exchange had become a common motive, with art practitioners and political dissenters, such as those involved in the Berkeley Free Speech Movement, interacting on the level of process itself – each, as Alfred Willener observes, expressing "a revolutionary desire for social emancipation ... the emancipation of the non-formal ... the desire to avoid being confined within a particular school, within existing rhythmic patterns."[6] Such convergences are not registered here at the expense of overriding considerations of the discursive domain of distinct disciplines, each with its own language and symbolic practices. Relationships between forms are not mimetically reflexive and material cannot be switched between completed spaces that are subsequently diminished into mere hosts for transferable arrangements. But it can nonetheless be productive to think of these in connection with each other, as an insight into ideas simultaneously arising across forms might call into consciousness the attitudes, tendencies, and meanings that shape a period.

On an immediate level, the Beat attraction to jazz inherited its associations with the liberal revolt against Puritanism accompanying the music's spread across the North in the 1920s, a trigger for the founding of "anti-jazz" societies across religious denominations and Henry Ford's location of degeneracy at the crossroads of liquor, trade unionism, and the "abandoned sensuousness" of "Nigger-Jew Jazz."[7] And, while bohemian leftists of the 1930s aligned themselves with boogie-woogie pianists such as Pinetop Smith and Meade Lux Lewis, the wartime home front sought bluesmen such as Lead Belly and Josh White for fundraising parties in progressive Hollywood circles.

With confidence in national credibility in decline by the late 1940s, a rebel identification with the practices of a disenfranchised minority was inevitable. Although by no means a popular phenomenon, the new jazz reflected unrest around black urban communities, and the word "bebop," which began as an onomatopoeic designation, soon came to denote dissent across US society, making an asset of alienation. Whereas John Clellon Holmes's novel *The Horn* (1958) documents the life of a penurious saxophonist named Edgar Pool, the earlier *Go* (1952) anticipates Kerouac's conflation of jazz and religious vocabularies ("altar," "holy," "prophecy," "ritual," "sacrament," "testament") and identifies the 1947 recording of Dexter Gordon and Wardell Gray's tenor duel in "The Hunt" as a generational "anthem," through which "something rebel and nameless ... spoke for them, and their lives knew a gospel for the first time ... it became an attitude toward life, a way of walking, a language and a costume."[8] And, while Lawrence Ferlinghetti saw "a natural affinity ... between the 'protest poet' and the jazz musician who blows 'dissent on the horn,'" Lawrence Lipton drew attention to the music's qualities of "ritual, healing or spiritual catharsis," which negated the sickness of mass conformity.[9] Hitching up to its appeal to dissidence in the crew-cut world, Lipton even provided a prescriptive jazz playlist for the Beatnik, rounded off by Ginsberg's "Holy the groaning saxophone! Holy the bop apocalypse! / Holy the jazzbands marijuana hipsters peace and junk and drums!"[10]

To Lipton, the sacred and ceremonial origins of music still lay close to the surface in jazz, giving voice to "the Dionysian, not the Apollonian, beat in music."[11] These concerns are anticipated by Beat progenitor Henry Miller in *The Colossus of Maroussi* (1941) in "prais[ing] God" for "the great Negro race which alone keeps America from falling apart" and mythologizing the jazzman as "barbarous" catalyst, "riffin' his way through the new land." Louis Armstrong features within a bohemian imaginary that groups Duke Ellington and Count Basie with Rimbaud and Isidore Ducasse, "bringing peace and joy to all the world" through "thick loving lips" that blow "one great big sour note like a rat bustin' open."[12]

Although removed from the "blackface" slumming endemic to Jazz Age writing, an inverse aristocratism based upon proximity to extrovert sexuality, such romantic incursions fail to reverse the common neglect of the music's performers and recoil from any critique of what Frank Kofsky calls the "cockroach capitalist" conditions of its production.[13] Kerouac similarly assigns a function to the improviser that is instinctive rather than cultural-historical: an attribution reinforced by the etymology of the word "jass," a colloquialism for fornication across West African coastal dialects, subsequently ditched by the politicized improvisers of the 1960s. "The drums were mad," notes Sal Paradise of the delirious music of the Mexican night in *On the Road* (1957):

> The mambo beat is the conga beat from Congo, the river of Africa and the world; it's really the world beat. Oom-*ta*, ta-poo-*poom*—oom-*ta*, ta-poo-*poom*... The final trumpet choruses that came with drum climaxes on conga and bongo drums, on the great mad Chattanooga record, froze Dean in his tracks for a moment till he shuddered and sweated; then when the trumpets bit the drowsy air with their quivering echoes, like a cavern's or a cave's, his eyes grew large and round as though seeing the devil, and he closed them tight.[14]

Kerouac's confused envy of indigenous energies rehearses Modernism's aesthetic mirroring of economic imperialism – three of the prostitutes in Picasso's *Les Demoiselles d'Avignon* (1907) sport African masks – and falls within Edward Said's definition of "Orientalism." Kerouac's stress on the music of "the happy, true-hearted, ecstatic Negroes of America" (149) and the mystique ascribed to the disaffiliate are fully brought to fruition in Norman Mailer's figure of the "White Negro," who embodies "the destructive, the liberating, the creative nihilism of the Hip," that "may break into the open with all its violence, its confusion, its ugliness and horror" in opposition to "the collective violence of the State."[15] Kerouac's admiration for the "Fellahin Indians of the world, the essential strain of the basic primitive, wailing humanity that stretches in a belt around the equatorial belly of the world," as he moves south of the border in *On the Road*, is equally typical of an anthropological perspective that bespeaks the hegemonic norms of the era.

Although he may fail to question the liberal stereotype of an untutored, nonindividualistic "Negro folk-art" free from commercial taint, much of Kerouac's work nevertheless demonstrates rare insight into the very episteme of improvisation. Moreover, his reception of musical improvisation's atemporal initiations, as previously apprehended by Oswald Spengler ("music alone ... can take us right out of this world ... and let us fondly imagine that we are on the verge of reaching the soul's final secret"[16]), is reiterated in the work of some contemporary African American writers. While Ted Joans's *Black Pow Wow of Jazz Poems* (1969) and *Afrodisia* (1970) are characterized by a dated fusion of the music with Black Nationalism and patriarchal eroticism, Amiri Baraka's 1963 tale "The Screamers" draws out the feral consciousness of the new jazz, which can whip an audience into insurrection: "We screamed and screamed at the clear image of ourselves as we should always be. Ecstatic, completed, involved in a secret communal expression. It would be the form of the sweetest revolution, to hucklebuck into the fallen capital, and let the oppressors lindy-hop out."[17] Bob Kaufman's "Battle Report" similarly invokes the title of a 1945 Parker track as a weapon against hostile mass society, spurring "infiltrat[ion]" of the polis: "At last, the secret code is flashed; / Now is the time, now is the time. / Attack: The sound of jazz. / The city falls."[18] Reproducing the jazz improviser's role in *On the Road*, both pieces politicize him as shamanic gatekeeper to the collective black psyche. Lorenzo Thomas accordingly draws attention to Kaufman's placement of Parker within a sacrificial environment that "encodes a more aggressive response to the racially motivated humiliations that frame the jazz artist's life."[19] But he simultaneously draws attention to Kaufman's measured and melancholic engagement with the music, which transcends ecstatic invocation and hipster idiom alike while nonetheless registering an identifiably Beat diction. Kaufman's "Walking Parker Home" is exemplary in its pile-up of laconic phrasal measures that internally trouble the urban narrative of power and test the limits of its representation:

> New York altar city/ black tears/ secret disciples
> Hammer horn pounding soul marks on unswinging gates
> Culture gods/ mob sounds/ visions of spikes
> Panic excursions to tribal Jazz wombs and transfusions
> Heroin nights of birth/ and soaring/ over boppy new ground.
> Smothered rage covering pyramids of notes spontaneously exploding
> Cool revelations/ shrill hopes/ beauty speared into greedy ears
> Birdland nights on bop mountains, windy saxophone revolutions.[20]

Such texts unleash potent energies in a nation petrified by fear of the black man, a concealed hostility underpinning many of the accusations of obscenity levied at Beat writing. Paradoxically, the force of such work comes less from the evocation of a primal energy released through archaic ceremony and more from an imaginative poetics that amplifies the music's emotional intensity. As Baraka concluded in 1965: "I have made theories, sought histories, tried to explain. But the music itself is not about any of those things."[21]

Having entered his fictions as a magical resource, Kerouac also reflects in *Visions of Cody* upon the shortfall in the capacity of language to register the "rawest peak" of "Frisco jazz" during "the age of the wild tenorman," who blew with "honest frenzy" through "regular-course developments of bop" in a vertical moment of release from Cold War neurosis:

> "What's the IT, Cody?" I asked him that night.
>
> "We'll all know when he hits it – there it is! he's got it! – hear – see everybody rock? It's the big moment of rapport all around that's making him rock; that's jazz; dig him; dig her; dig this place, dig these cats, this is all that's left, where else can you and go Jack?" It was absolutely true. We stood side by side sweating and jumpin in front of wild be-hatted tenormen blowing from their shoetops at the brown ceiling, … and wild women dancing, the ceiling roaring, people falling in from the street, from the door, no cops to bother anybody because it was summer, August 1949, and Frisco was blowing mad.[22]

The impossibility of transmitting the emotional impact of the music through available modes of textual notation is also performatively recorded by Corso in *Gasoline* (1958). In the volume's introduction, Ginsberg cites Corso's bid to imitate the approach of Parker and Miles Davis to composition, specifically starting with standard diction and measure before an "intentionally distracted diversed into my own sound."[23] The struggle to forge a mnemonic device that might convey the expressive vitality of witnessed live performance marks his poem "For Miles":

> Poet whose sound is played
> lost or recorded
> but heard
> can you recall that 54 night at the Open Door
> when you & bird
> wailed five in the morning some wondrous
> yet unimaginable score?[24]

As such passages indicate, the impact of jazz on Beat writing far transcends the issue of aspirational fetishism. Beyond the level of its image, the music's oral basis spurred the Beat shift in the focus of attention to speaking the poem: a recalibration of literary language for the registration of an American tongue shaped by metabolism as opposed to fixed metrics. Bop structures translate into what Kerouac calls "blowing phrases" or "breath separations of the mind,"[25] reaffirming Charles Olson's emphasis on "the HEAD, by way of the EAR, to the SYLLABLE / the HEART, by way of the BREATH, to the LINE."[26] "By 1955," reiterates Ginsberg, "I wrote poetry ... arranged by phrasing or breath groups into little short line patterns ... and long saxophone-like chorus lines I knew Kerouac would hear the *sound* of."[27]

Ginsberg's development of long adjectival measures is augmented by his attention to a soloist's phrasing and his embrace of a looser, often syncopated beat. Ellipsis features in "Howl" to disrupt the poem's discursive field, as in the line "who were expelled from the academies for crazy & publishing obscene odes on the windows of the skull" (9). The omission of "being" between "for" and "crazy" destabilizes the spatial perspective and renders subjectivity elusive: a transdisciplinary tactic owing as much to the jagged collisions of the new jazz as it does to the poet's emulation of Cézanne's junking of the dissolving facet. Parker's mastery of fluctuating tempos and placement of microaccents and hiatuses against the rhythm section's common-time beat proved revelatory to Ginsberg and his peers in demonstrating how to jettison the monotonous sense of foot associated with the iambic pentameter. The internalization of bop's impetus permitted a more choppy, refractive measure than the rigid "stride" accents of earlier styles, a quality Warren Tallman attributes to Kerouac's own musical correspondences. Whereas the narrative of his Kerouac's novel, *The Town and the City* (1950), is concomitant with the sentimental linearity of 1930s swing, Tallman identifies a bebop momentum in *On the Road* that yields a sonic "BIFF, BOFF, BLIP, BLEEP, BOP, BEEP, CLINCK, ZOWIE! Sounds break up. And are replaced by other sounds. The journey is NOW. The narrative is a Humpty Dumpty heap. Such is the condition of NOW."[28]

Beat work is thus scored partly for vocal performance and reinstates the bardic principle of rhetorical address, in contrast to the academy's traditional bias of silent interpretation. As Lipton observed, Beat writers, such as Whitman in the previous century, sought to restore poetry to its ancient role as social function or ritualized drama lyrically reintegrated with instruments. The contemporary experiments with musical accompaniment are an extension of this, complementing the impulse to transgress genre. Jazz antecedents for such readings range from the half-sung dialogues of Louis Armstrong's "That's When I'll Come Back to You" (1927) to Duke Ellington's verse drama *A Drum Is a Woman* (1956) and Bessie Smith's blues poetry to the bop scatting of Slim Gaillard, Dizzy Gillespie, and Jon Hendricks, all "black talk" transformations of standard speech. In 1958, Langston Hughes recorded *Weary Blues* alongside quintets led by

Henry "Red" Allen and Charles Mingus, whose bass playing also under-scored Hughes and Lonnie Elder's "Scenes in the City" on *Poetry and Jazz Symposium* (1957). After reading in public at New York's Village Vanguard, Kerouac produced a burst of recordings in 1959; while *Poetry for the Beat Generation* betrays little integration between the sensual, indeterminate push of the voice and Steve Allen's urbane piano, *Blues and Haikus* attains a more energetic empathy with "just the pure vibrating horn" blown by Zoot Sims and Al Cohn, the inflections of three-lined poems traded in call and response style with considerable verve.[29]

Such examples of cross-formal reciprocity nonetheless qualify as excep-tional. *Poetry Readings in the Cellar* (1957) by Ferlinghetti and Kenneth Rexroth, the latter of whom claimed to have first read with a jazz ensem-ble "in the late 20s, at the Green Mask in Chicago," reinforce a less than compelling sense of hybridity, the incongruity between the variable meters of the poetry and the rhythmic conservatism of the West Coast jazz tending to plague the form as a whole.[30] Ferlinghetti's wryly allusive "Autobiography," which features on the recording, was one of seven poems published in *A Coney Island of the Mind* (1958) "conceived specifically for jazz accompaniment and as such should be considered as spontane-ously spoken 'oral messages' rather than as poems written for the printed page." Whereas the poet stated that, "As a result of continued experimen-tal reading with jazz, they are still in a state of change," there is little to suggest an endemic contingency or thematic jazz orientation, beyond the pedestrian exchange of mimetic four-bar refrains with Bruce Lippincott's quintet on the LP version.[31] That ensemble's free-jazz accompaniment to Rexroth's antibourgeois jeremiad, "Thou Shalt Not Kill," lends color, but it also reduces earnestness to melodrama and adds fuel to the popular industry of vilification that would accompany the degradation of Beat into Beatnik by the decade's end.[32]

Beyond questions of overt collaboration, it is more productive to return to the consequences of formal collision via a shift in the symbiosis of a literary work's acoustic architecture and its visual culture. With regard to Kerouac's work in particular, such convergences testify to a profound grasp of bop's complexity of energy. Sonic and visual components are fused through con-trols of tempo, measure, and cadence and are spaced accordingly for the eye and ear. Pursuing a related struggle for liberation from standardized metrics and notation and addressing shared concerns of performance, the prosodic line mirrors the organization of a musical phrase into improvised sound patterns punctuated as unique pulses. Voice and print culture intermediate, but the ensuing works remain language configurations, despite the use of nonsemantic sounds and bebop's pace and cadence as paradigm. Kerouac's concrete notations of the sea in the coda to *Big Sur* (1962), for example, in no way comprise a substitution of musical score. These visual forms can be appreciated without knowledge of their sound–text dimensions even though that information adds to them.

The Personality of Bebop

With Parker at its core, bebop had evolved through a series of experimental associations in the Harlem underground at the turn of the 1940s as "a reaction by young musicians against the sterility and formality of swing [big band] as it moved to become a formal part of the mainstream American culture" (*Black Music* 16). Reverting to a small-group framework of rhythm section plus horns, bebop signaled the reemergence of individual and collective improvisation. Soloists such as Gillespie, Thelonious Monk, Fats Navarro, Parker, and Bud Powell released energies in celebration, violence, or anguish that were previously contained and neutralized within the over-organized big band ("Jazz and Fiction" 195).

To many of the established swing generation, bebop appeared an extreme music full of speeding tempos, shocking explosions, jagged accents, angular mixtures of consonance and dissonance, and manic switches between registers, requiring unsurpassed coordinations of nerve, muscle, and intellect. The undercurrent of unease was further emphasized by the separation of pulse and melody and by the devastation of causal logic. Surprising lines hung in the air, oscillating between the lyrical and the fitful and splintered beyond resolution. The notion of musical personality as conveyed through vehicles of referentiality was ditched via new expressive possibilities that fractured the allusive routines of cliché and artifice.

To Beat writers such virtuosity demonstrated how isolated fragments could be bound together at bewildering speed within the three-minute constraints of 78-rpm playback technology. Identifying disjunction as a "positive feature" of Parker's solos, Max Harrison assigns the synthesis of figures comprising "Klactoveedsedstene" (1947) – the title of which recalled not only Gaillard's "Vout"-speak and Gillespie's scatting but also Dada sound–text vocabularies without semantic reference – as an example of the alto saxophonist's ability to realize a composition from apparently unrelated shards ("Jazz and Fiction" 198). Stop-start lines work in quotations from popular melodies, replacing the narrative linearity of a previous jazz generation with an intertextual barrage. The order of sounds placed within the chorus frame is collage, a principle of *non*coherence, as suggested by the title of Parker's 1948 recording "Segments," rather than incoherence.

This is the prerogative that excites Beat writers, an application of procedures that yields no predictive results. Baraka's essay "Hunting Is Not Those Heads on the Wall" (1973) clarifies this issue in contending that a series of polished mannerisms emulating the technical facility of an artist cannot extend his or her innovative spirit, regardless of how disruptive the original model may have been. "A saxophonist who continues to 'play like' Charlie Parker," writes Baraka, "cannot understand that Parker wasn't certain that what happened had to sound like that."[33] As his thirteen-year recording career confirms, Parker's genius resided in a restless investigation of the forms an improvisation might take.

As witness to the instantaneous realization of form on the bandstand, Kerouac discerned new possibilities for "even greater complicated sentences & VISIONS" by transposing the immediacy of a group art that takes place in public over an appointed duration into a literary act ("So from now on just call me Lee Konitz").[34] The pressure on bop improvisers to turn it on at call is echoed within Kerouac's proposals: "As for my regular English verse, I knocked it off fast like the prose," he indicated to Ted Berrigan, "just as a ... jazz musician has to get out ... his statement within a certain number of bars, within one chorus, which spills over into the next, but he has to stop where the chorus page *stops*" ("Art of Fiction" 70). This illuminates the relationship between language and the unconscious in Kerouac's writing, which admits nonverbal signs and deliberately problematizes the dominance over the selection of materials traditionally enjoyed by authors. To this end, the "riff" or *obligato*, a rhythmic figure repeated with variations to instigate exchanges between soloist and ensemble, assumes prominence throughout his work as a free-associational spur, being analogous to his term "jewel center."

Tailored for the jam session and formalized by Count Basie, riff-based improvisation was the definitive element of 1930s Kansas style, stimulating the kind of heated saxophone trade-offs that drive Dean frantic in *On the Road*. In the passage where Sal's party departs for the West from Old Bull's house in Louisiana, the reiteration of "back" creates an *obligato*-like momentum akin to a soloist's rhetorical evocation of tension through rushing phrases together:

> We wheeled through the sultry old light of Algiers, back on the ferry, back toward the mud-splashed, crabbed old ships across the river, back on Canal, and out; on a two-lane highway to Baton Rouge in purple darkness; swung west there, crossed the Mississippi at a place called Port Allen. Port Allen – where the river's all rain and roses in a misty pinpoint darkness and where we swung around a circular drive in yellow foglight and suddenly saw the great black body below a bridge and crossed eternity again. (156)

Recalling Lester Young's signature use of "false fingering" to vary pitch quality over single notes, this approach is sustained through a percussive phrase ("Port Allen") in counterpoint to the dominant pulse, before releasing pent-up energies upon rejoining the ascendant line. Kerouac's prose admits Young's exhilaration of pace, with sound reinforcing sense through alliteration and assonance, forcing the mind back to the key word "wheeled" prior to slowing into the closing cadence.

Such shedding of consensus orders of syntax demands an attention to compositional planning beyond standard paragraphed form. The condition of surprise supplants an orthodox language geared toward habitual responses and reflects the stance of the improviser. In *Visions of Cody*, his most experimental novel, Kerouac adopts the soloist's attitude that anything can happen, the narratives of jazz being not deterministic structures but states of mind or preparations for dealing with constant change. The Dionysian topos of Neal Cassady energizes the text into any shape necessary, reflecting the post-bop orientation of Ornette Coleman's seminal *Free Jazz* (1960) and Jackson Pollock's "all-over" paintings with a "structure possessed of its own organization [which] in turn derives from the circumstances of its making."[35] The appearance of the writing is necessarily unfinished and ragged with inconsistencies, while the ongoing process of construction remains exposed.

The playful descriptions of Parker's "Irish St Patrick patootle stick" and Lionel Hampton "whal[ing] his saxophone at everybody with sweat, claps, jumping fools in the aisles" display a further debt to a defining element of jazz from its ragtime evolution.[36] Whereas Cab Calloway's *Dictionary of Hep* (1934) relates the origins of "jive talk" to the word "jibe," meaning an inherent sarcasm and infelicitousness, the parodic tendency is yet more pronounced in bebop through Gillespie's persona of scornful superiority and Parker's practice of inserting unlikely quotations in solos. The countless performances that conclude with a facetious rendering of "English Country Garden" are endemic to a broader tendency to substitute duplicity and disjunction for a rhetoric of mimesis. Such gestures move within a range of mid-century transgressions of fixed performance, embracing action painting, William S. Burroughs and Brion Gysin's splicing of audio-visual materials, and John Cage's use of the *I Ching* to help compose piano compositions. Kerouac similarly adopts indeterminate procedures to release the self from conscious identity and style via linguistic play. In the case of his *Blues* poems, linear sense is disrupted by the material strictures of the writerly act itself, which, corresponding to the ongoing nature of the twelve-bar form, shape the statement. "Sometimes the word-meaning can carry from one chorus into another, or not," he contends, "just like the phrase-meaning can carry harmonically from one chorus to the other, or not. It's all gotta be non stop ad libbing within each chorus, or the gig is shot."[37]

However, as the alternate takes of Parker's recordings illustrate, improvisation need not discount revision, and Kerouac's manuscripts display ample evidence of alteration. The palimpsest-like nature of the improviser's reworking of melody over the chords of a thirty-two-bar "standard" also characterizes his oeuvre, with each novel of the Duluoz Legend a reassessment of previously documented material. This tiered approach to recall is dramatized in *Desolation Angels* (1965) through the metaphor of saxophonist Bruce Moore's tendency "to carry the message along for several chorus-chapters," in which "his ideas get tireder than at first, he does give up at the right time – besides he wants to play a new tune – I do just that, tap him on the shoe-top to acknowledge he's right."[38] By implication performance possibilities are multiple. Analogous to the notion of perpetual rehearsal conveyed by the name of Charles Mingus's band, the Jazz Workshop, the anguished search for perfectibility in completion evaporates with no single interpretation designated authoritative. This carries into the nonstop, unexpurgated feel of the paragraphs of *The Subterraneans* (1958), each "written in one breath" (*Selected Letters* 451), with one such example evoking a nightclub with Parker at its radiating center:

> and up on the stand Bird Parker with solemn eyes who'd been busted fairly recently and had now returned to a kind of bop dead Frisco but had just discovered or been told about the Red Drum, the great new generation gang wailing and gathering there, so here he was on the stand, examining them with his eyes as he blew his now-settled-down-into-regulated-design "crazy" notes – the booming drums, the high ceiling ... the king and founder of the bop generation at least the sound of it in digging his audience digging his eyes, the secret eyes him-watching, as he just pursed his lips and let great lungs and immortal fingers work, his eyes separate and interested and humane, the kindest jazz musician there could be while being and therefore naturally the greatest –[39]

Kerouac introduces fluctuations of line-speed over pulse with connectives skipped and qualification phrases dumped, a means of replicating Parker's asymmetrical phrasing, with a single word or dash "intended as a release from the extent of the phrase ... as if a saxophonist drawing breath there" (*Selected Letters* 451). Parker's shift from "'crazy' notes" to a "now-settled-down-into-regulated-design" stands as a metacommentary for Kerouac's own narrative technique for micromapping the "telepathic shock and meaning-excitement" of perception: his erratic restarts and directional changes suggest a plateau or eternal middle, forgoing the expenditure of ecstasy in singular climax and dissipation (*Good Blonde* 69). Parker's ability to combine circumstances and bring group activity to an intense fabric that flares for an instant also inspires Kerouac's disconnection from systematized chronology ("Time stops"). As Dean explains in *On the Road*:

> Now, man, that alto man last night had IT … Up to him to put down what's on everybody's mind … and then he rises to his fate and has to blow equal to it. All of a sudden somewhere in the middle of a chorus he *gets it* – everybody looks up and knows; they listen; he picks it up and carries. Time stops. (206)

Kerouac's ability to hold heterophonic voices and styles in tension mirrors a jazz impulse rooted in the New Orleans band styles of Jelly Roll Morton and King Oliver. His bop prosody "deliberately scrambles all the codes," to apply Gilles Deleuze and Félix Guattari's terminology, "by quickly shifting from one to another, according to the questions asked him, never invoking the same genealogy, never recording the same event in the same way."[40] In so doing his narratives initiate an extensional thrust that Baraka identifies in trumpeter Don Cherry's noncadential contributions to Ornette Coleman's quartet, namely that "the completion of one statement simply reintroduces the possibility of more" (*Black Music* 170). Volatile new material erupts through Kerouac's description of Lester Young's chorus in "You Can Count On Me" from *Visions of Cody*, its fragmentary nature being a manifestation of his struggle to register a barely communicable vision, with lines that plunge into a barrage of clashing consonants and a swift meta-reference to the saxophonist:

> Lester is just like the river, the river starts in near Butte, Montana in frozen snow caps (Three Forks) and meanders on down across states and entire territorial areas of dun bleak land with hawthorn crackling in the sleet, picks up rivers at Bismarck, Omaha and St Louis just north, another at Kay-ro, another in Arkansas, Tennessee, comes deluging on New Orleans with muddy news from the land and a roar of subterranean excitement that is like the vibration of the entire land sucked of its gut in mad midnight, fevered, hot, the big mudhole rank clawpole old frogular pawed-soul titanic Mississippi from the North, full of wires, cold wood, and horn. (456)

The inconsistent tense shuffles temporalities, and stretches and contracts the action, in order to dramatize the dislocations of memory and perception. Patterned upon layered snap-units and dense word conjunctions, meaning emerges from rhythmic compression and a series of sonic and syntactic disconnections that never reveal their destination in advance, as with the earlier "Lester droopy porkpie hung his horn and blew bop lazy ideas inside jazz had everybody dreaming" (380). The question of narrative runs subordinate to the jazz-*bricoleur*'s joy in artifice, echoing Parker's rush to enter explorative action with the "head" statement accorded merely the briefest acknowledgment. As an accomplished improviser, Kerouac may similarly choose to retreat into the arena of inherited fictional styles or "licks," "so long as he can stuff it full of all the disjunctions that this code was designed to eliminate" (*Anti-Oedipus* 15).

The Beat convergence with jazz thus transcends literary homage to stimulate an adventurous reinvigoration of form across poem and novel alike. As the range of work discussed in this chapter indicates, it is in the formal emulation of the music's free play of signs, its multipersonal subjectivity, its flexing to assimilate thematically aberrant materials, and its metrical license that the influence of jazz can be most productively felt. Fed by its sensory experience, Beat writers use bebop not merely as metaphor but as mediated access to an all-encompassing euphoria that dissolves subject and environment: their means of asserting the prerogative of creative freedom enshrined within this most exhilarating and affirmative of twentieth-century art forms.

NOTES

1 W. E. B. DuBois, *The Souls of Black Folk* (1903; Millwood, NY: Kraus-Thompson, 1973), 12.
2 Julian Cowley, "Jazz and Fiction in Post-bebop America,"*Review of Contemporary Fiction* 34 (1987), 195.
3 Gregory Corso, *The Vestal Lady and Other Poems* (Cambridge, MA: R. Brukenfeld, 1955), 21.
4 Jack Kerouac, "The Beginning of Bop," *Good Blonde & Others* (San Francisco: Grey Fox, 1993), 113.
5 Jack Kerouac, *Mexico City Blues* (New York: Grove Press, 1959), np.
6 Alfred Willener, *The Action-Image of Society*, trans. A. M. Sheridan-Smith (London: Tavistock, 1970), 230.
7 Henry Ford, *The International Jew: The World's Foremost Problem* (Dearborn, MI: Dearborn Publishing, 1920), 187.
8 John Clellon Holmes, *Go* (1952; London: Penguin, 2006), 161.
9 Notes to *Poetry Readings in the Cellar* [LP](Fantasy LP, 1958).
10 Allen Ginsberg, *Howl and Other Poems* (San Francisco: City Lights, 1956), 27.
11 Lawrence Lipton, *The Holy Barbarians* (New York: Messner, 1959), 207, 215.
12 Henry Miller, *The Colossus of Maroussi* (1941; London: Penguin, 1950), 140–45.
13 Frank Kofsky, *Black Nationalism and the Revolution in Music* (New York: Pathfinder, 1970), 15.
14 Jack Kerouac, *On the Road* (1957; New York: Penguin, 1991), 270; ellipsis in original.
15 Norman Mailer, *Advertisements for Myself* (1959; Cambridge, MA: Harvard University Press, 1992), 319.
16 Oswald Spengler, *Perspectives of World History*, Vol. II of *The Decline of the West*, trans. Charles Atkison (New York: Alfred A. Knopf, 1926), 8.

17 Amiri Baraka, *LeRoi Jones/Amiri Baraka Reader* (New York: Thunder's Mouth, 1991), 176.

18 Bob Kaufman, *Solitudes Crowded With Loneliness* (New York: New Directions, 1965), 8.

19 Lorenzo Thomas, "'Communicating by Horns': Jazz and Redemption in the Poetry of the Beats and the Black Arts Movement," *African American Review* 26.2 (summer 1992), 292.

20 Bob Kaufman, *Cranial Guitar: Selected Poems* (Minneapolis: Coffee House Press, 1996), 102.

21 Amiri Baraka, *Black Music* (New York: William Morrow, 1968), 173.

22 Jack Kerouac, *Visions of Cody* (1973; London: Flamingo, 1992), 407.

23 Allen Ginsberg, "Introduction," Gregory Corso, *Gasoline* (San Francisco: City Lights, 1958), 14–15.

24 Corso, *Gasoline*, 50.

25 Ted Berrigan, "The Art of Fiction XLI: Jack Kerouac," *Paris Review* 43 (1968), 69.

26 Charles Olson, "Projective Verse," *Collected Prose* (Berkeley and Los Angeles: University of California, 1997), 242.

27 Allen Ginsberg, "Notes for *Howl and Other Poems*," *The Poetics of the New American Poetry*, ed. Donald Allen and Warren Tallman (New York: Grove, 1973), 318.

28 Warren Tallman, "Kerouac's Sound," *Tamarack Review* (spring 1959), 70.

29 Notes to *Blues and Haikus* [LP] (Hanover LP, 1959).

30 Kenneth Rexroth, "Disengagement: The Art of the Beat Generation," *A Casebook on the Beat*, ed. Thomas Parkinson (New York: Crowell, 1961), 188.

31 Lawrence Ferlinghetti, *A Coney Island of the Mind* (New York: New Directions, 1958), 15.

32 *The Beat Generation* [CD box set] (Rhino, 1992) collates several audio examples of such attacks.

33 Amiri Baraka, "Hunting Is Not Those Heads on the Wall," *Poetics of the New American Poetry*, 380.

34 Jack Kerouac, *1940–1956*, Vol. II of *Selected Letters*, ed. Ann Charters (New York: Viking, 1995), 327.

35 Robert Creeley quoted in Charles Olson, *Selected Writings* (New York: New Directions, 1967), 7.

36 Jack Kerouac, *Mexico City Blues* (1959; New York: Grove, 1990), 242 and *Good Blonde*, 118.

37 Jack Kerouac, *Book of Blues* (New York: Penguin, 1995), 1.

38 Jack Kerouac, *Desolation Angels* (1965; London: Paladin, 1990), 226–27.

39 Jack Kerouac, *The Subterraneans* (1958; New York: Grove, 1981), 13–14.

40 Gilles Deleuze and Félix Guattari, *Anti-Oedipus: Capitalism and Schizophrenia*, Vol. I, trans. Robert Hurley, Mark Seem, and Helen R. Lane (London: Athlone, 1984), 67.

18

DAVID STERRITT

The Beats and Visual Culture

The Beats took a strong interest in the moving-image media, seeing cinema and television as potentially powerfully allies in their quest for quintessentially modern forms of personal expression, cultural commentary, and social protest. Generally speaking, however, the movers and shakers of film, television, digital video, and the Internet have not reciprocated with as much enthusiasm. Only a limited number of commercial movies and television shows have explored Beat themes, portrayed Beat personalities, or adapted Beat literary works, and most of the films that do glance at the Beats tend to be superficial and insincere at best, and exploitive or downright insulting at worst. Beats have fared somewhat better outside the mainstream media, where a limited number of avant-garde filmmakers and video artists have engaged with their ideas. Various documentaries also delve into Beat territory, incorporating artifacts, interviews, and archival materials in efforts to illuminate Beat history and memorialize the contributions of Beat writers, thinkers, and fellow travelers.

Loosely speaking, Beat-related film and video can be grouped into those three categories: mass-audience movies and television shows, experimental works, and nonfiction works. This remains true in the twenty-first century, when cinematic treatment of the Beats has enjoyed something of an upsurge due to increased awareness of the Beats among younger generations, nostalgia felt by people who remember the original Beat scene, and the growing importance of visual media, as the primary locus of communication continues to shift from printed texts to electronically disseminated imagery.

Any informed appreciation of Beat-related visual culture must start with an understanding of the historical circumstances in which the Beat sensibility was born. American society after World War II was in some ways robust and healthy, in other ways anxious and uncertain. The United States had emerged from the war as the strongest, most prosperous power in the world. Yet the advance in material comforts did not bring a corresponding rise in psychological and spiritual contentment. Uneasy terms such as "lonely crowd" and "rat race" gained currency in journalism and entertainment. Voters elected Republican war hero Dwight D. Eisenhower to the presidency in 1952 and again in 1956, reinforcing a turn to conservative values that produced Cold War paranoia as a by-product. Gaps widened between rich and poor; suburbs took on a nondescript sameness; minority groups faced bigotry and segregation; consumption was fueled by aggressive advertising and the "planned obsolescence" of expensive goods. Marriage was a prerequisite for sex, in theory if not in practice, and, while the word "homophobia" had not been coined, the attitude was ubiquitous. Such was the postwar American society that the Beats confronted and opposed.

Movie Fans

The core Beats were enthusiastic moviegoers, and at times they considered making films as well as watching them, creating Hollywood magic that would somehow be free of Hollywood commercialism. It is not surprising that the Beats had a yen for movies, since motion pictures appeal to the eye and ear at once, and Beat writing tends to be *embodied* writing, committed to the evidence of the senses as well as flights of imagination and excursions into metaphysics.

As demonstrated in Chapter 17, Jack Kerouac was keenly attuned to the sounds and structures of modern jazz, which provided the basis for his spontaneous writing and his conviction that in-the-moment intuition is the best route to authentic creativity. His musical attachments were paired with visual ones, since he felt that words must grow organically from concrete images held continuously in consciousness, and woven into memory as well. "The object is set before the mind," he wrote in 1958, "either in reality ... or ... in the memory wherein it becomes the sketching from memory of a definite image-object."[1] He described his method as "blowing (as per jazz musician) on subject of image," thus linking sound and picture in a proto-cinematic manner.[2] In this way Kerouac regarded himself as the verbal equivalent of a visual artist, using words to capture and convey the images that swarmed in his mind's eye, but doing so with a musical sensibility that transforms static images into dynamic flows. Equally cinematic was Kerouac's capacity for recording the sights and sounds of the cultural environment in which he worked. Like an anthropologist or journalist, he didn't so much originate as chronicle the linguistic tenor of the current scene. He imagined making a movie in which his friends would appear as both real-life people and fictional characters, much as they do in his autobiographical novels.

Allen Ginsberg wrote in his diary at age eleven that films gave him "about the only relief from boredom" that otherwise seemed inescapable. Years later he described his landmark 1955 poem "Howl" as "a tragic custard-pie comedy of wild phrasing ... running along making awkward combinations [of images] like Charlie Chaplin's walk."[3] He spoke fondly of such irreverent underground films as Barbara Rubin's *Christmas on Earth* (1963) and Andy Warhol's *The Chelsea Girls* (1966), and he mused about making a Buddhist science-fiction film called *Burroughs on Earth*.

William S. Burroughs's personal mythology held that an insidious "reality film" predetermines the everyday world and that language offers the only means to contest its totalitarian control. Therefore, he concluded, "to think in concrete visual terms is almost essential to a writer." He favored movies with a subversive edge, such as two 1969 releases, Dennis Hopper's *Easy Rider* and Sam Peckinpah's *The Wild Bunch*. The influence of cinema on Burroughs's work is most vivid in his use of the cut-up method, which he acquired from Brion Gysin, an avant-garde writer and painter. Cut-ups are created by tearing, scissoring, folding over, or otherwise dividing materials – written texts, voice recordings, film strips, whatever – into segments that can then be rejiggered and spliced into new configurations. This technique has clear parallels with montage, the shot-to-shot cutting found in nearly all cinematic works. Using this and other aleatory procedures, such as shooting paint cans with a shotgun, Burroughs made countless texts, paintings, collages, photomontages, and tape-recorded works. The cut-up's great advantage, he asserted, is the room it allows for spontaneity and happenstance; the best writing "seems to be done almost by accident," and here was an invaluable tool for writers who previously "had no way to produce the accident of spontaneity."[4]

Mainstream Movies

Most mass-audience movies that claim to explore Beat interests or represent Beat personalities show little understanding of Beat ideas, sympathy for Beat positions, or respect for Beat lifestyles. Eisenhower-era Americans viewed Beats and so-called Beatniks with little more than bemused curiosity, often accompanied by a tinge of the lascivious or the morbid, thanks to popular scuttlebutt about free love, infrequent bathing, and an unhealthy interest in jazz.

In fact, stories about jazz musicians were useful vehicles for postwar filmmakers wishing to capitalize on public interest in the Beats while keeping a cautious distance. The blues, a type of jazz and folk music with a whiff of funkiness, evokes the Beats by association in *Pete Kelly's Blues*, directed by Jack Webb and released in 1955. The opening scenes depict a Southern funeral, during which an African American cornetist loses his instrument. The white title character, played by Webb with the staccato inflections that were his trademark, then wins the horn in a dice game on a freight car; this amps up the Beat undertones by hinting at rootlessness, off-the-cuff living, going "on the road" to seek one's destiny. We next encounter Kelly as a mature musician in a 1920s speakeasy, devoted to jazz and passionate about his cornet. Typically for this superficial film, the sonic ambience of a real jazz joint is missing; when a white singer (Peggy Lee) performs a ballad, her voice is luminously clear while the instrumental accompaniment fades into the background. Spontaneity and authenticity, key values of jazz and Beat culture, are muted by the technology of the Hollywood mixing room.

A presiding spirit of Martin Ritt's *Paris Blues* (1961) is the French poet Arthur Rimbaud, a favorite of Ginsberg, Kerouac, and other Beat writers who followed his recommendation to seek radical creative freedom by means of "long, intimidating, immense, and rational derangement of all the senses."[5] His incarnation in *Paris Blues*, played by Paul Newman, is Ram Bowen, a white American trombonist. The other main character, portrayed by Sidney Poitier, is Eddie Cook, a black saxophonist. Also on hand is a token character called Wild Man Moore, played by trumpeter Louis Armstrong, then a universally famous icon of African American culture. Subtract the "e" from Wild Man's last name and you have an uncommonly blunt signifier of dominant white attitudes toward African American people in American society and movies. Ram and Eddie respect his energy and spontaneity, however, and, although his part in the film is brief, his personality exudes charisma. No character in *Paris Blues* is actually Beat, and the film – set in Paris, comfortably removed from more familiar Beat locales such as Greenwich Village and North Beach, San Francisco – is primarily a romance wherein Ram and Eddie pair off with American tourists and must decide between returning to the United States and remaining in Paris, where Eddie's race is not stigmatized. *Paris Blues* has no genuine interest in Rimbaud or sensory derangement, but its engagement with sexuality is unusually direct for the period when it was made: Ram is allowed to manifest a Beat-like rejection of long-term commitment, preferring to enjoy "kicks while they last" and then move on. The filmmakers also seem sincere in their affection for the aesthetics of spontaneity shared by Beats and jazz musicians.

Exploitation Films

There is no better specimen of the Beat-related exploitation film – or Beatsploitation film – than *A Bucket of Blood*, a 1959 release from American International Pictures (AIP) written by Charles B. Griffith and directed by Roger Corman, who also produced it. Those credits are a trifecta of exploitation-picture expertise: Griffith and the hugely prolific Corman specialized in low-budget genre fare, and AIP specialized in bringing such fare to theaters. The milieu of *A Bucket of Blood* is the Beat coffeehouse, distinguishable from its square counterparts – traditional hangouts such as bars, saloons, and taverns – by the absence of alcohol (the square's drug of choice) and a general tolerance for marijuana, sexual freedom, and progressive entertainments such as jazz and poetry readings. Coffeehouses were sympathetic to liminal activities that would seem peculiar or excessive in "normal" settings. Since square society viewed them with suspicion, movie studios found them to be handy signifiers of strangeness and willful eccentricity.

A Bucket of Blood begins with a bearded Beatnik reciting a poem in the Yellow Door, a coffeehouse whose name suggests cowardly fear of the "real world" outside. The filmmakers clearly mean to satirize the Beats in this opening scene, but the details betray scant knowledge of Beat realities: the resident musician is a folk singer, not a jazz performer, and there is little evidence of loose sexuality. The main character is Walter Paisley (Dick Miller), a worker at the Yellow Door who wishes he were an artist like many patrons of the establishment. After accidentally killing a cat, he somehow gets the idea of enclosing it in clay, presenting it as a sculpture, and keeping the unpleasant facts of its creation to himself. When the patrons hail it as a masterpiece, Walter proceeds to repeat the process with a police officer, again receiving acclaim from the coffeehouse clique. His secret comes out after two more murders, whereupon he commits suicide. The last word comes from a Beatnik who sees Walter's body dangling from the noose: "I suppose he would have called it 'Hanging Man.' His greatest work."

A Bucket of Blood plays two aesthetic-ideological notions against the middle, depicting an environment centered on art and poetry while portraying its habitués as phony, pretentious, and (when discussing the prices of their wares) as mercenary as the capitalists they purportedly scorn. The poetry, paintings, and sculptures in the Yellow Door are ridiculous, disagreeable, and contagious, giving dull-witted Walter the idea that his clay-covered corpses are bona-fide works of art. The movie brandishes a spirit of tacky fun as it inveighs against self-indulgent art and nonconformist values, but its underlying attitude toward the Beat Generation is unmistakably snide.

Beat Girl (a.k.a. *Wild for Kicks*), a 1961 release directed by Edmond T. Greville for the English production arm of Metro-Goldwyn-Mayer (MGM), gives Beats a more sympathetic hearing. In one scene, a schoolgirl, Jennifer Linden (Gillian Hills), explains to her father that nuclear war may annihilate the world tomorrow, so "while it's *now* we live it up. Do everything. Feel everything. Strictly for kicks!" Family conflict propels the story, which interestingly contrasts two socially liminal places: the Off Beat, a coffeehouse for alienated teens, and Les Girls, a strip club for the older crowd. While the mood at the Off Beat is often boring and glum, the youngsters prefer it to the tedium at home. Evenings at Les Girls can be downright awful, fueled by liquor and anger that bring about a climactic murder. The film regards everyone – Beats and squares, youths and adults – as aimless and apathetic, but it appears that the Beats have some excuse, whereas the squares should have grown up by now.

The Beat Generation, a 1959 melodrama produced by Albert Zugsmith and directed by Charles F. Haas from a screenplay by Richard Matheson and Lewis Meltzer, also rests on an attraction–repulsion dynamic. After opening in a Beat coffeehouse where Louis Armstrong is singing an anti-Beat song, the film becomes a thriller about a police officer pursuing a quasi-Beatnik rapist who slips in and out of Beat milieus with ease, as does the film itself. Balancing the film's Beat-unfriendly side, however, a jive-talking character is allowed to weigh in against squares who merely "eat, sleep, go to work, vegetate." The film also displays a critical awareness of American misogyny, pointing to sexist bias in square culture and Beat counterculture alike. Such a critique is hard to find in most other Hollywood movies on Beat subjects.

It is certainly absent in The Subterraneans (1960), for instance, directed by Ranald MacDougall and produced by Arthur Freed, who is best known for his MGM musicals of the 1940s and 1950s. Based on Kerouac's 1958 novella, The Subterraneans may have attracted Freed by virtue of its music possibilities; along with topline actors Leslie Caron, Roddy McDowall, George Peppard, and Janice Rule, the film has a score by the illustrious André Previn and includes an impressive roster of jazz artists including singer Carmen McRae, drummer Shelley Manne, alto saxophonist Art Pepper, trumpeter Art Farmer, bassists Red Mitchell and Buddy Clark, pianist Russ Freeman, and the great baritone saxophonist Gerry Mulligan as a (fictional) priest. Peppard has the requisite good looks as the Kerouac character, Leo Percepied, but any true Beat vibes fall prey to the film's fundamental lack of authenticity, exemplified most glaringly by the fact that one of the novel's title characters, an African American woman named Mardou Fox, is played by Caron, a white French actress.

Other mainstream films about Beat subjects include John Byrum's Heart Beat (1980), a biopic with John Heard as Kerouac, Nick Nolte as Neal Cassady, and Sissy Spacek as Carolyn Cassady, and David Cronenberg's Naked Lunch (1991), a loose pastiche drawn from Burroughs's 1959 novel and from incidents in the writer's life. Critics have found little to praise in either film.

Television

Television's excursions into Beat territory have been superficial and few. The medium's most famous Beatnik was the work-avoiding, jazz-loving, girl-shy Maynard G. Krebs, a supporting character played by Bob Denver in *The Many Loves of Dobie Gillis* (1959–63), a CBS situation comedy. Maynard wore a shabby sweatshirt and sported a goatee, a basic Beatnik stereotype although most Beat writers never wore them. He punctuated every other sentence with "like" and yowled a panicky "*WORK!??!*" whenever he heard that distressing word. The principle behind this character was that the aimlessness, fecklessness, and scruffiness attributed to Beats in the popular imagination might seem humorous and endearing if embodied by an appealing figure. This proved to be true. Maynard was a likable Beat caricature whom squares and hipsters could laugh into inconsequentiality every week.

Route 66 (1960–64), another CBS series, featured Beat-like young men named Buzz and Todd who traversed America in a Corvette Stingray, finding adventure wherever they went. Kerouac resented the show as an unacknowledged theft from *On the Road* (1957), but virtually all Beat sensibilities had been lost in translation. Slightly more of the Beat spirit glimmered in *Johnny Staccato*, an NBC series that lasted for just one season (1959–60), allowing its private-eye hero (played by John Cassavetes, who also directed some episodes) to solve crimes in Greenwich Village and play the piano at Waldo's on MacDougal Street in his spare time. Well-known jazz figures such as Barney Kessel, Shelly Manne, and Red Norvo often joined the cast.

Cassavetes completed his first film, *Shadows*, in 1959. It focuses on two African American brothers, a jazz singer and a jazz trumpeter, and their sister, a light-skinned woman who does not "pass" for white but is mistaken for white by an attractive young man she meets. While the film is not specifically about Beats, the brothers have Beat proclivities in music, in dress, and in their one-day-at-a-time approach to life. The film itself is recognizably Beat in mood, temperament, and atmosphere. Cassavetes returned to jazz-related material in the more polished *Too Late Blues* (1961), starring actor and pop singer Bobby Darin as John "Ghost" Wakefield, a piano player caught in a self-made tangle of artistic idealism, personal pride, and hopes of making it big. Produced by Paramount Pictures, this was one of Cassavetes's rare studio ventures, and he felt that its integrity was fatally compromised by Hollywood commercialism, which he despised. In later years he used his earnings as a Hollywood star to finance independent productions influenced by nobody's sensibilities but his.

The Experimental and Avant-Garde

Cassavetes developed the basic materials of *Shadows* in improvisation sessions with the cast, and then refined the film through intensive editing and reshooting. The end product has a free-flowing, impressionistic style that forges a link between mass-audience movies about Beat subjects and radically unorthodox works that fully partake of the Beat spirit. Avant-garde cinema emerged well before the Beat era, but a modern wave of Beat-like poetic cinema began with such pioneers as Kenneth Anger and Maya Deren in the 1940s and continued with Beat-connected artists such as Antony Balch, Bruce Conner, and Ron Rice in the 1950s and 1960s. Although this field is too diversified to support generalizations, it is safe to remark that the rejection of mainstream aesthetics, the expression of deeply personal visions, and the elevation of spontaneity and impulsiveness are among its most consistent goals. All are hallmarks of the Beat sensibility as well.

Pull My Daisy, one of the quintessential Beat films, is a half-hour production directed by painter Alfred Leslie and photographer Robert Frank; its premiere took place in 1959, the year in which the US edition of *The Americans*, Frank's most celebrated book of photographs, was published. Frank supervised the film's camerawork and Leslie was in charge of the staging. Gregory Corso, Ginsberg, and Peter Orlovsky play significant roles, and Kerouac is the off-screen narrator. The action and dialogue derive from the third act of Kerouac's unproduced play *The Beat Generation*, and the film's title comes from its theme song, "The Crazy Daisy," a musical setting of a poem written by Ginsberg and Kerouac in 1949:

> Pull my Daisy
> Tip my cup
> All my doors are open
> Cut my thoughts for coconuts
> All my eggs are broke[6]

Pull My Daisy has the look and feel of a motion-picture jam session, but in fact it was carefully made. The action was filmed over a two-week period, the shots were planned with continuity editing in mind, and Kerouac's narration was constructed to a significant extent by the editors, with portions taken from three different recording sessions.[7] Like the film as a whole, it tempers Beat extemporaneity with cinematic professionalism.

The main character is Milo, a poet and railroad brakeman. Others include his wife, their little boy, Beatnik friends who pay a call, and a bishop who drops in with his mother and sister, putting everyone on good behavior that proves temporary. After much horseplay and wordplay, Milo leaves with the Beatniks for adventures in the city outside, and Kerouac's voiceover dismisses the feelings of Milo's wife about being left behind: "She'll get over it. Come on, Milo. Here comes sweet Milo, beautiful Milo, Hello, gang. Da da da da da." This kind of male-chauvinist bias underlies the entire film; the narration celebrates men and the directors relegate women to the background. This sexist perspective is sadly representative of the male Beats in general; notwithstanding the contributions of such talented, independent-minded women as Carolyn Cassady, Diane di Prima, Joyce Johnson, Hettie Jones, and Edie Parker, the Beat scene was predominantly a male scene, and *Pull My Daisy* makes no effort to transcend or even recognize that failing.

Before he became a filmmaker, Bruce Conner was a sculptor, graphic artist, collage and assemblage artist, and light-show designer. He joined the Beat scene when he moved to San Francisco in 1957, and Beat aesthetics never lost their importance for him. His first film, *A Movie* (1958), introduced him as a poet of "found footage," constructing radically original works by appropriating materials from preexisting films – educational movies, television commercials, industrial documentaries, training films, Hollywood features – and editing them into wholly new configurations. His films often recall the anti-art impulses of Dadaism, and a delicate Surrealism runs through later works such as *Take the 5:10 to Dreamland* (1976) and *Valse Triste* (1977), which recall the strangeness of the dreams that Kerouac recorded in his journals. Other films convey Conner's powerful opposition to racism, sexism, conformity, and other contemporary ills; examples include *Report* (1967), which unsparingly rebukes the exploitation of footage of the assassination of John F. Kennedy on commercial television, and *Marilyn Times Five* (1973), which uses repetition to drain pornography of its misogynistic power. Like many Beat artists, Conner cultivated a close involvement with jazz, pop, and classical music, and his free-associative manipulations of found footage recall Burroughs's cut-ups. Connor celebrates the Beat urge to break apart the products of orthodox culture, reveal their inner workings, and destroy their power to beguile and control.

Ron Rice, who made only a handful of films before his death at age twenty-nine in 1964, was a talented member of what might be called the Wandering Beat school of experimental cinema.[8] He hailed the Beats as those whose renunciation of material wealth leads to "a special grace, the freedom of the mind which enables them to Create and receive the Joy," and he shared Kerouac's dedication to in-the-moment spontaneity. "See where analysis has brought the human race, the world is on the brink of destruction," Rice wrote in a paper published after his death.[9] His films are populated by outsiders who amble along the margins of mainstream society. *The Flower Thief* (1960) stars the underground actor Taylor Mead as a childlike San Franciscan who visits a jazz club, faces a firing squad for urinating in public, and miraculously returns to life. The soundtrack blends atmospheric jazz with words portraying postwar America as a sick society with no sympathy for those who reject conformity. This is unalloyed Beat philosophy, although the hero's ingenuous nature and fondness for flowers also anticipate the hippie movement, which would transform and extend fundamental Beat values later in the 1960s. In his second film, *Senseless* (1962), Rice foregoes narrative in favor of an intuitive critique of Western sociopolitical values, and in his third, *Chumlum* (1964), he uses powerful colors and multiple superimpositions to etch a drug-inflected portrait of figures from the underground art scene. Rice's last film, *The Queen of Sheba Meets the Atom Man*, was left unfinished when he died; starring Mead as a clownish bumbler and Winifred Bryan as an African American earth mother, it presents what the Italian author Alberto Moravia called a "violent, childish, and sincere ... protest against an industrial world based on the cycle of production and consumption."[10]

Burroughs and the English filmmaker Antony Balch collaborated on several short experimental films in the 1960s, starting with the 1963 documentary *William Buys a Parrot*, which shows what its title suggests. The same year brought *Towers Open Fire*, an elliptical fantasy with a voiceover written and spoken by Burroughs, who also appears on screen. The slender narrative contains elements of cut-up discontinuity and other Burroughs hallmarks, such as the obliteration of a board of authoritarian Nova Mob-type executives by intrepid enemies of conspiratorial control. *The Cut-Ups* (1966) is a sustained display of discontinuous montage. Balch started the editing process by cutting four sequences of shots into foot-long sections and splicing these together in a recurring 1-2-3-4 order. The soundtrack similarly consists of a few tape-recorded phrases, which Balch cut into segments and recombined: "Yes. Hello. / Look at this picture. Does it seem to be persisting? / Good. Thank you." Visually, the film has a certain logic; in a segment organized around "rolling," for instance, one person employs a paint roller while somebody else rolls up a canvas and another person unrolls someone's underpants. Even sympathetic spectators may find that the film's visual puns, rhymes, and repetitions soon wear thin, but the soundtrack works quite well, refining spoken language into a music-like canon of irreducible sound. Although the figures seen in Balch's films carry less conceptual weight than their unseen counterparts in Burroughs's books, the movies work reasonably well as illustrations of Burroughs's idea that linear words and images are virus-like entities that subject humanity to endless conflict and confusion when misappropriated by control systems and the false realities they serve.

Beat Film in the Twenty-First Century

In 1999, writer-director Chuck Workman broke new ground with *The Source: The Story of the Beats and the Beat Generation*, a compilation film mixing documentary material with Beat poetry and prose recited by Johnny Depp (as charismatic, intense Kerouac), Dennis Hopper (as volatile, peculiar Burroughs), and John Turturro (as scruffy, freewheeling Ginsberg). A decade later, another cinematic hybrid affirmed the continuing viability of Beat movies. *Howl* (2010), directed by Rob Epstein and Jeffrey Friedman, uses four different formats to sketch the history of Ginsberg's magisterial poem: Ginsberg (James Franco) tells an unseen interviewer how "Howl" came to be written; a Hollywood cast reenacts the obscenity trial of Lawrence Ferlinghetti for publishing it; animations give graphic life to some of the poem's more vivid passages; and connective sequences evoke key moments in Beat history via archival footage and reconstructions. According to the filmmakers, about ninety-five percent of the dialogue comes directly from trial transcripts and interviews that Ginsberg gave.

Epstein and Friedman are best known for documentaries on gay subjects, and in some respects *Howl* is a continuation of their nonfiction work by other means, restaging history in ways that might be unacceptable in an orthodox documentary.[11] It is also a foray into historical fiction, using narrative techniques to explain and interpret the past. The animated sequences fall outside the usual categories of narrative and nonfiction, and have little to do with the official record; they are, however, well attuned to the Beat creative spirit. The past is a matter of moods and feelings as well as events and personalities, and the animations are perhaps the film's most original contribution to Beat historiography.

Ginsberg was not the most conventionally attractive of poets, but posthumously he has been well served by casting departments. Franco handsomely portrayed him in *Howl*, and in John Krokidas's *Kill Your Darlings* (2013) he was played by Daniel Radcliffe, the star of the Harry Potter movies. *Kill Your Darlings* retells a woeful incident in early Beat history: Burroughs's friend David Kammerer developed a strong attachment to a younger man named Lucien Carr, who enrolled at Columbia University in 1943. Kammerer followed him there. Before long Carr fell in love with a woman, putting Kammerer into a state of rage, and one night Carr came to Burroughs and Kerouac with the confession that he had just stabbed Kammerer to death in a violent altercation. With some hesitation, Carr surrendered to the police. Burroughs and Kerouac were arrested for not reporting the crime, although the consequences for them were not severe. Ginsberg was not arrested but was deeply shaken. Krokidas's film mines these events for melodrama, charging the *amour fou* narrative with quasi-Beat aesthetic flash.

Kerouac's years at Columbia were behind him when he wrote *On the Road*, which remains his most famous and influential novel. When it was published in 1957 he quickly imagined a screen version, deciding that he should take the role of Sal Paradise, his surrogate in the novel, opposite Marlon Brando as Dean Moriarty, the Neal Cassady character. He wrote to Brando, who did not write back, and there matters lay until 1980, when Francis Ford Coppola acquired the movie rights. After rejecting screenplay drafts by multiple writers, it wasn't until the 2010s that Coppola engaged director Walter Salles and screenwriter José Rivera to realize a film version of *On the Road* (2012). Their adaptation is moderately true to the novel's structure, following Sal (Sam Riley) and Dean (Garrett Hedlund) on trips to Denver, San Francisco, a Mexican brothel, an upscale Manhattan neighborhood, and many other places, interacting with friends, acquaintances, and relatives along the way. But missing from the film is the novel's insatiable curiosity about people, places, and things. Its psychological perceptions are also diminished, especially when Sal's ultimate decision to break with Dean is reduced from a bittersweet epiphany to a moment of everyday rudeness; while this is plausible in narrative terms, it lacks the emotional resonance of the novel's conclusion.

A second Kerouac adaptation in 2013, Michael Polish's *Big Sur*, ranks with the most evocative Beat movies. Jean-Marc Barr plays Kerouac as Kerouac portrays himself in his 1962 novel: he is a disillusioned middle-aged alcoholic, sickened by unsought fame and convinced that he must "get away to solitude again or die." Ferlinghetti lends him an isolated cabin in Northern California, where Kerouac settles down for a healing, restorative sojourn. "No booze, no drugs, no binges, no bouts with Beatniks and drunks and junkies and everybody," he says in voiceover; replacing them are nature, books, and contemplation. But in a mere four days he becomes bored and jaded; renouncing the solitary life, he races away for more "wino yelling with the gang." Later he returns to Big Sur, first with writer friends and later with Cassady's mistress. At the end he is in the cabin again, ravaged by delirium tremens and paranoid hallucinations. In the film's last moments he has a transcendent vision complete with a Christian cross before his eyes. But this is clearly wishful self-delusion by a man who (in reality) died an alcoholic's hemorrhagic death a few years later. Polish takes many artistic risks, downplaying dramatic scenes and unfolding long sequences with no dialogue. The strategies work remarkably well, however, and the excellent acting by Barr (Kerouac), Josh Lucas (Cassady), and Anthony Edwards (Ferlinghetti) is enhanced by their resemblance to the figures they portray. Also present are second-tier Beats little seen in other movies, including Cassady's wife Carolyn (Radha Mitchell), his lover Billie (Kate Bosworth), and the poets Philip Whalen (Henry Thomas), Michael McClure (Balthazar Getty), and Lew Welch (Patrick Fischler). Ginsberg is not a character in Polish's film, but its best moments radiate what the poet called "eyeball kicks," the jolts of cosmic awareness that distinguish visionary art from everyday perceptions. While no movie has yet captured the full rambunctious essence of the Beats, *Big Sur* is among the few that have come close.

Ginsberg once remarked that the meaning of the term Beat Generation is encapsulated by a sentence in Kerouac's great novel *Visions of Cody*, written soon after *On the Road* in the 1950s: "Everything belongs to me because I am poor."[12] In aspiration if not always in achievement, the Beats embraced a poverty of possessions and wealth, not of spiritual insights or iconoclastic vigor. Their notion of revolutionizing society through radical aesthetics was quixotic but not crazy, and, although prose and poetry were their primary vocations, they often supplemented their far-reaching literary innovations with bold excursions into visual media. Ginsberg emerged as a significant American photographer in the 1980s. Burroughs engaged in photography, calligraphy, book-cover design, and assemblage art in addition to his shotgun paintings, cut-up collages, and contributions to Balch's nonlinear films. Kerouac collaborated on Frank and Leslie's film *Pull My Daisy* and produced an impressive array of paintings, drawings, and sketches, some as stand-alone works and others as marginalia in his notebooks.[13]

Beat visual culture built a small but steady following in the years after the movement's heyday, and growing recognition of the Beats' productivity in areas beyond literature is part of the reason why Beat-related films have been visible in the theatrical and televisual marketplace more frequently in the twenty-first century than at any other time since the early 1960s. The latter-day movies also bespeak a heightened seriousness about Beat personalities and events. Imperfect as they are, Salles's *On the Road* and Krokidas's *Kill Your Darlings* are more involved with Beat history than are such faded items as Ritt's *Paris Blues* and Webb's *Pete Kelly's Blues*, and they largely avoid the exploitation-movie tactics found in the likes of Corman's *A Bucket of Blood* and MacDougall's *The Subterraneans*. Although the nostalgia of older viewers partly explains the rekindling of interest in the Beats, the renewal owes more to young people – be they punks, cyberpunks, GenXers, millennials, or none of the above – who carry on the Beats' distinctive synthesis of antiauthoritarian instincts, distrust of top-down thinking, and irreverence toward traditional rules of propriety and decorum. Beat cinema, more available than ever thanks to digital communications, both reflects and sustains the ongoing relevance of Beat ideas.

NOTES

1 Jack Kerouac, "Essentials of Spontaneous Prose," *The Portable Beat Reader*, ed. Ann Charters (New York: Penguin, 1992), 57–58.

2 Jack Kerouac, "Belief & Technique for Modern Prose," *Evergreen Review* 2.8 (spring 1959), 57.

3 Barry Miles, *Ginsberg: A Biography* (New York: Simon & Schuster, 1989), 187, 26, 334.

4 William S. Burroughs, "The Cut-Up Method of Brion Gysin," *Re/Search* 4/5 (1982), 35.

5 Benjamin Ivry, *Arthur Rimbaud* (Bath: Absolute Press, 1998), 24.

6 In a letter to Kerouac dated June 13, 1949, Ginsberg wrote that he "dreamed more stanzas of our poem"; lines are quoted here. Bill Morgan and David Stanford, eds., *Jack Kerouac and Allen Ginsberg: The Letters* (New York: Viking Penguin, 2010), 83–84.

7 Gerald Nicosia, *Memory Babe: A Critical Biography of Jack Kerouac* (London: Penguin, 1986), 583; Blaine Allan, "The Making (and Unmaking) of *Pull My Daisy*," *Film History* 2 (1988).

8 David Sterritt, *Mad to Be Saved: The Beats, the '50s, and Film* (Carbondale: Southern Illinois University Press, 1998), 205.

9 Ron Rice, "Diaries, Notebooks, Documents," *Film Culture* 39 (winter 1965), 113, 119.

10 Quoted from *L'Espresso* (Rome) in Jonas Mekas, "Movie Journal," *Village Voice* (February 25, 1965), 14.

11 Films they have codirected include *The Celluloid Closet* (TriStar Pictures, 1995) and *Paragraph 175* (Telling Pictures, 2000).

12 Allen Ginsberg, "A Definition of the Beat Generation," *Friction* 1 (winter 1982), 50; Jack Kerouac, *Visions of Cody* (New York: Penguin, 1993), 33.

13 See, for instance, Allen Ginsberg, *Photographs* (Santa Fe, NM: Twin Palms, 1991), which includes self-portraits as well as photos of assorted Beats and Beat-friendly artists; Jack Kerouac, *Departed Angels: The Lost Paintings* (New York: Da Capo, 2004), which contains reproductions of fifty paintings and an equal number of sketchbook pages; and Synne Genzmer and Colin Fallows, eds., *The Art of William S. Burroughs: Cut-Ups, Cut-Ins, Cut-Outs* (Vienna: Moderne Kunst Nürnberg, 2012), which presents photographs, paintings, collages, scrapbook materials, and other work.

FURTHER READING

Allen, Donald M., ed. *The New American Poetry*. New York: Grove Press, 1960.

Asher, Levi, ed. *Beats in Time: A Literary Generation's Legacy*. New York: Literary Kicks, 2011.

Baker, Deborah. *A Blue Hand: The Tragicomic, Mind-Altering Odyssey of Allen Ginsberg, a Holy Fool, a Rebel Muse, a Dharma Bum, and His Prickly Bride in India*. New York: Penguin, 2008.

Baro, Gene, ed. *"Beat" Poets*. London: Vista Books, 1961.

Bartlett, Lee, ed. *The Beats: Essays in Criticism*. Jefferson: McFarland, 1981.

Beckett, Larry. *Beat Poetry*. St. Andrews: Beatdom, 2012.

Belgrad, Daniel. *The Culture of Spontaneity: Improvisation and the Arts in Postwar America*. Chicago: University of Chicago Press, 1999.

Bockris, Victor. *Beat Punks*. Boston: Da Capo, 1998.

Burns, Glen. *Great Poets Howl: A Study of Allen Ginsberg's Poetry, 1943–1955*. New York: Lang, 1983.

Campbell, James. *This Is the Beat Generation: New York–San Francisco–Paris*. Berkeley: University of California Press, 2001.

Carr, Roy, Brian Case and Fred Deller. *The Hip: Hipsters, Jazz and the Beat Generation*. London: Faber & Faber, 1987.

Carroll, Paul, ed. *The Young American Poets*. Chicago: Big Table, 1968.

Charters, Ann, ed. *Beat Down to Your Soul: What Was the Beat Generation?* New York: Penguin, 2001.

  Beats and Company: A Portrait of a Literary Generation. Garden City: Doubleday, 1986.

  ed. *The Beats: Literary Bohemians in Postwar America, Parts I and II*. Detroit: Gale Research Company, 1983.

  Kerouac. 1973; New York: St. Martin's Press, 1987.

  ed. *Portable Beat Reader*. New York: Penguin, 1992.

Charters, Ann and Samuel Charters. *Brother Souls: John Clellon Holmes, Jack Kerouac, and the Beat Generation*. Jackson: University Press of Mississippi, 2010.

Davidson, Michael. *The San Francisco Renaissance: Poetics and Community at Mid-Century*. Cambridge: Cambridge University Press, 1991.

Dean, Tim. *Gary Snyder and the American Unconscious: Inhabiting the Ground*. New York: Palgrave, 1991.

Elkholy, Sharin N., ed. *The Philosophy of the Beats*. Lexington: University Press of Kentucky, 2012.

Ellis, R. J. *Liar! Liar! Jack Kerouac, Novelist*. London: Greenwich Exchange, 1999.

Fazzino, Jimmy. *World Beats: Beat Generation Writing and the Worlding of US Literature*. Hanover, NH: Dartmouth, 2016.

Feldman, Gene and Max Gartenberg, eds. *The Beat Generation and the Angry Young Men*. New York: Dell, 1958.

Ferlinghetti, Lawrence, ed. *City Lights Pocket Poets Anthology*. San Francisco: City Lights, 2015.

Fisher, Stanley, ed. *Beat Coast East: An Anthology of Rebellion*. New York: Excelsior Press, 1960.

Forsgren, Frida and Michael J. Prince, eds. *Out of the Shadows: Beat Women Are Not Beaten Women*. Norway: Portal Books, 2015.

Foster, Edward Halsey. *Understanding the Beats*. Columbia: University of South Carolina Press, 1992.

French, Warren. *Jack Kerouac: Novelist of the Beat Generation*. Boston: Twayne, 1986.

Garcia-Robles, Juan. *At the End of the Road: Jack Kerouac in Mexico*. Minneapolis: University of Minnesota Press, 2014.

Gawthrop, Rhonda and Chrystal McCluny. *Surf's Beat Generation: An Art and Cultural Revolution in Orange County from 1953–1964*. New York: Grand Central Press, 2016.

Geis, Deborah, ed. *Beat Drama: Playwrights and Performances of the "Howl" Generation*. London: Bloomsbury, 2016.

George-Warren, Holly. *The Rolling Stone Book of the Beats: The Beat Generation and American Culture*. New York: Hyperion, 1999.

Gifford, Barry and Lawrence Lee. *Jack's Book: An Oral Biography of Jack Kerouac*. New York: St. Martin's Press, 1978.

Gonnerman, Mark, ed. *A Sense of the Whole: Reading Gary Snyder's Mountains and Rivers without End*. New York: Counterpoint, 2015.

Grace, Nancy M. *Jack Kerouac and the Literary Imagination*. New York: Palgrave, 2007.

Grace, Nancy M. and Jennie Skerl, eds. *The Transnational Beat Generation*. New York: Palgrave, 2012.

Gray, Timothy. *Gary Snyder and the Pacific Rim*. Iowa City: University Press of Iowa, 2006.

Halberstam, David. *The Fifties*. New York: Villard Books, 1993.

Harris, Oliver. *William Burroughs and the Secret of Fascination*. Carbondale: Southern Illinois University Press, 2003.

Harris, Oliver and Ian MacFadyen, eds. *Naked Lunch@50: Anniversary Essays*. Carbondale: Southern Illinois University Press, 2009.

Hemmer, Kurt, ed. *Encyclopedia of Beat Literature*. New York: Facts on File, 2007.

Holladay, Hilary. *Herbert Huncke: The Times Square Hustler Who Inspired Jack Kerouac and the Beat Generation*. Tucson: Schaffner Press, 2015.

Holladay, Hilary and Robert Holton, eds. *What's Your Road, Man? Critical Essays on Jack Kerouac's On the Road*. Carbondale: Southern Illinois University Press, 2009.

Holton, Robert. *On the Road: Kerouac's Ragged American Journey*. Boston: Twayne, 1999.

Honan, Park, ed. *The Beats: An Anthology of "Beat" Writing*. London: Dent & Sons, 1987.

Horemans, Rudi, ed. *Beat Indeed!* Antwerp: Exa, 1985.

Hrebeniak, Michael. *Action Writing: Jack Kerouac's Wild Form.* Carbondale: Southern Illinois University Press, 2006.

Hunt, Tim. *Kerouac's Crooked Road: Development of a Fiction.* 1981; Berkeley: University of California Press, 1996.

The Textuality of Soulwork: Jack Kerouac's Quest for Spontaneous Prose. Ann Arbor: University of Michigan Press, 2014.

Hyde, Lewis, ed. *On the Poetry of Allen Ginsberg.* Ann Arbor: University of Michigan Press, 1985.

Johnson, Joyce. *The Voice Is All: The Lonely Victory of Jack Kerouac.* New York: Viking, 2012.

Johnson, Ronna C. and Nancy M. Grace, eds. *Breaking the Rule of Cool: Interviewing and Reading Women Beat Writers.* Jackson: University Press of Mississippi, 2004.

eds. *Girls Who Wore Black: Women Writing the Beat Generation.* New Brunswick: Rutgers University Press, 2002.

Jones, James T. *Jack Kerouac's Duluoz Legend: The Mythic Form of an Autobiographical Fiction.* Carbondale: Southern Illinois University Press, 1999.

A Map of Mexico City Blues: Jack Kerouac as Poet. Carbondale: Southern Illinois University Press, 1992.

Jones, Jim. *Use My Name: Jack Kerouac's Forgotten Families.* Ontario: ECW Press, 1999.

Jones, LeRoi, ed. *The Moderns: An Anthology of New Writing in America.* New York: Corinth Books, 1963.

Katz, Eliot. *The Poetry and Politics of Allen Ginsberg.* St. Andrews: Beatdom, 2015.

Knight, Arthur and Kit Knight, eds. *The Beat Vision: A Primary Sourcebook.* New York: Paragon House, 1987.

Knight, Brenda. *Women of the Beat Generation.* San Francisco: Conari Books, 1996.

Krim, Seymour, ed. *The Beats.* Greenwich, CT: Gold Medal Books, 1960.

Lee, A. Robert, ed. *The Beat Generation Writers.* London: Pluto Books, 1996.

Modern American Counter Writing: Beats, Outriders, Ethnics. New York: Routledge, 2010.

Lydenberg, Robin. *Word Cultures: Radical Theory and Practice in William S. Burroughs' Fiction.* Urbana: University of Illinois Press, 1987.

Maher, Paul. *Kerouac: The Definitive Biography.* New York: Taylor Trade, 2004.

Marler, Regina. *Queer Beats: How the Beats Turned America On to Sex.* Berkeley: Cleis Press, 2004.

Maynard, John. *Venice West: The Beat Generation in Southern California.* New Brunswick: Rutgers University Press, 1991.

McIntosh, Martin, ed. *Beatsville.* Melbourne: Outré Gallery Press, 2003.

McNally, Dennis. *Desolate Angel: Jack Kerouac, the Beat Generation, and America.* Cambridge, MA: Da Capo Press, 2003.

Melehy, Hassan. *Kerouac: Language, Poetics, and Territory.* London: Bloomsbury, 2016.

Miles, Barry. *The Beat Hotel.* New York: Grove, 2000.

Call Me Burroughs: A Life. New York: Twelve, 2014.

Ginsberg: A Biography. New York: Simon and Schuster, 1989.

William Burroughs, El Hombre Invisible. London: Virgin, 1992.

Morgan, Bill. *The Beats Abroad: A Global Guide to the Beat Generation.* San Francisco: City Lights, 2016.

I Celebrate Myself: The Somewhat Private Life of Allen Ginsberg. New York: Viking, 2006.

The Typewriter is Holy: The Complete, Uncensored History of the Beat Generation. New York: Free Press, 2010.

Morgan, Ted. *Literary Outlaw: The Life and Times of Williams S. Burroughs.* New York: Holt, 1988.

Mortenson, Erik. *Capturing the Beat Moment: Cultural Politics and the Poetics of Presence.* Carbondale: Southern Illinois University Press, 2011.

Mottram, Eric. *William Burroughs: The Algebra of Need.* Buffalo: Intrepid Press, 1971.

Murphy, Timothy. *Wising Up the Marks: The Amodern William Burroughs.* Berkeley: University of California Press, 1997.

Myrsiades, Kostas, ed. *The Beat Generation: Critical Essays.* New York: Peter Lang, 2002.

Newhouse, Thomas. *The Beat Generation and the Popular Novel in the United States, 1945–1970.* Jefferson: McFarland, 2000.

Nicosia, Gerald. *Memory Babe: A Critical Biography of Jack Kerouac.* 1983; Berkeley: University of California Press, 1994.

Olson, Kirby. *Gregory Corso: Doubting Thomist.* Carbondale: Southern Illinois University Press, 2002.

Parkinson, Thomas, ed. *A Casebook on the Beat.* New York: Crowell, 1961.

Peabody, Richard, ed. *A Different Beat: Writings by Women of the Beat Generation.* London: Serpent's Tail, 1997.

Raskin, Jonah. *Allen Ginsberg's "Howl" and the Making of the Beat Generation.* Berkeley: University of California Press, 2004.

Rosen, Ralph and Sheila Murnaghan, eds. *The Hip Sublime: Beat Writers and the Classical Tradition.* Columbus: Ohio State University Press, 2017.

Russell, Jamie. *Queer Burroughs.* New York: Palgrave, 2001.

Scheiderman, David and Philip Walsh, eds. *Retaking the Universe: William S. Burroughs in the Age of Globalization.* London: Pluto Press, 2004.

Schumacher, Michael. *Dharma Lion: A Critical Biography of Allen Ginsberg.* New York: St. Martin's Press, 1992.

Shinder, Jason, ed. *The Poem that Changed America: "Howl" Fifty Years Later.* New York: Farrar, Straus and Giroux, 2006.

Skau, Michael. *"A Clown in a Grave": Complexities and Tensions in the Works of Gregory Corso.* Carbondale: Southern Illinois University Press, 1999.

Skerl, Jennie. *William S. Burroughs.* Boston: Twayne, 1985.

ed. *Reconstructing the Beats.* New York: Palgrave, 2004.

Skerl, Jennie and Robin Lydenberg, eds. *William S. Burroughs at the Front: Critical Reception, 1959–1989.* Carbondale: Southern Illinois University Press, 1991.

Stephenson, Gregory. *The Daybreak Boys: Essays on the Literature of the Beat Generation.* Carbondale: Southern Illinois University Press, 1990.

Sterritt, David. *The Beats: A Very Short Introduction.* New York: Oxford University Press, 2013.

Mad to Be Saved: The Beats, the '50s, and Film. Carbondale: Southern Illinois University Press, 1998.

Screening the Beats: Media Culture and the Beat Sensibility. Carbondale: Southern Illinois University Press, 2004.

Theado, Matt. *Understanding Jack Kerouac.* Columbia: University of South Carolina Press, 2000.

ed. *The Beats: A Literary Reference.* New York: Carroll & Graf, 2003.

Tietchen, Todd F. *The Cubalogues: Beat Writers in Revolutionary Havana.* Gainesville: University Press of Florida, 2010.

Tonkinson, Carole, ed. *Big Sky Mind: Buddhism and the Beat Generation.* New York: Riverhead, 1995.

Trigilio, Tony. *Allen Ginsberg's Buddhist Poetics.* Carbondale: Southern Illinois University Press, 2007.

Tytell, John. *Naked Angels: Kerouac, Ginsberg, Burroughs.* New York: McGraw-Hill, 1976.

Writing Beat and Other Occasions of Literary Mayhem. Nashville: Vanderbilt University Press, 2014.

Van Minnen, Cornelius A., Jaap van der Bent, and Mel van Elteren, eds. *Beat Culture: The 1950s and Beyond.* Amsterdam: VU University Press, 1999.

Waldman, Anne, ed. *The Beat Book: Writings from the Beat Generation.* Boston: Shambala, 1999.

Waldman, Anne and Laura Wright, eds. *Beats at Naropa.* Minneapolis: Coffee House Press, 2009.

Warner, Simon. *Text and Drugs and Rock 'n' Roll: The Beats and Rock Culture.* London: Bloomsbury, 2013.

Watson, Steven. *The Birth of the Beat Generation: Visionaries, Rebels, and Hipsters, 1944–1960.* New York: Pantheon, 1995.

Weidman, Rich. *The Beat Generation FAQ: All that's Left to Know about the Angelheaded Hipsters.* St. Andrews: Backbeat, 2015.

Weinreich, Regina. *Kerouac's Spontaneous Poetics.* 1987; New York: Thunder's Mouth Press, 2002.

Whaley, Preston. *Blows Like a Horn: Beat Writing, Jazz, Style, and Markets in the Transformation of US Culture.* Cambridge, MA: Harvard University Press, 2004.

Wilentz, Elias, ed. *The Beat Scene.* New York: Corinth Books, 1960.

Woznicki, John R., ed. *The New American Poetry Fifty Years Later.* Bethlehem, PA: Lehigh University Press, 2015.

INDEX

Cambridge Companions to...
AUTHORS

TOPICS